POST-COLONIAL STUDIES

'Not quite a dictionary but an invaluable reference tool nonetheless, its identification of *key* terms remains as useful as its definitions of those terms.'
Professor Antoinette Burton, University of Illinois

This best-selling key guide, now in its second edition, provides an
essential key to understanding the issues which characterize post-
colonialism, explaining what it is, where it is encountered and why it
is crucial in forging new cultural identities. As a subject, post-colonial
studies stands at the intersection of debates about race, colonialism,
gender, politics and language. Key topics covered include:

- borderlands
- transnational literatures
- neo-imperialism
- neo-liberalism
- ecofeminism.

Post-Colonial Studies: The Key Concepts is fully updated and cross-
referenced throughout. With additional further reading this book has
everything necessary for students and anyone keen to learn more
about this fascinating subject.

Bill Ashcroft teaches at the University of Hong Kong and the
University of NSW, **Gareth Griffiths** at the University of Western
Australia and **Helen Tiffin** at Queen's University, Canada. They are
the editors of *The Post-Colonial Studies Reader* and the authors of
The Empire Writes Back, both published by Routledge.

POST-COLONIAL STUDIES

The Key Concepts
Second edition

*Bill Ashcroft, Gareth Griffiths
and Helen Tiffin*

Routledge
Taylor & Francis Group

LONDON AND NEW YORK

First published 2000
by Routledge
2 Park Square, Milton Park,
Abingdon, Oxon, OX14 4RN

Second edition published 2007

Simultaneously published in the USA and Canada
by Routledge
270 Madison Avenue, New York, NY 10016

Routledge is an imprint of the Taylor & Francis Group, an informa business

© 2000, 2007 Bill Ashcroft, Gareth Griffiths and Helen Tiffin

Typeset in Bembo by
Keystroke, 28 High Street, Tettenhall, Wolverhampton
Printed and bound in Great Britain by
TJ International Ltd, Padstow, Cornwall

British Library Cataloguing in Publication Data
A catalogue record for this book is available from the British Library

Library of Congress Cataloging in Publication Data
Ashcroft, Bill, 1946–
Post colonial studies : the key concepts / Bill Ashcroft,
Gareth Griffiths & Helen Tiffin. – 2nd ed.
p. cm.
Previous ed. published under title: Key concepts in post-colonial studies.
"Simultaneously published in the USA and Canada by Routledge."
Includes bibliographical references and index.
1. Colonies–Dictionaries. 2. Decolonization–Dictionaries.
3. Postcolonialism–Dictionaries. 4. Ethnic attitudes–Dictionaries.
5. Race relations–Dictionaries. I. Griffiths, Gareth, 1943– II. Tiffin, Helen.
III. Ashcroft, Bill, 1946– . Key concepts in post-colonial studies. IV. Title.
JV22.A84 2008
325'.303—dc22
2007018708

ISBN10: 0–415–42856–4 (hbk)
ISBN10: 0–415–42855–6 (pbk)
ISBN10: 0–203–44997–5 (ebk)

ISBN13: 978–0–415–42856–9 (hbk)
ISBN13: 978–0–415–42855–2 (pbk)
ISBN13: 978–0–203–44997–4 (ebk)

CONTENTS

INTRODUCTION TO THE SECOND EDITION

Since the publication of *Post-Colonial Studies* nearly ten years ago the subject has expanded and diversified both in its impact and significance, in fields as varied as globalization, environmentalism, transnational-ism, the sacred, and even economics, through the significance of the spread of neo-liberalism. The controversies in the field, particularly, circulating around the term 'post-colonial/postcolonial' itself continue unabated, but the relevance of neo-imperialism and the issues emerg-ing from the engagements of post-colonized societies in a 'glocal' age have demonstrated the usefulness of post-colonial analysis. From the perspective of this decade it is possible to look back at the 1990s and see how important the humanities in general and post-colonial discourse in particular were to developing a new language to address the problems of global culture and the relationships between local cultures and global forces. This occurred because the classical narratives of Modernity in which social theory was mired – dependency theory and centre–periphery models – were unable to explain the multi-directional flow of global exchanges, a flow that was most noticeable in cultural exchange. One significant example of this multi-directional flow is the phenomenon of the Black Atlantic, which reveals the amazing complexity and productivity of African cultures in the Atlantic. The history of such flows reveals that the multi-directional and transcultural nature of global culture is not a new phenomenon.

Many of the issues and problems surrounding the topic of global-ization (the place of the 'glocal'; the function of local agency under the pressure of global forces; the role of imperialism in globalization; the connection between imperialism and neoliberal economics) are addressed, and continue to be addressed by the post-colonial analysis of imperial power. Thus, although we need to be careful about falsely prescribing post-colonial theory as a panacea, and should keep in mind the firm grounding of post-colonial discourse in the historical phenomenon of colonialism, the field of post-colonial studies has provided useful strategies for a wider field of global analysis. Post-colonial literary and cultural production in particular has demonstrated the insistent reality of local agency, an agency that can address simple dualistic approaches to the local and global.

One of the most persistent and controversial topics of contemporary politics is the issue of the environment. Global warming has demonstrated the devastating effects of the industrial revolution and the unfettered pursuit of capital expansion. The environment, and attendant topics such as ecofeminism, ecological imperialism, environmentalism, speciesism have all taken an increasingly prominent place in post-colonial thought because it has become clear that there is a direct connection between colonialist treatment of indigenous flora and fauna and treatment of colonized and otherwise dominated subjects and societies. The devastation of colonized place (and potentially of the planet) paved the way for the devastation of societies. Until now the destruction of the physical and human environments have become the same thing.

Increasingly, post-colonial theory has been found useful in examining a variety of colonial relationship beyond the classic colonizing activities of the British Empire. The concept of boundaries and borders has been crucial in the imperial occupation and domination of indigenous space. And the question of borders and borderlands has now become a pressing issue in an age of increasingly hysterical border protection. Cultural borders are becoming recognized as a critical region of colonial and neo-colonial domination, of cultural erosion, and of class and economic marginalization. The field of post-colonial studies now includes the vexed subjects of contemporary neo-colonialism: the identities and relationships of Chicano, Latino and hybrid subjectivities of various kinds. These subjects, who slip between the boundaries of the grand narratives of history and nation, are becoming an increasingly important constituency for post-colonial studies.

Another issue that has become more prominent, because more complex than previously regarded, is the issue of the sacred. Religion, the impact of missions and the nature and function of a 'post-colonial sacred' are becoming increasingly prevalent in what some refer to as a 'post-secular age'. There can be no doubt that the aggressive articulation of religious dogma, the failure of dialogue and the increasingly polarized globe have offered unprecedented global dangers. But these realities also offer opportunities for an analysis of the kinds of complex hybridized developments of the sacred that have been revealed by post-colonial analysis.

One of the terms emerging from post-colonial studies seems to circumvent some of the perceived problems inherent in descriptions such as 'post-colonial' and diaspora. 'Transnational' as an adjective is growing in use since it extends to migrant, diasporic and refugee communities not directly emerging from the colonial experience. The increasing flow of populations, the mobility of individuals, the increased crossing of borders and the blurring of the concept of 'home' have produced a range of transnational literatures and other forms of cultural production that extend the field of the post-colonial in productive ways.

Some more familiar terms in post-colonial studies have been included in this second edition, such as 'double colonization', 'first nations' and 'translation'. Others, such as 'whiteness' have already blossomed into a virtual field of their own. Many of these terms are central to post-colonial studies, others are shared with other fields of study; some, like 'race' are broader than post-colonial studies itself. But all the words in this Key Concepts will be used at some stage in the field and will be useful for students and writers as they engage this increasingly vibrant field.

LIST OF KEY CONCEPTS

Aboriginal/indigenous peoples
Abrogation
African American and
    post-colonial studies
Agency
Allegory
Alterity
Ambivalence
Anti-colonialism
Apartheid
Appropriation
Authentic/authenticity
Binarism
Black Atlantic
Black Studies/black
    consciousness
Borderlands
Cannibal
Caribbean/West Indian
Cartography
Catachresis
Catalysis
Centre/margin (periphery)
Chromatism
Class and post-colonialism
Colonial desire
Colonial discourse
Colonial patronage
Colonialism
Commonwealth

Commonwealth Literature
Comprador
Contact zone
Contrapuntal reading
Counter-discourse
Creole
Creolization
Culturaldiversity/cultural
    difference
Cultural tourism
Decolonization
Dependency theory
Deracinate
Diaspora
Discourse
Dislocation
Double colonization
Ecofeminism
Ecological imperialism
Empire
Environmentalism
Essentialism/strategic
    essentialism
Ethnicity
Ethnography
Ethno-psychiatry/
    ethno-psychology
Eurocentrism
Exile
Exotic/exoticism

Exploration and travel
Fanonism
Feminism and post-colonialism
Filiation/affiliation
First nations
Frontier
Globalization
Glocalization
'Going native'
Hegemony
Hybridity
Imperialism
Indentured labour
Independence
Interpellation
Liminality
Magic realism
Manicheanism
Marginality
Mestizo/mestizaje/métisse
Metonymic gap
Metropolis/metropolitan
Middle Passage
Mimicry
Miscegenation
Missions and colonialism
Modernism and post-colonialism
Modernity
Mulatto
Multitude
Nation language
Nation/nationalism
National allegory
National liberation movements
Native
Nativism
Négritude
Neo-colonialism/
    neo-imperialism
Neo-liberalism

New Literatures
Orality
Orientalism
Other
Othering
Palimpsest
Pidgins/creoles
Place
Post-colonial body
Post-colonialism/Postcolonialism
Post-colonial reading
Post-colonial state
Postcolony
Primitivism
Race
Rastafarianism
Religion and the post-colonial
Rhizome
Savage/civilized
Settler
Settler colony
Slave/slavery
Speciesism
Subaltern
Subject/subjectivity
Surveillance
Syncretism
Synergy
Testimonio
Third World (First, Second,
    Fourth)
Transculturation
Transnational literatures
Translation
Universalism/universality
Washington Consensus
Whiteness
World system theory
Worlding

POST-COLONIAL STUDIES

ABORIGINAL/INDIGENOUS PEOPLES

Indigenous peoples are those 'born in a place or region' *(OED)*. The term 'aboriginal' was coined as early as 1667 to describe the indigenous inhabitants of places encountered by European explorers, adventurers or seamen. While the terms 'aboriginal' and 'aborigine' have been used from time to time to describe the indigenous inhabitants of many **settler colonies**, they are now most frequently used as a shortened form of 'Australian Aborigine' to describe the indigenous inhabitants of Australia. The adjective 'aboriginal' has been more frequently used as the generic noun in recent times, the term 'aborigine' being considered by many to be too burdened with derogatory associations. Furthermore, the feeling that the term fails to distinguish and discriminate among the great variety of peoples who were lumped together generically as 'aborigines' by the colonial white settlers has been resisted with the assertion of special, local terms for different peoples and/or language groups such as the use of South-Eastern Australian terms like Koori, Queensland terms such as Murri and Western Australian terms such as Nyoongah. So far, though, no single term has been accepted as a general term by all the various peoples concerned, and the generic term most frequently used for the descendants of all pre-colonial indigenes is 'Australian Aboriginal peoples'.

In the Americas the term 'aborigines' gained currency as a generic term for indigenous peoples as it did in Australia. Terms such as 'Indian' and later 'Amerindian', which, like Aboriginal in Australia, accrued derogatory connotations, were employed by settler-invaders (and their descendants). In the twentieth century, terms generated by indigenous peoples themselves, such as 'First Nations', 'Native Americans' have replaced the older settler-invader nomenclatures. The term has also been, and is still used to describe the descendants of the earliest inhabitants of other regions, such as the 'orang asli' of Malaysia and Indonesian Borneo (Kalimantan) or the original inhabitants of the Indian sub-continent now referred to as the 'scheduled tribes' and Andaman Islanders.

(See **settler colony, Third World**.)

ABROGATION

Abrogation refers to the rejection by post-colonial writers of a normative concept of 'correct' or 'standard' English used by certain classes or groups, and of the corresponding concepts of inferior 'dialects' or 'marginal variants'. The concept is usually employed in conjunction with the term **appropriation**, which describes the processes of English adaptation itself, and is an important component of the post-colonial assumption that all language use is a 'variant' of one kind or another (and is in that sense 'marginal' to some illusory standard). Thus abrogation is an important political stance, whether articulated or not, and even whether conscious or not, from which the actual appropriation of language can take place.

In arguing for the parity of all forms of English, abrogation offers a counter to the theory that use of the colonialist's language inescapably imprisons the colonized within the colonizer's conceptual paradigms – the view that 'you can't dismantle the master's house with the master's tools'. Abrogation implies rather that the master's house is always adaptable and that the same tools offer a means of conceptual transformation and liberation.

Although abrogation has been used to describe the rejection of a standard language in the writing of post-colonial literatures, it can, like **appropriation** be used to describe a great range of cultural and political activities – film, theatre, the writing of history, political organization, modes of thought and argument. Individuals who are involved in these things may abrogate any centralizing notion of the 'correct', or standard, way of doing things and re-define the practice in a different setting.

Further reading: Ashcroft *et al.* 2002, Ziff and Rao 1997.

AFRICAN AMERICAN AND POST-COLONIAL STUDIES

Recent work in post-colonial studies by United States' scholars has stressed the relationship between post-colonial theory and the analysis of African American culture (DuCille 1996). In practice, the exponents of African American culture have often engaged with classic post-colonial theorists such as Fanon, though not always in an uncritical way. African American studies has been one of the most influential of recent intellectual, social and political movements, not only affecting the US but also influencing many people who have suffered oppression from racial discrimination in other parts of the world. It has had a widespread and often quite separate development from post-colonial studies, to which it is related only in a complex and ambiguous way.

Most post-colonial theorists who have engaged with the issue have seen the study of black culture in the Americas as, in part, the study of one of the world's major **diasporas**. In this respect, the history of African Americans has some features in common with other movements of oppressed diasporic peoples. Many groups were moved against their will from their homelands to serve the economic needs of empire in the societies that evolved from the wave of European expansion from the sixteenth century onwards. Comparative studies of these movements are a productive development in recent post-colonial theory, not least in the consideration of the different effects of these large-scale events on individual groups that such studies reveal.

Early formulations of African American Studies in the United States and elsewhere reflected the complex relationship between the African source cultures and their adopted societies, as they interacted with other influences in the new regions to which Africans were taken (see **négritude**). The fact that the bulk of African peoples were shipped under conditions of **slavery** makes the relationship between that institution and the wider practices of imperialism central to an understanding of the origins of African American culture. It also sheds light on the violence that was often hidden beneath the civilizing rhetoric of imperialism (DuCille 1996). Beyond this prime fact of oppression and violence, however, the relationships between the newly independent American societies, the wider diasporic black movement, and the modern independence movements in Africa itself, remain complex.

The history of the struggle for self-determination by African Americans is historically intertwined with wider movements of diasporic African struggles for independence. For example, figures like Jamaican born Marcus Garvey assumed a central role in the American struggle for self-determination. The 'Back to Africa' movement that he initiated, and which has affinities with the modern West Indian movement of **Rastafarianism**, supported the various movements to return African Americans to Africa. The national flag of Liberia, which was founded specifically to facilitate the return of freed black slaves to their 'native' continent, still bears the single star of Garvey's Black Star shipping company. In addition, many of the dominant figures in early African nationalism, such as Alexander Crummell, were ex-slaves or the children of slaves who had their ideas formed in the struggle for African American freedom (see de Moraes-Farias and Barber 1990; Appiah 1992).

Of course, African American studies are also concerned much more directly with the history and continuing effects of specific processes of race-based discrimination within US society. In this regard, African

American studies investigates issues that share certain features with other US groups affected by racial discrimination, such as the Chicano community. These studies have relevance to movements for the freedom of **indigenous** peoples, such as Native American Indians or Inuit peoples, despite their very different historical backgrounds (one group being victims of invasive settlement and the other of slavery and exile). Distinctions also need to be made between these various groups and linguistically and racially discriminated groups such as Chicanos, a great many of whom are part of a more recent wave of immigration, though some, of course, are the descendants of peoples who lived in parts of the US long before the current dominant Anglo-Saxon peoples. Other groups, such as the descendants of French Creoles, also occupy places contiguous in some respects to these latter Spanish speaking peoples, though their history and their treatment within US society may have been very different. For this, and other reasons, critics have often hesitated to conflate African American studies or the study of any of these other groups with post-colonial theory in any simple way. The latter may offer useful insights, but it does not subsume the specific and distinctive goals and history of African American studies or Native American studies or Chicano studies as distinctive academic disciplines with specific political and social struggle in their own right.

Further reading: DuCille 1996; Flint 2006; Gòkè-Paríolá 1996; Gruesser 2005; Hanchard 1997; McInturff 2000; Mostern 2000; Olson and Worsham 1999; Schueller 2003; Singh and Schmidt 2000; Wise 1995; Zeigler 1996; Zeigler and Osinubi 2002.

AGENCY

Agency refers to the ability to act or perform an action. In contemporary theory, it hinges on the question of whether individuals can freely and autonomously initiate action, or whether the things they do are in some sense determined by the ways in which their identity has been constructed. Agency is particularly important in post-colonial theory because it refers to the ability of post-colonial subjects to initiate action in engaging or resisting imperial power. The term has become an issue in recent times as a consequence of post-structuralist theories of **subjectivity**. Since human subjectivity is constructed by ideology (Althusser), language (Lacan), or discourse (Foucault), the corollary is that any action performed by that subject must also be to some extent a consequence of those things. For the colonial discourse theory of Bhabha and Spivak, which concurs with much of the post-structuralist position on subjectivity, the question of agency has been a troublesome one. However, many theories in which the importance of political action is paramount take agency for granted. They suggest that although it may be difficult for subjects to escape the effects of those forces that 'construct' them, it is not impossible. The very fact that such forces may be recognized suggests that they may also be countermanded.

Further reading: Ashcroft 1994; Bhabha 1994; Fanon 1952; Parry 1987, 1994; Slemon 1994: Leonard 2005; Werbner and Stoller 2002.

ALLEGORY

The simplest definition of allegory is a 'symbolic narrative' in which the major features of the movement of the narrative are all held to refer symbolically to some action or situation. Allegory has long been a prominent feature of literary and mythic writing throughout the world, but it becomes particularly significant for post-colonial writers for the way in which it disrupts notions of orthodox history, classical realism and imperial representation in general. Allegory has assumed an important function in imperial discourse, in which paintings and statues have often been created as allegories of imperial power. Consequently, one form of post-colonial response to this has been to **appropriate** allegory and use it to respond to the allegorical representation of imperial dominance.

Fredric Jameson made a controversial suggestion, in 'Third World Literature in the era of multi-national capitalism' (1986), that all Third World literatures, indeed all Third World cultural constructions, are 'necessarily' **national allegories**. Aijaz Ahmad vigorously criticized the homogenizing nature of this statement (see 1992). But Stephen Slemon suggested that what is really wrong with the suggestion is that it simply takes a Euro-centric literary notion of allegory and applies it to colonized societies. Slemon suggests that we might rather see allegory as a function of the 'conditions of postcoloniality'. This is because allegory has always been a dominant mode of colonial representation and therefore becomes a particularly valuable form in which post-colonial literature may conduct forms of **counter-discourse**.

This means, firstly, that post-colonial cultures may use allegory to 'read' the text of colonialism (Slemon 1987a: 11). So much of the life of the colonized subject has been constructed by, that is, metaphorically 'written' by, colonialism that allegory becomes a way in which such writing may be contested. But there are many other ways in which allegory has been used by post-colonial writers. One group of post-colonial allegories, such as Ayi Kwei Armah's 'An African fable', for example, seeks to contest colonialist or Euro-centric notions of history. In other texts, such as Lamming's *Natives of My Person*, or Coetzee's *Waiting for the Barbarians*, allegory is employed to expose the ways in which the allegorical form is used in the colonizing process. Thus in the Coetzee text, for example, the life of a magistrate isolated on the boundaries of an unnamed empire, and his peaceful relations with the people beyond the boundary, is disrupted when they are re-classified as 'barbarians' by the visit of an egregious secret policeman. This causes the magistrate to realize for the first time the full truth about the society in which he lives. Although such texts do not deal directly with specific colonial situations, they present a powerful allegory of underlying colonial ideology.

In other texts again, such as Randolph Stow's *Tourmaline* or Kofi Awoonor's *This Earth My Brother*, the use of the allegorical form seeks to replace monolithic traditions with a cross-cultural pluralism. In Stow's novel, for example, the small Western Australian mining town of Tourmaline is opened up to a perspective that places it in an older landscape of the Dreaming traditions of Australian Aboriginal cultures. The limited world of the small white town is framed by the huge forces of desert and sky, not merely as back-drops, but as symbols of a different and more integrated way of conceiving of the human relationship with nature and the natural world. In these latter cases, a 'post-colonial' allegory contests and disrupts the narrative assumptions of colonialism, such as the inevitability of 'development', of 'progress', of 'civilization', the dominance of the chronological view of history, the Euro-centric view of 'the real'. By reinforcing the fact that 'real' events occupy various horizons of meaning, post-colonial allegory becomes a common strategy of resistance in post-colonial texts.

Further reading: Ahmad 1992, 1995a; Buchanan 2003; Franco 1997; Hulme 2005; Jameson 1986; San Juan 1996; Schmidt 2000; Slemon 1987a; Szeman 2006.

ALTERITY

Alterity is derived from the Latin *alteritas*, meaning 'the state of being other or different; diversity, otherness'. Its English derivatives are alternate, alternative, alternation, and alter ego. The term *alterité* is more common in French, and has the antonym *identité* (Johnson and Smith 1990: xviii).

The term was adopted by philosophers as an alternative to 'otherness' to register a change in the Western perceptions of the relationship between consciousness and the world. Since Descartes, individual consciousness had been taken as the privileged starting point for consciousness, and 'the "other" appears in these [post-Enlightenment] philosophies as a reduced "other," as an epistemological question' (xix). That is, in a concept of the human in which everything stems from the notion that 'I think, therefore I am', the chief concern with the other is to be able to answer questions such as 'How can I know the other?', 'How can other minds be known?' The term 'alterity' shifts the focus of analysis away from these philosophic concerns with otherness – the 'epistemic other', the other that is only important to the extent to which it can be known – to the more concrete 'moral other' – the other who is actually located in a political, cultural, linguistic or religious context (xix). This is a key feature of changes in the concept of **subjectivity**, because, whether seen in the context of ideology, psychoanalysis or discourse, the 'construction' of the subject itself can be seen to be inseparable from the construction of its others.

Literary theorists commonly see the most influential use of alterity in Mikhail Bakhtin's description of the way in which an author moves away from identification with a character (Todorov 1984). The novelist must understand his or her character from within, as it were, but must also perceive it as other, as apart from its creator in its distinct alterity. Importantly, dialogue is only possible with an 'other', so alterity, in Bakhtin's formulation, is not simply 'exclusion', but an apartness that stands as a precondition of dialogue, where dialogue implies a transference across and between differences of culture, gender, class and other social categories. This is related to his concept of 'exotopy' or 'outsideness', which is not simply alienness, but a precondition for the author's ability to understand and formulate a character, a precondition for dialogue itself.

In post-colonial theory, the term has often been used interchangeably with otherness and difference. However, the distinction that initially held between otherness and alterity – that between otherness as a philosophic problem and otherness as a feature of a material and discursive location – is peculiarly applicable to post-colonial discourse. The self-identity of the colonizing subject, indeed the identity of imperial culture, is inextricable from the alterity of colonized others, an alterity determined, according to Spivak, by a process of **othering**. The possibility for potential dialogue between racial and cultural others has also remained an important aspect of the use of the word, which distinguishes it from its synonyms.

Further reading: Bhabha 1984b; Fazzini 2004; Harris 2004; Johnson and Smith 1990; Slemon 1987b; Taussig 1993; Todorov 1984.

AMBIVALENCE

A term first developed in psychoanalysis to describe a continual fluctuation between wanting one thing and wanting its opposite. It also refers to a simultaneous attraction toward and repulsion from an object, person or action (Young 1995: 161). Adapted into colonial discourse theory by Homi Bhabha, it describes the complex mix of attraction and repulsion that characterizes the relationship between colonizer and colonized. The relationship is ambivalent because the colonized subject is never simply and completely opposed to the colonizer. Rather than assuming that some colonized subjects are 'complicit' and some 'resistant', ambivalence suggests that complicity and resistance exist in a fluctuating relation within the colonial subject. Ambivalence also characterizes the way in which colonial discourse relates to the colonized subject, for it may be both exploitative and nurturing, or represent itself as nurturing, at the same time.

Most importantly in Bhabha's theory, however, ambivalence disrupts the clear-cut authority of colonial domination because it disturbs the simple relationship between colonizer and colonized. Ambivalence is therefore an unwelcome aspect of colonial discourse for the colonizer. The problem for colonial discourse is that it wants to produce compliant subjects who reproduce its assumptions, habits and values – that is, 'mimic' the colonizer. But instead it produces ambivalent subjects whose **mimicry** is never very far from mockery. Ambivalence describes this fluctuating relationship between mimicry and mockery, an ambivalence that is fundamentally unsettling to colonial dominance. In this respect, it is not necessarily disempowering for the colonial subject; but rather can be seen to be *ambi-valent* or 'two-powered'. The effect of this ambivalence (the simultaneous attraction and repulsion) is to produce a profound disturbance of the authority of colonial discourse.

Ambivalence therefore gives rise to a controversial proposition in Bhabha's theory, that because the colonial relationship is always ambivalent, it generates the seeds of its own destruction. This is controversial because it implies that the colonial relationship is going to be disrupted, regardless of any resistance or rebellion on the part of the colonized. Bhabha's argument is that colonial discourse is *compelled* to be ambivalent because it never really wants colonial subjects to be exact replicas of the colonizers – this would be too threatening. For instance, he gives the example of Charles Grant, who, in 1792, desired to inculcate the Christian religion in Indians, but worried that this might make them 'turbulent for liberty' (Bhabha 1994: 87). Grant's solution was to mix Christian doctines with divisive caste practices to produce a 'partial reform' that would induce an empty imitation of English manners. Bhabha suggests that this demonstrates the conflict within imperialism itself that will inevitably cause its own downfall: it is compelled to create an ambivalent situation that will disrupt its assumption of monolithic power.

Robert Young has suggested that the theory of ambivalence is Bhabha's way of turning the tables on imperial discourse. The periphery, which is regarded as 'the borderline, the marginal, the unclassifiable, the doubtful' by the centre, responds by constituting the centre as an 'equivocal, indefinite, indeterminate ambivalence' (1995: 161). But this is not a simple reversal of a binary, for Bhabha shows that both colonizing and colonized subjects are implicated in the ambivalence of colonial discourse. The concept is related to **hybridity** because, just as ambivalence 'decentres' authority from its position of power, so that authority may also become hybridized when placed in a colonial context in which it finds itself dealing with, and often inflected by, other cultures. The hybridity of Charles Grant's suggestion above, for instance, can be seen as a feature of its ambivalence. In this respect, the very engagement of colonial discourse with those colonized cultures over which it has domination, inevitably leads to an ambivalence that disables its monolithic dominance.

Further reading: Bhabha 1984a, 1985, 1996; Burton 2004; Papastergiadis 1996; Young 1995.

ANTI-COLONIALISM

The political struggle of colonized peoples against the specific ideology and practice of colonialism (see **colonization**). Anti-colonialism

11

signifies the point at which the various forms of opposition become articulated as a resistance to the operations of colonialism in political, economic and cultural institutions. It emphasizes the need to reject colonial power and restore local control. Paradoxically, anti-colonialist movements often expressed themselves in the appropriation and subversion of forms borrowed from the institutions of the colonizer and turned back on them. Thus the struggle was often articulated in terms of a discourse of anti-colonial 'nationalism' in which the form of the modern European nation-state was taken over and employed as a sign of resistance (see **nation/nationalism**). The sometimes arbitrary arrangements of colonial governance – such as the structures of public administration and forums for local political representation – became the spaces within which a discourse of anti-colonial nationalism was focused and a demand for an independent postcolonial nation-state was formed (see Anderson 1983; Chatterjee 1986, 1993).

Anti-colonialism has taken many forms in different colonial situations; it is sometimes associated with an ideology of racial liberation, as in the case of nineteenth-century West African nationalists such as Edward Wilmot Blyden and James Africanus Horton (ideologies that might be seen as the precursors of twentieth-century movements such as **négritude**). Conversely, it may accompany a demand for a recognition of cultural differences on a broad and diverse front, as in the Indian National Congress which sought to unite a variety of ethnic groups with different religious and racial identities in a single, national independence movement.

In the second half of the twentieth century, anti-colonialism was often articulated in terms of a radical, Marxist discourse of liberation, and in constructions that sought to reconcile the internationalist and anti-élitist demands of Marxism with the nationalist sentiments of the period (National Liberation Fronts), in the work and theory of early national liberationist thinkers such as C.L.R.James, Amilcar Cabral and Frantz Fanon, (see **Fanonism, national liberation**). Such anti-colonial, national liberation movements developed the Marxist idea of a revolutionary cadre to explain the crucial role of the European (colonial) educated intelligentsia in the anti-colonial struggle. These movements argued that the peasant/proletarian needed to be led to a practice of liberation – through various stages of local and national affiliation – by a bourgeois élite who would eventually, in Cabral's dramatic formulation, 'commit suicide' by developing a popular and local social practice in which they would be assimilated.

Cabral, in particular, developed this idea of the need to empower and recognize the local as a specific and distinct feature of post-colonial politics in ways that radicalized the more rigid and orthodox practices of post-Stalinist Marxist thought. Unlike later nationalist formulations of the new bourgeois post-independence élites, however, there is here no sentimental or mythologized attachment to an idealized pre-colonial condition. The local is perceived to be fully corrigible and involved in an inevitable *process* of historical change:

> the working masses and in particular the peasants, who are usually illiterate and have never moved beyond the boundaries of their village or their region, come into contact with other groups and lose those complexes of their own that constricted them in their relationships with other ethnic and social groups. They realise their crucial role in the struggle. They break the bonds of the village universe. They integrate progressively into their country and the world. . . . The armed liberation struggle implies, therefore, a veritable forced march along the road to cultural progress.
>
> (Cabral, January 1969)

(See also the account offered by Edward Said (1993: 264) of the contrastive and more progressive discourse of nationalism employed by these early anticolonialist figures compared with the regressive discourse of some modern post-colonial nationalists.)

Cabral's contribution has received less recognition than that of Fanon, whose political practice was arguably less developed, though his theories of the formation of colonial consciousness were among the most powerful contributions to the creation of an effective anti-colonial discourse. Anti-colonialism frequently perceived resistance to be the product of a fixed and definitive relationship in which colonizer and colonized were in absolute and implacable opposition. As such it was less a feature of **settler colonies**, where a more obvious form of complicity occurred between the colonial power and the settler in, for example, their suppression of the **indigenous peoples**. Settler colonies illustrate the power of filiative modes of cultural representation to effect a stronger and more complete **hegemony** of the colonial culture. In settler colonies, the struggle to articulate the underlying economic and political discriminations of a colonial relationship, that is to move to an awareness of the limited and affiliative connections of the colony and the colonial power, is central to any anti-colonial impulse. In settler colony situations, resistance at the level of cultural practice may occur before the political importance of such resistance is articulated or perceived.

Further reading: Cabral 1973; Davidson 1994; Fanon 1961; Gandhi 2006; Goswami 2005; Hawes 2003; Ngugi 1981a; Pratt 2004; Simpson 2004; Slemon 1990.

APARTHEID

An Afrikaans term meaning 'separation', used in South Africa for the policy initiated by the Nationalist Government after 1948 and usually rendered into English in the innocuous sounding phrase, 'policy of separate development'. Apartheid had been preceded in 1913 and 1936 by the Land Acts which restricted the amount of land available to black farmers to 13 per cent. But in 1948 the Apartheid laws were enacted, including the Population Registration Act, which registered all people by racial group; the Mixed Amenities Act, which codified racial segregation in public facilities; the Group Areas Act, which segregated suburbs; the Immorality Act, which illegalized white–black marriages; and the establishment of the so-called Bantustans, or native homelands, to which a large proportion of the black population was restricted.

Theoretically, the establishment of the Bantustans was supposed to provide a solution to the racial tension of South Africa by providing a series of designated territories or homelands in which the different races could develop separately within the state. But since the white minority retained for themselves the bulk of the land, and virtually all of the economically viable territory, including the agriculturally rich areas and the areas with mining potential, it was, in practice, a means of institutionalizing and preserving white supremacy. Since the economy required a large body of non-white workers to live in close proximity to white areas, for which they provided cheap labour, the Group Areas Act led to the development of specific racially segregated townships, using low-cost housing, such as the notorious Soweto area (South West Townships) south of Johannesburg. Under the same Act, people of African, Cape Coloured or Indian descent were forcibly removed from urban areas where they had lived for generations. The notorious and still unreconstructed District Six in central Capetown, bulldozed and cleared of its mixed race inhabitants under the Act, is an often cited example of this aspect of apartheid policy.

The policy of segregation extended to every aspect of society, with separate sections in public transport, public seats, beaches, and many other facilities. Further segregation was maintained by the use of Pass Laws which required non-whites to carry a pass that identified them, and which, unless it was stamped with a work permit, restricted their access to white areas. The racist basis of the policy was nowhere more apparent, and nowhere more bizarre in its application, than in the frequent redesignations of races conducted by the government, in which individuals were reclassified as Black, Coloured, Indian or White. Most of these rectifications were, predictably, downwards within the white-imposed hierarchy of race. The process demonstrated the sheer fictionality of suggesting that these racial divisions were either fixed or absolute, as did the necessity of passing a law against **miscegenation** between the races. The so-called Immorality Act, designed to preserve 'racial purity', indicated the desire to rewrite the fact that the societies of Southern Africa had for centuries intermingled culturally and racially.

The term apartheid acquired very widespread resonance, and it became commonly used outside the South African situation to designate a variety of situations in which racial discrimination was institutionalized by law. An extreme instance of this is when the post-structuralist philosopher and cultural critic Jacques Derrida employed the term in an influential essay, suggesting that it had acquired a resonance as a symbol that made it an archetypal term of discrimination and prejudice for later twentieth-century global culture (Derrida 1986).

Further reading: Alexander 1996; Collett 2002; Coombes 2003; Jacobs 2004; Lapping 1987; Pechey 1994; Price and Rosberg 1980; Richmond 1994; Sono 1999; Woods 1986.

APPROPRIATION

A term used to describe the ways in which post-colonial societies take over those aspects of the imperial culture – language, forms of writing, film, theatre, even modes of thought and argument such as rationalism, logic and analysis – that may be of use to them in articulating their own social and cultural identities. This process is sometimes used to describe the strategy by which the dominant imperial power incorporates as its own the territory or culture that it surveys and invades (Spurr 1993: 28). However, post-colonial theory focuses instead on an exploration of the ways in which the dominated or colonized culture can use the tools of the dominant discourse to resist its political or cultural control.

Appropriation may describe acts of usurpation in various cultural domains, but the most potent are the domains of language and textuality. In these areas, the dominant language and its discursive forms are appropriated to express widely differing cultural experiences, and to interpolate these experiences into the dominant modes of representation to reach the widest possible audience. Chinua Achebe (quoting James Baldwin), noted that the language so used can 'bear the burden of another experience', and this has become one of the most famous declarations of the power of appropriation in post-colonial discourse. However, the very use of the colonial language has been opposed by writers such as Ngugi wa Thiong'o (Ngugi 1981a), who, after a successful career as a writer in English, has renounced the language of the former colonizer to write his novel and plays in Gikuyu. Nevertheless, Ngugi continues to appropriate the novel form itself, and it has been argued that the very success of his political tactic of renouncing English has relied on his reputation as a writer in that tongue.

Many other non-English speaking writers who have chosen to write in English do so not because their mother tongue is regarded by them as inadequate, but because the colonial language has become a useful means of expression, and one that reaches the widest possible audience. On the other hand, writers such as Ngugi argue that since access to English in the post-colonial societies themselves is often restricted to an educated élite, this 'wider' audience is largely outside the country, or restricted to the **comprador** class within the society. The debate has been a persistent and unresolved one.

These arguments based on the political effect of choosing English as a medium of expression are frequently contested by the alternative claim that language itself somehow embodies a culture in a way that is inaccessible to speakers of another language. Those critics and writers who appropriate ex-colonial languages to their own use argue that although language may create powerful emotive contexts through which local identities are formed, and whilst the use of non-indigenous languages may, as a result, appear to such communities to be less **authentic** than texts in indigenous languages, such languages do not, in themselves, constitute an irrecoverably alien form, and they may be appropriated to render views that are just as powerful in constructing anti-colonial texts. They may also effect further results that texts in the indigenous languages cannot do so easily, offering a different mode of post-colonial resistance to cultural hegemony.

By appropriating the imperial language, its discursive forms and its modes of representation, post-colonial societies are able, as things stand, to intervene more readily in the dominant discourse, to interpolate their own cultural realities, or use that dominant language to describe those realities to a wide audience of readers. Many writers feel, however, that as well as encouraging translation between all the languages used in the various post-colonial societies (including translations of indigenous languages into English and into other indigenous languages), it is equally important to insist on the need for metropolitan institutions and cultural practices to open themselves up to indigenous texts by encouraging the learning and use of these languages by metropolitan scholars.

Further reading: Ashcroft, Griffiths and Tiffin 2002; Butler 1997; Fuchs 2000; Hart 1997; Pennycook 2002; Ziff and Rao 1997.

AUTHENTIC/AUTHENTICITY

The idea of an authentic culture is one that has been present in many recent debates about post-colonial cultural production. In particular, the demand for a rejection of the influence of the colonial period in programmes of **decolonization** has invoked the idea that certain forms and practices are 'inauthentic', some decolonizing states arguing for a recuperation of authentic pre-colonial traditions and customs. The problem with such claims to cultural authenticity is that they often become entangled in an **essentialist** cultural position in which fixed practices become iconized as authentically **indigenous** and others are excluded as hybridized or contaminated. This has as its corollary the danger of ignoring the possibility that cultures may develop and change as their conditions change.

Significantly, this was not as common a feature of the work of the early anti-colonialist writers working with a Marxist model of culture (see **anti-colonialism**). Later post-structuralist models have found the issue much more difficult to resolve, reflecting, perhaps, the political problem of discovering a firm ground for material practice in an analysis that emphasizes the radical instability of signs and the fundamental and persistent difficulty of 'grounding' systems in an objective, material, extra-discursive 'space'. In some respects, cultural **essentialism**, which is theoretically questionable, may be adopted as a strategic political position in the struggle against imperial power. Clearly, certain kinds of practices are peculiar to one culture and not to others, and these may serve as important identifiers and become the means by which those cultures can resist oppression and oppose homogenization by global forces.

However, the emergence of certain fixed, stereotypical representations of culture remains a danger. The tendency to employ generic signifiers for cultures that may have many variations within them may override the real differences that exist within such cultures. Markers of cultural difference may well be perceived as authentic cultural signifiers, but that claim to authenticity can imply that these cultures are not subject to change. The use of signifiers of authenticity may be a vital part of the attempt by many subordinated societies to argue for their continued and valid existence as they become inevitably hybridized and influenced by various social and cultural changes. But too rigid a definition can militate against such resistance if they are used to police and license the determining boundaries of the culture by the dominant group (Griffiths 1994: 6).

Further reading: D'Cruz 2001; Fee 1989; Fenwick 2000; Ganguly 2002; Griffiths 1994.

BINARISM

From 'binary', meaning a combination of two things, a pair, 'two', duality *(OED)*, this is a widely used term with distinctive meanings in several fields and one that has had particular sets of meanings in post-colonial theory.

The concern with binarism was first established by the French structural linguist, Ferdinand de Saussure, who held that signs have meaning not by a simple reference to real objects, but by their opposition to other signs. Each sign is itself the function of a binary between the signifier, the 'signal' or sound image of the word, and the signified, the significance of the signal, the concept or mental image that it evokes. Saussure held that although the connection between the signifier and signified is arbitrary (that is, there is no necessity in nature for the link between the word 'dog' and the signified dog), once the link is established, it is fixed for everyone who speaks that language.

While signs mean by their difference from other signs, the binary opposition is the most extreme form of difference possible – sun/moon; man/woman; birth/death; black/white. Such oppositions, each of which represents a binary system, are very common in the cultural construction of reality. The problem with such binary systems is that they suppress ambiguous or interstitial spaces between the opposed categories, so that any overlapping region that may appear, say, between the categories man/woman, child/adult or friend/alien, becomes impossible according to binary logic, and a region of taboo in social experience.

Contemporary post-structuralist and **feminist** theories have demonstrated the extent to which such binaries entail a violent hierarchy, in
which one term of the opposition is always dominant (man over woman,
birth over death, white over black), and that, in fact, the binary
opposition itself exists to confirm that dominance. This means that any
activity or state that does not fit the binary opposition will become
subject to repression or ritual. For instance, the interstitial stage between
child and adult – 'youth' – is treated as a scandalous category, a rite of
passage subject to considerable suspicion and anxiety. Subsequently,
the state between the binarism, such as the binary colonizer/colonized,
will evidence the signs of extreme ambivalence manifested in **mimicry**,
cultural schizophrenia, or various kinds of obsession with identity, or will
put energy into confirming one or other side of the binarism, e.g.
Anglocentrism or nationalism.

The binary logic of **imperialism** is a development of that tendency
of Western thought in general to see the world in terms of binary
oppositions that establish a relation of dominance. A simple distinction
between centre/margin; colonizer/colonized; metropolis/empire;
civilized/primitive represents very efficiently the violent hierarchy
on which imperialism is based and which it actively perpetuates. Binary
oppositions are structurally related to one another, and in colonial
discourse there may be a variation of the one underlying binary –
colonizer/colonized – that becomes rearticulated in any particular text
in a number of ways, e.g.

colonizer	:	colonized
white	:	black
civilized	:	primitive
advanced	:	retarded
good	:	evil
beautiful	:	ugly
human	:	bestial
teacher	:	pupil
doctor	:	patient

The binary constructs a scandalous category between the two terms
that will be the domain of taboo, but, equally importantly, the structure can be read downwards as well as across, so that colonizer, white,
human and beautiful are collectively opposed to colonized, black,
bestial and ugly. Clearly, the binary is very important in constructing
ideological meanings in general, and extremely useful in imperial
ideology. The binary structure, with its various articulations of the

underlying binary, accommodates such fundamental binary impulses within imperialism as the impulse to 'exploit' and the impulse to 'civilize'. Thus we may also find that colonizer, civilized, teacher and doctor may be opposed to colonized, primitive, pupil and patient, as a comparatively effortless extension of the binary structure of domination. In fact, of course, as we are increasingly aware, the one depends on the other in a much more complex way than this simplistic binary structure suggests, with the 'civilizing mission' of the former categories acting as the cloak for the naked exploitation of those consigned to their binary opposites, and the former category all too often acting to conceal and justify the latter, as Conrad showed so graphically in *Heart of Darkness*.

Binary distinctions are not necessarily motivated by a desire to dominate. David Spurr (1993: 103) discusses the ways in which Rousseau, in the *Essay on the Origin of Languages*, attempts to validate the 'life and warmth' of Oriental languages such as Arabic and Persian. But in employing the 'logic and precision' of Western writing to do so, Rousseau effectively negates these languages because they become characterized by a primitive lack of rational order and culture. Although setting out to applaud such languages, he succeeds in confirming the binary between European science, understanding, industry and writing on the one hand, and Oriental primitivism and irrationality on the other.

It may be argued that the very domain of post-colonial theory is the region of 'taboo' – the domain of overlap between these imperial binary oppositions, the area in which ambivalence, hybridity and complexity continually disrupt the certainties of imperial logic. Apart from illuminating the interstitial spaces, post-colonial theory also disrupts the structural relations of the binary system itself, revealing the fundamental contradictions of a system that can include, for instance, the binaries civilized/primitive or human/bestial along with doctor/patient or enlightener/enlightened. In this way it uncovers the deep ambivalence of a structure of economic, cultural and political relations that can both debase and idealize, demonize and eroticize its subjects.

Perhaps one of the most catastrophic binary systems perpetuated by imperialism is the invention of the concept of **race**. The reduction of complex physical and cultural differences within and between colonized societies to the simple opposition of black/brown/yellow/white is in fact a strategy to establish a binarism of white/non-white, which asserts a relation of dominance. By thus occluding the vast continuum of ethnic variation, relegating the whole region of ethnicity, racial mixture and cultural specificity to one of taboo or otherness, imperialism draws the concept of race into a simple binary that reflects its own logic of power. The danger for anti-colonial resistance comes when the binary opposition is simply reversed, so that 'black', for instance, or 'the colonized' become the dominant terms. This simply locks the project of resistance into the semiotic opposition set up by imperial discourse.

Much contemporary post-colonial theory has been directed at breaking down various kinds of binary separation in the analysis of colonialism and imperialism. For instance, Guyanese novelist and critic Wilson Harris' attempt to break down the binaristic structuration of language precedes the poststructuralists' efforts in European theory. Thus in a novel such as *Ascent to Omai*, for example, this process is continually foregrounded, as the following extract makes clear:

> 'Do you remember?' the judge addressed the hidden *personae* in his pack, blurred masks or readers looking over his shoulder backwards into the future: flicked the pages of his book like an expert gambler with currencies of time obverse and reverse. On the one side *judge* on the other *judged*. On one side again *father* on the other *son*. On one side still again *ancient* on the other *modern*.
>
> (Harris 1970: 86)

An important consequence of this disruption of imperial binary systems is a particular emphasis on the interactive and dialectical effects of the colonial encounter. Imperial binarisms always assume a movement in one direction – a movement from the colonizer to the colonized, from the explorer to the explored, from the surveyor to the surveyed. But just as post-colonial identity emerges in the ambivalent spaces of the colonial encounter, so the dynamic of change is not all in one direction; it is in fact **transcultural**, with a significant circulation of effects back and forth between the two, for the engagement with the colonies became an increasingly important factor in the imperial society's constitution and understanding of itself.

Further reading: Russell 2006.

BLACK ATLANTIC

The term Black Atlantic was employed first by the Black British critic Paul Gilroy (Gilroy 1993). In that study, he addressed the cultural and historical linkages, which unified the peoples of African descent on both sides of the ocean that had been the scene of the **diaspora** of black Africans resulting from the Atlantic slave-trade across the infamous Middle Passage and the so-called 'triangular trade,' which flowed from it between Africa, the Americas and Europe, a trade which had a powerful effect on modern economies. For Gilroy the important point is not just to register this linkage as an historical event, but to show how the ongoing effects of that exchange remain the constituting factor in a discursive economy that continues to dominate the social and political practices of the modern world in societies as diverse as the United States, Brazil, Britain and in the independent colonies of Africa, the Caribbean and the Americas. His contention is that all those societies, and indeed the economic and political framework of the Atlantic region as a whole, have been determined in large part by the linkages formed in that first era of mercantilism and expansion when the principal cargo was the bodies of black Africans. In this foundational work Gilroy stresses the interdependence of all the cultures which depended on this exchange of enslaved bodies across the Black Atlantic. Thus he analyses the cross-influence of black intellectuals, who worked not within specific and isolated nations or states but within a transnational framework in which their work flourished and cross-fertilized.

It is Gilroy's contention therefore that far from being a limited or marginalised experience the black experience prefigured many of the problems and issues which were faced later by all peoples dealing with the emerging transnational and globalized conditions of the modern world. Recently the term has been recruited in the concept of a Black Atlantic Literature, which traces the interconnections and influences which have occurred between writers and artists across the region. It has also been extended back into studies of earlier periods of black cultural exchange into the mediaeval period (Campbell 2006) and into many discussions of music and popular culture which take up the issues raised in the final chapter of Gilroy's 1993 book which deals with these cultural forms. In fact, as a brief online search will show, the term has now become a shorthand reference to any and all projects which have a transcultural dimension across one or more sections of the black African **diasporic** cultures of the region.

In the work that has followed, Gilroy himself has produced a series of studies of the effects of this historical process on contemporary social interaction in societies such as Britain (Gilroy 2002, 2004). Although critical of the failure of **neo-liberalism** to address the racism endemic in these cultures, he has not turned away from an attempt to discuss how the descendants of these intersecting cultures can forge effective means of working within a single polity. The deeply ironic turn of his earlier study of racism in British life *Ain't No Black in the Union Jack!* (1987) has yielded more recently to the more hopefully titled *After Empire: Melancholia or Convivial Culture?* (2004) in the introduction to which he argues that for all its limitations 'beleaguered multiculture [needs to be defended] against the accusations of failure' (2004: xi). In part this has been a response to the conservative attacks on the idea of multiculture which have erupted in many societies across the region and elsewhere since the 9/11 attacks on the World Trade Centre and the Pentagon in 2001. Gilroy argues that, instead of the failed discourse of official multiculturalism, which has done little to address real, ongoing and indeed increasing cultural and racial prejudices, he suggests that we might develop the idea of 'conviviality'. He uses this term 'to refer to the processes of cohabitation and interaction that have made multiculture an ordinary feature of social life in Britain's urban areas and in post-colonial cities elsewhere. I hope an interest in the workings of conviviality will take off from the point where "multiculturalism" broke down'. (2004: xi). Gilroy is careful to note that he does not mean that racism has disappeared. But the term which stresses shifts in interpersonal relations 'introduces a measure of distance from the pivotal term "identity," which has proved to be such an ambiguous resource in the analysis of **race, ethnicity**, and politics. The radical openness that brings conviviality alive makes a nonsense of closed, fixed, reified identity and turns attention towards the always-unpredictable mechanisms of identification.' (2004: xi) Gilroy's later work, though far less sombre in tone, has some elements in common with Mbembe's work on the **post-colony**, at least in its stress on the analysis of actual daily practice and the interactive processes of social production. It is also interesting to compare its critique of simplistic models of identity with some of the recent accounts of identity politics in texts on **whiteness** such as Hill 2004.

Further reading: Campbell 2006; Gilroy 1987, 1993, 2004.

BLACK STUDIES/BLACK CONSCIOUSNESS

This was one of the earliest models for cross-cultural studies of peoples affected by colonization, and centred on African peoples who had been transported, enslaved or otherwise made diasporic by **colonialism** and by **slavery**. It developed mainly in the United States. In the nineteenth century, black American intellectuals such as Frederic Douglas (circa 1817–1895), Booker T. Washington (1856–1901) and W.E.B. du Bois (1868–1963), men who had either been born slaves or were the children of slaves, as well as others like Marcus Garvey (1887–1940), a Jamaican who settled in the United States, had developed a body of texts and institutions dedicated to black education and black development. Many colleges were founded, through their inspiration, to educate black Americans. These included Wilberforce College, Lincoln College, Howard Universuty, Tuskegee Institute and Fisk University. These intellectuals advocated an investigation of the distinctiveness of the African cultural elements in black American and Caribbean societies. Cultural historians such as Paul Gilroy have argued that these links across and between the various regions where black diasporic intellectuals had emerged formed a crucial part of the emergence of a distinctive and transnational movement, which he has dubbed the Black Atlantic.

The widespread growth of Black (variantly African American or African Caribbean) Studies followed the Civil Rights activism of the 1960s. Black Studies rapidly established itself in United States institutions as a powerful model to investigate any and all aspects of the African negro **diaspora**. It encouraged investigations of African origins for American and Caribbean language usage and cultural practices (see **creole**), and examined the cross-cultural influence on Africa itself of American and Caribbean intellectuals such as Alexander Crummell (1819–1898) and Edward Wilmot Blyden (1832–1912), who had been so influential there in the nineteenth century with the founding of colonies of freed slaves in Liberia and Sierra Leone. Influenced in part by the example of the francophone movement of **négritude**, Black Studies both predated and outlasted that movement. In the 1960s it embraced many of the ideas developed by **Fanonist** thinkers and, in the form of the black consciousness movement, sought to redress the negative self-image created in many black people by their long history of enslavement and discriminatory treatment, treatment made inescapable, as Fanon had noted, by the visibility of their perceived 'difference' ('The Fact of Blackness' in Fanon 1952: 109–140).

Various movements in different parts of the world have embraced elements of the black consciousness programme, for example in Australia and New Zealand, where Australian Aboriginal and Maori groups have used the concept of 'blackness' as an ethnic signifier, and among the many diasporic 'peoples of colour' who now make up an increasing proportion of the people of the old European metropolitan centre where the term 'black' has been employed to identify a new **ethnicity** (Hall 1989).

Further reading: Appiah and Gates 1995; Baker and Diawara 1996; Blassingame 1971; Bracey 2003; Butler 1981; Chrisman 2000, 2005; Joyce 2005; Mercer 1994; Moikabu 1981; White 1985.

BORDERLANDS

The idea of the border is clearly crucial to **post-colonial** studies and manifests itself in concerns with the constructed boundaries between peoples, nations and individuals. The idea of the border is implicit in the outreach of European cultures in the colonial period. The region which this aggressive **diasporic** movement of European settlers reached at any point became defined as the **frontier**. The settled area adjacent to this was also known sometimes as the borderlands. Contemporary transcultural studies have suggested that such borderland spaces can be spaces of energy, when they question fixities and release the potential for change and revision (Anzaldua 1987, Glissant 1989, Harris 1983). This is because these **liminal** spaces act to problematise and so dismantle the binary systems which bring them into being. It is this idea of the deconstructive potential of the space where two cultures encounter one another which also underlies the idea of the transformative energy of the **contact zone** (Pratt 1992).

The term has been especially important in studies of the US–Mexican borderlands, spaces which have been occupied at various periods by the two **nation** states of Mexico and the United States and which remain profoundly **hybridized** in many aspects of their culture. The so-called **mestizo** (literally mixed) cultures of this region resulting from a long period of **transcultural** exchange between the various ethnic populations, extends to the cultural expression of the region eg. musical forms, food (Tex-Mex cuisine) etc. But this admixture has had only the most superficial effect on the underlying power differences, which the border enforces. The borderland of the South-West remains the space where the United States most actively polices its difference from the rest of the Americas, differences rooted in racial, linguistic and economic factors which feed the idea of this as a region of threat and potential dissolution. The principal stress is on the exclusion of so-called illegals, Mexicans seeking to cross into the US for economic reasons. But since the attacks on the World Trade Centre and the Pentagon in 2001 the South-West border region has been seen as a potential threat to national security. As a result a physical barrier has been constructed along most of its length. The long border with Canada to the north, although also subject to more stringent regulations since 2001 has been seen as less dangerous, emphasizing the fact that the south-west is a borderland where more threatening forms of difference, racial and economic, are rendered visible.

Further reading: Anzaldua 1987; Ashcroft 2001a; Hennessy 2007.

CANNIBAL

This term for an eater of human flesh is of particular interest to post-colonial studies for its demonstration of the process by which an imperial Europe distinguishes itself from the subjects of its colonial expansion, while providing a moral justification for that expansion. The *OED* definition of 'cannibal' reads: 'A man (*esp.* a savage) that eats human flesh; a man-eater, an anthropophagite. Originally proper name of the man-eating Caribs of the Antilles' (Hulme 1986: 16). This definition is itself a very good demonstration of two related features of colonial discourse: the separation of the 'civilized' and the 'savage', and the importance of the concept of cannibalism in cementing this distinction. To this day, cannibalism has remained the West's key representation of primitivism, even though its first recording, and indeed most subsequent examples, have been evidence of a rhetorical strategy of imperialism rather than evidence of an objective 'fact'.

According to Peter Hulme, the first recording of the term 'canibales' is found in Columbus' journal, where he writes that the local Arawaks regarded a particular island with great trepidation saying:

> that this land was very extensive and that in it were people who had one eye in the forehead, and others whom they called 'canibales'. Of these last they showed great fear, and when they saw that this course was being taken, they were speechless, he says, because these people ate them and because they were very warlike.
>
> (Hulme 1986: 16–17)

Quite apart from the questions surrounding the validity of this journal – 'a transcription of an abstract of a copy of a lost original' – Columbus' 'record' is far from being an observation that those people called 'canibales' ate other people. It is a report of other people's words, spoken in a language of which he had no prior knowledge, and associated with the obviously dubious report of people with one eye in their forehead.

Why was it that the canibales were so readily accepted as man-eaters? Why was it that the term cannibal so readily displaced 'anthropophagite' as a description of those who ate human flesh? In essence Peter Hulme's explanation is that there was an implicit struggle occurring within Columbus' journal, as there was in European consciousness generally, over how the New World was to be depicted: a struggle between the rhetorical tropes of idealization and debasement, between Oriental civilization and savagery. With the report of the canibales, the discourse of savagery triumphs in Columbus' writing as the journal writer declares 'the Caniba are nothing else than the people of the Grand Khan' – the idealized Oriental civilization is displaced by the definitive primitivism of man-eating cannibals, and the demonization of the 'primitive' **other** in imperial discourse becomes (almost from this moment it seems) increasingly naturalized. The merging of 'cannibal' and 'primitive' into a virtually synonymous relationship extends to the present day as the pre-eminent sign of the power of 'othering' maintained by imperial discourse.

The eating of human flesh on occasions of extremity or transgression, or in ritual, has been recorded from time to time as a feature of many societies, but the emergence of the word cannibal was an especially powerful and distinctive feature of the rhetoric of empire. The superseding of 'anthro-pophagy' by 'cannibalism' was not a simple change in the description of the practice of eating human flesh, it was the replacement of a descriptive term with an ontological category. From the time of Columbus, 'cannibal' became synonymous with the savage, the primitive, the 'other' of Europe, its use a signification of an abased state of being. In this sense the term came to play an important part in the moral justification for imperial rule.

Further reading: Berglund 2006; Colás 2001; Hulme 1986; Kilgour 1993; Motohashi 1999; Obeyesekere 1992; Sanborn 1998; Sanday 1986; Shaw 2001; Slemon 1992.

CARIBBEAN/WEST INDIAN

The terms 'Caribbean' and 'West Indian' are often used interchangeably to refer to the island nations of the Caribbean Sea and territories on the surrounding South and Central American mainland (such as Guyana and Belize). More accurately, however, the term 'Caribbean' refers to all island nations located in the area (and mainland Guyana and Belize), while 'West Indian' refers only to those nations that were formerly

British colonies, e.g. Jamaica, Trinidad, Barbados, St Lucia, St Vincent, Antigua, Dominica, Guyana (and sometimes Belize).

The origins of the two terms also differ, with 'Caribbean' deriving from a corruption of the Spanish 'caribal', itself generally considered to be a 'mishearing' of an Amerindian word. 'West Indies' arose in contrast to the designation 'East Indies', the 'spice islands' of Asia and Columbus' intended destination when he 'discovered' the Caribbean in 1492.

(See **cannibal**.)

Further reading: Baugh 2000; Childs, Weber *et al.* 2006; Chin 2006; Dash 2003; Döring 2002; Hogan 2000; Murdoch 1999; Murray 2000; Puri 2004; Taylor 1995.

CARTOGRAPHY (MAPS AND MAPPING)

Both literally and metaphorically, maps and mapping are dominant practices of colonial and post-colonial cultures. Colonization itself is often consequent on a voyage of 'discovery', a bringing into being of 'undiscovered' lands. The process of discovery is reinforced by the construction of maps, whose existence is a means of textualizing the spatial reality of the other, naming or, in almost all cases, renaming spaces in a symbolic and literal act of mastery and control. In all cases the lands so colonized are literally reinscribed, written over, as the names and languages of the indigenes are replaced by new names, or are corrupted into new and Europeanized forms by the cartographer and explorer. This was a long-standing feature of colonialism and not restricted to distant unknown lands. Irish playwright Brian Friel graphically illustrates this in *Translations*, which deals with the mapping and renaming of the West of Ireland by the English army in the nineteenth century, a process in which the native Irish (Gaelic) culture is literally overwritten by English imperialism.

Maps also inscribe their ideology on territory in numerous ways other than place-names. The blank spaces of early maps signify a literal *terra nullius*, an open and inviting (virginal) space into which the European imagination can project itself and into which the European (usually male) explorer must penetrate. Such blank spaces invite other cultural superscriptions, such as the elaborately drawn monsters and sub-human wild-men (**savages**) of most early maps. Imaginative transferences are frequent. Thus early maps of Australia (*Terra Incognita* or *Terra Incognita Australis* as it was known in the seventeenth century when the first

European maps of the northern coast-line were drawn) show an interior populated by elephants and pygmies. Similarly the so-called **cannibals** of the Indies (a term derived from the corruption of the Spanish name for the Carib peoples) appear frequently on maps of the interior of Africa. Indeed, by the early twentieth century, the term is almost synonymous with Africans in popular literature and humour, as witness the numerous cartoons that represent cannibals as black people with bones through their noses roasting missionaries in a pot.

The fictionality of the narratives of such processes of 'discovery', which the process of mapping objectifies, is emphasized by the role of the native guide in such explorations, who leads the explorer to the interior. The prior knowledge of the land that this dramatizes, and which cannot be wholly silenced in the written accounts of these explorations, is ignored, and literally silenced by the act of mapping, since the **indigenous people** have no voice or even presence that can be heard in the new discourse of scientific measurement and written texts that cartography implies. They figure, if at all, only as illustration – savages, cannibals or monsters. The allegorization of space (and its hierarchization) is also defined by maps, first by the decision as to which projection to favour, since this privileges some land-spaces over others; or by the decision to orient all maps on a North–South axis; or by the creation of a body of special maps that divide the land into such 'objective' categories as climatic regions, population densities and, not least, natural resources.

Maps can also serve as (allegorical) tools of exploitation. In his analysis of Mercator's Atlas, José Rabasa (1993) demonstrates how the projection map became a major tool of **Euro-centrism**, defining European latitudes as pivotal reference points for the conception of a world hierarchy, and embodying as geographical fact European attitudes about the nature of the world. In effect, the European map created what has remained the contemporary geographical world reality. The definition of cultures as tropical in a world where temperate is the norm, or as densely populated or thinly populated, or as resource rich or poor, are essential discriminations upon which a practice of exploitation or control can be erected. That these techniques also feature in such modern controlling discourses as 'development' studies illustrates how persistently the sciences of cartography and mapping have contributed to the establishment and reestablishment of the various world orders of the last few centuries.

Although **ethnography** (the supposedly objective scientific description of 'primitive' peoples and cultures) has frequently borne the brunt of anti-colonial attacks as being the principal intellectual discourse of colonization, it is worth noting that geography and geographers, and the science of cartography, played at least as important a role in underpinning the objects and values of the colonial enterprise. The Royal Geographical Society was a prime mover in the imperial conquests of the 'undiscovered' regions of the world, and it is significant that as Kipling's *Kim* illustrates (the cover of the Head of the Secret Service in that text, Creighton Sahib, is that of the Director of the General Survey of India), the colonial mapper and surveyor was frequently the most ubiquitous figure of imperial control.

Further reading: Carter 1987; Clifford 1997; Hiatt 2005; Huggan 1995; Mignolo 1995a; Rabasa 1993; Ryan 1994.

CATACHRESIS

The application of a term to a thing that it does not properly denote *(OED)*. Originally referring to grammatical 'misuse', this term is used by Gayatri Spivak in a way that is close to the meaning of **appropriation**. Catachresis is the process by which the colonized take and reinscribe something that exists traditionally as a feature of imperial culture, such as parliamentary democracy. When Spivak speaks, for instance, of the ability of the subaltern 'to catachretize parliamentary democracy' (1991: 70), she means 'the insertion and the reinscription of something which does not refer literally to the correct narrative of the emergence of parliamentary democracy' (70). That is, while parliamentary democracy emerges from a specific European history and culture, its adoption into, and adaptation by, the culture of the postcolonial society, including the assertion, for instance, that there exists a pre-colonial native tradition of parliamentary democracy, may offer an empowering avenue of self-determination to the subaltern subject. Another common and empowering catechresis is the application of the term 'nation' to a social group in existence before colonization, such as the 'Zulu nation', the 'Aboriginal nation', the 'Sioux nation'.

Further reading: Prakash 1997; Spivak 1991, 2000.

CATALYSIS

A term adopted by Guyanese novelist and critic Denis Williams to describe processes of racial change and racial intermixing in New World societies, a formulation that deliberately challenges the 'melting-pot' model. A catalyst, as Williams notes, is 'a body which changes its surrounding substance without itself undergoing any change' (1969: 10). For Williams, American societies are 'crucibles in which catalysts of greater or lesser potency operate'. The process of catalysis in such New World societies challenges the very concepts of race purity and its obverse, 'miscegenation', since it is what both makes the societies unique and gives them a potency lacking in Old World cultures that fetishize pure-race ancestry.

Arguing that this process is 'more dramatically marked' in Guyanese society than among any other New World peoples, Williams notes that in catalysis:

> the sperm is continually invested with a new skin, a new mask. There is no warrant from one generation to another as to the form in which this sperm will be handed on; unlike in [*sic*] the Old World Societies our culture inherently lacks those restraining institutions which act as checks and safeguards for the continued purity of the sperm, tribal, religious, social or psychic taboos which secure and protect the continuity of the line. No New World individual might pronounce with absolute certainty on what his grandchildren are racially likely to be. . . . There are no Africans in the New World; there is only the African sperm in various states of catalysis, and it is this fact of catalysis which constitutes our difference from all other peoples of the world.
>
> (1969: 11–12)

According to Williams, this process of catalysis becomes a distinguishing feature of the reality of 'the New World man' and also becomes the focus for 'the release of his original energies' (14). For him, New World philosophy must arise out of this energizing tension. It is generated out of the mutual insecurities created by the pressure of several racial groups qualifying and diminishing the self-image of the other. Although, on the face of it, this might seem to be a negative thing, the energy produced is the source of great creative potential. 'The resulting uneasiness, the sense of psychic erosion, the self questioning' causes a catalytic reaction that leads to a new totality.

· This qualifying process is also associated in Williams' view with a 'lack of union with the ancestral gods of the soil', another feature distinguishing New World from Old World cultures. Williams also draws a distinction between the New World societies of the Americas and

31

those of, for instance, Australia and New Zealand, which he regards as filiative cultures on the Old World model.

Williams concludes that since 'reality' for Guyanese and other New World societies 'hinges on the fact of the human in infinite process of catalysis', the emphasis is necessarily on the present. 'It is the minute nature and definition of this present viewed in the fluctuating individual consciousness that seems to me crucial in assessing our cultural situation and in realising this situation in our works of art' (35). Catalysis is thus different from **creolization**, **hybridization** or **transculturation** even though it involves historically determined colonial racial and cultural 'mixing' and the creative products of these 'exchanges'.

Further reading: Williams 1969.

CENTRE/MARGIN (PERIPHERY)

This has been one of the most contentious ideas in post-colonial discourse, and yet it is at the heart of any attempt at defining what occurred in the representation and relationship of peoples as a result of the colonial period. Colonialism could only exist at all by postulating that there existed a **binary** opposition into which the world was divided. The gradual establishment of an empire depended upon a stable hierarchical relationship in which the colonized existed as the **other** of the colonizing culture. Thus the idea of the savage could occur only if there was a concept of the civilized to oppose it. In this way a geography of difference was constructed, in which differences were mapped (**cartography**) and laid out in a metaphorical landscape that represented not geographical fixity, but the fixity of power.

Imperial Europe became defined as the 'centre' in a geography at least as metaphysical as physical. Everything that lay outside that centre was by definition at the margin or the periphery of culture, power and civilization. The colonial mission, to bring the margin into the sphere of influence of the enlightened centre, became the principal justification for the economic and political exploitation of colonialism, expecially after the middle of the nineteenth century.

The idea is contentious because it has been supposed that attempts to define the centre/margin model function to perpetuate it. In fact, post-colonial theorists have usually used the model to suggest that dismantling such binaries does more than merely assert the independence of the marginal, it also radically undermines the very idea of such a centre, deconstructing the claims of the European colonizers to a unity and a fixity of a different order from that of others. In this sense the dismantling of centre/margin (periphery) models of culture calls into question the claims of any culture to possess a fixed, pure and homogenous body of values, and exposes them all as historically constructed, and thus corrigible formations.

Further reading: Brah 1996; Brennan 2005; Castillo 1999; Clifford 1997; Harding and Narayan 2000; Huggan 2001; Marriott 2000; Mignolo 2000a; Sarkowsky 2002; Smyth 2000.

CHROMATISM

From 'chromatic' (1603) meaning 'of or belonging to colour or colours' *(OED)*, this term is used to refer to the essentialist distinction between people on the basis of colour. It is sometimes used in conjunction with the term 'genitalism', a distinction between men and women based on the obvious biological difference between male and female. Both terms are employed to indicate the fallacy of making simplistic and stereotypical distinctions of **race** and gender and to suggest that the range of difference within these categories is a matter of representation and discursive construction.

CLASS AND POST-COLONIALISM

Like 'gender' and **race**, the concept of class intersects in important ways with the cultural implications of colonial domination. It is clear that economic control was of significant, if not primary importance in imperialism, and that economic control involved a reconstruction of the economic and social resources of colonized societies. Consequently, class was an important factor in colonialism, firstly in constructing the attitudes of the colonizers towards different groups and categories of the colonized ('natives'), and increasingly amongst the colonized peoples themselves as they began to employ colonial cultural discourse to describe the changing nature of their own societies. However, it is less clear to what degree categories like class were able to be employed as descriptors of colonized societies without undergoing profound modifications to accommodate their cultural differences from Europe.

The first contention to be answered is the notion that the kinds of inequity and injustice, exclusion and oppression found in post-colonial societies is *simply* explicable in terms of class. Is the condition of the colonized themselves simply referable to universal notions of class identification, so that they can be absorbed into some general category such as the international proletariat without a need of further culturally discrete distinctions? The **Eurocentric** and **universalist** bias of such a contention is obvious. Nevertheless, it is clear that in many ways the idea of a **binarism** between a proletarian and an owning class was a model for the **centre's** perception and treatment of the **margin**, and a model for the way in which imperial authority exercised its power within the colonies.

This conjunction is hardly surprising given the fact that ideas of class and race were deeply intertwined in nineteenth-century European thought, with figures like Gobineau, sometimes called 'the father of modern racism', motivated in his production of a theory of race and degeneration by his own aristocratic fear of the degeneracy produced by the emerging power of the new urban bourgeoisie (Biddiss 1970). The legitimization of sociopolitical (class group) interests by appeals to racial origins was a strong feature of nineteenth-century French thought, as myths of origin, Germanic and Gallic, were employed to legitimate different positions in the class struggles of the time. A similar association can be found in much nineteenth-century English thought, with appeals by literary texts to ideas of Norman and Saxon blood as features of a similar if less violent debate between the aristocracy and the new bourgeoisie.

The concentration of manufacturing in England and the use of colonies as sources of raw materials meant that colonial societies exercised no control over the 'means of production'. At the same time, a modern class analysis involves more than simply identifying the owners of the means of production and the wage-slaves of classic Marxism. It involves identifying the specific and complex array of class interests and affiliations that are established in the wake of capital investment in the colonies. It also involves an analysis of the ways in which the colonized themselves replicate the groupings of the capitalist system, with the emergence of distinctive forms of 'native' capitalists and workers whose social role will often be the result of an intersection of their place in the new social and economic structures with their own, older social and economic formations.

The question of class in colonial societies is further complicated by the kinds of cultural particularities that intersect with general economic categories. For Marx, as for Engels, the universal grouping of all pre-capitalist societies as either feudal or 'Asiatic' meant in effect that any detailed analysis of sociopolitical groups in non-European societies was effectively precluded. Thus one thing Marx himself did not account for, indeed perhaps could not account for, given the resolutely Eurocentric orientation of his models of society, was the fact that class does not transfer across cultures in a simple way, even when those cultures are deeply reconstructed along lines of capital accumulation.

For example, any analysis of ideas of 'class' in societies such as India, in which traditional caste divisions, replicating economic and social disadvantages from generation to generation, may be overlaid by modern, post-industrial forces, needs to take into account the ways in which models of class-divided groups, such as workers or capitalists, often cross and conflict with the older caste boundaries. Where these identities and differences coincide, they may reinforce the kinds of privileges or oppressions that a classic Marxist class analysis would emphasize. Even those **settler** societies, such as Australia, that would seem to reproduce the existing class structure of Britain more exactly than any other kind of colony, clearly do not do so in any unproblematic way. Thus, though they may reproduce many aspects of the imperial centre and may even perceive themselves to be filiatively related to it, they often construct opposing myths of their democratic or classless nature, or operate along lines of internal division based on perceived racial or religious differences ('Irish Catholic convictism' for example) that have completely different orientations from that of the officially acknowledged 'Mother Country'. Such myths of egalitarianism or democracy clearly do not reflect economic truths since inequalities of wealth prevail in all these colonial situations, but they may well reflect self-perceptions that are important aspects of the construction of a new national mythology and identity.

Since recent post-colonial theory has tended to concentrate on the issues of **race**, **ethnicity**, and, to a lesser extent, gender in the colonialist definitions and opposing self-definitions of colonized peoples, the importance of class has been downplayed. Few if any attempts have been made to see how the formation of categories such as race, gender and class, both historically and in modern practice, intersect and coexist. The need to find ways of articulating the importance of economic structures to the formation of these categories of analysis is increasingly clear. An analysis of class has a crucial, if complex, role to play in emphasizing the link between representation and material practice in post-colonial discourse. This revision is necessary because in the final analysis the means of representation and the means of production act together reflexively to create the complex conditions of the various colonial and post-colonial societies.

Further reading: Ahmad 1992.

COLONIAL DESIRE

This term, employed by Robert Young in a recent study (1995), indicates the extent to which colonialist discourse was pervaded by sexuality. The idea of colonization itself is grounded in a sexualized discourse of rape, penetration and impregnation, whilst the subsequent relationship of the colonizer and colonized is often presented in a discourse that is redolent of a sexualized exoticism. Thus, even the positive features of colonial attitudes in discourses such as **orientalism**, reflect an eroticized vision that is fundamentally reductive. Ideas of the seductive but enervating world of the 'native', to which the colonizer yields at his (or even more her) peril, lead to formulations such as **going native**, which embody the simultaneous lure and threat of the **other**. As Young has shown, the discourse of colonialism is pervaded by images of transgressive sexuality, of an obsession with the idea of the hybrid and miscegenated, and with persistent fantasies of inter-racial sex. He concludes that sexuality is the direct and congruent legacy of the commercial discourse of early colonial encounters, the traffic of commerce and the traffic of sexuality being complementary and intertwined:

> as in that paradigm of respectability, marriage, economic and sexual exchange were intimately bound up, coupled with each other, from the very first. The history of the meanings of the word 'commerce' includes the exchange both of merchandise and of bodies in sexual intercourse. It was therefore wholly appropriate that sexual exchange and its miscegenated product, which captures the violent antagonistic power relations of sexual and cultural diffusion, should become the dominant paradigm through which the passionate economic and political trafficking of colonialism was conceived.
>
> (Young 1995: 181–182)

Further reading: Dissanayake and Wickramagamage 1993; Docker 1992; McClintock 1995; Young 1995.

COLONIAL DISCOURSE

This is a term brought into currency by Edward Said who saw Foucault's notion of a **discourse** as valuable for describing that system within which that range of practices termed 'colonial' come into being. Said's *Orientalism*, which examined the ways in which colonial discourse operated as an instrument of power, initiated what came to be known as colonial discourse theory, that theory which, in the 1980s, saw colonial discourse as its field of study. The best known colonial discourse theorist, apart from Said, is Homi Bhabha, whose analysis posited certain disabling contradictions within colonial relationships, such as **hybridity**, **ambivalence** and **mimicry**, which revealed the inherent vulnerability of colonial discourse.

Discourse, as Foucault theorizes it, is a system of statements within which the world can be known. It is the system by which dominant groups in society constitute the field of truth by imposing specific knowledges, disciplines and values upon dominated groups. As a social formation it works to constitute reality not only for the objects it appears to represent but also for the subjects who form the community on which it depends. Consequently, colonial discourse is the complex of signs and practices that organize social existence and social reproduction within colonial relationships.

Colonial discourse is greatly implicated in ideas of the centrality of Europe, and thus in assumptions that have become characteristic of **modernity**: assumptions about history, language, literature and 'technology'. Colonial discourse is thus a system of statements that can be made about colonies and colonial peoples, about colonizing powers and about the relationship between these two. It is the system of knowledge and beliefs about the world within which acts of colonization take place. Although it is generated within the society and cultures of the colonizers, it becomes that discourse within which the colonized may also come to see themselves. At the very least, it creates a deep conflict in the consciousness of the colonized because of its clash with other knowledges (and kinds of knowledge) about the world. Rules of inclusion and exclusion operate on the assumption of the superiority of the colonizer's culture, history, language, art, political structures, social conventions, and the assertion of the need for the colonized to be 'raised up' through colonial contact. In particular, colonial discourse hinges on notions of race that begin to emerge at the very advent of European imperialism. Through such distinctions it comes to represent the colonized, whatever the nature of their social structures and cultural histories, as 'primitive' and the colonizers as 'civilized'.

Colonial discourse tends to exclude, of course, statements about the exploitation of the resources of the colonized, the political status accruing to colonizing powers, the importance to domestic politics of the development of an empire, all of which may be compelling reasons for maintaining colonial ties. Rather it conceals these benefits in statements about the inferiority of the colonized, the primitive nature of other **races**, the barbaric depravity of colonized societies, and therefore the duty of the imperial power to reproduce itself in the colonial society, and to advance the civilization of the colony through trade, administration, cultural and moral improvement. Such is the power of colonial discourse that individual colonizing subjects are not often consciously aware of the duplicity of their position, for colonial discourse constructs the colonizing subject as much as the colonized. Statements that contradict the discourse cannot be made either without incurring punishment, or without making the individuals who make those statements appear eccentric and abnormal.

Further reading: Ashcroft 2001b; Barker *et al.* 1994; Bhabha 1983, 1984a; 1994, 1996; Chrisman and Williams 1993; Hulme 1989; Lazarus 1993; Mohanty 1995; Parry 1995; Pennycook 1998; Said 1978; Spivak 1987.

COLONIAL PATRONAGE

Patronage is a term that refers to the economic or social power that allows cultural institutions and cultural forms to come into existence and be valued and promoted. Patronage can take the form of a simple and direct transaction, such as the purchase or commissioning of works of art by wealthy people, or it can take the form of the support and recognition of social institutions that influence the production of culture. The patronage system may even, in one sense, be said to be the whole society, in so far as a specific society may recognize and endorse some kinds of cultural activities and not others. This is especially true in colonial situations where the great differences between the colonizing and colonized societies means that some forms of cultural activity crucial to the cultural identity of the colonized, and so highly valued by them, may simply be unrecognizable or, if recognized at all, grossly undervalued by the dominant colonial system.

The dominance of certain ethno-centric ideas from European culture at the time of the colonization of other cultures, such as nineteenth-century romantic, liberal-humanist assumptions, concealed such communal cultural systems by promoting the idea that the only significant cultural product is that concerned with and produced by individuals. Post-colonial cultures resist such a concealment because it is impossible to discuss the culture of such societies without recognizing the power of colonial institutions, ideologies and patronage systems in validating some forms of culture and denying the validity of others. The privileging of writing and other inscriptive arts over the **oral** and the performative arts, as well as over other kinds of signifying practices such as sculpture, painting, carving, weaving, ceramics – the whole body of material inscription beyond the written – offers a classic example of such privileging.

Colonial powers instituted these privileges through patronage systems that preferred and encouraged written forms over orality. In the hands of the early missionary patrons, the acquisition of literacy was seen as the mark of civilization, and being raised to a 'civilized' state was a concomitant of, if not an absolutely necessary precondition for, salvation. This cultural hierarchy was reinforced by Colonial Educational Systems and Colonial Literature Bureaux, whose task was to develop certain forms of communication, such as written texts in the indigenous and colonial languages – newspapers, journals and various kinds of fiction – to encourage the development of a class of colonials willing to participate in colonial modes of social and artistic production (see **hegemony**). Literature was given support, while oral practices were seen as primitive and were thus neglected or actively discouraged. Although some colonial administrations recognized and even encouraged writing in the indigenous languages, they often did so in ways that transformed local forms of cultural production and encouraged the colonized to accept the superiority of European practices over the local. Thus, for example, in Northern Nigeria, Hausa was encouraged by the Colonial Literature Bureau in the region as a language of expression, in accordance with the policies of 'indirect rule' that the British administration in West Africa favoured. But traditional, religious forms were discouraged, while modern forms such as the short fictional narrative were actively promoted. This was seen as consistent with the colonial policy of 'modernization' which resulted in the supplanting of local cultural practices by imported European ones.

Patronage systems continued to influence the development of post-colonial cultures into and beyond the period of independence, as publishers actively promoted some forms of expression over others (see Lefevere 1983; Griffiths 1996). The control exercised by missionary presses and Colonial Literature Bureaux is obvious, but it may be just as powerfully exercised by the more hidden forces of patronage operated by foreign-owned publishing companies or other media outlets and by the location of the prominent journals of critical assessment in the erstwhile metropolitan centres (Mitchell 1992). The dispute about language choice often intermeshes with these issues of patronage and control, as does the issue of the control of the ownership of the copyright to editions of texts in various designated world or local 'markets'. As culture is increasingly commodified, the ownership of these agencies for commissioning, licensing and distribution can have profound effects, not only on the pricing and availability of material, but on the selection of the art forms and genres, themes and styles of products that are actively promoted.

Further reading: Altbach 1975; Barringer and Flynn 1998; Griffiths 1997; Griffiths 2000; Lefevere 1983; Viswanathan 1989.

COLONIALISM

The term colonialism is important in defining the specific form of cultural exploitation that developed with the expansion of Europe over the last 400 years. Although many earlier civilizations had colonies, and although they perceived their relations with them to be one of a central *imperium* in relation to a periphery of provincial, marginal and barbarian cultures, a number of crucial factors entered into the construction of the post-Renaissance practices of **imperialism**. Edward Said offers the following distinction: '"imperialism" means the practice, the theory, and the attitudes of a dominating metropolitan centre ruling a distant territory; "colonialism", which is almost always a consequence of imperialism, is the implanting of settlements on distant territory' (Said 1993: 8).

The scale and variety of colonial settlements generated by the expansion of European society after the Renaissance shows why the term colonialism has been seen to be a distinctive form of the more general ideology of imperialism. Although Said's formula, which uses 'imperialism' for the ideological force and 'colonialism' for the practice, is a generally useful distinction, European colonialism in the post-Renaissance world became a sufficiently specialized and historically specific form of imperial expansion to justify its current general usage as a distinctive kind of political ideology.

The fact that European post-Renaissance colonial expansion was coterminous with the development of a modern capitalist system of economic exchange (see **world system theory**) meant that the perception of the colonies as primarily established to provide raw materials for the burgeoning economies of the colonial powers was greatly strengthened and institutionalized. It also meant that the relation between the colonizer and colonized was locked into a rigid hierarchy of difference deeply resistant to fair and equitable exchanges, whether economic, cultural or social.

In colonies where the subject people were of a different race, or where minority indigenous peoples existed, the ideology of race was also a crucial part of the construction and naturalization of an unequal form of intercultural relations. **Race** itself, with its accompanying racism and racial prejudice, was largely a product of the same post-Renaissance period, and a justification for the treatment of enslaved peoples after the development of the **slave** trade of the Atlantic Middle Passage from the late sixteenth century onwards. In such situations the idea of the colonial world became one of a people intrinsically inferior, not just outside history and civilization, but genetically pre-determined to inferiority. Their subjection was not just a matter of profit and convenience but also could be constructed as a natural state. The idea of the 'evolution of mankind' and the survival of the fittest 'race', in the crude application of Social Darwinism, went hand in hand with the doctrines of imperialism that evolved at the end of the nineteenth century.

The sexist exclusivity of these discourses (man, mankind, etc.) demonstrated their ideological alliance with patriarchal practices, as numerous commentaters have noted (see **feminism and post-colonialism**). As a result of these new formulations, colonization could be (re)presented as a virtuous and necessary 'civilizing' task involving education and paternalistic nurture. An example of this is Kipling's famous admonition to America in 1899 to 'Take up the White Man's Burden' after their war against Spain in the Philippines rather than follow their own anti-colonial model and offer the Filipinos independence and nationhood (Kipling 1899: 323–4). In this period, and for these reasons, colonialism developed an ideology rooted in obfuscatory justification, and its violent and essentially unjust processes became increasingly difficult to perceive behind a liberal smoke-screen of civilizing 'task', paternalistic 'development' and 'aid'. The development of such territorial designators as 'Protectorates', 'Trust Territories', 'Condominiums', etc. served to justify the continuing process of colonialism as well as to hide the fact that these territories were the displaced sites of increasingly violent struggles for markets and raw materials by the industrialized nations of the West.

In the case of the non-indigenous inhabitants of **settler colonies**, the idea of a cultural inferiority exceeded that of mere provincial gaucherie as race permeated even the construction of 'white' settlers. These were frequently characterized as having wholly degenerated ('**gone native**') from contact with other races, as in the case of white Creoles in the West Indies (Brathwaite 1971), or, in the case of settler colonies such as Canada or Australia, as having developed specific limited colonial characteristics (physical prowess, sporting ability) but not others (cultural and social sophistication). The same practice of characterizing 'colonial' peoples by signifiers of naivety, of social and cultural provinciality and of originary taint ('Irishness', for example, was imported from the internal discriminations of Britain in the Victorian period to its colonialist constructions of both America and Australia) was a feature of English texts even as late as the early twentieth century.

This was so even for Americans, despite independence and the radical shift in their own power position in the world at large after American industrialization in the late nineteenth century (see, for example, the presentation of Americans in such late nineteenth-century and early twentieth-century texts as Conan Doyle's Sherlock Holmes stories, or Shaw's *Man and Superman*). Thus the negative construction of self was as important a feature of self-representation for settler colonies as for colonies of occupation where race and the idea of an alien or decayed civilization were a feature of colonial discrimination. (Although Canada had achieved independent status in the 1870s and Australia became an independent Federation in 1900, the people of both these settler colonies retained many symbolic links that emphasized their continuing dependence on the imperial centre; thus, for example, Australians did not carry separate and distinctive national passports until 1946). By the end of the nineteenth century, colonialism had developed into a system of ahistorical categorization in which certain societies and cultures were perceived as intrinsically inferior.

In Britain, at least, and arguably elsewhere too, by the end of the nineteenth century, a domestic programme for the function of Empire could be clearly discerned, as Victorian society faced increasing internal dissension and division (Disraeli's 'Two Nations'). The doctrine of the New Imperialism was in many ways Disraeli's response to his perception that Britain was divided into two nations of rich and poor, industrial and non-industrial. Empire became the principal ideological unifier across class and other social divisions in Britain. It was to be the principal icon of national unity in the face of the widely perceived social threat of class unrest and revolution that had arisen in post-industrial British society. An **other** (the colonized) existed as a primary means of defining the colonizer and of creating a sense of unity beneath such differences as class and wealth and between the increasingly polarized life of the industrialized cities that developed the wealth and that of the traditional countryside to which its beneficiaries retreated or retired. The colonialist system permitted a notional idea of improvement for the colonized, via such metaphors as parent/child, tree/branch, etc., which in theory allowed that at some future time the inferior colonials might be raised to the status of the colonizer. But in practice this future was always endlessly deferred.

It is significant that no society ever attained full freedom from the colonial system by the involuntary, active disengagement of the colonial power until it was provoked by a considerable internal struggle for self-determination or, most usually, by extended and active violent opposition by the colonized. It is one of the great myths of recent British colonial history in particular that the granting of independence to its colonies was the result of a proactive and deliberate policy of enlightenment on the part of the British people, a policy that distinguished British colonialism from the inferior and more rapacious European brands. Such readings are, of course, part of the construction of the ideology of late nineteenth-century imperialism in which literary representation played a vigorous part, whether actively, as in the work of Kipling, or in a more ambivalent way in the works of Conrad. Despite the anti-imperial strain in some of his writing, Conrad continues to distinguish actively between the English model of colonialism, which has 'an ideal at the back of it', and the mere rapacity of the imperialism of 'lesser breeds' of imperialists. These specious distinctions are projected back into the narratives of the rapacious Spanish conquistadores, though the British treatment of the Indians in Virginia differed from that of the Spanish only in quantity not in the degree of its brutality (Hulme 1986).

Even the granting of Dominion status or limited independence to white settler cultures was the result of long constitutional and political struggles and was made dependent on the retention of legal and constitutional links with the Crown that limited the right of those societies to conduct their own affairs and to develop their own systems of justice or governance. In such societies, of course, the indigenous peoples were not granted even the most limited form of citizenship under these new constitutional models. In Western Australia, for example, even in the 1920s, the Government Department that had charge of Aboriginal affairs was called the Department of Fisheries, Forests, Wildlife and Aborigines. Recent attempts to 'offload' the guilt of colonial policies onto the colonial 'settlers' as a convenient scapegoat emphasize the periods when metropolitan, government policy was more enlightened than that of the local settlers. But in general such ideological discriminations were in no sense alien to the spirit of the metropolitan, colonial powers that had set up these colonies, nor did this essentially discriminatory attitude on the part of the 'home' country change after the granting of federal or dominion status. Racial discrimination was, in the majority of cases, a direct extension of colonial policy and continued to receive both overt and covert support from the ex-colonial powers as well as from the newly emerging power of America throughout the period up to and even after the Second World War.

Such policies of racial discrimination reached their nadir in South African apartheid, which had its roots in earlier colonial discriminatory policies (Davidson 1994). In the case of societies where the factor of race was less easily resolved by such internal discriminatory categorizations, the importance of racial discrimination was even more obvious. British India and European African colonies, for example, had to engage in a long and frequently bloody process of dissent, protest and rebellion to secure their independence. It is also significant that in those cases where European colonial powers held on longest, for example the Portuguese colonies, they were often able to do so and indeed were encouraged to do so by the degree to which their colonial governments were really only a front for a 'broader imperialism', as Amilcar Cabral himself noted (see **anti-colonialism**). Similarly, the nationalist government in South Africa was able to survive only because it was supported by the investment of those very countries who were supposedly opposed to the regime. Thus **colonialism**, far from disappearing as the century goes on, too often merely modified and developed into the **neo-colonialism** of the post-independence period.

Further reading: Croizier *et al.* 2002; Dirlik 2005; Dixon and Heffernan 1991; Eagleton 1990; Easton 1964; Ferro 1997; Fieldhouse 1981; Hart 2003; Havinden and Meredith 1993; Hogan 2000; Kent 1992; Loomba 2005; Prakash 1995; Reiss 2004; Ukai and Harrington 2005; Wesseling 1997.

COMMONWEALTH

Formerly the British Commonwealth of Nations, i.e. the political community constituted by the former British Empire and consisting of the United Kingdom, its dependencies and certain former colonies that are now sovereign nations.

COMMONWEALTH LITERATURE

Broadly, the literatures of the former British Empire and Commonwealth, including that of Britain. In practice, however, the term has generally been used to refer to the literatures (written in English) of colonies, former colonies (including India) and dependencies of Britain, excluding the literature of England. (The term has sometimes included literatures written in 'local' languages and oral performance; and it has been used to include the literatures of Wales, Scotland and Ireland.)

The rise of the study of national literatures written in English (outside Britain) begins with the study of 'American' literature (i.e. the literature of the United States). But those literatures that came to be collectively studied as literatures of the Commonwealth were beginning to be considered within their own national contexts from the late 1940s onwards. However, the concept of 'Commonwealth Literature' as a separate disciplinary area within English studies began in the early 1960s in both the United States and England. In the United States it was formulated as the study of literatures written in a 'world' language in Joseph Jones' *Terranglia: The Case for English as a World Literature* (1965), and as Commonwealth literature in A.L. McLeod's *The Commonwealth Pen* (1961), a work dedicated to R.G. Howarth whose comparative grounding in South African and Australian literatures had proved inspirational for a number of early Commonwealth Literature scholars. The journal *World Literature Written in English* began in 1966 and was appearing regularly by 1971; its precursor, the *CBC Newsletter*, was published from 1962 to 1966; a division of the MLA (ethno-centrically entitled 'World Literatures in English outside the United States and Britain') was constituted in the early 1960s. In England the first international Commonwealth Literature Conference was held in Leeds in 1964 and the Association for Commonwealth Literature and Language Studies formed. (The Leeds meeting followed conferences held at Makerere, Uganda, on the role of English as an overseas language, and at Cambridge, England, on the teaching of English literature overseas). *The Journal of Commonwealth Literature* began in 1965 and the third major journal devoted exclusively to theory and criticism of commonwealth literatures (*Kunapipi*) was published in 1979 (the journal subsequently became a leading journal in establishing the shift to the use of the term post-colonial literatures).

Contemporary post-colonial studies represent the intersection of Commonwealth literary studies and what is usually now referred to as '**colonial discourse** theory'. As Peter Hulme notes in his essay 'Subversive Archipelagoes' (1989), colonial discourse is 'a formulation of recent currency which can perhaps be best understood as designating a conceptual area first marked out by Edward Said's *Orientalism*' although, as Hulme notes, 'much of the work in the area published after *Orientalism* obviously had its genesis long before'.

Like *Orientalism*, which established future developmental lines for colonial discourse theory, the papers delivered at the 1964 Leeds Conference, in particular D.E.S. Maxwell's 'Landscape and Theme', set some of the terms that dominated Commonwealth post-colonial criticism and theory for the next decade. But much that happened at Leeds had already been determined by the growth of nationalist (literary) movements and traditions of cultural critique in Commonwealth countries, a growth based on an understanding of the both deliberate and adventitious uses of English literature as a means of colonialist control throughout Britain's former empire. In the 1960s, the initiation of American literature courses in a number of Commonwealth universities, together with the rise of nationalist cultural sentiment, destablized both the hitherto unquestioned centrality of British literature in English Department curricula and the grounds on which much of that study was based, particularly the notion of 'literary universality'. The Leeds Conference and the 1960s questioning of such Anglo-centric assumptions could themselves also be traced to a history of colonial (and racial) resistance and critique, of which the negritude movement of the 1930s and 1940s is a prominent example.

Commonwealth post-colonial critics, less engaged by Continental philosophies than colonial discourse theorists, initially concentrated their energies on rendering creative writing in English in Commonwealth countries visible within a discipline of literary studies whose assumptions, bases and power were deeply and almost exclusively invested in the literatures of England (or at best the United Kingdom). In fighting for the recognition of post-colonial Commonwealth writing within academies whose roots and continuing power depended on the persisting cultural and/or political centrality of the imperium, and in a discipline whose manner and subject matter were the focal signs and symbols of that power – British literature and its teaching constantly reified, replayed and reinvested the colonial relation – nationalist critics were forced to conduct their guerrilla war within the terms and framework of an English literary critical practice. In so doing they initially adopted the tenets of Leavisite and/or New Criticism, reading post-colonial texts within a broadly Euro-modernist tradition, but one whose increasing and inevitable erosion was ensured by the anti-colonial pressures of the literary texts themselves. Forced from this New Critical hermeticism into a socio-cultural specificity by such local anti-colonial pressures, Commonwealth post-colonialism increasingly took on a localized orientation *and* a more generally theoretical one, bringing it closer to the concerns of what would become its developing 'sister' stream, colonial discourse theory.

Commonwealth post-colonialism remains primarily committed to the literary text, even though it has increasingly turned as well to imperial documents and the discourse of empire, and it has remained, following the Leeds Conference, both predominantly nation-based and determinedly comparative in its practice. Tending increasingly during the 1970s to the anti-colonial, it challenged the centrality of English values and the English canon, and raised the important issue of the continuing interpellative effects of English literary education. Such anti-colonialist arguments were necessarily accompanied by calls for the institutional introduction of national or regional literatures. Most significantly, in terms of future debate within the field, it retained its historical basis in the institutions and practices of British colonialism (and in resistance to these), continuing to include the study of the settler colonies as being crucial for the understanding of imperialism, resistance and the post-colonial.

The more broadly post-structuralist or colonial discourse theory stream, by contrast, with its basis in European philosophy and politics has generally been less interested in contemporary writing by the formerly colonized and the politics of anti-colonial pedagogy within the academies. It has been considerably less focused on creative writing (with the exception of British imperial works). Above all, perhaps, on the basis of its philosophical groundings, it has rejected the national as a kind of 'false consciousness', thereby bringing it into conflict with the Commonwealth Literature stream, much of whose important early anti-colonial work was necessarily grounded in the national as a decolonizing counter to both pre- and post-independence Anglo-interpellation.

Further reading: Amur *et al.* 1985; Ashcroft *et al.* 1989; Bennett 2003; Boehmer 1995, 1998; Brahms 1995; Goodwin 1992; Head 2006; Hulme 1989; Jones 1965; King 1974, 1983, 1996; Mohanram and Rajan 1996; New 1975; Riemenschneider 1983; Rutherford *et al.* 1992; Spivak 2005; Talib 2002; Thieme 1996; Tiffin 1983, 1984.

COMPRADOR

A Portuguese word meaning 'purchaser', *comprador* was originally used to refer to a local merchant acting as a middleman between foreign producers and a local market. Marxists have used it to refer specifically to those local bourgeoisie who owe their privileged position to foreign monopolies and hence maintain a vested interest in colonial occupation. In post-colonial theory the term has evolved a broader use, to include the intelligentsia – academics, creative writers and artists – whose independence may be compromised by a reliance on, and identification with, colonial power.

The notion of a *comprador* class, whether of capitalists or intellectuals, assumes the existence of a clear hierarchical structure of cultural and material relations, for it is arguable that nobody in a colonized society can ever fully avoid the effects of colonial and neo-colonial cultural power. In post-colonial societies it is by no means the bourgeoisie alone who have gained 'access to' popular cultural media such as television or consumables such as Coca-Cola. The assumption that a comprador class is necessarily and identifiably distinct from the rest of the society is therefore somewhat questionable. The word continues to be used to describe a relatively privileged, wealthy and educated élite who maintain a more highly developed capacity to engage in the international communicative practices introduced by colonial domination, and who may therefore be less inclined to struggle for local cultural and political independence.

CONTACT ZONE

The term was first used by Pratt as part of a **transcultural** pedagogic exercise to try and involve students in understanding their own subject-position in transcultural negotiation and confrontation.

> The lecturer's traditional (imagined) task – unifying the world in the class eyes by means of a monologue that rings equally coherent, revealing, and true for all, forging an ad hoc community, homogeneous with respect to ones own words – this task became not only impossible but anomalous and unimaginable. Instead, one had to work in the knowledge that whatever one said was going to be systematically received in radically heterogeneous ways that we were neither able nor entitled to prescribe.
>
> (Pratt 1991)

The term was then developed by Pratt to describe social spaces where 'disparate cultures meet, clash and grapple with each other, often in highly asymmetrical relations of dominance and subordination-like colonialism, slavery, or their aftermaths as they are lived out across the globe today' (Pratt 1992: 4). Since then the term has proliferated. As the advertisement for a notable conference held at the University of Wisconsin-Madisonin 2001 expressed it: 'In the past ten years, the explosion of work across the disciplines on contact zones, **borderlands**,

transculturation, migrations, cultural and commercial traffic, and the various forms of resulting **hybridity**, **métissage**, **mestizaje**, and **créolité** has developed the term far beyond her original formulation. Interactions between global and local, transnational and **national**, identity and **difference**, conjuncturalism and identity politics, space and time have become important areas of research as the study of culture, society, and power has become increasingly comparative, historical, and global in scope' (http://btcs.wisc.edu/contactzone.htm). What this suggests is that the contact zone is an extremely useful and flexible term for the many complex engagements which characterize the post-colonial space and its encounters. The term has had considerable usage in recent studies of settler/indigene relations in societies such as Australia. (See Carter 1992; Somerville and Perkins 2003) Studies like the last which are produced by non-indigenous and indigenous collaborators seek to make the contact zone a space of engagement where the inequalities of the relations between the parties engaged can be confronted if not resolved. This is very much in the spirit of Pratt's initial exercise.

Further reading: Pratt 1992.

CONTRAPUNTAL READING

A term coined by Edward Said to describe a way of reading the texts of English literature so as to reveal their deep implication in imperialism and the colonial process. Borrowed from music, the term suggests a responsive reading that provides a counterpoint to the text, thus enabling the emergence of colonial implications that might otherwise remain hidden. Thus a reading of Jane Austen's *Mansfield Park*, for instance, can reveal the extent to which the privileged life of the English upper classes is established upon the profits made from West Indian plantations, and, by implication, from the exploitation of the colonized. By thus stressing the affiliations of the text, its origin in social and cultural reality rather than its filiative connections with English literature and canonical criteria, the critic can uncover cultural and political implications that may seem only fleetingly addressed in the text itself. 'As we look back at the cultural archive,' says Said, 'we begin to reread it not univocally but *contrapuntally* (1993: 59). The overarching implication is the extent to which English society and culture was grounded on the ideology and practices of imperialism.

Further reading: Said 1993.

COUNTER-DISCOURSE

A term coined by Richard Terdiman to characterize the theory and practice of symbolic resistance. Terdiman examines the means of producing genuine change against the 'capacity of established discourses to ignore or absorb would-be subversion' (1985: 13) by analysing nineteenth-century French writing. He identifies the 'confrontation between constituted reality and its subversion' as 'the very locus at which cultural and historical change occurred' (13).

Terdiman's work focused exclusively on French literature, but his term has been adopted by post-colonial critics to describe the complex ways in which challenges to a dominant or established discourse (specifically those of the imperial centre) might be mounted from the periphery, always recognizing the powerful 'absorptive capacity' of imperial and neo-imperial discourses. As a practice within post-colonialism, counter-discourse has been theorized less in terms of historical processes and literary movements than through challenges posed to particular texts, and thus to imperial ideologies inculcated, stabilized and specifically maintained through texts employed in colonialist education systems.

The concept of counter-discourse within post-colonialism thus also raises the issue of the subversion of canonical texts and their inevitable reinscription in this process of subversion. But Terdiman's general address to this problem is also useful here, in that an examination of the ways in which these operate as naturalized controls exposes their 'contingency and permeability'. Thus, such challenges are not simply mounted against the texts as such but address the whole of that discursive colonialist field within which imperial texts – whether anthropological, historical, literary or legal – function in colonized contexts.

Further reading: Slemon 1987a; Terdiman 1985; Tiffin 1987, 1995.

CREOLE – see PIDGINS/CREOLES

The English term 'creole' is derived from the Portuguese *Criolulu* (Spanish *criollo*) meaning 'native', via the French *créole*, meaning indigenous. 'Creole' originally referred to a white (man) of European descent, born and raised in a tropical colony. The meaning was later extended to include indigenous natives and others of non-European origin. The term was subsequently applied to certain languages spoken by Creoles in and around the Caribbean and in West Africa, and then more generally to other languages of similar type that had arisen in similar circumstances (see Romaine 1988: 38).

From the seventeenth century to the nineteenth, however, the most common use of the term in English was to mean 'born in the West Indies', whether white or negro. Although, therefore, the term had 'no connotation of colour' *(OED)*, it increasingly conjured, in European eyes, the 'threat' of colonial miscegenation.

Historically, and today, the word has been used in quite different ways by different societies. As the Caribbean historian Edward Brathwaite notes,

> in Peru the word was used to refer to people of Spanish descent who were born in the New World. In Brazil, the term was applied to Negro slaves born locally. In Louisiana, the term was applied to the white francophone population, while in New Orleans it applied to mulattoes. In Sierra Leone, 'creole' refers to descendants of former New World slaves, Maroons and 'Black Poor' from Britain who were resettled along the coast and especially in Freetown, and who form a social élite distinct from the African population. In Trinidad, it refers principally to the black descendants of slaves to distinguish them from East Indian immigrants. When used with reference to other native groups, an adjectival prefix – French creole, Spanish creole – is used. In Jamaica, and the old settled English colonies, the word was used in its original Spanish sense of criollo: born into, native, committed to the area of living, and it was used in relation to both white and black, free and slave.
>
> (Brathwaite 1974: 10)

CREOLIZATION

The process of intermixing and cultural change that produces a creole society. While the creolization processes might be argued to be going on throughout the world, the term has usually been applied to 'new world' societies (particularly the Caribbean and South America) and more loosely to those post-colonial societies whose present ethnically or racially mixed populations are a product of European colonization. According to Edward Brathwaite, creolization 'is a cultural process' – 'material, psychological and spiritual – based upon the stimulus/response of individuals within the society to their [new] environment and to each other'. Although 'the scope and quality of this response and interaction' are 'dictated by the circumstances of society's foundation and composition', they produce a totally 'new construct' (1971: 11).

Brathwaite stresses that creolization is not a product but a process incorporating aspects of both acculturation and interculturation, the 'former referring . . . to the process of absorption of one culture by another; the latter to a more reciprocal activity, a process of inter-mixture and enrichment, each to each'. In his Jamaican case study, Brathwaite traces the ways in which the processes of creolization began as a result of slavery:

> and therefore in the first instance involving black and white, European and African, in a fixed superiority/inferiority relationship, tended first to the culturation of white and black to the new Caribbean environments; and, at the same time, because of the terms and the conditions of slavery, to the acculturation of black to white norms. There was at the same time, however, significant interculturation going on between these two elements.
>
> (Braithwaite 1971: 11)

Creolization, as described by Brathwaite, is specific to, and is best understood in the context of, Caribbean history and societies. But Brathwaite's model of creolization can be compared with, and be seen to be doing some of the same work discussed under the rubric of 'hybridization', though creolization has generally received more historically specific discussion. Robert Young terms an 'unconscious **hybridity**, whose pregnancy gives birth to new forms of amalgamation rather than contestation' or 'the French métissage, the imperceptible process whereby two or more cultures merge into a new mode' as creolization, in contrast to a Bakhtinian hybridity which he regards as more 'contestatory' (1995: 21).

Further reading: Berman 2006; Bongie 1998; Brathwaite 1971, 1981, 1995, 1995a; Colás 1995; Gates 1991; Lang 2000; Memmi 1965; Simmons-McDonald 2003; Young 1995.

CULTURAL DIVERSITY/CULTURAL DIFFERENCE

In common usage, these terms both refer interchangeably to the variety of cultures and the need to acknowledge this variety to avoid universal prescriptive cultural definitions. However, Homi Bhabha, in the essay 'The commitment to theory' (1988), employs the terms as oppositions to draw a distinction between two ways of representing culture. Bhabha argues that it is insufficient to record signifiers of cultural *diversity* which merely acknowledge a range of separate and distinct systems of behaviour, attitudes and values. Such a framework may even continue to suggest that such differences are merely aberrant or **exotic**, as was implicit in imperialistic ethnographies. References to cultural diversity based on an assumption of 'pre-given cultural "contents" and customs' give rise to anodyne liberal notions of multiculturalism, cultural exchange or the culture of humanity.

Cultural *difference*, on the other hand, suggests that cultural authority resides not in a series of fixed and determined diverse objects but in the process of how these objects come to be known and so come into being. This process of coming to be known is what brings into being and discriminates between the various 'statements *of* culture or *on* culture' and gives authority to the production of the fields of references by which we order them. By stressing the process by which we know and can know cultures as totalities, the term 'cultural difference' emphasizes our awareness of the 'homogenising effects of cultural symbols and icons' and places the emphasis on a questioning attitude towards 'the authority of cultural synthesis in general' (Bhabha 1994: 20).

The 'difference' Bhabha emphasizes here is clearly connected with the radical **ambivalence** that he argues is implicit in all colonial discourse. He insists that this same ambivalence is implicit in the act of cultural interpretation itself since, as he puts it, the production of meaning in the relations of two systems requires a 'Third Space'. This space is something like the idea of deferral in poststructuralism. While Saussure suggested that signs acquire meaning through their difference from other signs (and thus a culture may be identified by its difference from other cultures), Derrida suggested that the 'difference' is also 'deferred', a duality that he defined in a new term '*différance*'. The 'Third Space' can be compared to this space of deferral and possibility (thus a culture's difference is never simple and static but ambivalent, changing, and always open to further possible interpretation). In short, this is the space of **hybridity** itself, the space in which cultural meanings and identities always contain the traces of other meanings and identities. Therefore, Bhabha argues, 'claims to inherent originality or purity of cultures are untenable, even before we resort to empirical historical instances that demonstrate their hybridity'.

This view is not incompatible with Fanon's idea of the development of a radical and revolutionary native intelligentsia. In fact it is specifically invoked as the defining condition for such a radical native intelligentsia as opposed to a *comprador*-class or **neo-colonialist** native élite, which merely positions itself within a totalized and controlled metaphor of cultural diversity. Such an élite, which invokes unchanging and fixed **nativist** forms, can never fully oppose the control of the dominant culture, since they define culture as fixed and unprogressive. Yet, ironically, it may be their very in-betweenness that allows a revolutionary potential for embracing change in members of the same group of native intelligentsia as **Fanonist** thought acknowledges. Bhabha suggests that 'for Fanon the liberatory "people" who initiate the productive instability of revolutionary cultural exchange are themselves the bearers of a hybrid identity . . . and they construct their culture from the national text translated into modern Western forms of information technology, language, dress . . . [transforming] the meaning of the colonial inheritance into the liberatory signs of a free people of the future' (38). Despite Bhabha's intervention in many post-colonial discussions, the terms continue to be used interchangeably in the way defined at the beginning of this entry.

Further reading: Bhabha 1994.

CULTURAL TOURISM

After independence many colonized cultures sought various ways to preserve their traditional practices. One of the most controversial and disputed methods has been the establishment of cultural tourism, that is, the use of culture as an attraction for foreign tourists. Such tourism has also become an increasingly important part of the economy for many post-colonial states. Of course, the use of cultural practices to attract visitors is part of the tourist industry in most countries, eg. the use of Britain's castles and stately homes, or the use of the American West and its traditions in so-called 'dude ranches'. But in post-colonial cultures it is especially problematic since it engages with the broader issue of the **exoticization** of such cultures. The issue revolves around the control of the process. Who controls the process and who benefits from it? These are crucial questions. In some parts of the world they are tied into issues related to the preservation of specific art forms. Elsewhere they are related to issues of land ownership and control. For example, in the Kimberley region of Western Australia the local Mowanjum community has engaged in a process of renewing the sacred *wanjina* images originally painted on rock faces. They have used these images to create artwork, which has been sold to raise money for education and health facilities. But they also see the process as one which keeps the traditional culture alive and passes it on to the new generation (See Blundell and Woolagoodja 2005). In South Africa and in parts of Australia the local communities have regained control of sacred areas that had been incorporated in National Parks. They have continued to allow access to these areas under their control to encourage tourism, which creates wealth for the community. Notable examples include the Uluru region (the erstwhile Ayer's Rock) in central Australia and the Gemsbok National Park in the Kalahari region of Southern Africa. These have become sites in which traditional cultural practices are displayed as part of a cultural tourism controlled by the local communities (See Carruthers 2003).

Although such examples show cultural tourism in a positive light it is also clear that it has considerable potential for the further exploitation of post-colonial peoples and may be recruited to **neo-colonial** agendas. This more exploitative form of tourism has a long history, and has a clear link with the process of **exoticizing** the 'native,' which underlay the display of living peoples in the colonial period. This process continues in the more frankly commercial ventures, such as the 'cultural villages' which can be found in locations as far apart as the West Indies, South Africa and South-East Asia. But it may also be seen to be extended by some of the ways in which post-colonial cultures continue to be represented within discourses such as development and heritage studies. Even projects such as the UNESCO Cultural Heritage programmes, are in danger of exploiting the very material and people they seek to 'preserve'. There is also the danger of regarding such 'preserved' cultures as fixed and unchanging, as embodying some **essential** and **authentic** tradition, which is rendered inflexible. This has consequences for the politics of such communities and their ability to appropriate and adapt the practices of their invaders to resist them (See Griffiths 1994). Some might argue that cultural tourism is a case of just this process of **appropriation** in action, as in the Mowanjum instance cited above. Nevertheless even the most liberal of such ventures are potentially engaged in a commodification of the culture and even of the bodies of the colonized and this has been recognized. The UNESCO website on cultural heritage quotes its own Universal Declaration on Cultural Diversity 2001 which 'seeks to address this concern by emphasizing the Organization's commitment to the "fruitful diversity of . . . cultures" in a spirit of dialogue and openness, taking into account the risks of identity-based isolationism and standardization associated with **globalization**' (www.unesco.org/ culture/heritage/). But it is significant that it recognizes the very real nature of those risks in an increasingly globalized world.

Further reading: Appadurai 1986; Blundell 2000; Carruthers 2006; Griffiths 2007; Huggan 2001; Hulme 2000.

DECOLONIZATION

Decolonization is the process of revealing and dismantling colonialist power in all its forms. This includes dismantling the hidden aspects of those institutional and cultural forces that had maintained the colonialist power and that remain even after political independence is achieved. Initially, in many places in the colonized world, the process of resistance was conducted in terms or institutions appropriated from the colonizing culture itself. This was only to be expected, since early nationalists had been educated to perceive themselves as potential heirs to European political systems and models of culture. This occurred not only in **settler colonies** where the white colonial élite was a direct product of the system, but even in colonies of occupation. Macaulay's infamous 1835 Minute on Indian Education had proposed the deliberate creation in India of just such a class of 'brown white men', educated to value European culture above their own. This is the *locus classicus* of this **hegemonic** process of control, but there are numerous other examples in the practices of other colonies.

Whether in India, Africa or the West Indies in the nineteenth and early twentieth centuries, the first nationalists were also modernizers, whose programme was less to effect a rejection of colonialist culture than to adopt its practices. This process of political and cultural 'brokerage', as some historians have called it, involved these early decolonizers in a profound complicity with the imperial powers from which they sought to emerge as free agents. Their general attitudes and practices were necessarily imbued with the cultural and social values they had been taught to regard as those of a modern, civilized state (de Moraes-Farias and Barber 1990). Consequently, political independence did not necessarily mean a wholesale freeing of the colonized from colonialist values, for these, along with political, economic and cultural models, persisted in many cases after independence.

In colonies where a majority culture or cultures had been invaded and suppressed or denigrated by colonialist practices, the process of resisting and overthrowing these assumptions has been more obviously active. The powerful designation of **neo-colonialism** to denote the new force of global control operating through a local élite or *comprador* class was coined by the Ghanaian independence leader Kwame Nkrumah (1965). As a socialist, Nkrumah restricted his concept of the neo-colonial operations of imperialism to the operation of the global capitalism of the West.

The **globalization** of the modern world economy has meant that political independence has not effected the kinds of changes in economic and cultural control that the early nationalists might have expected. It has even been argued by some recent commentators that the colonial powers deliberately avoided granting independence until they had, through internal discriminations and hegemonic educational practices, created an élite (*comprador*) class to maintain aspects of colonial control on their behalf but without the cost or the opprobrium associated with the classic colonial models.

As well as direct and indirect economic control, the continuing influence of **Eurocentric** cultural models privileged the imported over the indigenous: colonial languages over local languages; writing over orality and linguistic culture over inscriptive cultures of other kinds (dance, graphic arts, which had often been designated 'folk culture'). Against all these occlusions and overwritings of pre-colonial cultural practices, a number of programmes of decolonization have been attempted. Notable among these have been those that seek to revive and revalue local languages. The pressure of the global economy means that élite communication is dominated by the use of the ex-colonial languages, notably the new 'world language' of English, whose power derives from its historical use across the largest of the modern empires and from its use by the United States.

In post-colonial societies in which alternatives exist, it has been suggested that a return to indigenous languages can restructure attitudes to the local and the indigenous cultures, and can also form a more effective bridge to the bulk of the population whose lives have continued to be conducted largely in their mother tongues. Thus, decolonizing processes that have advocated a return to indigenous language use have involved both a social programme to democratize culture and a programme of cultural recuperation and re-evaluation. In Africa, the work of Ngugi wa Thiong'o has been at the forefront of this decolonizing model (Ngugi 1981a, 1986, 1993). But it has also had considerable advocacy in India where, due to the unbroken power of local languages and their literary traditions throughout the colonial period, a strong drive to revalue the literatures and other arts employing Indian languages has occurred in recent times (Ahmad 1992; Devy 1992). It is important, though, not to assume that these cultures remained untouched, and indeed the forms they often now employ, such as the novel, prose fiction, drama, magazines and television soap-opera, reflect an energetic engagement with dominant practices.

Only the most extreme forms of decolonization would suggest that precolonial cultures can be recovered in a pristine form by programmes of decolonization (see **nativism**). More recently, for example, some post-colonial African critics (Appiah 1992; Gikandi 1992; Mudimbe 1994) have questioned the bases on which such extreme decolonizing projects have been erected, arguing from a variety of different perspectives that the systems by which, to use Mudimbe's phrase, 'African worlds have been established as realities for knowledge' are always multiple and diverse, and are implicated in colonial and European orders of knowledge as much as in local ones. For example, Kenyan critic Simon Gikandi has argued that many decolonizing practices 'were predicated on the assumption that African cultures and selves were natural and holistic entities which colonialism had repressed, and which it was the duty of the African writer, in the period of decolonization to recover (if only the right linguistic and narrative tools could be developed), there is now an urgent need to question the ideological foundations on which the narratives of decolonization were constructed' (Gikandi 1992: 378).

Gikandi's analyses critique the simple equation of national narratives and decolonizing processes and argue that discourses of **nationalism** and national liberation (or, in some later texts, of the disillusioning failure of such narratives and such nationalist discourses) are increasingly inadequate ways of analysing and correcting the problems and conflicts of the post-independence condition. For Gikandi, the task faced by African writers now, and by implication by writers in many post-colonial societies, is 'to theorise adequately . . . the problematic of power and the state' (see **post-colonial state**). Thus Gikandi argues that formulations of decolonization, such as Ngugi's in novels like *Matigari*, are 'both a symptom of the problems which arise when the narrative of decolonization is evoked in a transformed post-colonial era and a commentary on the problematics of a belated national narrative' (Gikandi 1992: 379).

The projects of other writers, such as Salman Rushdie, who embrace a 'transnational' identity and seek to critique the contemporary post-colonial state, are often dismissed as not contributing to a decolonizing process. But this is to assume an absolute contiguity between decolo-nization and narratives of nation and nationalism, which arguments like Gikandi's seriously call into question. In fact, the borders and images of the post-colonial nation may be fictions that allow free passage to the continuing control of the **neo-colonialism** of multinational com-panies and global monetary institutions. Decolonization, whatever else it may be, is a complex and continuing process rather than something achieved automatically at the moment of **independence**.

In the **settler colonies** this process can also be seen to occur in a different form. Although they were permitted political independence on the inherited British model at a relatively early stage, they often continued to suffer what the noted Australian commentator A.A. Phillips wittily characterized as 'a cultural cringe' from which they were not released by their nominal political 'independence' (Phillips 1958, 1979). Similarly, they have frequently been far less successful than other kinds of colonies in dismantling the colonialist elements in their social institutions and cultural attitudes. This is to some extent because of the peculiar hegemonic strength exerted by notions of a **filiative** connection with the Imperial centre, reiterated in phrases such as 'sons and daughters of Empire'. Such connections tended to keep the settler colonies more dependent on the apron strings of their colonial masters (Docker 1978), usually at the expense of the recognition of the rights of their indigenous peoples.

Further reading: Ahmad 1992; Appiah 1992; Betts 2004; Brydon and Tiffin 1993; Chamberlain 1999; Coutinho 1992; Crawford 2002; Devy 1992; Docker 1978; Duara 2003; Gikandi 1992; de Moraes-Farias and Barber 1990; Moreiras 2004; Mudimbe 1994; Nederveen Pieterse and Parekh 1995; Newsom 2001; Ngugi 1981a, 1986, 1993; Nkrumah 1965; Okonkwo 1999; Phillips 1979; Rothermund 2006; Shi-xu and Servaes 2005; Spivak 1993; Springhall 2001; Young 1998.

DEPENDENCY THEORY

Dependency theory offers an explanation for the continued impov-erishment of colonized 'Third World' countries on the grounds that underdevelopment is not internally generated but a structural condition of global capitalism itself. It thus presents a similar argument to **world**

system theory in that it explains underdevelopment as consequent on the global structure of domination, rather than an early stage in a process of development. Such 'underdeveloped' countries are usually formerly colonized states that are actually prevented, by the forces of global capitalism, from independent development. The economic rationale of colonization, by establishing colonies as producers of raw materials and foodstuffs for the industrialized metropolitan centres, played a major part in retarding the industrialization and development of those regions.

In drawing attention to this history, dependency theory thus challenges the hypotheses of modernization theory which explains underdevelopment in terms of the lack of certain qualities in 'underdeveloped' societies such as drive, entrepreneurial spirit, creativity and problem-solving ability. Writers such as André Gunder Frank (1979) dismiss modernization theory's argument that underdevelopment is a natural state caused by internal forces and show that it is the form of capitalist development of the West that is responsible for the continued underdevelopment of the 'Third World'.

However, dependency theory has been criticized for a tendency to offer a static analysis of the relation between developed and under-developed states and is thus unable to provide a convincing explanation of such phenomena as the 'Tiger' economies of South-East Asia. Nevertheless, it has been valuable for revealing the ethno-centric bias of modernization theory and for showing that the global system of capital prevents peripheral economies from developing in a manner more appropriate to their cultures and values.

Further reading: Blomstrom and Hettne 1984; Darby 1997; Franco 1975; Frank 1979; Ghosh 2000; Pidd 2004; Seers 1981; B. C. Smith 2003; Wallerstein 1980.

DERACINATE

Literally, to pluck or tear up by the roots; to eradicate or exterminate. The root of the word thus has no direct relation to 'race', but as its emphasis in both English and French has shifted to 'uprooted from one's national or social environment' (as in the French *déraciné*), it has increasingly been associated with racial identity. The European slave trade and plantation slavery not only uprooted Africans from their home environments, but, through centuries of systematic racial denigration, alienated enslaved Africans from their own racial characteristics. (The 'Black is Beautiful' movement of the mid-twentieth century in both the United States and the Caribbean represents systematic attempts by blacks to counter the deracination consequent on plantation slavery.)

DIASPORA

From the Greek meaning 'to disperse' *(OED)*. Diasporas, the voluntary or forcible movement of peoples from their homelands into new regions, is a central historical fact of colonization. Colonialism itself was a radically diasporic movement, involving the temporary or permanent dispersion and settlement of millions of Europeans over the entire world. The widespread effects of these migrations (such as that which has been termed **ecological imperialism**) continue on a global scale. Many such 'settled' regions were developed historically as planta-tions or agricultural colonies to grow foodstuffs for the metropolitan populations, and thus a large-scale demand for labour was created in many regions where the local population could not supply the need.

The result of this was the development, principally in the Americas, but also in other places such as South Africa, of an economy based on **slavery**. Virtually all the slaves shipped to the plantation colonies in the Americas were taken from West Africa through the various European coastal trading enclaves. The widespread slaving practised by Arabs in East Africa also saw some slaves sold into British colonies such as India and Mauritius, whilst some enslaving of Melanesian and Polynesian peoples also occurred in parts of the South Pacific to serve the sugar-cane industry in places like Queensland, where it was known colloquially as 'blackbirding'.

After the slave trade, and when slavery was outlawed by the European powers in the first decades of the nineteenth century, the demand for cheap agricultural labour in colonial plantation economies was met by the development of a system of indentured labour. This involved transporting, under indenture agreements, large populations of poor agricultural labourers from population rich areas, such as India and China, to areas where they were needed to service plantations. The practices of slavery and indenture thus resulted in world-wide colonial diasporas. Indian populations formed (and form) substantial minorities or majorities in colonies as diverse as the West Indies, Malaya, Fiji, Mauritius and the colonies of Eastern and Southern Africa. Chinese minorities found their way under similar circumstances to all these regions too, as well as to areas across most of South-East Asia (including the Dutch East Indian colonies, in what is now Indonesia) and the Spanish- and later American-dominated Philippines.

The descendants of the diasporic movements generated by colonialism have developed their own distinctive cultures which both preserve and often extend and develop their originary cultures. Creolized versions of their own practices evolved, modifying (and being modified by) indigenous cultures with which they thus came into contact. The development of diasporic cultures necessarily questions **essentialist** models, interrogating the ideology of a unified, 'natural' cultural norm, one that underpins the **centre/margin** model of colonialist discourse. It also questions the simpler kinds of theories of **nativism** which suggest that **decolonization** can be effected by a recovery or reconstuction of pre-colonial societies. The most recent and most socially significant diasporic movements have been those of colonized peoples back to the metropolitan centres. In countries such as Britain and France, the population now has substantial minorities of diasporic ex-colonial peoples. In recent times, the notion of a 'diasporic identity' has been adopted by many writers as a positive affirmation of their hybridity.

Further reading: Brah 1996; Braziel and Mannur 2003; Brown and Coelho 1987; Carter 1996; Chow 1993; Gellner 2006; Gunew 2004; Hall 1996; Hayes Edwards 2003; Institute of Commonwealth Studies 1982; Mishra 1996a, 1996b; S. Mishra 2006; Nelson 1993; Rajan and Mohanram 1995; Ramraj 1996; Rath 2000; Roy 1995; Thompson 1987; West-Pavlov 2005.

DISCOURSE

This is a much used word in contemporary theory and in post-colonial criticism is mostly employed in such terms as **colonial discourse**, which is specifically derived from Foucault's use of the concept. Discourse was originally used from about the sixteenth century to describe any kind of speaking, talk or conversation, but became increasingly used to describe a more formal speech, a narration or a treatment of any subject at length, a treatise, dissertation or sermon. More recently, discourse has been used in a technical sense by linguists to describe any unit of speech longer than a sentence.

However, the Foucauldian sense of the term has little to do with the act of speaking in its traditional sense. For Foucault, a discourse is a strongly bounded area of social knowledge, a system of statements within which the world can be known. The key feature of this is that the world is not simply 'there' to be talked about, rather, it is through discourse itself that the world is brought into being. It is also in such a discourse that speakers and hearers, writers and readers come to an understanding about themselves, their relationship to each other and their place in the world (the construction of **subjectivity**). It is the 'complex of signs and practices which organises social existence and social reproduction'.

There are certain unspoken rules controlling which statements can be made and which cannot within the discourse, and these rules determine the nature of that discourse. Since a virtually limitless number of statements can be made within the rules of the system, it is these rules that characterize the discourse and that interest analysts such as Foucault. What are the rules that allow certain statements to be made and not others? Which rules order these statements? Which rules allow the development of a classificatory system? Which rules allow us to identify certain individuals as authors? These rules concern such things as the classification, the ordering and the distribution of that knowledge of the world that the discourse both enables and delimits.

A good example of a discourse is medicine, in mundane terms we simply think of medicine as healing sick bodies. But medicine represents a system of statements that can be made about bodies, about sickness and about the world. The rules of this system determine how we view the process of healing, the identity of the sick and, in fact, encompass the ordering of our physical relationship with the world. There are certain principles of exclusion and inclusion that operate within this system; some things can be said and some things cannot. Indeed we cannot talk about medicine without making a distinction between different kinds, such as 'Western' and 'Chinese' medicine. For these are two discourses in which the body and its relationship to the world are not only different but virtually incompatible. This explains the very great resistance in Western medicine to forms of healing that do not accord with its positivistic idea of the body. Until such practices as acupuncture or herbal remedies could be incorporated into the positivistic framework of Western medicine, by being incorporated into other 'scientific' statements, they were rejected as charlatanism or superstition (they did not concur with 'truth'). It is only very gradually that such rules of exclusion, which keep a discourse intact, can be modified, because the discourse maintains not just an understanding of the world, but in a real sense the world itself. Such incursions, when not controlled, may represent a very great threat to the authority of the discourse.

Discourse is important, therefore, because it joins power and knowledge together. Those who have power have control of what is known and the way it is known, and those who have such knowledge have power over those who do not. This link between knowledge and power is particularly important in the relationships between colonizers and colonized, and has been extensively elaborated by Edward Said in his discussion of **Orientalism**, in which he points out that this discourse, this way of knowing the 'Orient', is a way of maintaining power over it. Said's work lays more stress on the importance of writing and literary texts in the process of constructing representations of the other than does Foucault's, whose concern is more widely distributed across a variety of social institutions. Said's insistence on the central role of literature in promoting colonialist discourse is elaborated in his later work (Said 1993), where he argues that the nineteenth-century novel comes into being as part of the formation of Empire, and acts reflexively with the forces of imperial control to establish imperialism as the dominant ideology in the period. This emphasis has made Said's work of especial interest to those concerned with post-colonial literatures and literary theory.

Foucault's view of the role of discourse though is even wider, and more pervasive, since he argues that discourse is *the* crucial feature of **modernity** itself. For the discourse of modernity occurs when what is said, the 'enunciated', becomes more important than the saying, the 'enunciation'. In classical times, intellectual power could be maintained by rhetoric, by the persuasiveness of the speaker 'discoursing' to a body of listeners. But gradually the 'will to truth' came to dominate discourse and statements were required to be either true or false. When this occurred, it was no longer the act of discourse but the subject of discourse that became important. The crucial fact for post-colonial theory is that the 'will to truth' is linked to the 'will to power' in the same way that power and knowledge are linked. The will of European nations to exercise dominant control over the world, which led to the growth of empires, was accompanied by the capacity to confirm European notions of utility, rationality, discipline as truth.

We can extend our example, therefore, to talk about 'Eurocentric discourse', or the 'discourse of modernity', that is, a system of statements that can be made about the world that involve certain assumptions, prejudices, blindnesses and insights, all of which have a historical provenance, but exclude other, possibly equally valid, statements. All these statements and all that can be included within the discourse thus become protected by the assertion of 'truth'.

Further reading: Ashcroft 1999; Bauman 1998; Bhabha 1994; Chrisman and Williams 1994; Ezzaher 2003; Foucault 1971; Gikandi 2004; Harrison 2003; Hulme 1989; Lazarus 1993, 1994; McHoul and Grace 1993; Said 1978, 1983; Tiffin 1995.

DISLOCATION

A term for both the occasion of displacement that occurs as a result of imperial occupation and the experiences associated with this event. The phenomenon may be a result of transportation from one country to another by slavery or imprisonment, by invasion and settlement, a consequence of willing or unwilling movement from a known to an unknown location. The term is used to describe the experience of those who have willingly moved from the imperial 'Home' to the colonial margin, but it affects all those who, as a result of colonialism, have been placed in a location that, because of colonial **hegemonic** practices, needs, in a sense, to be 'reinvented' in language, in narrative and in myth. A term often used to describe the experience of dislocation is Heidegger's term *unheimlich* or *unheimlichkeit* – literally 'unhousedness' or 'not-at-home-ness' – which is also sometimes translated as 'uncanny' or 'uncanniness'.

Nineteenth-century Australian writers show this process of dislocation in action: for example, novelist Marcus Clark, who speaks of the 'uncanny nature' of the Australian landscape's 'funereal gloom', or the poet Barron Field who declared that 'All the dearest allegories of human life are bound up with the infant and slender green of spring, the dark redundance of summer, and the sere and yellow leaf of Autumn . . . I can therefore hold no fellowship with Australian foliage' (Carter 1987: 43). The implication of Field's remarks is that Australia exists outside of 'real' or 'normal' experience, and in terms of the assumptions of imperial discourse is unknowable until the place is brought under control by language. But it is here, in the attempt to convert the uncolonized 'space' into colonized 'place', that dislocation becomes most obvious. Because the words to describe the new place adequately cannot be found in the language brought with the early settlers, new terms must necessarily be invented. The necessity of dislocation does indeed become the mother of invention. Hence the disruptive and 'disorienting' experience of dislocation becomes a primary influence on the regenerative energies in a post-colonial culture.

In a similar way, the extreme form of physical, social and individual dislocation involved in the institution of slavery has led some Caribbean critics, such as Dennis Williams, Wilson Harris and Edouard Glissant, to suggest that dislocation is the key to a release of a distinctive form of cultural energy. Harris employs the sign of the Caribbean limbo dance or 'gateway', the dance that some speculate may reproduce the forced and literal dislocation of the slave's body in the cramped conditions of the slaver's holds, to signify the process of dismantling and rebirth that generated the distinctive **catalytic** cultures of the New World. The resulting restructuring generates new and powerful forms of culture which, whilst having their roots in an African origin, are able to bring forth a new 'Adamic' possibility of renewal and regeneration (Walcott 1974). **Diasporic** communities formed by forced or voluntary migration may all be affected by this process of dislocation and regeneration too, and this has certainly been argued by some recent critics of the diasporic and migrant experience. (See essays in Rajan and Mohanram 1995.)

Finally, dislocation in a different sense is also a feature of all invaded colonies where indigenous or original cultures are, if not annihilated, often literally dislocated, i.e. moved off what was their territory. At best, they are metaphorically dislocated, placed into a hierarchy that sets their culture aside and ignores its institutions and values in favour of the values and practices of the colonizing culture. Many post-colonial texts acknowledge the psychological and personal dislocations that result from this cultural denigration, and it is against this dislocating process that many modern **decolonizing** struggles are instituted.

See also **Fanonism**.

Further reading: Bery *et al.* 2000; Glissant 1989; Harris 1981; Huggan 2000; Rajan and Mohanram 1995. Williams 1969

DOUBLE COLONIZATION

A term coined in the mid-1980s, and usually identified with Holst-Petersen and Rutherford's *A Double Colonization: Colonial and Post-Colonial Women's Writing* published in 1985. The term refers to the observation that women are subjected to both the colonial domination of empire and the male domination of patriarchy. In this respect empire and patriarchy act as analogous to each other and both exert control over female colonial subjects, who are, thus, doubly colonized by imperial/patriarchal power. Feminist theory has propounded that women have been marginalized by patriarchal society and consequently the history and concerns of feminist theory have paralleled developments in post-colonial theory which foregrounds the marginalization of the colonial subject.

However, post-colonial nationalisms do not necessarily alleviate this situation but may entrench rather than dismantle the power of patriarchy, so that women's struggle against 'colonial' domination often continues after national independence. Post-colonial feminism continues to analyse the perpetuation of gender bias and 'double colonization' even in post-independence states, seeing the persistence of 'neo-colonial' domination of women in national patriarchies. There is considerable disagreement, however, among post-colonial feminists about whether imperialism or patriarchy is the force most urgently in need of contesting. One, perhaps most celebrated example is Hazel Carby's *White Woman Listen* (1982), but similar issues are addressed by Mohanty (1984), Suleri (1992) and others.

Further reading: Carby (1982), Holst-Petersen and Rutherford (1985), Mohanty (1984), Suleri (1992).

ECOFEMINISM

Ecofeminism has become an increasingly important field in both contemporary feminist and environmental studies. Although, as Diamond and Orenstein note, ecofeminism is really 'a new term for an ancient wisdom' (Mies and Shiva 1993: 13), it first came to prominence in the early 1980s, its bases in feminist philosophy, environmental activism and the European and American peace movements of the late 1970s. The term itself was first used by Françoise d'Eauborne in 1980 (Mies and Siva 1993: 13) and was increasingly adopted by both scholars and environmental activists. Organised in response to the Three Mile Island nuclear disaster, the 1980 'Women and Life on Earth: A Conference on Eco-Feminism' focused on 'the connections between feminism, militarization, healing and ecology' (Mies and Shiva 1993: 14). The adoption of the term had also been preceded by much women's poetry and fiction in the 1960s and 70s, and has gained increasing prominence through the work of philosophers Val Plumwood and Karen Warren. It has also been adopted by other disciplines through the writing and activism of Arundhati Roy and Vandara Shiva.

Ecofeminism stresses the indissoluble connectedness – both physical and conceptual – of the earth itself, and all life on it. Humans, as a part of this community depend on earth and sea, and the life this generates for survival; but they are even more fundamentally of it, one component part of the living whole. As Val Plumwood notes, the basic interconnectedness of all matter and psyche is such a 'truism' that it is puzzling that it should need to be remarked at all. 'But the reason why this message of continuity and dependency is so revolutionary in the context of the modern world is that the dominant strands of Western culture have for so long denied it, and have given us a model of human identity as only minimally and accidentally connected to the earth' (Plumwood 1993: 6). Even though we all have a 'formal knowledge of evolutionary biology', this disconnection 'remains deeply and fatally entrenched in modern conceptions of the human and of nature,' continuing to 'naturalize domination in both human and non-human spheres' (1993: 6).

Ecofeminists, however, reject the notion that 'man's freedom and happiness depend on an *ongoing process* of emancipation from nature, and an independence from and dominance over natural processes by the power of reason and rationality' (Mies and Shiva 1993: 6). The tenets of Enlightenment reason rely for their continuing power on a number of linked and hierarchized **binarisms**: nature and culture; black and white; civilization and savagery; the human and the animal. As Mies and Shiva argue, 'wherever women acted against ecological destruction or/and the threat of atomic annihilation, they immediately became aware of the connection between patriarchal violence against women, other people and nature' (14). The 'corporate and military warriors' aggression against the environment was perceived almost physically as an aggression against our female body' (14).

To stop the exploitation and despoliation of, in Plumwood's phrase, the 'more than human' world, radical changes in Western and Western-derived capitalist thinking are required. Central to such rethinking is the dismantling of those dangerous and divisive dualisms of patriarchal economies whose modern roots in Western cultures are traceable to the dictates of reason. Reason is interrogated not, as Plumwood stresses, to instantiate the unreasonable, but to understand the historically and philosophically contingent bases of the subjugation of women, non-western people and the natural world.

Western rationality, which still assumes that the basis of human civilization consists in a progressive detachment from 'nature', also dominated the colonial period. The more closely associated with nature non-European peoples and women were considered to be, the more 'inherently' inferior they were; inferiority ensured and justified patriarchal/Western civilization's destruction and domination of other lands and peoples. Land itself, cast as a female and 'new' to Europeans, was 'ripe' for conquering and taming.

The legacy of the dominant discourse, as ecofeminists recognize, is environmental devastation and on-going destruction of plants, animals and other subject peoples in the name of capitalist 'progress' identified as 'civilization.' Ecofeminism thus seeks to establish – or in the case of some colonized cultures, to *re*-establish, a sense of interconnectedness of being, through ontological change and political activism replicating the philosophy of connectedness in an amalgam of theory and practice. As its affirmation of the shared ground of all being suggests, ecofeminism (especially in the United States) has strong spiritual as well as political and scholarly dimensions; modern retrieval of the traditional confluence of material and spiritual being intimately connected to place and the earth in many pre-colonized cultures.

Further reading: Mies and Shiva 1993; Plumwood 1993; Warren 2000.

ECOLOGICAL IMPERIALISM

A term coined by Alfred W. Crosby (Crosby 1986) to describe the ways in which the environments of colonized societies have been physically transformed by the experience of colonial occupation. According to this thesis, imperialism not only altered the cultural, political and social structures of colonized societies, but also devastated colonial ecologies and traditional subsistence patterns.

Crosby makes a convincing case for the success of European imperialism as having a primarily 'biological and ecological component'. European diseases were unwittingly (and more rarely deliberately) introduced to other parts of the globe, where they decimated indigenous populations and thus facilitated European military and technological conquest. More importantly, introduced crops and livestock not only supported conquering armies and colonizing populations but, in what Crosby calls 'the Neo-Europes' (**settler colonies**), radically altered the entire ecology of the invaded lands in ways that necessarily disadvantaged indigenous peoples and annihilated or endangered native flora and fauna on which their cultures (and sometimes their very lives) depended. The 'Neo-Europes' located in those temperate zones of the northern and southern hemispheres (e.g. Canada, USA, Australia, New Zealand, Argentina) that most closely approximated the climate of Europe quickly became the major exporters of European food crops, even though their native biotas were considerably different and varied. 'The regions that today export more foodstuffs of European provenance – grains and meats – than any other lands on earth had no wheat, barley, rye, cattle, pigs, sheep, or goats whatsoever five hundred years ago' (Crosby 1986: 7). Arguably this has led to one of the most profound ecological changes the world has seen.

The current famines in sub-Saharan Africa can be directly related to the European insistence on the repetitive cultivation of cash crops for export to the metropolitan centres in place of the traditional crop rotation that had kept the desert at bay. As a major form of Euro-spatialization, and as a most effective means of social and territorial control, ecological imperialism cannot be underestimated. Its range of meaning can be extended into the neo-colonial arena in the current Western (or 'multinational') patenting of **'third world'** plant and animal species and in the global destruction (sponsored by both Western and Asian companies) of, for instance, rain-forests.

Recently it has been argued that current Western ecological aware-ness also has its roots in Empire (Grove 1994). In India and the Caribbean, Europeans encountered attitudes to the natural world that differed radically from their own and were more generally 'conserva-tionist', respectful or animistic. European policies in the colonies frequently had to reach compromises with these differing attitudes.

Further reading: Crosby 1986; Grove 1994; Verdesio 2002.

EMPIRE

This term outlined by Hardt and Negri in the book of that name, refers to a phenomenon arising from the increasing globalization of the world, transcending the power of even the strongest sovereign nations. Empire refers to something very different from those empires that have been the traditional consequence of imperialism: the extra-territorial extensions of sovereign nations beyond their own boundaries. For Hardt and Negri, Empire now 'establishes no territorial centre of power and does not rely on fixed boundaries or barriers. It is a *decentred and deterritorializing* apparatus of rule that progressively incorporates the entire global realm within its open, expanding frontiers' (2001: xii). Empire is thus a liminal and decentred principle of power underlying the operation of global capital. The emergence of Empire has many consequences, one of which is to scramble the distinction between First, Second and Third worlds, as the relationship between Capital, labour and markets transcends both national and regional distinctions.

Hardt and Negri reject the simplistic equation of US economic power and Empire. The US does have a privileged position in Empire, but not because of its extension of traditional imperialism, nor its similarities to European empires, but because of its differences. 'Imperialism is over. No nation will be world leader in the way modern European nations were' (2001: xiv). Empire has no geographical limits, but effectively encompasses the spatial totality of the world; it has no historical limits, but 'suspends history' and fixes the present state of affairs forever; it has no class limits but operates at all registers of the social order. While the operation of Empire is 'bathed in blood' the *concept* of empire is always dedicated to peace. However, according to them, this new order of global control, despite its enormous powers of oppression and destruction, leads to new possibilities for the forces of liberation. These forces they conceptualise as originating in the **multitude** – a collectivity that is naturally and inevitably disposed towards liberation. Rather than simply resisting Empire, the **multitude** will reorganise these new processes and put them towards new ends.

Further reading: Hardt and Negri (2001)

ENVIRONMENTALISM

Perhaps the most significant change in the orientation of the Humanities in the second half of the twentieth century has been the questioning of a once taken-for-granted anthropocentrism. Since the Enlightenment, Western epistemology has relegated the extra-human world to the sciences, while the study of the human became the province of the Humanities. It is only relatively recently that the disciplines of, for instance, History, Anthropology, Philosophy, Literature and Cultural Studies have begun to reclaim the 'natural' environment as crucial to the understanding of human 'being' (both past and present) and as of intrinsic worth. The enigma of place, the nature of indigeneity, the relationship between landscape and language, settler incursions with the consequent destruction of integrated biotas, colonial exploitation of resources and enforced cash-cropping (sometimes leading to desertification) have all been subjects of post-colonial study, especially in relation to genocide and the wholesale dispossession of indigenous peoples. But it is only recently that the influences and impacts on the extra-human environment have been studied, both for their own importance and because of the increasing recognition that the more-than-human is indissolubly interwoven with the human past, present, and now future. This increasing emphasis on the 'more-than-human' is environmentalism.

Environmentalism in post-colonial discourse has its beginings in Alfred Crosby's account of the impact of European incursions into the Americas and the Pacific (see **Ecological imperialism**). The conquest and colonization of so many extra-European environments produced irreversible changes in land use, in flora and fauna and frequently damaged beyond repair traditionally balanced relations between indigenous communities and their environments, a relationship – unlike that of their conquerors – crucial to their understanding of their 'being' as *of* the land rather than merely on it. (These very different ontologies are particularly evident in the land claim disputes between Aboriginal and settler-descent peoples which continue today in what Alfred Crosby termed the 'Neo-Europes'. Europeans see land in terms of individual ownership, while many native traditions regarded it as the essential part of a communal (w)holism.

Imperial incursions and colonization have been regarded as environmentally destructive, yet as Richard Grove argues, the perception of what had already been lost in Europe – the sense of *intrinsic* connection between the 'more-than-human' and the human, and thus the urgency of environmental preservation – became strikingly evident in Europe's colonies, particularly in the late nineteenth century when the world's first National Parks were consequently established in the United States and New Zealand.

The legacies of that colonial past, together with neo-colonial environmental exploitation and outright destruction have energized environmental activism world wide, from the tragic case of Ken Saro Wiwa to Arundhati Roy's protest against the Namada dam project, to the desert walk for food in the S.W. United States. Much environmentalism in theory and practice has emanated from former imperial centres such as Europe and the United States. While belated recognition of the crucial importance of other forms of life on earth is both welcome and necessary, its export and sometimes imposition on post-colonized cultures invites the obvious charge of hypocrisy and generates resentment against former imperial states, which, having degraded their own and their colonies' environments in the 'interests' of progress and 'development', now encourage (or impose) the theory and practices of environmental preservation on other peoples. This also frequently creates division within post-colonized cultures themselves, where, for instance, peoples are moved off their traditional lands to make way for game parks, essentially for the benefit of wealthy tourists (see Wolch, Elder and Emmel). Demands for the 'global' preservation of endangered species frequently clash with the policies of post-colonized governments eager to use their regained environmental sovereignty in the interests of a modern capitalism from which it is difficult for them to escape. Clashes between 'local' and 'global' environmental interests are explored in Amitav Ghosh's *The Hungry Tide* (2004).

The British eco-critic Dominic Head has prioritized the 'fundamental social restructuring associated with deep ecology' over the 'provisional management strategies' of environmentalism (Head 1999: 27). For Head, as for Lawrence Buell, environmental crises and Western thought are intrinsically interwoven. 'Western metaphysics and ethics need revision before we can address today's environmental problems (Buell 1995: 2). We need, argues Buell, 'better ways of imagining nature and humanity's relation to it' (Buell 1995: 2). Ironically, some of the cultures destroyed by colonization had existed for centuries in such better ways.

Further reading: Adams and Mulligan 2003; Buell 1995, 2005; Ghosh 2004; Guha and Martinez 1997; Head 1999; Plumwood 1993, 2002.

ESSENTIALISM/STRATEGIC ESSENTIALISM

Essentialism is the assumption that groups, categories or classes of objects have one or several defining features exclusive to all members of that category. Some studies of race or gender, for instance, assume the presence of essential characteristics distinguishing one race from another or the feminine from the masculine. In analyses of culture it is a (generally implicit) assumption that individuals share an essential cultural identity, and it has been a topic of vigorous debate within post-colonial theory. The Cartesian claim *Cogito ergo sum* (I think therefore I am) was the basis for the stress on the individual consciousness and the centrality of the idea of the human subject in the dominant intellectual discourse of the eighteenth and nineteenth centuries. The displacement of this Enlightenment concern for the individual by poststructuralist views of **subjectivity** put considerable pressure on contemporary cultural theory to revise this dominant way of conceiving of human behaviour.

Colonial discourse theory stressed this also when it drew attention to the ways of speaking and thinking that **colonialism** employed to create the idea of the inferiority of the colonial subject and to exercise **hegemonic** control over them through control of the dominant modes of public and private representation. Drawing on the critiques of language by post-structuralist theorists such as Jacques Derrida, Jacques Lacan and Michel Foucault, colonial discourse theory contended that essentialist cultural categories were flawed. This criticism was extended by various writers to the institutions through which individual subjectivity achieved a sense of identity, for example ideas of **race** or **nation**.

The political purpose of this critique was, in part, to expose the falsity of this mode of representing the colonial subject as an **other** to the Self of the dominant colonial culture.

Ironically, then, the very process of displacing the essentialist modes of identity ran counter to the pragmatic use of such concepts in various local agendas designed to recover a sense of self-worth and difference. The basis of the **National Liberation Movements** of the 1960s and 1970s was a recognition of the need to recover or develop a local identity and a sense of distinction damaged by imperial and colonizing discourses. At the same time, theorists warned of the dangers of simply reversing the categories of oppressed and oppressor without critiquing the process by which such simple binaries had come into being in the first place. They also warned of the dangers of creating a new indigenous élite who would act merely as **neo-colonial** puppets for the old forces of the colonizing powers.

Theorists such as Gayatri Spivak drew attention to the dangers of assuming that it was a simple matter of allowing the subaltern (oppressed) forces to speak, without recognizing that their essential subjectivity had been and still was constrained by the discourses within which they were constructed as **subaltern**. Her controversial question 'Can the Subaltern Speak?' (Spivak 1985b), was frequently misinterpreted to mean that there was no way in which subaltern peoples could ever attain a voice (see **agency**). Such negative misreadings of Spivak's position inevitably produced counter-claims from critics such as Benita Parry who asserted the political necessity of maintaining the idea of oppositionality between the binary divisions such as black–white, colonizer–colonized, oppressed-oppressor (Parry 1987). In fact, Spivak's essay is not an assertion of the inability of the subaltern voice to be accessed or given agency, but only a warning to avoid the idea that the subaltern can ever be isolated in some absolute, essentialist way from the play of discourses and institutional practices that give it its voice.

In response to this negative interpretation of her earlier work, perhaps, and in an attempt to reassert the political force resident in her theory, Spivak spoke of the need to embrace a strategic essentialism, in an interview in which she acknowledged the usefulness of essential-ist formulations in many struggles for liberation from the effects of colonial and neo-colonial oppression. She remarked, 'I think we have to choose again strategically, not universal discourse but essentialist discourse. I think that since as a deconstructivist . . . I cannot in fact clean my hands and say I'm specific. In fact I must say I am an essentialist from time to time (Spivak 1984–5: 183). And, again in the same interview she remarked, 'I think it's absolutely on target . . . to stand against the discourses of essentialism, . . . [but] *strategically* we cannot' (184).

The argument suggests that in different periods the employment of essentialist ideas may be a necessary part of the process by which the colonized achieve a renewed sense of the value and dignity of their pre-colonial cultures, and through which the newly emergent post-colonial **nation** asserts itself. However, as critics such as Edward Said have argued (Said 1993), the early National Liberation theorists such as Fanon, Cabral and James were always fully aware of the dangers of essentialism, and were always critical of the application of such essentialist discourses as nationalism and race in the construction of the modern **post-colonial state**.

Further reading: Parry 1987; Said 1993; Spivak 1984–5, 1985b, 1990.

ETHNICITY

Ethnicity is a term that has been used increasingly since the 1960s to account for human variation in terms of culture, tradition, language, social patterns and ancestry, rather than the discredited generalizations of **race** with its assumption of a humanity divided into fixed, genetically determined biological types. Ethnicity refers to the fusion of many traits that belong to the nature of any ethnic group: a composite of shared values, beliefs, norms, tastes, behaviours, experiences, consciousness of kind, memories and loyalties (Schermerhorn 1974: 2). A person's ethnic group is such a powerful identifier because while he or she chooses to remain in it, it is an identity that cannot be denied, rejected or taken away by others. Whereas race emerged as a way of establishing a hierarchical division between Europe and its 'others', identifying people according to fixed genetic criteria, ethnicity is usually deployed as an expression of a positive self-perception that offers certain advantages to its members. Membership of an ethnic group is shared according to certain agreed criteria, even though the nature, the combination and the importance of those criteria may be debated or may change over time.

Indeed, few terms are used in such a variety of ways or with such a variety of definitions – Isajaw (1974) deals with twenty-seven definitions of ethnicity in the United States alone. This is possibly because ethnic groups, although they may seem to be socially defined, are distinguished both from inside and outside the group on the basis of cultural criteria, so that the defining characteristics of a particular 'ethnicity' have usually depended upon the various purposes for which the group has been identified. Not every ethnic group will possess the totality of possible defining traits, but all will display various combinations to varying degrees. Furthermore, both ethnicity and its components are relative to time and place, and, like any social phenomenon, they are dynamic and prone to change.

The simplest, and perhaps narrowest, definition of an ethnic group therefore might be

> A group that is socially distinguished or set apart, by others and/or by itself, primarily on the basis of cultural or national characteristics.

Indeed the word ethnic comes from the Greek *ethnos*, meaning 'nation'. In its earliest English use the word 'ethnic' referred to culturally different 'heathen' nations, a sense that has lingered as a connotation. Some contemporary uses of the term identify ethnicity with national groups in Europe, where, with some exceptions, such as the Basques, the link between ethnicity and nationality has appeared justified. The first use of ethnic group in terms of national origin developed in the period of heavy migration from Southern and Eastern European nations to the USA in the early twentieth century. The *name* by which an ethnic group understands itself is still most often the name of an originating nation, whether that nation still exists or not (e.g. Armenia). The term 'ethnicity' however, really only achieves wide currency when these 'national' groups find themselves as minorities within a larger national grouping, as occurs in the aftermath of colonization, either through immigration to settled colonies such as USA, Canada, Australia, New Zealand, or by the migration of colonized peoples to the colonizing centre. One further consequence of this movement is that older European nations can no longer claim to be coterminous with a particular ethnic group but are themselves the heterogeneous and, in time, hybridized, mixture of immigrant groups.

A feature of the use of the term is that the element of marginalization evident in the earliest uses of 'ethnic' often seems to remain implied in contemporary usage. Where it originally referred to heathen nations, it now suggests groups that are not the mainstream, groups that are not traditionally identified with the dominant national mythology. Thus in **settler colonies** of the British Empire the dominant Anglo–Saxon group is usually not seen as an ethnic group because its ethnicity has constructed the mythology of national identity. Such an identification is not limited to colonial experience, but does reveal the 'imperialistic' nature of national mythology, and the political implications of any link between ethnicity and nation.

Given the fact that 'ethnicity' comes into greatest contemporary currency in the context of immigration, we might therefore further define ethnicity in its contemporary uses as:

> a group or category of persons who have a common ancestral origin and the same cultural traits, who have a sense of peoplehood and of group belonging, who are of immigrant background and have either minority or majority status within a larger society.
>
> (Isajaw 1974: 118)

The perception of common ancestry, both real and mythical, has been important both to outsiders' definitions and to ethnic groups' self-definitions. Max Weber saw ethnic groups broadly as 'human groups that entertain a subjective belief in their common descent – because of similarities of physical type or of customs or both, or because of memories of colonization or migration – in such a way that this belief is important for the continuation of the nonkinship communal relationships' (1968a: 389).

In a 1974 study of twenty-seven definitions of ethnicity, only one included the trait 'immigrant group', while twelve included 'common national or geographic origin', eleven included 'same culture or customs', ten included 'religion' and nine included 'race or physical characteristics'. However, the intervening decades have seen a great change in the ways in which the term 'ethnicity' is used: there are fewer ethnic groups in which religion has the greatest influence in the way its members see its character; the concept of race – with some notable exceptions, such as African Americans – has become more and more distinct from ethnicity because of the greater specificity of the latter (a 'racial' group may subsume several ethnic groups); in the societies in which ethnicity is most discussed, the practical and social implications of the group's status as an immigrant group have often outweighed memories of a common national origin. Recent studies have revealed that ethnic groups are not necessarily marginalized cultural groups, but that all ethnic groupings, and indeed the concept of ethnicity itself, have come to exert a powerful political function. Regardless of the status of the particular group, its ethnicity is a key strategy in the furtherance of group political interests and political advancement.

Inasmuch as group power is always a favoured solution to individual powerlessness, the ethnic group is a salient formation in the bid for political power within a society. However, the impermeability of an ethnic group's borders, the difficulty of moving in, and indeed out, of the group, along with its tendency to cut across class divisions, set it apart from other political groupings such as trade unions and political parties and suggests that its political nature is often largely unconscious. Nevertheless, the 'ethnic revolution', as Fishman (1985) calls it, was a direct consequence of the use, from the 1960s, of cultural identity and the assertion of ethnicity in political struggle.

To encompass the variety and complexity of social and cultural features constituting ethnicity, a more elaborate definition might be developed from Schermerhorn (1970: 12):

> A collectivity within a larger society having real or putative common ancestry (that is, memories of a shared historical past whether of origins or of historical experiences such as colonization, immigration, invasion or slavery); a shared consciousness of a separate, named, group identity; and a cultural focus on one or more symbolic elements defined as the epitome of their peoplehood. These features will always be in dynamic combination, relative to the particular time and place in which they are experienced and operate consciously or unconsciously A significant feature of this definition is the function of those 'symbolic elements' that may provide a sense of ethnic belonging. Examples of such symbolic elements are: kinship patterns, physical contiguity, religious affiliation, language or dialect forms, tribal affiliation, nationality, physical features, cultural values, and cultural practices such as art, literature and music. Various combinations of these elements ('one or more') may be privileged at different times and places to provide a sense of ethnicity.

This definition accommodates the complex status of groups such as black Americans or black British, whose identity may be putatively constructed along racial as well as ethnic lines. The 'ethnic revolution' of the 1960s saw the construction of various such *new* ethnicities (ethnogenesis) which were much more consciously political in origin than other, increasingly attenuated ethnic connections in contemporary society. Indeed, black ethnicity in America and Britain becomes more intricately dependent upon politics in the process of ethnic legitimation than is evident with white ethnic groups.

Ethnic identities thus persist beyond cultural assimilation into the wider society and the persistence of ethnic identity is not necessarily related to the perpetuation of traditional cultures. In most cases, a very few features of traditional culture need to be selected as 'symbolic elements' around which ethnic identity revolves, and individuals need experience very few of the defining criteria (e.g. common ancestry) to consider themselves members of the group. No ethnic group is completely unified or in complete agreement about its own ethnicity and no one essential feature can ever be found in every member of the group. Nevertheless, this dynamic interweaving of identifying features has come to function as an increasingly potent locus of identity in an increasingly migratory, globalized and hybridized world.

Further reading: Darias 2000; Drew 1999; Fishman 1985; Gunew 1997; Hall 1989; Isajaw 1974; Olson and Worsham 1999; Schermerhorn 1970, 1974; Singh and Schmidt 2000; Sollors 1986, 1996; Weber 1968.

ETHNOGRAPHY

Ethnography is that field of anthropological research based on direct observation of and reporting on a people's way of life. It is the basic methodology employed by cultural anthropologists and consists of two stages: fieldwork, which is the term used for the process of observing and recording data; and reportage, the production of a written description and analysis of the subject under study. Historically, ethnography concerned itself principally with recording the life and habits of peoples from societies not the observer's own – usually distant locales, distant, that is, geographically or culturally from the West, and seen as different from the normative European cultures. Anthropology began as a kind of natural history, a study of the peoples encountered along the frontiers of European expansion.

Anthropology is thus the term for the broad discipline in which ethnography is located. When the discipline began, these alternative cultures were constructed through a notion of the **exotic**, which differentiated them from the European, or of the primitive, which saw them in a Darwinian way as stages in the 'development' of man, ideas that were clearly useful to **colonial discourse** in constructing a hierarchy of cultures. For this reason, anthropology and ethnographic discourse have often been critiqued in post-colonial texts as classic examples of the power of Western discourse to construct its primitive **others**.

To its proponents, on the other hand, ethnography is simply a social research method whereby the ethnographer 'participates, overtly or covertly, in people's daily lives for an extended period of time, watching what happens, listening to what is said, asking questions; in fact collecting whatever data are available to throw light on the issues with which he or she is concerned' (Hammersley and Atkinson 1983: 2). Thus it is a form of participant observation which attempts to gather data, 'on location', that will lead to an understanding of a particular social or cultural group.

However, criticism of ethnography argues that none of these activities – watching, listening, asking or collecting – is a neutral, value free act, nor does it exist beyond the assumptions and prescriptions of the **discourse** of the participant's own culture. Not even the concept of knowledge itself can be value free, because *what* is known depends upon *how* it is known, that is, cultural knowledge is 'constructed' rather than 'discovered' by ethnography. Indeed the most vigorous criticism suggests that ethnography itself, as a 'science', has historically existed precisely to locate the observed subjects in a particular way, to **interpellate** them as Europe's others. Some of the more critical accounts (e.g. Asad 1973) have argued that anthropology itself was not simply a child of colonialism, in that colonization opened up areas of research and ethnographers provided information to colonial administrations, but rather that it was 'colonialism's twin' (Fardon 1990: 6). Anthropology reproduced versions of the colonized subject that both were motivated by and rationalized the exclusion and exploitation of those subjects by imperial discourse itself. This critical account of the role of anthropology and ethnography is put strongly by Richard Fardon:

> Anthropology necessarily reproduced versions of assumptions deeply embedded in a predatory European culture . . . the inversion of a self-image was generalized to some fictive collectivity based on geography, skin colour, tribe or whatever. To counterpose to an enlightened Europe we produced an African heart of darkness; to our rational, controlled west corresponded an irrational and sensuous Orient; our progressive civilization differed from the historical cul-de-sacs into which Oriental despots led their subjects; our maturity might be contrasted with the childhood of a darker humanity, but our youth and vigour distinguished us from the aged civilizations of the east whose splendour was past. . . .

Subtly, not so subtly, and downright crassly, we produced our exemplar others; now, we pride ourselves that we see through the mirrors we set up, no longer dazzled by the pleasing images of ourselves they reflected. The temporal transpositions have been rendered transparent for what they were: artifices of imagination in the service of power.

(Fardon 1990: 6)

More recently, ethnography itself has experienced vigorous debates about its methodology; between the claims of 'positivism' and 'naturalism', for instance, and about the status of reflexivity, the extent to which the ethnographer is conscious of his or her own **subject** position. There has been considerable debate between structuralists and ethnographers adopting a phenomenological or ethno-methodological approach. Since the advent of contemporary revelations of its own provisional textuality, ethnography has had increasingly to address the issue of whether there is an underlying conflict between the earlier claims about its ability to make objective representative statements about the conditions of human life in the world. This is necessarily associated with arguments that assert that human life can be known only through specific and therefore limited representations which inevitably reflect the power relations between those who represent and those who are represented.

One influential response to this question of representation and power has been James Clifford's insistence that ethnography is itself a form of writing and should be approached from the point of view of its textuality. Clifford's argument is that, with the demise of colonialism, 'the West can no longer present itself as the unique purveyor of anthropological knowledge about others' (1988: 22). In *Writing Culture* he takes up Clifford Geertz's suggestion that it is anthropologists' practice, especially their writing, that should be examined. He distinguishes four main areas governing the reading and writing of ethnography: 'language, rhetoric, power and history' (Clifford 1986: 25), with his own emphasis being on the first two. Clifford demonstrates that ethnography, like any discourse, operates with its own set of rules, proscriptions and assumptions; it is a form of writing that may be examined using the techniques of reading more familiar to literary criticism.

Ultimately, Clifford is optimistic about ethnography's ability to shake off its Western epistemological legacy, and in *The Predicament of Culture* (1988) he surveys several modes of ethnographic writing that may do so. While ethnographic writing 'cannot entirely escape the reductionist use of dichotomies and essences, it can at least struggle self-consciously to avoid portraying abstract ahistorical 'others' (1988:23). Despite the earlier role of ethnography in the colonial enterprise, Clifford propounds the need for a decentred ethnographic practice, a form of ethnographic writing that takes into account, and overcomes, its colonial history and the difficulties concerning the subject position of the ethnographer: 'It is more than ever crucial for different peoples to form complex concrete images of one another, as well as of the relationships of knowledge and power that connect them' (23). One consequence of such a position has been a form of localized ethnography that interrupts the **surveillance** of the process and produces knowledge from the point of view of the local subject (Fardon 1990).

Contemporary ethnography vigorously asserts its ability to produce useful, complex, 'thick' descriptions that seek to take the position of the observer and the problem of surveillance into account. Taking the dispute to the opposing camp, some anthropologists have gone further and argued that they, in fact, take far more account of the 'differences' between cultures than their critics. For example, they have drawn attention to the fact that they acknowledge the material inscriptive elements of cultures far more effectively than more textually oriented disciplines such as cultural studies, which, despite its claims to study a wide variety of social practices, has still largely concentrated on forms similar to or analogous in their significatory structures to Western cultural ideas of inscription and communication.

Anthropology has also tried to overcome the paralysis that extreme forms of post-structuralist critique would impose on all 'fieldwork' by engaging constructively with the issues of representation and discrimination in anthropological definitions of its subject's goals and range. In particular, anthropology has tried to reorientate itself towards the study of groups or sections of the cultures within the metropolitan spheres, breaking down the idea that sociology deals with 'us' and anthropology with 'them'. Forming links with other disciplines, with which in the past it had tended to compete, such as sociology, psychology and linguistics, contemporary cultural anthropology seeks to take its core practice of 'fieldwork' and ethnographic description into societies and sub-groups much closer to the observer's own culture. Ethnographic studies in the past few decades – studies of youth gangs in North American cities, gender in British rural villages, working-class youths in English schools – are offered as examples that suggest that it is in fact possible to reach some effective and meaningful descriptions that help us to understand social and cultural phenomena.

Contemporary ethnography, then, is concerned with describing and differentiating cultures in ways that acknowledge its own perspectives and role. A recent development has been the increasing internationalization of the discipline with major studies by, amongst many others, Kenyan, Nigerian, South African, Indian, Brazilian, Indonesian and Mexican anthropologists. Although in itself this is no answer to critiques of the substantive, philosophical basis of ethnography, the fact that in recent times substantial contributions to the discipline have been made by people in the erstwhile 'target' communities themselves has helped to focus attention on the possibility of a more 'self-ascriptive' mode of social and cultural analysis employing modern ethnographic methodologies.

Further reading: Appadurai 1991; Asad 1973; Boon 1982; Clifford 1986, 1988; Fardon 1990; Ingold 1996; Mignolo and Shiwy 2003; Nederveen Pieterse 1992; Raheja 2002; Stocking 1983; Thomas 1994.

ETHNO-PSYCHIATRY/ETHNO-PSYCHOLOGY

A particularly significant development in classic **ethnography** in colonial situations occurred from the 1920s onwards and had a negative influence on the representation of colonized peoples. This was the application of psychiatric and psychological theories to the construction of models of the so-called 'native mind' or 'native personality'. Just as ethnography could be employed to control the colonized by creating scientific models of their culture that stressed those features that suited the colonial purposes, so ethno-psychiatry could suggest that there were certain ineradicable mental 'sets' that prevented 'natives' from exercising the same degree of control or responsibility as the colonial settlers. This form of pseudo-scientific construction was deeply embedded in the assumptions underlying the notion of race itself – that physical characteristics indicated deeply embedded psychological, intellectual and behavioural differences between racial groups.

The combining of race models with fashionable discourses such as psychiatry proved particularly powerful and useful in colonies with a large indigenous majority, such as Kenya or Rhodesia (Zimbabwe), as settlers came into conflict with their home governments over the long-term goals of colonization. Such disputes centred on whether the natives could be 'made ready' for self-government (the official British and European government policies on most colonies in the period), or would always remain dependent on white expertise and white support (the preferred settler position). Ironically, the ideas of the proponents of this kind of psychiatric model were used by later anti-colonialist theorists, such as Fanon, who took the idea of a 'native mind' and employed it to suggest that certain colonial disorders were the direct result of the construction of the native as inferior and as deformed. Of course, Fanon did not accept the **essentialist** ideas that underlay colonial ethnopsychiatric models and critiqued the idea that the 'native' was a natural category, demonstrating how the mental deformations of the patients in Algerian psychiatric wards were the direct result of the racist policies of the colonial administration.

Further reading: Carothers 1953; D'Andrade 1995; Fanon 1961.

EUROCENTRISM

The conscious or unconscious process by which Europe and European cultural assumptions are constructed as, or assumed to be, the normal, the natural or the universal. The first, and possibly most potent sign of Eurocentrism, as José Rabasa explains (1993), was the specific projection employed to construct the Mercator Atlas itself, a projection that favoured the European temperate zones in its distribution of size. This map of the world is not merely an objective outline of discovered continents, but an 'ideological or mythological reification of space' which opens up the territories of the world to domination and appropriation. 'The world' only acquired spatial meaning after different regions had been inscribed by Europeans, and this inscription, apart from locating Europe at the top of the globe or map, established an ideological figuration, through the accompanying text and illustrations, which firmly centralized Europe as the source and arbiter of spatial and cultural meaning.

By the eighteenth century this conception of a collective 'Europe' constructed as a sign of superiority and in opposition to the rest of the world's cultures had become firmly consolidated. Then, as now, such collective constructions existed in a troubled or ambivalent relationship with an alternative stress on the nationalism of emerging individual European nation-states and their particular cultures. European colonization of the rest of the globe, which accelerated in the eighteenth century and reached its apogee in the nineteenth, actively promoted or facilitated Eurocentrism through exploration, conquest and trade. Imperial displays of power, both in the metropolitan centres and at the colonial peripheries, and assertions of intellectual authority in colonialist institutions such as schools and universities, and through the civil service and legal codes, established European systems and values as inherently superior to indigenous ones.

Edward Said's *Orientalism* examines the ways in which Eurocentrism not only influences and alters, but actually produces other cultures. **Orientalism** is 'a way of coming to terms with the orient that is based on the orient's special place in European western experience' (1978: 1) or 'the western style for dominating, restructuring and having author-ity over the orient' (3). This authority is, in Said's view, a product of a systematic 'discipline' by which European culture was able to construct and manage the Orient during the post-Enlightenment period.

Eurocentrism is masked in literary study by concepts such as literary universality, in history by authoritative interpretations written from the point of view of the victors, and in early anthropology by the unconscious assumptions involved in the idea that its data were those societies defined as 'primitive' and so opposed to a European norm of development and civilization. Some cultural critics have argued that anthropology as a discipline in its classic, unrevised form came into being in such a close relationship with colonization that it could not have existed at all without the prior existence of Eurocentric concepts of knowledge and civilization. Eurocentrism is also present in the assumptions and practices of Christianity through education and mission activity, as well as in in the assumed superiority of Western mathematics, cartography, art and numerous other cultural and social practices which have been claimed, or assumed, to be based on a universal, objective set of values.

Further reading: Blaut 1993; Chakrabarty 2000; Dirlik 1999; Dussel 1993; Dussel and Mendieta 1998; Ferro 1997; Kanth 2005; Lazarus 2002; Rabasa 1993; Shohat 1994.

EXILE

The condition of exile involves the idea of a separation and distancing from either a literal homeland or from a cultural and ethnic origin. Critics such as Andrew Gurr (1981) have suggested that a distinction should be drawn between the idea of exile, which implies involun-tary constraint, and that of expatriation, which implies a voluntary act or state. In a sense, only the first generation of free settlers (of all the many peoples of the varied colonial societies) could be regarded as expatriates rather than exiles. For those born in the colonies, the idea of expatriation (defined as a state voluntarily entered into) needs to be revised. However, if the term is restricted, as Gurr suggests, to refer to those who cannot return to the 'place of origin', even if they wish to do so, then exile becomes a characteristic of a number of different colonial conditions. For example, it helps to account for the tension involved in constructing a distant place as 'home' by native-born descendants of the colonizers.

The degree and tenacity with which such native-born colonizers perceive the metropolitan colony as 'home' differs, of course, between 'settler-invader' colonies and colonies of occupation. Discourses of **race** and **ethnicity** were, however, in both a feature that conflicted with desires to claim a special status for the 'native-born' colonizer. In settler colonies, the 'native-born' colonial wished to claim an insider knowledge but wished to retain a 'racial' distinction from the 'native', for example Kipling's character Kim. In settler colonies, the settler also often wished to preserve a racial distinction from the 'natives' that depended on retaining a linkage with the absent homeland. As they formed specific attachments to the new space, tensions arose that were central to the continued preoccupation with issues of 'identity' in settler colony discourses. A classic text illustrating this process is that by the Australian woman writer Henry Handel Richardson, whose hero in *The Fortunes of Richard Mahony* (1917) shuttles to and fro between Australia and Europe, unable to find a sense of wholly belonging in either space, so ambivalent is his identity. The situation of the increasingly large number of **diasporic** peoples throughout the world further problematizes the idea of 'exile'. Where is the place of 'home' to be located for such groups? In the place of birth (*nateo*), in the displaced *cultural community* into which the person is born, or in the *nation-state* in which this diasporic community is located? The emergence of new ethnicities that cross the boundaries of the diasporic groups' different cultural, geographical and linguistic origins also acts to problematize these categories further (e.g. Black British; see Hall 1989).

Exile was also produced by colonialism in another way, as pressure was exerted on many colonized peoples to exile themselves from their own cultures, their languages and traditions. The production of this 'in-between' class, 'white but not quite', was often a deliberate feature of colonial practice. As Gauri Viswanathan (1989) has shown, it was the basis for the development of the education system in India following Macaulay's notorious Minute on Indian Education. It was also the condition of many of the creolized intellectuals of West Africa (de Moraes-Farias and Barber 1990). The possibilities shown by this class of colonially educated 'natives' to broker their position into a radical and nationalist political strategy does not mean that they did not suffer a form of profound exile. Such conditions of localized alienation or exile could sometimes contribute to the generation of new social and cultural practices and the questioning of old traditions.

Exile continues to be an ambivalent state in post-colonial studies, particularly in the work of Edward Said. While for him it is an almost necessary condition for true critical worldliness, 'the achievements of any exile are permanently undermined by his or her sense of loss' (1984: 49). While it is 'the unhealable rift forced between a human being and a native place' (49), nevertheless, the canon of modern Western culture 'is in large part the work of exiles' (49). This tension between personal desolation and cultural empowerment is the tension of exile in Said's own work, a tension which helps explain his own deep investment in the link between the text and the world. Consequently, Said's view of the intellectual is of a person whose detachment from the centres of power, whose ability to 'speak truth to power' is deeply enhanced by the experience of exile despite the debilitating sense of loss it engenders (Said 1994: 47–64).

Further reading: Barkan 1998; Chambers and Curti 1996; Gunew 2004; Gurr 1981; Said 1984, 1994,1999; Ward 2002.

EXOTIC/EXOTICISM

The word exotic was first used in 1599 to mean 'alien, introduced from abroad, not indigenous'. By 1651 its meaning had been extended to include 'an exotic and foreign territory', 'an exotic habit and demeanour' (OED). As a noun, the term meant 'a foreigner' or 'a foreign plant not acclimatized'.

During the nineteenth century, however, the exotic, the foreign, increasingly gained, throughout the empire, the connotations of a stimulating or exciting difference, something with which the domestic could be (safely) spiced. The key conception here is the introduction of the exotic from abroad into a domestic economy. From the earliest days of European voyages, exotic minerals, artefacts, plants and animals were brought back for display in private collections and museums and live specimens were cultivated, in Kew Gardens, for example, or in the many private and public zoos established in the period. Peoples of other cultures were also brought back to the European metropoles and were introduced in fashionable salons or travelled as popular entertainment. Omai from the Society Islands, Bennelong from Australia, and later the 'Hottentot Venus' from South Africa, were displayed in European capitals as exotics. Not only indigenes from the colonies but those Europeans deemed to have had exotic experiences could also be exhibited or exhibit themselves, e.g. Eliza Fraser, who had been shipwrecked and survived among Australian aborigines, was displayed as a woman who had lived amongst savages.

The key point here, however, is made by Renate Wasserman that, 'Indians exhibited at Royal courts or turkeys and parrots in cages' could be seen as 'innocent signifiers' of an exotic other, one that could titillate the European public imagination while offering no threat since such exotics were, in her terms, 'non-systematic' (1984: 132). Isolated from their own geographical and cultural contexts, they represented whatever was projected onto them by the societies into which they were introduced. Exotics in the metropoles were a significant part of imperial displays of power and the plenitude of empires.

When the English language and the concepts it signified in the imperial culture were carried to colonized sites, through, for instance, English education, the attribution of exoticism as it applied to those places, peoples or natural phenomena usually remained unchanged. Thus schoolchildren in, for instance, the Caribbean and North Queensland could regard and describe their own vegetation as 'exotic' rather than trees like the oak or yew that were 'naturalized' for them as domestic by the English texts they read.

Further reading: Appadurai 1986; Arnold 2003; Célestin 1996; Forsdick 2001; Gualtieri 1996; Huggan 2001; Nederveen Pieterse 1992; Thomas 1994; Wasserman 1984, 1994.

EXPLORATION AND TRAVEL

European exploration of other parts of the globe began with the actual movements out of Europe by land routes to the 'East', and by sea across the Mediterranean and into the Atlantic. Although there are many legendary accounts of early voyages, and considerable historical evidence of extensive, even intercontinental, travel by peoples such as the Vikings in the Dark and Middle Ages, European travel beyond the traditional fringes of the Mediterranean appears to have taken a giant leap forward in the early Renaissance. This was partly due to the decline of the Muslim control of the so-called Middle and Far East, which allowed travellers to proceed under the *Pax Mongolica* as far as China (Marco Polo), and partly due to the development of effective navigational aids and the advances in mapping (see **cartography**). Such advances meant that early sea-going explorers such as the Portuguese and the Spanish could venture further afield and risk leaving the coast-hugging voyages of the fifteenth century to start voyaging out into the Atlantic itself to discover the off-shore islands of the Canaries and the Azores, perhaps the earliest of all European 'colonies', which they occupied in the early sixteenth century.

In addition to such physical explorations, however, 'travel' also began as the imaginative construction of other people and places. This intermixing of actual exploratory voyages with fictive representations of otherness rooted in the imaginative practice of the Middle Ages persists through and beyond the actual eighteenth-century circum-navigation of the globe and the extensive travels in the land-mass interiors that followed in the nineteenth century. Of course, the idea of exploration and discovery in such travelling is profoundly Euro-centric, since what explorers purportedly discovered was invariably already known to local indigenous peoples, many of whom led white explorers to local land-marks, rivers and sources of food that enabled them to survive. Yet these discoveries were credited to the European explorers as though such places had not existed beforehand.

Renaissance sea voyages led to the widespread seizure of the goods of indigenous peoples as loot. Travel and exploration in the period was seen as strictly and unashamedly commercial and exploitative in purpose. During the eighteenth century, however, new kinds of travellers began to emerge, especially the scientific travellers in search of new geographical and biological information, and the missionaries who began increasingly to travel to spread the Christian religion and who, like the scientific explorers, saw their interaction with the people of the worlds they entered as essentially benign. Initially, these new kinds of travellers were often sponsored by trading companies or were attached to government expeditions. But they rapidly developed independent scientific and religious institutions to support their work, such as The Royal Geographical Society or the various Missionary Societies, a development that allowed them ostensibly to distance themselves from commercial and military expeditions and to portray themselves as harmless knowledge seekers in contrast to rapacious traders and military expeditionary forces of conquest. However, their travels and their accounts of these travels, whether ostensibly factual or fictionally embellished, were as effectively 'capturing' as commercial exploitation or conquest. Such knowledge also directly facilitated exploitation and intervention, processes whose real effects are reflected in phrases like 'the opening up of Africa'. Such a phrase also suggests the gendering of landscape and the associations between sexuality and exploration and conquest. 'Virgin territories' (never virgin, but the inhabitants were considered to be uncivilized and thus having no legal rights of ownership) were opened up by exploration to trade and settlement, their original inhabitants killed, displaced or marginalized within European settler communities. In extreme cases where peoples were seen to be without organizational forms recognizable as such to European eyes, as in Australia, the land was declared literally empty, a *terra nullius*.

Accounts of European travel and reports of explorations to the Royal Society helped produce and maintain ideas of Europe itself, ideas framed by Europe's sense of its difference from the places and cultures that were being explored and reported on. The knowledge produced by exploratory travel of these various groups is at the heart of the control of the new possessions. Once 'explored' and so 'known', these territories were possessed and able to be catalogued as under the control or influence of one or other of the colonizing powers. Such travel accounts were quickly appropriated to fictional forms in works as diverse as *The Tempest, Gulliver's Travels* and *Robinson Crusoe*. In fact, the latter has been seen by many critics as the first modern novel, suggesting that the development of this powerful new genre and the discovery of new lands and their imaginative transformation are closely aligned (see Watt 1957 and Said 1993).

Contemporary tourism, it can be argued, is in many ways the modern extension of this possession by exploration. The tourist enters the territory of the 'other' in search of an exotic experience. Early tourism parodied the exploration of earlier exploratory periods, with bands of Victorian gentlemen and ladies roped together to explore the lower Alps or the slopes of Vesuvius. Modern tourism divides between the contemporary form of this in the adventure or safari tour, and the mass form of modern comfort tourism in which the experience is typically stereotyped, packaged and reduced to an easily consumed product. In effect, the tourist, ostensibly in search of the new, is actually seeking the already known. In the same way that early travellers' experience was coloured by expectations formed over centuries of superstitious imagining, so the modern tourist travels to discover those stereotypical experiences already presented as **exotic**. Where signifiers of stereotyped exotic difference are absent (such as palm trees, white sand beaches, etc.) they are constructed as part of so-called resort developments. The idea of the tropical ceases to refer to an actual geographical reality that may involve such discomforting actualities as mosquitoes, mangrove swamps and poisonous fauna, as well as human poverty and exploitation, instead it becomes an imaginative construct that says more about the European fantasy than the actual location in which it finds its setting. Tourism also functions, therefore, as part of the process of cultural and economic control whereby economies of underdeveloped countries are constructed by and made dependent on external institutions and multinational companies (see **neo-colonialism**).

Further reading: Abernethy 2000; Armstrong and Hestertun 2006; Arnold 2003; Blunt and McEwan 2002; Clark 1999; Clifford 1997; Hall 2004; Huggan 1989; Huggan 2000; Kincaid 1988; Korte 2001; Korte and Matthias 2000; Leer 1992; Mignolo 1995a; Mills 1991; Pratt 1992; Ryan 1994; Scott 2001.

FANONISM

A term for the anti-colonial liberationist critique formulated by the Martiniquan psychiatrist Frantz Fanon (1925–1961). Fanon's work in Algeria led him to become actively involved in the Algerian liberation movement and to publish a number of foundational works on racism and colonialism. These include *Black Skin, White Masks* (1952, translated 1968), a study of the psychology of racism and colonial domination. Just before his death he published *The Wretched of the Earth* (1961), a broader study of how **anti-colonial** sentiment might address the task of **decolonization**. In these texts Fanon brought together the insights he derived from his clinical study of the effects of colonial domination on the psyche of the colonized and his Marxist derived analysis of social and economic control. From this conjuction he developed his idea of a ***comprador*** class, or élite, who exchanged roles with the white colonial dominating class without engaging in any radical restructuring of society. The black skin of these *compradors* was 'masked' by their complicity with the values of the white colonial powers. Fanon argued that the native intelligentsia must radically restructure the society on the firm foundation of the people and their values.

However, Fanon, like other early National Liberationist figures such as the Trinidadian C.L.R. James and the Cape Verdean Amilcar Cabral, did not advocate a naive view of the pre-colonial. Fanon's nationalism was always what Edward Said in *Culture and Imperialism* has defined as 'critical nationalism', that is, formed in an awareness that pre-colonial societies were never simple or homogeneous and that they contained socially prejudicial class and gender formations that stood in need of reform by a radical force. As Said has noted '[Fanon's] notion was that unless national consciousness at its moment of success was somehow changed into social consciousness, the future would not hold liberation but an extension of imperialism' (1993: 323). For Fanon, the task of the national liberator, often drawn as he himself was from a colonially educated élite, was to 'join the people in that fluctuating movement which they are *just* giving a shape to . . . which will be the signal for everything to be called into question' (1952: 168) (see **cultural diversity/cultural difference**).

Although Fanon is sometimes recruited to the banner of a naive form of **nativism**, he took a more complicated view of tradition and the pre-colonial as well as of its role in the construction of the modern **post-colonial state**. Fanon, of course, recognized and gave a powerful voice to the fact that for the new national leaders 'the passionate search for a national culture which existed before the colonial era finds its legitimate reason in the anxiety shared by many indigenous intellectuals to shrink away from that western culture in which they all risk being swamped' and to 'renew contact once more with the oldest and most pre-colonial springs of their people' (1961: 153–4). But he also recognized the danger that such pasts could be easily mythologized and used to create the new élite power groups, masquerading as the liberators of whom he had warned.

> A national culture is not a folklore, nor an abstract populism that believes it can discover the people's true nature. It is not made up of the inert dregs of gratuitous actions, that is to say actions which are less and less attached to the ever present reality of the people. A national culture is the whole body of efforts made by a people in the sphere of thought to describe, justify and praise the action through which that people has created itself and keeps itself in existence.
>
> (1961: 154–5)

Throughout his historical analysis, Fanon never lost sight of the importance of the subjective consciousness and its role in creating the possibilities for the **hegemonic** control of the colonized subject, and of the **neo-colonial** society that followed political independence. In studies such as 'The Fact of Blackness' (1952) he addressed the importance of the visible signs of racial difference in constructing a discourse of prejudice, and the powerful and defining psychological effects of this on the self-construction of black peoples. Much of Fanon's work gives definition to the radical attempt to oppose this in the discourses of the **black consciousness** movement that emerged in America and Britain in the 1960s and which drew much of its inspiration from Fanon's work. Although it might be argued that later theorists such as Amilcar Cabral presented a more effective political programme for implementing the radical transformation of the native colonial intelligentsia in what Cabral called, in a memorable phrase, 'a veritable forced march along the road to cultural progress' (Cabral 1973), it was in the interweaving of the specific and personal with the general and social that Fanon's distinctive and profoundly influential contribution was made.

Further reading: Fanon 1952, 1959, 1961.

FEMINISM AND POST-COLONIALISM

Feminism is of crucial interest to post-colonial discourse for two major reasons. First, both patriarchy and imperialism can be seen to exert analogous forms of domination over those they render subordinate. Hence the experiences of women in patriarchy and those of colonized subjects can be paralleled in a number of respects, and both feminist and post-colonial politics oppose such dominance. Second, there have been vigorous debates in a number of colonized societies over whether gender or colonial oppression is the more important political factor in women's lives. This has sometimes led to division between Western feminists and political activists from impoverished and oppressed countries; or, alternatively, the two are inextricably entwined, in which case the condition of colonial dominance affects, in material ways, the position of women within their societies. This has led to calls for a greater consideration of the construction and employment of gender in the practices of imperialism and colonialism.

Feminism, like post-colonialism, has often been concerned with the ways and extent to which representation and language are crucial to identity formation and to the construction of **subjectivity**. For both groups, language has been a vehicle for subverting patriarchal and imperial power, and both discourses have invoked essentialist arguments in positing more authentic forms of language against those imposed on them. Both discourses share a sense of disarticulation from an inherited language and have thus attempted to recover a linguistic authenticity via a pre-colonial language or a primal feminine tongue. However, both feminists and colonized peoples, like other subordinate groups, have also used **appropriation** to subvert and adapt dominant languages and signifying practices.

The texts of feminist theory and those of post-colonialism concur on many aspects of the theory of identity, of difference and of the inter-pellation of the subject by a dominant discourse, as well as offering to each other various strategies of resistance to such controls. Similarities between 'writing the body' in feminism and 'writing place' in post-colonialism; similarities between the strategies of bisexuality and cultural syncreticity; and similar appeals to nationalism may be detected (Ashcroft 1989).

In the 1980s, many feminist critics (Carby 1982; Mohanty 1984; Suleri 1992), began to argue that Western feminism, which had assumed that gender overrode cultural differences to create a universal category of the womanly or the feminine, was operating from hidden, universalist assumptions with a middle-class, Euro-centric bias. Feminism was therefore charged with failing to account for or deal adequately with the experiences of Third World women. In this respect, the issues concerning gender face similar problems to those concerned with **class**. Mohanty, for instance, criticizes

> the assumption that all of us of the same gender, across classes and cultures, are somehow socially constituted as a homo-geneous group identified prior to the process of analysis. . . . Thus, the discursively consensual homogeneity of 'women' as a group is mistaken for the historically specific material reality of groups of women.
>
> (Mohanty 1984: 338)

Domatila Barrios de Chungara's *Let Me Speak* demonstrates how the material reality of different groups of women can lead to very different perceptions of the nature of political struggle. When she was invited to the International Women's Year Tribunal in Mexico City in 1974, the difference between the feminist agenda of the tribunal and her own political struggle against oppression in the Bolivian tin mines became very clear. In her view, the meeting's World Plan of Action 'didn't touch on the problems that are basic for Latin American women' (Barrios de Chungara 1977: 201). The overlap between patriarchal, economic and racial oppression has always been difficult to negotiate, and the differences between the political priorities of First and Third World women have persisted to the present. Such differences appear to be those of emphasis and strategy rather than those of principle, since the interconnection of various forms of social oppression materially affects the lives of all women.

More recently, feminism has been concerned that categories like gender may sometimes be ignored within the larger formation of the colonial, and that post-colonial theory has tended to elide gender differences in constructing a single category of the colonized. These critics argue that colonialism operated very differently for women and for men, and the 'double colonization' that resulted when women were subject both to general discrimination as colonial subjects and specific discrimination as women needs to be taken into account in any analysis of colonial oppression (Spivak 1985a, 1985b, 1985c and 1986; Mohanty 1984; Suleri 1992). Even post-independence practices of anti-colonial nationalism are not free from this kind of gender bias, and constructions of the traditional or pre-colonial are often heavily inflected by a contemporary masculinist bias that falsely represents 'native' women as quietist and subordinate.

One illuminating account of the connections between race and gender as a consequence of imperial expansion is Sander L. Gilman's 'Black bodies, white bodies' (1985), which shows how the representation of the African in nineteenth-century European art, medicine and literature, reinforced the construction of the sexualized female body. The presence of male or female black servants was regularly included in paintings, plays and operas as a sign of illicit sexual activity. 'By the nineteenth century the sexuality of the black, both male and female, becomes an icon for deviant sexuality in general' (228). Furthermore, the 'relationship between the sexuality of the black woman and that of the sexualized white woman enters a new dimension when contemporary scientific discourse concerning the nature of black female sexuality is examined' (231). Notorious examples of prurient exoticism, such as the Hottentot Venus displayed on tour in England, provide material examples of the ways in which signs of racial otherness became instrumental in the construction of a (transgressive) female sexuality.

In settler colonies, although women's bodies were not directly constructed as part of a transgressive sexuality, their bodies were frequently the site of a power discourse of a different kind. As critics like Whitlock have argued, they were perceived reductively not as sexual but as reproductive subjects, as literal 'wombs of empire' whose function was limited to the population of the new colonies with white settlers.

Further reading: Alexander and Mohanty 1977; Bahri 2004; Boehmer 2005; Bulbeck 1998; Chang 2001; Donaldson 1993; Emberley 1993; Frankenberg 2001; Gandhi 1998; Harding 2000; Holst-Petersen and Rutherford 1985; hooks 1997; Hyam 1990; Jarratt 2000; Katrak 1996; Lionnet 1995; Loomba

2005; McClintock 1995; Mann 1995; Meyer 1996; Mills 2003; Minh-ha 1995; Mohanram 1999; Mongia 1996; Morgan 2006; Rajan 1993; Ray 2000; Spivak 1999; Suleri 1992; Weedon 1999; Whitlock 1995; Wisker 2000; Wynter 1990.

FILIATION/AFFILIATION

This pair of terms was brought to prominence by Edward Said, who suggested that patterns of 'filiation' (heritage or descent) that had acted as a cohering force in traditional society were becoming increasingly difficult to maintain in the complexity of contemporary civilization and were being replaced by patterns of 'affiliation'. While filiation refers to lines of descent in nature, affiliation refers to a process of identification through culture.

Said promotes affiliation as a general critical principle because it frees the critic from a narrow view of texts connected in a filiative relationship to other texts, with very little attention paid to the 'world' in which they come into being. For instance, his initial use of the terms suggested that canonical English literature tended to be approached filiatively, the literature being regarded as self-perpetuating and literary works having their most important hermeneutic relationships to the literature that had gone before. By contrast, an affiliative reading allows the critic to see the literary work as a phenomenon in the world, located in a network of non-literary, non-canonical and non-traditional affiliations. In this sense, affiliation is seen positively as the basis of a new kind of criticism in which a recognition of the affiliative process within texts may free criticism from its narrow basis in the European canon.

While filiation suggests a Utopian domain of texts connected serially, homologously and seamlessly with other texts, affiliation is that which enables a text to maintain itself as a text, the 'status of the author, historical moment, conditions of publication, diffusion and reception, values drawn upon, values and ideas assumed, a framework of consensually held tacit assumptions, presumed background, and so on' (Said 1983: 174–175). Affiliation sends the critical gaze beyond the narrow confines of the European and canonically literary into this cultural texture. 'To recreate the affiliative network is therefore to make visible, to give materiality back to the strands holding the text to society, author and culture' (175). This concern with the materiality of the text also allows him to read the texts of English literature 'contrapuntally' to see the extent to which they are implicated in the broad political project of **imperialism**. The political and social world becomes available to the scrutiny of the critic, specifically the non-literary, the non-European and above all, the political dimension in which all literature, all texts can be found (21). Traditionally assumed to be connected filiatively to the discourse of 'English literature', the text can now be seen to be affiliated with the network of history, culture and society within which it comes into being and is read.

Said has also used the concept to describe the way in which the network of affiliation links colonized societies to imperial culture. Cultural identities are understood as 'contrapuntal ensembles' (1993: 60), and the often hidden affiliations of both imperial and colonial cultures are amenable to a **contrapuntal reading**. Clearly, the concept of affiliation is useful for describing the ways in which colonized societies replace filiative connections to indigenous cultural traditions with affiliations to the social, political and cultural institutions of empire. Affiliation refers to 'that implicit network of peculiarly cultural associations between forms, statements and other aesthetic elaborations on the one hand and, on the other, institutions, agencies, classes, and amorphous social forces' (174). Said links the concept to Gramsci's notion of **hegemony** by suggesting that the affiliative network itself is the field of operation of hegemonic control, and this may be particularly evident in the case of the control of imperial culture.

The tendency for affiliation to reproduce filiation has implications far beyond the activity of the critic. For there is an affiliative process constantly at work in colonized societies: an implicit network of assumptions, values and expectations that continually places and replaces the colonized subject in a filiative relation with the colonizer. This indicates one way in which the affiliative process maintains its obdurate strength in colonial societies. Affiliation invokes an image of the imperial culture as a parent, linked in a filiative relationship with the colonized 'child'. Thus, while filiation gives birth to affiliation, in colonized societies the reverse is also true.

Clearly, this move from filiation to affiliation specifically invokes the hegemonic power of a dominant imperial culture. Filiation is not limited to racial or genealogical ancestry; its real force comes from its suggestion of a cultural and psychological inheritance. Filiation is a powerful ideological consequence of the capacity of imperialist discourse to control representation and invoke networks of affiliation. It becomes a fundamental way of structuring relationships between empires and colonies, since it is by this process that the cultural power of the imperial centre and the sustainable rule of the mechanisms of state are maintained.

Further reading: Said 1983.

FIRST NATIONS

This is a term for Native American peoples, originating, and used mainly in Canada, to refer to an indigenous American Indian community officially recognized as an administrative unit by the federal government or functioning as such without official status (OED). In practice it refers to the indigenous peoples located in the region of North America that is now Canada who are not Inuit or Métis. The term was coined in 1980 to replace 'Indian band' which has legal recognition in Canadian Law. Although referred to in the past as Aboriginal peoples, (a term increasingly used to refer only to Australian Aboriginal peoples), the indigenous people of North America are variously referred to as Native Americans or 'Indians' (US). The concept, if not the term 'First nation' is growing in frequency in the US with terms such as the 'Six Nations' referring to the peoples of the Iroquois confederacy.

The concept of 'Nation' in reference to indigenous peoples is a recently developed **catachresis** that emphasises their historical, ancestral and communal relationship with the land. Whereas 'nation' refers to a large body of people united by common descent, history, culture, or language, inhabiting a particular state or territory (OED) this term is now recognized as referring to both nation-states and First Nations as a recognition of the latter's special claim to a communal identification within the context of national law. This has allowed bodies such as The First Nations Development Institute to work to restore Native control over cultural assets such as land, human potential, cultural heritage, or natural resources. In general, members of First Nations make no claim to nation-state status but to a communal identity that in fact precedes the nation-state, and in particular the colonial nations of Canada and the US.

Further reading: Battiste and Barman (1995); Muckle (1998)

FRONTIER

The idea of a frontier, a boundary or a limiting zone to distinguish one space or people from another, is clearly much older and used more widely than in colonial and post-colonial theory. There is, for example, a broad study of frontier history in American Studies, beginning with the so-called 'Turner thesis' advanced by Frederick Jackson Turner in 1893 (see Taylor 1971; Philp and West 1976). Turner theorized that

American development could be explained by the existence of a vast area of free land into which American settlement advanced westward. Turner saw the frontier as the essential guarantor of American democratic freedoms, because whenever social conditions put pressure on employment or when political restraints tended to impede freedom, individuals could escape to the free conditions of the frontier. Men would not accept inferior wages and a permanent position of social insubordination, he believed, when a promised land of freedom and equality was open to everyone for the taking. Significantly, Turner also observed that the open frontier was already an environment of the past and that Americans should of necessity move on to another chapter of history.

Regardless of the validity of his thesis as a whole (and it has been severely critiqued as largely unproven by empirical evidence), few will quarrel with his assertion that the American frontier experience has been central to self-perceptions of identity in the United States as a result of its ubiquity in mass culture. It is, of course, significant that the frontier is perceived by Turner primarily as a shaping force on the westward expanding settler population, and little interest is shown in the perception of this expansion by the indigenous populations of the so-called frontier. Thus recent accounts by historians and others of native American reactions to the westward expansion are a necessary corrective to this dominant myth of the West as a land of freedom and escape. For the Indians, the frontier experience was very different (Berkhofer 1978). The centrality of the idea to settler American self-perceptions may have had a great deal to do with the popularity of the term, and frontier studies have always been a major component of American studies ever since. The term has also been internationalized by modern American historians such as McNeill who took the idea of the frontier and argued that it should be seen as one of the most dominant tropes of recent world history (McNeill 1983).

Nevertheless, in its more recent use within post-colonial cultures, it has taken on a particular local significance. Colonial frontiers were created as imperial discourse sought to define and invent the entities it shaped from its conquests. The numerous ruler-straight frontiers of imperial maps indicate how colonial **cartography** existed as much to invent as to record actual features and distinctions between various places and peoples. The frontier or boundary that limited the space so defined was a crucial feature in imagining the imperial self, and in creating and defining (**othering**) those others by which that 'self' could achieve definition and value. That which lies 'beyond the pale' (itself a metaphor invoking one of the earliest delimiting frontiers of colonial

Ireland, the fence between the Protestant enclave of Dublin and the wild, Catholic lands beyond) is often defined literally as the other, the dark, the savage and the wild.

As well as literal frontiers, the discourse of empire was metaphorically concerned to delineate boundaries and frontiers, inventing categories for which the spatial was always and only a loose image for a perceived or desired racial, cultural or gendered divide. 'East is East and West is West, and never the twain shall meet' wrote Kipling (1889), suggesting that the idea of a West and East had less physical than metaphysical boundaries. Even the creation of some literal juncture, 'East of Suez', seems less than physically specific, since Egypt, the land of the joining frontier, has been at different times defined both as the cradle of European civilization and the heart of the exotic and dangerous Orient, as discourses shift and meet on a terrain of abstraction to which frontiers and spatial categories refer only as metonyms.

The idea of a frontier civilization implies a civilization where rules of law and social graces wither as man reverts to a state of nature. The frontier then becomes a place of **savagery**. But it is also frequently imagined as a place where men (the pronoun is deliberate) can test themselves and where the effete weakness of the civilized can be bred into a renewed strength (Low 1996). This ambivalence is always present in construction of settler frontier narratives, as the idea of civilization is both upheld and critiqued from the rude but vigorous perspective of the frontier world. Significantly, frontier narratives by women are far less romantic and more often emphasize the harsh daily realities of survival (Moodie 1852).

Further reading: Billington 1966; Janiewski 1998; McNeill 1983; Philp 1986; Taylor 1971; Thorpe 1996; Turner 1961, 1962; Weber and Rausch 1994.

GLOBALIZATION

Globalization is the process whereby individual lives and local communities are affected by economic and cultural forces that operate world-wide. In effect it is the process of the world becoming a single place. Globalism is the perception of the world as a function or result of the processes of globalization upon local communities.

The term has had a meteoric rise since the mid-1980s, up until which time words such as 'international' and 'international relations' were preferred. The rise of the word 'international' itself in the eighteenth century indicated the growing importance of territorial states in organizing social relations, and is an early consequence of the global perspective of European **imperialism**. Similarly, the rapidly increasing interest in globalization reflects a changing organization of world-wide social relations in this century, one in which the 'nation' has begun to have a decreasing importance as individuals and communities gain access to globally disseminated knowledge and culture, and are affected by economic realities that bypass the boundaries of the state. The structural aspects of globalization are the nation–state system itself (on which the concepts of internationalism and international co-operation are based), global economy, the global communication system and world military order.

Part of the complexity of globalism comes from the different ways in which globalization is approached. Some analysts embrace it enthusiastically as a positive feature of a changing world in which access to technology, information services and markets will be of benefit to local communities, where dominant forms of social organization will lead to universal prosperity, peace and freedom, and in which a perception of a global environment will lead to global ecological concern. For this group, globalism is a term 'for values which treat global issues as a matter of personal and collective responsibility' (Albrow 1994: 4). Others reject it as a form of domination by 'First World' countries over 'Third World' ones, in which individual distinctions of culture and society become erased by an increasingly homogeneous global culture, and local economies are more firmly incorporated into a system of global capital. For this group, globalism 'is a teleological doctrine which provides, explains and justifies an interlocking system of world trade'. It has 'ideological overtones of historical inevitability', and 'its attendant myths function as a gospel of the global market' (Ferguson 1993a: 87). The chief argument against globalization is that global culture and global economy did not just spontaneously erupt but originated in and continue to be perpetuated from the centres of capitalist power. Neither does globalization impact in the same way, to the same degree, nor equally beneficially upon different communities.

Proponents of 'critical globalism' take a neutral view of the process, simply examining its processes and effects. 'Critical globalism refers to the critical engagement with globalization processes, neither blocking them out nor celebrating globalization' (Nederveen Pieterse 1995: 13). Thus, while critical globalists see that globalization 'has often perpetuated poverty, widened material inequalities, increased ecological degradation, sustained militarism, fragmented communities, marginalized subordinated groups, fed intolerance and deepened crises of democracy', they also see that it has had a positive effect in 'trebling world per capita income since 1945, halving the proportion of the world living in abject poverty, increasing ecological consciousness, and possibly facilitating disarmament, while various subordinated groups have grasped opportunities for global organisation' (Scholte 1996: 53).

As a field of study, globalization covers such disciplines as international relations, political geography, economics, sociology, communication studies, agricultural, ecological and cultural studies. It addresses the decreasing agency (though not the status) of the nation-state in the world political order and the increasing influence of structures and movements of corporate capital. Globalization can also be 'a signifier of travel, of transnational company operations, of the changing pattern of world employment, or global environmental risk' (Albrow 1994: 13). Indeed, there are compelling reasons for thinking globally where the environment is concerned. As Stuart Hall puts it, 'When the ill winds of Chernobyl came our way, they did not pause at the frontier, produce their passports and say "Can I rain on your territory now?"' (1991: 25).

The importance of globalization to post-colonial studies comes first from its demonstration of the structure of world power relations which stands firm in the twentieth century as a legacy of Western imperialism. Second, the ways in which local communities engage the forces of globalization bear some resemblance to the ways in which colonized societies have historically engaged and appropriated the forces of imperial dominance. In some respects, globalization, in the period of rapid **decolonization** after the Second World War, demonstrates the transmutation of imperialism into the supra-national operations of economics, communications and culture. This does not mean that globalization is a simple, unidirectional movement from the powerful to the weak, from the central to the peripheral, because globalism is **transcultural** in the same way that imperialism itself has been. But it does demonstrate that globalization did not simply erupt spontaneously around the world, but has a history embedded in the history of imperialism, in the structure of the **world system**, and in the origins of a global economy within the ideology of imperial rhetoric.

The key to the link between classical imperialism and contemporary globalization in the twentieth century has been the role of the United States. Despite its resolute refusal to perceive itself as 'imperial', and indeed its public stance against the older European doctrines of colonialism up to and after the Second World War, the United States had, in its international policies, eagerly espoused the political domi-nation and economic and cultural control associated with imperialism. More importantly, United States society during and after this early expansionist phase initiated those features of social life and social relations that today may be considered to characterize the global: mass production, mass communication and mass consumption. During the twentieth century, these have spread transnationally, 'drawing upon the increasingly integrated resources of the global economy' (Spybey 1996: 3).

Despite the balance between its good and bad effects, identified by critical globalists, globalization has not been a politically neutral activity. While access to global forms of communication, markets and culture may indeed be worldwide today, it has been argued by some critics that if one asks how that access is *enabled* and by what ideological machinery it is advanced, it can be seen that the operation of globalization cannot be separated from the structures of power perpetuated by European imperialism. Global culture is a continuation of an imperial dynamic of influence, control, dissemination and hegemony that operates according to an already initiated structure of power that emerged in the sixteenth century in the great confluence of **imperialism**, capitalism and **modernity**. This explains why the forces of globalization are still, in some senses, centred in the West (in terms of power and institutional organization), despite their global dissemination.

However, the second reason for the significance of globalization to postcolonial studies – how it is engaged by local communities – forms the focus of much recent discussion of the phenomenon. If globalism is not simply a result of top–down dominance but a transcultural process, a dialectic of dominant cultural forms and their appropriation, then the responses of local communities becomes critical. By appropriating strategies of representation, organization and social change through access to global systems, local communities and marginal interest groups can both empower themselves and influence those global systems. Although choice is always mediated by the conditions of subject formation, the belief that one has a choice in the processes of changing one's own life or society can indeed be empowering. In this sense, the appropriation of global forms of culture may free one from local forms of dominance and oppression or at least provide the tools for a different kind of identity formation.

The more recent directions of globalization studies concern the development of 'global culture', a process in which the strategies, techniques, assumptions and interactions of cultural representation become increasingly widespread and homogeneous. But, as Featherstone and Lash point out, 'only in the most minimalist sense can one speak of a "global society" or a "global culture", as our conceptions of both society and culture draw heavily on a tradition which was strongly influenced by the process of nation-state formation' (Featherstone *et al.* 1995: 2). However, global culture can be seen to be focused in mass culture, in what Stuart Hall calls a 'new globalization'. 'This new kind of globalization is not English, it is American. In cultural terms, the new kind of globalization has to do with a new form of global mass culture' (1991: 27). New globalization has two dominant features: one is that it is still centred in the West; the other is a peculiar form of homogenization, a form of cultural capital that does not attempt to produce mini versions of itself but operates through other economic and political élites (28).

The most active area of debate in globalization studies therefore appears to be the style and nature of the process by which external and internal forces interact to produce, reproduce and disseminate global culture within local communities. This is because one of the key questions at the centre of this interaction is the nature and survival of social and cultural identity. The interpenetration of global and local cultural forces is present in all forms of social life in the twentieth century. But the extent to which globalization exhibits the effects of domination by the powerful centres of global culture, and the extent to which it offers itself to transformation by peripheral communities, is still a matter of debate.

Further reading: Albrow 1994; Albrow and King 1990; Behdad 2005; Brennan 2004; Brydon 2001a, 2001b; Cheah 1999; Dirlik 1999; Featherstone 1990; Featherstone et al. 1995; Gikandi 2001; Hoogvelt 2001; Huggan 2004; Hulme 2005; King 1991; Kofman and Youngs 1996; Koshy 2005; McCallum and Faith 2005; Mignolo 2000a; Robertson 1992; Spybey 1996.

GLOCALIZATION

First popularized in the English-speaking world by the British sociologist Roland Robertson in the 1990s, and later developed by Zygmaunt Bauman, the term 'glocal' and the process noun 'glocalization' are formed by blending the words 'global' and 'local'. Both terms became aspects of business jargon during the 1980s, originating in Japan, but its use for post-colonial studies has been principally in its foregrounding of local agency against a seemingly relentless global culture. Globalization is itself always local and while globalization operates according to 'flows', the agency of the local ensures that the flow is very often reciprocal. According to Robertson 'it makes no good sense to define the global as if the global excludes the local. In somewhat technical terms defining the global in such a way suggests that the global lies beyond all localities, as having systemic properties over and beyond the attributes of units within a global system.' (1995: 34). The concept is present in slogans such as 'think globally, act locally' but it has accompanied the greatly nuanced view of the relationship between the local and the global that has been introduced by post-colonial studies.

The concept is important to post-colonial studies because it can be understood in terms of the **transcultural** relationships pertaining between colony and imperial centre in imperialism. As with classical imperialism, the impact of colonial incursion was not simply one-way, oppressive and hierarchical but reciprocal, transcultural and eventually transformative. This is perhaps most clearly demonstrated in the capacity of post-colonial literatures to appropriate the language, forms and genres of English literature and transform the discipline. Both literary writing and its transcultural scenario emphasise the **agency** of the local and of individual subjects and colonial communities to interpolate the discourses of imperial power.

The relationship between the local and global has been of particular interest to post-colonial theorists such as Dirlik, Appadurai, Bhabha and Spivak, This involvement of post-colonial theorists in the discourse of cultural globalization has been so pronounced that Simon Gikandi has suggested that its 'cultural turn' has been entirely due to the intervention of post-colonial discourse over the last two decades. Globalization and post-colonialism 'have at least two important things in common: they are concerned with explaining forms of social and cultural organization whose ambition is to transcend the boundaries of the nation-state, and they seek to provide new vistas for understanding cultural flows that can no longer be explained by a homogenous Eurocentric narrative of development and social change' (Gikandi 2001: 627).

The language of post-colonialism provided a way of talking about the engagement of the global by the local, particularly local cultures, and, most importantly, provided a greatly nuanced view of globalization that developed from its understanding of the complexities of imperial relationships. This language needed to be adopted because by the 1990s globalization could no longer be explained in terms of traditional social science models. Globalization constitutes what Appadurai calls 'a complex overlapping, disjunctive order that cannot any longer be understood in terms of existing centre-periphery models' (Appadurai 1996: 32).

Further reading: Appadurai 1996; Bauman 1998; Gikandi 2002; Robertson 1995.

'GOING NATIVE'

The term indicates the colonizers' fear of contamination by absorption into native life and customs. The construction of **native** cultures as either primitive or degenerate in a binary discourse of colonizer/ colonized led, especially at the turn of the century, to a widespread fear of 'going native' amongst the colonizers in many colonial societies. Variants occur such as 'going Fantee' (West Africa) and 'going troppo' (Australian), which suggest that both the associations with other races and even the mere climate of colonies in hot areas can lead to moral and even physical degeneracy. The threat is particularly associated with the temptation posed by inter-racial sex, where sexual liaisons with 'native' peoples were supposed to result in a contamination of the colonizers' pure stock and thus their degeneracy and demise as a vigorous and **civilized** (as opposed to **savage** or degenerate) **race**. But 'going native' could also encompass lapses from European behaviour, the participation in 'native' ceremonies, or the adoption and even enjoyment of local customs in terms of dress, food, recreation and entertainment. Perhaps the best known canonical example of the perils of going native is Kurtz in Conrad's *Heart of Darkness*, a character who seems to embody the very complex sense of vulnerability, primitivism and horror of the process.

Further reading: Torgovnik 1990.

HEGEMONY

Hegemony, initially a term referring to the dominance of one state within a confederation, is now generally understood to mean domination by consent. This broader meaning was coined and popularized in the 1930s by Italian Marxist Antonio Gramsci, who investigated why the ruling class was so successful in promoting its own interests in society. Fundamentally, hegemony is the power of the ruling class to convince other classes that their interests are the interests of all. Domination is thus exerted not by force, nor even necessarily by active persuasion, but by a more subtle and inclusive power over the economy, and over state apparatuses such as education and the media, by which the ruling class's interest is presented as the common interest and thus comes to be taken for granted.

The term is useful for describing the success of imperial power over a colonized people who may far outnumber any occupying military force, but whose desire for self-determination has been suppressed by a hegemonic notion of the greater good, often couched in terms of social order, stability and advancement, all of which are defined by the colonizing power. Hegemony is important because the capacity to influence the thought of the colonized is by far the most sustained and potent operation of imperial power in colonized regions. Indeed, an 'empire' is distinct from a collection of subject states forcibly controlled by a central power by virtue of the effectiveness of its cultural hegemony. Consent is achieved by the **interpellation** of the colonized subject by **imperial** discourse so that **Euro-centric** values, assumptions, beliefs and attitudes are accepted as a matter of course as the most natural or valuable. The inevitable consequence of such interpellation is that the colonized subject understands itself as peripheral to those Euro-centric values, while at the same time accepting their centrality.

A classic example of the operation of hegemonic control is given by Gauri Viswanathan, who shows how 'the humanistic functions traditionally associated with the study of literature – for example, the shaping of character or the development of the aesthetic sense or the disciplines of ethical thinking – can be vital in the process of sociopolitical control' (1987: 2). Such control was maintained by the British government when it took responsibility for education in India after the Charter Act of 1813. Searching for a method of communicating the values of Western civilization to Indians which avoided offending their Hindu sensibilities, the administration discovered the power of English literature as a vehicle for imperial authority. 'The strategy of locating authority in these texts all but effaced the sordid history of colonialist expropriation, material exploitation, and class and race oppression behind European world dominance . . . the English literary text functioned as a surrogate Englishman in his highest and most perfect state' (Viswanathan 1987: 23). This Englishman was, at the same time, the embodiment of universal human values. As Viswanathan puts it, the 'split between the material and the discursive practices of colonialism is nowhere sharper than in the progressive refraction of the rapacious, exploitative and ruthless actor of history into the reflective subject of literature' (22–23). This refraction is a precise demonstration of one mode of hegemonic control. It proved a particularly effective one because the discourse of English literature was disseminated with its attendant spiritual values, cultural assumptions, social discriminations, racial prejudices and humanistic values more or less intact.

Further reading: Bharucha 1997; Gramsci 1988, 1991; Olson and Worsham 1999; San Juan 1995; Viswanathan 1989.

HYBRIDITY

One of the most widely employed and most disputed terms in post-colonial theory, hybridity commonly refers to the creation of new **transcultural** forms within the contact zone produced by colonization. As used in horticulture, the term refers to the cross-breeding of two species by grafting or cross-pollination to form a third, 'hybrid' species. Hybridization takes many forms: linguistic, cultural, political, racial, etc. Linguistic examples include **pidgin** and **creole** languages, and these echo the foundational use of the term by the linguist and cultural theorist Mikhail Bakhtin, who used it to suggest the disruptive and trans-figuring power of multivocal language situations and, by extension, of multivocal narratives. The idea of a polyphony of voices in society is implied also in Bakhtin's idea of the carnivalesque, which emerged in the Middle Ages when 'a boundless world of humorous forms and manifestations opposed the official and serious tone of medieval ecclesiastical and feudal culture' (Holquist 1984: 4).

The term 'hybridity' has been most recently associated with the work of Homi K.Bhabha, whose analysis of colonizer/colonized relations stresses their interdependence and the mutual construction of their subjectivities (see **mimicry and ambivalence**). Bhabha contends that all cultural statements and systems are constructed in a space that he calls the 'Third Space of enunciation' (1994: 37). Cultural identity always emerges in this contradictory and ambivalent space, which for Bhabha makes the claim to a hierarchical 'purity' of cultures untenable. For him, the recognition of this ambivalent space of cultural identity may help us to overcome the **exoticism** of **cultural diversity** in favour of the recognition of an empowering hybridity within which cultural difference may operate:

> It is significant that the productive capacities of this Third Space have a colonial or postcolonial provenance. For a willing-ness to descend into that alien territory . . . may open the way to conceptualizing an *inter*national culture, based not on

the exoticism of multiculturalism or the *diversity* of cultures, but
on the inscription and articulation of culture's *hybridity*.

(Bhabha 1994: 38)

It is the 'in-between' space that carries the burden and meaning of
culture, and this is what makes the notion of hybridity so important.

Hybridity has frequently been used in post-colonial discourse to
mean simply cross-cultural 'exchange'. This use of the term has been
widely criticized, since it usually implies negating and neglecting
the imbalance and inequality of the power relations it references. By
stressing the transformative cultural, linguistic and political impacts on
both the colonized and the colonizer, it has been regarded as replicating
assimilationist policies by masking or 'whitewashing' cultural differences.

The idea of hybridity also underlies other attempts to stress the
mutuality of cultures in the colonial and post-colonial process in expressions of syncreticity, cultural **synergy** and **transculturation**. The
criticism of the term referred to above stems from the perception that
theories that stress mutuality *necessarily* downplay oppositionality, and
increase continuing post-colonial dependence. There is, however, nothing in the idea of hybridity as such that suggests that mutuality negates
the hierarchical nature of the imperial process or that it involves the
idea of an **equal** exchange. This is, however, the way in which some proponents of **decolonization** and **anti-colonialism** have interpreted
its current usage in **colonial discourse** theory. It has also been subject
to critique as part of a general dissatisfaction with colonial discourse
theory on the part of critics such as Chandra Talpade Mohanty,
Benita Parry and Aijaz Ahmad. These critiques stress the textualist and
idealist basis of such analysis and point to the fact that they neglect
specific local differences.

The assertion of a shared post-colonial condition such as hybridity has
been seen as part of the tendency of discourse analysis to de-historicize
and de-locate cultures from their temporal, spatial, geographical and
linguistic contexts, and to lead to an abstract, globalized concept of
the textual that obscures the specificities of particular cultural situations.
Pointing out that the investigation of the discursive construction
of colonialism does not seek to replace or exclude other forms such
as historical, geographical, economic, military or political, Robert Young
suggests that the contribution of colonial discourse analysis, in which
concepts such as hybridity are couched,

provides a significant framework for that other work by
emphasising that all perspectives on colonialism share and have

to deal with a common discursive medium which was also that of colonialism itself: . . . Colonial discourse analysis can therefore look at the wide variety of texts of colonialism as something more than mere documentation or 'evidence'.

(Young 1995: 163)

However, Young himself offers a number of objections to the indiscriminate use of the term. He notes how influential the term 'hybridity' was in **imperial** and colonial discourse in negative accounts of the union of disparate races – accounts that implied that unless actively and persistently cultivated, such hybrids would inevitably revert to their 'primitive' stock. Hybridity thus became, particularly at the turn of the century, part of a colonialist discourse of racism. Young draws our attention to the dangers of employing a term so rooted in a previous set of racist assumptions, but he also notes that there is a difference between unconscious processes of hybrid mixture, or creolization, and a conscious and politically motivated concern with the deliberate disruption of homogeneity. He notes that for Bakhtin, for example, hybridity is politicized, made contestatory, so that it embraces the subversion and challenge of division and separation. Bakhtin's hybridity 'sets different points of view against each other in a conflictual structure, which retains "a certain elemental, organic energy and openendedness"' (Young 1995: 21–22). It is this potential of hybridity to reverse 'the structures of domination in the colonial situation' (23), which Young recognizes, that Bhabha also articulates. 'Bakhtin's intentional hybrid has been transformed by Bhabha into an active moment of challenge and resistance against a dominant colonial power . . . depriving the imposed imperialist culture, not only of the authority that it has for so long imposed politically, often through violence, but even of its own claims to **authenticity**' (23).

Young does, however, warn of the unconscious process of repetition involved in the contemporary use of the term. According to him, when talking about hybridity, contemporary cultural discourse cannot escape the connection with the racial categories of the past in which hybridity had such a clear racial meaning. Therefore 'deconstructing such essentialist notions of race today we may rather be repeating the [fixation on race in the] past than distancing ourselves from it, or providing a critique of it (27). This is a subtle and persuasive objection to the concept. However, more positively, Young also notes that the term indicates a broader insistence in many twentieth-century disciplines, from physics to genetics, upon 'a double logic, which goes against the convention of rational either/or choices, but which is repeated in science in the split between the incompatible coexisting logics of classical and quantum physics' (26). In this sense, as in much else in the structuralist and poststructuralist legacy, the concept of hybridity emphasizes a typically twentieth-century concern with relations within a field rather than with an analysis of discrete objects, seeing meaning as the produce of such relations rather than as intrinsic to specific events or objects.

Whilst assertions of national culture and of pre-colonial traditions have played an important role in creating **anti-colonial** discourse and in arguing for an active **decolonizing** project, theories of the hybrid nature of post-colonial culture assert a different model for resistance, locating this in the subversive **counter-discursive** practices implicit in the colonial ambivalence itself and so undermining the very basis on which imperialist and colonialist discourse raises its claims of superiority.

Further reading: Bakhtin 1981, 1994; Bhabha 1994; Kraniauskas 2004; Puri 2004; Radhakrishnan 2000; Ramazani 2001; Smith 2004; Stoneham 2000; Young 1995; for opposing views see Ahmad 1992; S. Mishra 1996; Parry 1987; Smyth 2000.

IMPERIALISM

In its most general sense, imperialism refers to the formation of an empire, and, as such, has been an aspect of all periods of history in which one nation has extended its domination over one or several neigh-bouring nations. Edward Said uses imperialism in this general sense to mean 'the practice, theory, and the attitudes of a dominating metropolitan centre ruling a distant territory', (Said 1993: 8), a process distinct from **colonialism**, which is 'the implanting of settlements on a distant territory'. However, there is general agreement that the word imperialism, as a conscious and openly advocated policy of aquiring colonies for economic, strategic and political advantage, did not emerge until around 1880. Before that date, the term 'empire' (particularly the British variety) conjured up an apparently benevolent process of European expansion whereby colonies *accrued* rather than were *acquired*. Around the mid-nineteenth century, the term 'imperialism' was used to describe the government and policies of Napoleon III, self-styled 'emperor', and by 1870 was used disparagingly in disputes between the political parties in Britain. But from the 1880s imperialism became a dominant and more transparently aggressive policy amongst European states for a variety of political, cultural and economic reasons.

The expansionist policies pursued by the modern industrial powers from 1880 have been described as 'classical imperialism' (Baumgart 1982: 5). The year 1885, when the Berlin Congo Conference ended and the 'scramble for Africa' got underway, has been regarded as the beginning of classical imperialism. But the 'scramble' itself really began earlier, in 1879, when the rivalry between Britain and France became intense in West Africa, and intensified further in 1882, when Egypt was occupied, and the Treaty of Brazza-Moroko initiated the struggle for the Congo. At the turn of the century, both European and American commentators enthusiastically advocated a policy of imperialism, because the idea of expansion could be seen, and was presented, in terms of the improvement of the lot of the 'barbaric nations'.

The significant feature of imperialism then is that, while as a term used to describe the late nineteenth-century policy of European expansion it is quite recent, its historical roots run deep, extending back to Roman times. Derived from the Latin word *imperium* to describe its sovereignty over the Mediterranean world, the term *Imperium populi Romani* was not merely rhetorical, it defined the sovereignty invested in the people and bestowed by the people on its magistrates abroad. It was this Republican use of the term that Cicero defended against the notion of the monarchical *Imperium Romanum* instituted by Caesar Augustus, a power invested in the *imperator* to whom all the people must show allegiance. However, the *imperium* was the creation and instrument of a self-perpetuating oligarchy, something that has remained relevant to modern imperialism. It is clear that the Roman empire has had more impact than any before it in modelling the strategies, techniques and rhetoric on which subsequent imperial practice has been based. Koebner claims that the modern concept of Empire 'unfailingly recalls the Roman Empires of the past' (Koebner 1961: 18).

Imperialism in its more recent sense – the acquisition of an empire of overseas colonies – is associated with the Europeanization of the globe which came in three major waves: the age of discovery during the fifteenth and sixteenth centuries; the age of mercantilism during the seventeenth and eighteenth centuries; and the age of imperialism in the nineteenth and early twentieth centuries. Europeanization was chiefly effected not by governments and states, but rather by those hundreds of thousands of colonists, merchants, missionaries and adventurers who permeated the non-European world. This general Europeanization of the globe is much harder to trace, but it is important to understand the extent to which European imperialism is grounded on this **diaspora** of ordinary travellers, explorers, missionaries, fortune hunters and settlers over many centuries.

Both the Roman internationalist and Carolingian dynastic senses of imperialism were very different from that which emerged as a consequence of the development of the nation-state. Hobson makes the point that colonialism 'is a natural overflow of nationality', its test being 'the power of colonists to transplant the civilization they represent to the new natural and social environment in which they find themselves' (1902: 7). But it is clear that mercantilism, or mercantile capitalism (that is, the 'merchant' capitalism that existed before the Industrial Revolution), was a significant feature of the European acquisition of colonies, and one tied up with national sentiment. During the mercantilist age, which began roughly with Cromwell's Navigation Act of 1651, rivalry between the European powers was based no longer on religion but on the competitive acquisition of wealth, particularly gold and silver, and its consolidation through the discouragement of imports by tariffs and the encouragement of exports through bounties and rebates. The principle was that one nation's gain was another's loss, since the world's wealth was thought to be a fixed quantity. (Adam Smith critiqued the mercantile system in the *Wealth of Nations* published in 1776, pointing out the absurdity of confusing material wealth with money.) But mercantilism was important to its supporters because 'its purpose was not to maximise welfare, but to promote the economic and political independence of the nation-state' (Lichteim 1971: 51). All European powers in the mercantalist age believed that the acquisition of colonies was beneficial, if only to deprive competitors of potential wealth.

Surprisingly, empire building did not die out with the end of mercantilism and slavery but increased apace during the nineteenth century. Hobsbawm in *Industry and Empire* (1968) proposes that the earlier British empire was crucial in promoting the industrial transformation of 1750–1850 which in turn gave rise to the second British empire. His argument is that the Industrial Revolution could not have occurred in Britain but for the possession of a colonial empire that provided outlets far in excess of anything the home markets could offer. Industrialization entailed a sudden expansion of productive capacity possible only in a country that occupied a key position within the evolving world economy. Imperialism at this time was an unspoken assumption rather than a concrete doctrine.

After 1815, Britain ruled the seas and began to establish itself as the world's factory, so major colonial annexations were unnecessary. Economic penetration could take the place of military conquest, and this was facilitated by the doctrine of free trade that Britain preached because it could undersell the manufactures of its competitors. Robinson and

Gallagher (1981) have called this a time of 'informal imperialism'. By the 1880s capital was beginning to stagnate and so an openly imperialist movement, that is, one not content with the invisible 'imperialism of free trade', but one that called for a protective tariff wall to be built around the empire, rapidly rose to prominence. The debate over imperialism occupied an entire generation from 1880 to 1914, and its effect upon European public opinion has been seen by many historians as a factor in the outbreak of the First World War in 1914.

Although Lenin's analysis of imperialism in *Imperialism, The Highest Stage of Capitalism* (1916) has become perhaps the most influential in twentieth-century political economy, this specifically economic definition of the term was developed from J.A. Hobson, whose disgust with the war in South Africa led to his book *Imperialism* in 1902. Hobson asserted that as a nation enters the machine economy it becomes more difficult for its manufacturers, merchants and financiers to dispose profitably of their economic resources, so they prevail upon government to acquire colonies in order to provide markets. As production at home exceeds the growth in consumption, and more goods are produced than can be sold at a profit, more capital exists than can be profitably invested. 'It is this economic condition of affairs that forms the taproot of imperialism' (1902: 71).

There are several arguments against purely economic views of European imperialism, not the least of which is the argument by historians such as Robinson and Gallagher that there was a continuation of imperial policy that became openly aggressive only in the 1880s. Empirical studies reveal that the flow of profit from colony to metropolis was not as great as had often been supposed during this period. Such was Prime Minister Disraeli's reluctance about maintaining costly colonies that Britain's involvement in the post-1880s scramble is better explained by political strategy and competitive nationalism than by economic considerations.

More importantly for post-colonial theory, there was a continuous development of imperial rhetoric and of imperial representation of the rest of the globe from at least the fifteenth century. As a continuous practice, this had much more to do with the desire for, and belief in, European cultural dominance – a belief in a superior right to exploit the world's resources – than pure profit. Said observes that the rhetoricians of imperialism after 1880 'deploy a language whose imagery of growth, fertility, and expansion, whose teleological structure of property and identity, whose ideological discrimination between 'us' and 'them' had already matured elsewhere – in fiction, political science, racial theory, travel writing' (Said 1993: 128). This is, of course, the most significant omission from accounts by economic theorists of imperialism: that the ideological grounding, the language of cultural dominance, the ideology of race and the civilizing mission of European cultural dominance had been accelerating since the eighteenth century.

The nineteenth-century growth in the activity of humanitarian organizations and missionary societies, which provided continuity between imperial policies before and after 1880, was a powerful impulse of classical imperialism. This, allied with the growth in **exploration and travel**, the perception of the new lands as regions of adventure and renewal where the Anglo-Saxon race could regenerate, or as 'el dorados', sites of fabulous wealth, provided very compelling motivation for the movement of European peoples to the colonial margins. Clearly there is a case for arguing the existence of different kinds of imperialisms clustered around the philanthropic and exploitative, and indeed the worst colonialist scandals were exposed by humanitarian and missionary organizations. But the subtle way in which the two could become enmeshed can be seen in the work of David Livingston, whose claim was that 'Christianity, Commerce and Civilization' must go hand in hand. His aim was to promote legal trade and thus eradicate slavery and exploitation, to which end he encouraged the building of roads and railways and the establishing of steamship routes. But this very conjunction demonstrates the extent to which the European presence in Africa, whatever its purposes, involved a profound cultural imperialism which, along with the arbitrary geo-political division of the continent, proved ultimately disabling to African societies.

In the end, however, it was the control of the means of representation rather than the means of production that confirmed the hegemony of the European powers in their respective empires. Economic, political and military dominance enabled the dissemination of European ideas through the powerful agencies of education and publishing. But it was the power of imperial discourse rather than military or economic might that confirmed the **hegemony** of imperialism in the late nineteenth century. By 1914, the age of 'classical imperialism' had come to an end, but by this time imperialism had demonstrated its protean nature, its ability to change centres, to adapt to the changing dynamic of world power and ultimately to develop into globalism, arguably its natural successor in the late twentieth century.

Further reading: Abernethy 2000; Ansell-Pearson *et al.* 1997; Baumgart 1982; A. Burton 2003; Chrisman 2003; Darby 1998; Hobsbawm 1968; Hobson 1902; Koebner 1961; Koebner and Schmidt 1964; Lenin 1916; Lichteim 1971; Prakash 1995; Robinson and Gallagher 1981.

INDENTURED LABOUR

see **slave/slavery**

INDEPENDENCE

In post-colonial usage this usually refers to the achievement by a colony of full self-government. Independence took a variety of forms and occurred at different times and in different guises, according to the diversity of colonialist practices. **Settler colonies** achieved political independence considerably earlier than others because, despite the degree to which they had also been constructed as marginal by **colonial discourse**, they were not identified by signs of difference such as race and religion. The period after the Second World War saw an upsurge of new independent states. India and Pakistan were 'granted' independence in 1947, as were the majority of African states in 1960. But it is worth noting how long the process of achieving independence took to complete. Some countries in the Caribbean, for instance, did not become independent until the 1980s. Nor did independence always occur in a simple and final form. Thus Malaya achieved its independence in 1957 but Singapore, never entirely and happily located in the newly formed Federation of Malaysia, became independent in its present form only after a further separation in 1965.

The forces of **neo-colonialism** and **globalization** are clearly part of the contentious problem of whether independence really meant the end of colonial control or merely its mutation. Disputes about the term 'independence' overlap those about the term **post-colonial** itself. For example, whether it is best employed only to designate the period after independence, on the grounds that this is essential to discriminate between the radical shifts in relationship at different historical periods (notably between the colonial and post-colonial – here meaning post-independence – periods). Others argue that **post-colonialism** is absolutely and only congruent with overt resistance and opposition (**anti-colonialism**) and that independence has often simply meant the installation of a neo-colonial form of government by local élites (a **comprador** class). Yet others have argued that the desig-nation of the post-colonial as covering the whole period from the moment of colonization allows us to see such continuations of control even whilst we record the various moments of resistance, of which political independence is clearly the most crucial. The whole problem of defining and discriminating between the periods of the colonial/post-colonial is much more problematic than is often suggested; and the moment of independence, whilst a crucial signifier of a profound historical shift, is not in itself as definitive or absolute as has sometimes been implied. If the danger of one approach is to homogenize and eradicate historical difference, the danger of the other is to occlude the ongoing continuities and the elements of colonial influence that continue to mark post-colonial politics and the **post-colonial state**, even after it achieves political independence.

Further reading: Barrington 2006; Ngugi 1986; Nkrumah 1965.

INTERPELLATION

see **subject/subjectivity**

LIMINALITY

This term derives from the word 'limen', meaning threshold, a word particularly used in psychology to indicate the threshold between the sensate and the subliminal, the limit below which a certain sensation ceases to be perceptible. The sense of the liminal as an interstitial or in-between space, a threshold area, distinguishes the term from the more definite word 'limit' to which it is related.

The importance of the liminal for post-colonial theory is precisely its usefulness for describing an 'in-between' space in which cultural change may occur: the **transcultural** space in which strategies for personal or communal self-hood may be elaborated, a region in which there is a continual process of movement and interchange between different states. For instance, the colonized subject may dwell in the liminal space between **colonial discourse** and the assumption of a new 'non-colonial' identity. But such identification is never simply a movement from one identity to another, it is a constant process of engagement, contestation and **appropriation**.

Homi Bhabha quotes the art historian Renée Green's characterization of a stairwell as a 'liminal space, a pathway between upper and lower areas, each of which was annotated with plaques referring to blackness and whiteness' (Bhabha 1994: 4) to indicate how the liminal can become a space of symbolic interaction. That is, the stairwell, the liminal, prevents identities from polarizing between such arbitrary designations as 'upper' and 'lower', 'black' and 'white'. In a sense one could say that post-colonial discourse itself consistently inhabits this liminal space, for the polarities of imperial rhetoric on one hand, and national or racial characterization on the other, are continually questioned and problematized.

For Bhabha the liminal is important because liminality and **hybridity** go hand in hand. This 'interstitial passage between fixed identifications opens up the possibility of a cultural hybridity that entertains difference without an assumed or imposed hierarchy' (1994: 4). He further employs liminality to show that 'post-modernity, post-coloniality, post-feminism' are meaningless if the 'post' simply means 'after'. Each of these represents a liminal space of contestation and change, at the edges of the presumed monolithic, but never completely 'beyond'. The present can no longer be envisaged as a break or a bonding with the past or future; our presence comes to be revealed in its 'discontinuities, its inequalities, its minorities'.

Further reading: Bhabha 1994.

MAGIC REALISM

This term, which has a long and quite distinctive history in Latin American criticism, was first used in a wider post-colonial context in the foundational essay by Jacques Stephen Alexis, 'Of the magical realism of the Haitians' (Alexis 1956). Alexis sought to reconcile the arguments of post-war, radical intellectuals in favour of social realism as a tool for revolutionary social representation, with a recognition that in many post-colonial societies a peasant, pre-industrial population had its imaginative life rooted in a living tradition of the mythic, the legendary and the magical. The term became popularized when it was employed to characterize the work of South American writers widely translated into English and other languages, such as Gabriel García Marquez. It tended to be used indiscriminately during the 'Boom' period of the 1960s and 1970s by some critics who saw it as a defining feature of all Latin American writing, in stark contrast to its older, more specific usage in Latin American criticism, a usage that differed in marked ways from the recent rather loose and generalized use of the term (Zamora and Faris 1995).

However, its origins in the 1950s lay in the specific need to wed Caribbean social revolution to local cultural tradition. Mythic and magical traditions, Alexis argued, far from being alienated from the people, or mere mystifications, were the distinctive feature of their local and national cultures, and were the collective forms by which they gave expression to their identity and articulated their difference from the dominant colonial and racial oppressors. They were, in other words, the modes of expression of that culture's reality. Radical social visions of art and culture thus regarded myth and magic as integral. For Alexis, 'The treasure of tales and legends, all the musical, choreographic and plastic symbolism, all the forms of Haitian popular art are there to help the nation in accomplishing the tasks before it.' More recently, the term has been used in a less specific way to refer to the inclusion of any mythic or legendary material from local written or oral cultural traditions in contemporary narrative.

The material so used is seen to interrogate the assumptions of Western, rational, linear narrative and to enclose it within an indigenous metatext, a body of textual forms that recuperate the pre-colonial culture. In this way it can be seen to be a structuring device in texts as varied as Salman Rushdie's *Midnight's Children*, Ben Okri's *The Famished Road*, Keri Hulme's *The Bone People* or Thomas King's *Green Grass, Running Water*. In texts like these and many others, the rational, linear world of Western realist fiction is placed against alter/native narrative modes that expose the hidden and naturalized cultural formations on which Western narratives are based. Although the term has been useful, its increasingly ubiquitous use for any text that has a fabulous or mythic dimension has tended to bring it into disrepute with some critics who suggest that it has become a catch-all for any narrative device that does not adhere to Western realist conventions.

Further reading: Alexis 1956; S. Baker 1991; Durix 1998; Faris 2004; Molloy 2005; Parkinson and Faris 1995; Slemon 1988a, 1995.

MANICHEANISM

This term is adapted from the 'Manichaean heresy' of the third century AD which propounded a dualistic theology, according to which Satan was represented as coeternal with God. Matter was evil and God by His nature could not intervene in the world of evil matter. Thus Christ could not have been born into the flesh and had to be only spirit – a heresy against the doctrine of Christ's dual nature as both Man and God. The implication that the two realms of spirit and matter were always and eternally separate and could never be linked implies an extreme form of binary structure, and it is this to which contemporary post-colonial usage refers. The concept was popularized by Abdul JanMohammed (1983, 1985) who developed Frantz Fanon's identification of the Manichaean nature of the implacable opposition of colonizer and colonized.

In the field of post-colonial studies, Manicheanism is a term for the **binary** structure of **imperial** ideology. JanMohammed uses the uncompromisingly dualistic aspect of the concept to describe the process by which imperial discourse polarizes the society, culture and very being of the colonizer and colonized into the Manichean categories of good and evil. The world at the boundaries of civilization is perceived as uncontrollable, chaotic, unattainable and ultimately evil, while the civilized culture is the embodiment of good. The consequences of this for **colonial discourse** are that the colonizer's assumption of moral superiority means that 'he will not be inclined to expend any energy in understanding the worthless alterity of the colonized' (1985: 18). Much literature of cultural encounter,

> instead of being an exploration of the racial Other . . . affirms its own ethno-centric assumptions; instead of actually depicting the outer limits of 'civilization', it simply codifies and preserves the structures of its own mentality. While the surface of each colonialist text purports to represent specific encounters with specific varieties of the racial Other, the subtext valorizes the superiority of European cultures, of the collective process that has mediated that representation. Such literature is essentially specular: instead of seeing the native as a bridge toward syncretic possibility, it uses him as a mirror that reflects the colonialist's self image.
>
> (JanMohammed 1985: 19)

Borrowing from Lacan, JanMohammed claims that colonialist literature can be divided into 'imaginary' and 'symbolic' modes. The writer of the 'imaginary' text tends to 'fetishize a nondialectical, fixed opposition between the self and the native. Threatened by a metaphysical alterity that he has created, he quickly retreats to the homegeneity of his own group.' Writers of 'symbolic' texts tend to be more open to a modifying dialectic of self and Other, and it is this preparedness to consider the possibility of syncretism that is the most important factor distinguishing it from the 'imaginary' text. Ultimately, according to JanMohammed, it is the ability to bracket the values and bases of imperialist culture that determines the success of the symbolic text and its ability to subvert or avoid the economy of Manichean allegory.

Further reading: JanMohammed 1983, 1985.

MARGINALITY

Being on the margin, marginal. The perception and description of experience as 'marginal' is a consequence of the binaristic structure of various kinds of dominant discourses, such as patriarchy, **imperialism** and **ethno-centrism**, which imply that certain forms of experience are peripheral. Although the term carries a misleading geometric implication, marginal groups do not necessarily endorse the notion of a fixed centre. Structures of power that are described in terms of 'centre' and 'margin' operate, in reality, in a complex, diffuse and multi-faceted way. The marginal therefore indicates a *positionality* that is best defined in terms of the limitations of a subject's access to power.

However, marginality as a *noun* is related to the verb 'to marginalize', and in this sense provides a trap for those involved in resistance by its assumption that power is a function of centrality. This means that such resistance can become a process of replacing the centre rather than deconstructing the binary structure of centre and margin, which is a primary feature of post-colonial discourse. Marginality unintentionally reifies centrality because it is the centre that creates the condition of marginality. In simple terms we could ask 'Who are the marginal?' 'Marginal to what?' We might be tempted to reply spontaneously, 'imperialism marginalizes, the colonized people are marginalized'. But they are neither *all* marginalized nor *always* marginalized. Imperialism cannot be reduced to a structure, a geometry of power that leaves some particular races on the margin. It is continuous, processual, working through individuals as well as upon them. It reproduces itself within the very idea of the marginal. Therefore, despite its ubiquity as a term to indicate various forms of exclusion and oppression, the use of the term always involves the risk that it endorses the structure that established the marginality of certain groups in the first place.

Further reading: Gunew 1994; Jordan and Weedon 1995; Orgun 2000; Spivak 1996.

MESTIZO/MESTIZAJE/MÉTISSE

These terms, respectively Spanish and French in origin, semantically register the idea of a mixing of races and/or cultures. Initially, they emerged from a **colonial discourse** that privileged the idea of racial purity and justified racial discrimination by employing the quasi-scientific precursors of physical anthropology to create a complex and largely fictional taxonomy of racial admixtures (mulatto, quadroon, octaroon, etc.).

Mestizo differs from Creole and from *métisse* in so far as its usage reflects the older, large-scale Spanish and Portuguese settlement of their South American and Meso-American possessions. This early settlement led to an intensive cultural and racial exchange between Spaniards and Portuguese settlers and the native Indians, in many cases prior to the influence of black African slaves upon this cultural mélange. The relatively early date of this colonizing process, and the equally early date at which Spanish and Portuguese colonies in the Americas achieved their independence, means that in Latin American cultural discourses the idea of *mestizo* is much more developed as a positive 'national' cultural sign, as a sign of shared if disputed indigeneity.

Both terms have gradually moved from a pejorative to a positive usage, as they have begun to reflect a perception in these cultures that **miscegenation** and interchange between the different cultural **diasporas** had produced new and powerful **synergistic** cultural forms, and that these cultural and racial exchanges might be the place where the most energized aspects of the new cultures reside. These terms have not been used widely to describe aspects of cultures outside the Caribbean, the Americas and the Indian Ocean regions. The dominance of the use of **creole** as a generic term in linguistics and in wider cultural studies as well as in general discourse stems from its early adoption into English as the standard term, though English writers have occasionally used mestizo to indicate some of the special nuances discussed above. The use of the Spanish term ***mestizaje*** has also become prevalent, particularly in Latin American studies, and is used to describe the cultural processes attendant to a long history of **miscegenation** by emphasizing **heterogeneity** and **transculturation**. *Mestizaje* is employed most commonly in cultural and linguistic analyses to denote plurality and is a key feature of Latin American regionalist discourse.

Further reading: Alonso 2004; Chanady 1995, 2003; Cornejo Polar 1997; Cornejo Polar and Dennis 2004a, 2004b; Echeverría 1998; Glissant 1981, 1989; Harris 1983; Hildebrant 1992; Klor de Alva 1995; Miller 2004; Moraña 2002; Pérez Torres 2006; Vilanova 1977.

METONYMIC GAP

This is a term for what is arguably the most subtle form of abrogation. The metonymic gap is that cultural gap formed when appropriations of a colonial language insert unglossed words, phrases or passages from a first language, or concepts, allusions or references that may be unknown to the reader. Such words become synechdochic of the writer's culture – the part that stands for the whole – rather than representations of the world, as the colonial language might. Thus the inserted language 'stands for' the colonized culture in a metonymic way, and its very resistance to interpretation constructs a 'gap' between the writer's culture and the colonial culture. The local writer is thus able to represent his or her world to the colonizer (and others) in the metropolitan language, and at the same time to signal and emphasize a difference from it. In effect, the writer is saying 'I am using your language so that you will understand my world, but you will also know by the differences in the way I use it that you cannot share my experience.'

There are many ways in which the language can do this: syntactic fusion; neologisms; code-switching; untranslated words. An example of the latter occurs in Ngugi's *A Grain of Wheat*, in which Gikonyo sings a song to his future wife Mumbi in Gikuyu (Ashcroft 1989b: 61). The song itself it densely ironic and yet inaccessible to a non-Gikuyu reader. It reiterates that absence that lies at the point of interface between the two cultures. The insertion of a Gikuyu song in the text presents a cultural 'gap' that emphasizes difference yet situates it in a way that makes the piece accessible.

Further reading: Ashcroft 1989b.

METROPOLIS/METROPOLITAN

'Metropolis' is a term used binaristically in colonial discourse to refer to the 'centre' in relation to a colonial periphery. In Greek history, a metropolis was the parent state of a colony. The first specific use of the term to cover the modern colonial situation, in which 'metropolitan' means 'belonging to or constituting the mother country', is listed in the *OED* as 1806. The metropolis in European thought was always constituted as the seat of culture, and this meaning is readily transferred to the imperial/colonial relationship. There is frequent slippage in the use of the term to cover 'mother country' (England, France) or, metonymically, their chief cities, London and Paris. (Oswald Spengler claimed that at the turn of the century the seat of world power was, in practical terms, focused in four cities.)

Since the binarism inherent in the concept connotes a **centre** and a **periphery**, colonies are by definition constructed as peripheral to the metropolitan 'centres'. Post-colonial writers such as V.S. Naipaul have attempted to question or dismantle/disrupt this hierarchized binary by exposing the idea of an imperial 'centre' as chimeric. Since the 'centre' can never be found, the distinction between metropolis and colony, centre and periphery necessarily collapses. In practical terms, however, control of publishing and distribution was (and in many cases still is) centred in the European (and, latterly, North American) metropoles, and, together with the migration of artists and intellectuals to Paris, London and Madrid, reinforced (and to some extent still reinforces) the cultural power of 'the metropolis'.

While there are obvious similarities here between the empires of England, France and Spain, it should be noted that the ways in which their empires were administered and the attitudes of colonials to the different 'centres' varied significantly. In the empire of France, cultural power was invested almost exclusively in a Parisian intellectual élitism that rendered the rest of France as culturally 'peripheral' as the African or Antillean colonies. Colonial intellectuals who migrated to Paris could share in that 'cultural capital'. By contrast, although the controlling cultural institutions of the British Empire were generally collected in London, significant cultural differences between colonies and 'the metropolitan' remained in a **binaristic** hierarchy more usually formulated as 'England and the colonies' or 'Britain and the colonies'. Colonial writers and artists could succeed in London, but their primary affiliation was usually regarded as being with their colonial homelands. As these writers became increasingly prominent, however, Britain has widened its metropolitan self-concept to include contemporary post-colonial writers originally from Australia, Africa, India and Pakistan under the label of 'British'.

Further reading: Ball 2004; McLeod 2004; Spengler 1926; Stoneham 2000.

MIDDLE PASSAGE

(see **slave/slavery**)

MIMICRY

An increasingly important term in post-colonial theory, because it has come to describe the **ambivalent** relationship between colonizer and colonized. When colonial discourse encourages the colonized

124

subject to 'mimic' the colonizer, by adopting the colonizer's cultural habits, assumptions, institutions and values, the result is never a simple reproduction of those traits. Rather, the result is a 'blurred copy' of the colonizer that can be quite threatening. This is because mimicry is never very far from mockery, since it can appear to parody whatever it mimics. Mimicry therefore locates a crack in the certainty of colonial dominance, an uncertainty in its control of the behaviour of the colonized.

Mimicry has often been an overt goal of imperial policy. For instance, Lord Macaulay's 1835 *Minute to Parliament* derided Oriental learning, and advocated the reproduction of English art and learning in India (most strategically through the teaching of English literature). However, the method by which this mimicry was to be achieved indicated the underlying weakness of imperialism. For Macaulay suggested that the riches of European learning should be imparted by 'a class of inter-preters between us and the millions whom we govern – a class of persons Indian in blood and colour, but English in tastes, opinions, in morals, and in intellect' (Macaulay 1835). In other words, not only was the mimicry of European learning to be **hybridized** and therefore ambivalent, but Macaulay seems to suggest that imperial discourse is compelled to make it so in order for it to work.

The term mimicry has been crucial in Homi Bhabha's view of the ambivalence of colonial discourse. For him, the consequence of suggestions like Macaulay's is that mimicry is the process by which the colonized subject is reproduced as 'almost the same, but not quite' (Bhabha 1994: 86). The copying of the colonizing culture, behaviour, manners and values by the colonized contains both mockery and a certain 'menace', 'so that mimicry is at once resemblance and menace' (86). Mimicry reveals the limitation in the authority of colonial discourse, almost as though colonial authority inevitably embodies the seeds of its own destruction. The line of descent of the 'mimic man' that emerges in Macaulay's writing, claims Bhabha, can be traced through the works of Kipling, Forster, Orwell and Naipaul, and is the effect of 'a flawed colonial mimesis in which to be Anglicized is emphatically not to be English' (1994: 87).

The consequences of this for post-colonial studies are quite profound, for what emerges through this flaw in colonial power is *writing*, that is, post-colonial writing, the ambivalence of which is 'menacing' to colonial authority. The menace of mimicry does not lie in its concealment of some real identity behind its mask, but comes from its '*double* vision which in disclosing the ambivalence of colonial discourse also disrupts its authority' (88). The 'menace' of post-colonial writing, then, does not necessarily emerge from some automatic opposition to colonial discourse, but comes from this disruption of colonial authority, from the fact that its mimicry is also potentially mockery. While Macaulay's interpreter, or Naipaul's 'mimic man' (discussed below), are appropriate objects of a colonial chain of command, they are also 'inappropriate' colonial subjects because what is being set in motion in their behaviour is something that may ultimately be beyond the control of colonial authority. This 'inappropriateness' disturbs the normality of the dominant discourse itself. The threat inherent in mimicry, then, comes not from an overt resistance but from the way in which it continually suggests an identity not quite like the colonizer. This identity of the colonial subject – 'almost the same but not white' (89) – means that the colonial culture is always potentially and strategically insurgent.

Mimicry can be both ambivalent and multi-layered. In his novel *The Mimic Men*, V.S. Naipaul opens with a very subtle description of the complexity of mimicry when he describes his landlord:

> I paid Mr Shylock three guineas a week for a tall, multi-mirrored, book-shaped room with a coffin-like wardrobe. And for Mr Shylock, the recipient each week of fifteen times three guineas, the possessor of a mistress and of suits made of cloth so fine I felt I could eat it, I had nothing but admiration. . . . I thought Mr Shylock looked distinguished, like a lawyer or businessman or politician. He had the habit of stroking the fore of his ear inclining his head to listen. I thought the gesture was attractive; I copied it. I knew of recent events in Europe; they tormented me; and although I was trying to live on seven pounds a week I offered Mr Shylock my fullest, silent compassion.
>
> (Naipaul 1967: 7)

This deeply ironic passage uncovers the way in which both **hegemony** and mimicry work. Although the title suggests a disparagement of the tendency to emulate the colonizer, the complexity and potential insurgency of mimicry emerges in this passage. The narrator not only copies the habits of the landlord, but mimics the guilt of a post-war Europe concerning the Jews, a guilt that is embedded also in a cultural familiarity with the implications of the name 'Shylock' (the Jew who demanded repayment of a pound of flesh in Shakespeare's *Merchant of Venice*). He is encouraged to mimic a compassion for the one exploiting him. But the very irony of the passage suggests an inversion, a mockery just under the surface; not a mockery of Shylock but of the whole process of colonization that is being enacted in the narrator's mimicry and cultural understanding. The mimicry of the post-colonial subject is therefore always potentially destabilizing to colonial discourse, and locates an area of considerable political and cultural uncertainty in the structure of imperial dominance.

Further reading: Bhabha 1984a, 1994; Castro-Klarén 1999; Huggan 1994, 1997; McQuillan 2002; Parry 1987.

MISCEGENATION

Miscegenation, the sexual union of different races, specifically whites with negroes (*OED*), has always haunted European colonizers and their settler descendants (see **apartheid**). Colonialist practice was obsessed with the products of such unions, particularly in those areas where black and white had also been further hierarchized as slave and free. Nineteenth-century slave-owners developed extensive codifications of the various divisions of admixture resulting from miscegenation. French colonizers, for example, developed no fewer than 128 differing degrees of pigmentation to distinguish between the children of mixed race relations. Since the maintenance of absolute difference between Europeans and others, colonizers and colonized, was crucial to military and administrative control, miscegenation raised the constant spectre of ideological (and sometimes external) destabilization of imperial power. Yet, as theorists such as Bhabha have suggested, the very process of insisting on racial difference may mask a hidden and opposite fascination, as the colonizer sees a menacing **ambivalence** in the ways in which the colonized is both like and unlike. As some critics have argued, the fear of miscegenation thus stems from a desire to maintain the separation between **civilized** and **savage**, yet that binary masks a profound longing, occluding the idea of the inevitable dependence of one on the existence of the other.

One of the earliest theorists of **race**, Gobineau, expressed this ambivalence in his long and influential essay 'Essai sur l'inegalité des races humaines', emphasizing, as Robert Young notes, that there is a positive as well as a negative feature to racial admixture which 'accords with the consistent tendency for the positive to intermingle with the negative, growth with degeneration, life with death' (Young 1995: 115). Young also notes that in this respect Gobineau looks forward to modern ideas concerning the tendency of the socially repressed to return symbolically, citing Stallybrass and White's argument that 'disgust always bears the imprint of desire. These low domains, apparently expelled as 'Other' return as the objects of nostalgia, longing and fascination' (Stallybrass and White 1986: 191). Paradoxically, then, race is seen as the marker of civilization, and racial purity its pre-eminent pre-condition. Yet if civilization must be spread, then the road to the one must lead to the decline of the other. That is, as Gobineau expressed it, 'If mixtures of blood are, to a certain extent, beneficial to the mass of mankind, if they raise and ennoble it, this is merely at the expense of mankind itself, which is stunted, abased, enervated, and humiliated in the persons of its noblest sons' (Gobineau 1853–5: 1, 410, translated by Young).

Further reading: Anderson 1991; Fitz 2002; Gobineau 1853–5, 1856; Lemire 2002; Moore 2000; J.D. Smith 1991; Young 1995.

MISSIONS AND COLONIALISM

The role of missions and missionaries in the development of colonization was crucial. In the words of one historian 'The explosive expansion of Christianity in Africa and Asia during the last two centuries constitutes one of the most remarkable cultural transformations in the history of mankind. Because it coincided with the spread of European economic and cultural hegemony, it tends to be taken for granted as a reflex of imperialism' (Etherington, 2005: 1). As a result for a long while both imperial historians and radical revisers of their work either ignored altogether or radically simplified the complex role religion (See **religion and the post-colonial**) and their instrument, the Christian missions, played for good and bad in the spread of empire. In the last few years we have seen a growth of studies of missions, which have treated the role they played with a new seriousness and which have detailed their importance in the story of colonization.

These new studies emphasized that although the story of Euro-American expansion and the story of missions are deeply intertwined, the relations between them are far more complex than has often been suggested. Radical critics of missions who argue that missions are the forerunners of more direct control. ('First the missionary, then the Consul, and at last the invading army' (Hobson 1938: 204)) see missionaries as conscious precursors of imperialism. They forget the role missionaries also played in acting as a buffer between harsh government policy and indigenous peoples, and especially between settlers and indigenes in settler colonies. In fact, the role of missions in providing education, and so increasing literacy, was construed as a dangerous act by many traders and settlers. It is also certainly the case that many of the first generation of nationalist anti-colonial activists were mission educated. While their oppositional stance was certainly not a conscious product of mission intention it was an undeniable offshoot of the mission emphasis on modernization. Apart from education, this included missionaries' involvement in medical and health issues and their broad concerns for the effects of practices such as slavery on the rights of individuals, especially groups such as women and children who were seen as particularly vulnerable (Scott and Griffiths 2005).

From a literary viewpoint missions had a special role to play in many colonial situations. Of course missions and their role have featured in many post-colonial literary accounts. For the most part these accounts have emphasized the negative impact of missions, as might be expected. As with the general historical accounts however, more complex readings of mission involvement in colonial texts are now emerging (see Griffiths, 2005). Mission presses were often the first places in which colonized peoples were able to find a voice, even though they did so under conditions of patronage which were deeply constraining. Despite this, the degree to which they succeeded in speaking through these constraints is remarkable. Missions and their role exemplify once again how colonized peoples could appropriate and subvert colonial institutions and bend them to their own ends even under the most unpromising of conditions.

Further reading: Dangaremba 1988; Etherington 2005; Griffiths 2005; Hobson 1902.

MODERNISM AND POST-COLONIALISM

Modernism is a twentieth-century European movement in the creative arts that sought to break with the dominant conventions of nineteenth-century art, such as realism, linear narrativity, perspective and tonality. Although modernism is usually defined as a European movement, it has been argued that the encounter with African cultures in the so-called 'scramble for Africa' period of the 1880s and 1890s was crucial to the development of a modernist aesthetic. While the European powers were engaged in violently suppressing the 'savage' cultures of Africa, they were importing into Europe, as loot, the revelation of an alternative view of the world in the form of African masks, carvings and jewellery – artefacts that were often stored in museum basements until displayed in the early decades of the twentieth century. These African works, together with those from other so-called 'primitive' cultures, such as Papua New Guinea and the South Pacific, North American Indian and Inuit, were seen as products of societies preserved in time, reflecting primitive and aboriginal impulses common to all people. Their art reflected a 'stage' in the development of 'civilized' art.

However, from its inception, this ethnographic view was accompanied by a more fearful and complex vision in which primitive art was seen as expressive of the other, darker side of European man, whose civilization might thus be considered merely a veneer. This fear is expressed in works such as Conrad's *Heart Of Darkness* and Yeats' *Savage God*. But in the reaction of artists as diverse as Jarry, Rimbaud, Artaud, Lawrence and Picasso, a more radical critique was formulated in which the claims of European art to universal validity were questioned and in which the claims of Europe to being a unique civilization were exposed as a veneer on a deeper, 'universal' savagery. This view appears to have been vindicated when the claims of nineteenth-century Europe to be civilized collapsed in the horrors of the mass destruction of the First World War.

Further reading: Bray and Middleton 1979; Esty 2004; Eysteinsson 1990; Fokkema 1984; Friedman 2006; Lazarus 2005; McDougall 1998; McGee 1992; Nunes 1994; Peretti 1995; Rajadhyaksha 1998; Ramazani 2006; Richards 2000; Ruthven 1968; Smith 1992; Weston 1996.

MODERNITY

The term 'modern' derives from the late fifth-century Latin term *modernus* which was used to distinguish an officially Christian present from a Roman, pagan past. 'Modern' was used in the medieval period to distinguish the contemporary from the 'ancient' past. But 'modernity' has come to mean more than 'the here and now': it refers to modes of social organization that emerged in Europe from about the sixteenth century and extended their influence throughout the world in the wake of European exploration and colonization. Three momentous cultural shifts around the year 1500 – the discovery of the 'new world', the Renaissance and the Reformation – had, by the eighteenth century, come to constitute 'the epochal threshold between modern times and the middle ages' (Habermas 1981: 5). The emergence of the French Enlightenment saw the development of the idea that modernity was a distinctive and superior period in the history of humanity, a notion that became habitual as successive generations saw their own 'present' as enjoying a prominent position within the modern. As European power expanded, this sense of the superiority of the present over the past became translated into a sense of superiority over those pre-modern societies and cultures that were 'locked' in the past – primitive and un-civilized peoples whose subjugation and 'introduction' into modernity became the right and obligation of European powers.

The concept of modernity is therefore significant in the emergence of **colonial discourse**. Modernity is fundamentally about conquest, 'the imperial regulation of land, the discipline of the soul, and the creation of truth' (Turner 1990: 4), a **discourse** that enabled the large-scale regulation of human identity both within Europe and its colonies. The emergence of modernity is co-terminous with the emergence of **Euro-centrism** and the European dominance of the world effected through imperial expansion. In other words, modernity emerged at about the same time that European nations began to conceive of their own dominant relationship to a non-European world and began to spread their rule through **exploration, cartography** and **coloniz-ization**. Europe constructed itself as 'modern' and constructed the non-European as 'traditional', 'static', 'prehistorical'. The imposition of European models of historical change became the tool by which these societies were denied any internal dynamic or capacity for development.

Understanding modernity as a discourse rather than an epoch involves seeing it as characterized by major discontinuities separating modern *social institutions* from traditional social orders. Giddens identifies three: the pace of change, the scope of change, and the nature of modern institutions. The advent of various technologies inititated an ever accelerating pace of change, and the scope of this change came to affect the entire globe (Giddens 1990: 6). Many social forms and processes are not found in pre-modern societies: the nation-state, the dependence on inanimate power sources, the commodification of products and wage labour, formal schooling, the secularization of values and norms, and the predominance of urban forms of life. These differences dis-tinguish the modern from the pre-modern past, but also distinguish colonizing Europe from colonized cultures, thus becoming the source of profound misunderstanding and dislocation.

Apart from the distinctiveness of modern social institutions, and the many other reinforcing processes that accompany them, modernity can be characterized by developments in philosophical thought. The conception of modernity as a period that was superior to the past, buttressed as it was by the replacement of divine providence with the autonomous rational human mind, effectively ended the veneration of tradition and paved the way for the Enlightenment philosophical project of developing 'a rational organisation of everyday social life' (Habermas 1981:9). In turn, of course, this characteristic of Enlightenment thought consolidated the assumption of European cultural authority as its influence spread throughout the world. Science and rationality were assumed to be the only possible course for modern consciousness, and modern (i.e. European) social institutions were then, and are still, regarded as creating 'vastly greater opportunities for human beings to enjoy a secure and rewarding existence than any type of pre-modern system' (Giddens 1990: 7).

Rationality became such a core feature of 'modern' thought that its origin as a specifically European mode of thinking was forgotten by the time Europe came to dominate the world in the nineteenth century. Modernity became synonymous with 'civilized' behaviour, and one more justification for the 'civilizing mission' of European imperialism. Weber in particular regarded rationalization as a key component of modernization, but for him it was also a key to its ambiguity. Modernization brings with it considerable possibilities: the erosion of univocal meaning, the endless conflict of polytheistic values, the threat of the confinement of bureaucracy. Rationalization makes the world orderly and reliable, but it cannot make the world meaningful. If Weber is correct, it would suggest that imperialism not only is a key aspect of the emergence of modernity and its connection with an aggressive European self-image, but also creates the cultural conditions for the (post-colonial) disruptions that modernity brings to European society.

Contemporary debate interrogates the relationship between modernity and post-modernity. Theorists such as Habermas see modernity as an unfinished project and the 'post-modern' as simply a stage of modernity, while others see the post-modern as a sign of the dissolution of modernity. Post-modernity may also be characterized as offering a different set of discontinuities from modernity. However, it would appear that the revolution in social organization and philosophical thought, and the geographical expansion that modernity entailed, still remains a fundamental constitutive feature of social life in contemporary times.

Further reading: Ashcroft 2005; Barlow 2005; Bartolovich and Lazarus 2002; Burton 2003; Chakrabarty and Bhabha 2002; Comaroff and Comaroff 1993; J. Ferguson 2005; Friedman 2006; Gardiner 2001; George 2003; Giddens 1990; Gikandi 2000; Habermas 1981, 1987; Koundoura 2002; Lazarus 2002; Lloyd 2003; Mignolo 1995a, 1995b, 2001; Moore and Sanders 2001; Murray 1997a; Parry 2002, 2002a; Scott 1996; Turner 1990.

MULATTO

From the Spanish word for 'young mule' (1595), refering to the progeny of a European and a negro *(OED)*. The term is sometimes used interchangeably with ***mestizo/mestizaje/métisse*** to mean a mixed or miscegenated society and the culture it creates. However, its usage is usually confined to the classifications of miscegenation employed in **racist** slave discourse, specifically referring to a slave who is one half white.

MULTITUDE

This is the word used by Hardt and Negri to describe the location of the forces of liberation that are opposed to, but are themselves an integral part of **Empire**. The multitude, like Empire itself, is a concept that transcends geographical, historical and class boundaries, but in which the utopian hope of liberation is completely and optimistically focused. The reason for this is that the multitude is not simply an oppressed victim of Empire but is a part of Empire itself. The authors see Empire as composed of two phenomena, a juridical structure and 'the plural multitude of productive, creative subjectivities of globalization' (2001: 60). The significant thing about the multitude is that it is not merely negatively oppositional but is itself the source of new subjectivities that work towards the 'liberation of living labour.' The multitude exists in a constant ambivalent relationship with Empire. 'The de-territorializing power of the multitude is the productive force that sustains Empire and at the same time the force that calls for and makes necessary its destruction.' (61). Another way of putting this is that the multitude, whose province is the local, is both the field of operation of globalization and the origin of its transformation and hence the agent of the potential destruction of Empire because Empire cannot exist without it.

Further reading: Hardt and Negri (2001)

NATION LANGUAGE

Edward Kamau Brathwaite's term for culturally specific forms of Caribbean English. Brathwaite sees nation language as heavily influenced by the African heritage in Caribbean cultures, and contends that while the language used in, for instance, Jamaica, may be English in terms of its lexical features, 'in its contours, its rhythm and timbre, its sound explosions, it is not English, even though the words, as you hear them, might be English to a greater or lesser degree' (Brathwaite 1984: 311). Brathwaite suggests that this language is the result of a specific cultural experience when he says

> it is an English which is not the standard, imported, educated English, but that of the submerged, surrealist experience and sensibility, which has always been there and which is now increasingly coming to the surface and influencing the perception of contemporary Caribbean people.
>
> (Brathwaite 1984: 311)

Brathwaite takes pains to distinguish nation language from 'dialect', which, he contends, is thought of as 'bad English', the kind of English used in caricature and parody. This is similar to the contention of a number of post-colonial linguists and theorists that all language is localized, heterogeneous and 'variant', and that the concept of a standard English is a construction of imperial rhetoric that constantly separates 'centre' from 'margin'. Such a standard English is subverted by nation language which 'is like a howl, or a shout or a machine-gun or the wind or a wave. It is also like the blues' (311). Nation language is first of all based on an **oral** tradition; the language is based as much on sound as it is on song, the noise it makes being part of the meaning. The communal nature of the language is thus important, 'the noise and sounds that the maker makes are responded to by the audience and are returned' (312). Nation language is thus a lived, dynamic and changing phenomenon, not merely a linguistic structure. It is something that people *do*, and the constitutive environment of language is as important as the utterance.

Further reading: Brathwaite 1981, 1984.

NATION/NATIONALISM

The idea of the nation is now so firmly fixed in the general imagination, and the form of state it signifies so widely accepted, that it is hard to realize how recent its invention has been. In 1882, the French Orientalist Ernest Renan, addressing an audience at the Sorbonne in a lecture entitled 'What is a nation?', felt it necessary to remind his audience of the historical beginnings of the idea of a nation:

Nations . . . are something fairly new in history. Antiquity was unfamiliar with them; Egypt, China and ancient Chaldea were in no way nations. They were flocks led by a Son of the Sun or by a Son of Heaven. Neither in Egypt nor in China were there citizens as such. Classical antiquity had republics, municipal kingdoms, confederations of local republics and empires, yet it can hardly be said to have had nations in our understanding of the term.

(quoted in Bhabha 1990: 9)

Renan traces the emergence of the nation-state to the break-up of the classic and mediaeval empires, locating its cultural provenance in a specifically European political and social environment. That nations were and are profoundly unstable formations, always likely to collapse back into sub-divisions of clan, 'tribe', language or religious group, is nothing new, and the false tendency to assign this unstable condition to specific regions or conditions ('balkanization', 'the Third World', 'underdeveloped countries') is reflected in contemporary discussion of national questions.

As thinkers as early as Renan were aware, nations are not 'natural' entities, and the instability of the nation is the inevitable consequence of its nature as a social construction. This myth of nationhood, masked by ideology, perpetuates nationalism, in which specific identifiers are employed to create exclusive and homogeneous conceptions of national traditions. Such signifiers of homogeneity always fail to represent the diversity of the actual 'national' community for which they purport to speak, and, in practice, usually represent and consolidate the interests of the dominant power groups within any national formation.

Constructions of the nation are thus potent sites of control and domination within modern society. This is further emphasized by the fact that the myth of a 'national tradition' is employed not only to legitimize a general idea of a social group ('a people') but also to construct a modern idea of a nation-state, in which all the instrumentalities of state power (e.g. military and police agencies, judiciaries, religious hierarchies, educational systems and political assemblies or organizations) are subsumed and legitimized as the 'natural' expressions of a unified national history and culture. Timothy Brennan comments on this modern collapsing of the two concepts of nation and nation-state:

As for the 'nation' it is both historically determined and general. As a term, it refers both to the modern nation-state

135

and to something more ancient and nebulous – the '*natio*' – a local community, domicile, family, condition of belonging. The distinction is often obscured by nationalists who seek to place their own country in an 'immemorial past' where its arbitrariness cannot be questioned.

(Bhabha 1990: 45)

The confusion of the idea of the nation with the practice and power of the nation-state makes nationalism one of the most powerful forces in contemporary society. It also makes it an extremely contentious site, on which ideas of self-determination and freedom, of identity and unity collide with ideas of suppression and force, of domination and exclusion.

Yet for all its contentiousness, and the difficulty of theorizing it adequately, it remains the most implacably powerful force in twentieth-century politics. Its displacement has proved to be very difficult even within internationally oriented movements such as Marxism, at least in the Stalinist form in which it emerged in the Soviet Union and its client states. It is, perhaps, not insignificant that Stalin himself was an expert on the so-called Nationalities Question, and that he was one of the most ruthless advocates of the suppression of 'national differences', despite his own minority origins as a Georgian rather than a so-called Great Russian.

The complex and powerful operation of the idea of a nation can be seen also in the great twentieth-century phenomenon of global capitalism, where the 'free market' between nations, epitomized in the emergence of multinational companies, maintains a complex, problematic relationship With the idea of nations as natural and immutable formations based on shared collective values (see **globalization**). Modern nations such as the United States, with their multi-ethnic composition, require the acceptance of an overarching national ideology (*in pluribus unum*). But global capitalism also requires that the individual be free to act in an economic realm that crosses and nullifies these boundaries and identities. The tensions between these two impulses, increasing rapidly as modern communications make global contact a daily reality, are amongst the most important and as yet unresolved forces in the modern world.

Nations and nationalism are profoundly important in the formation of colonial practice. As Hobson puts it:

Colonialism, where it consists in the migration of part of a nation to vacant or sparsely peopled foreign lands, the emigrants carrying with them full rights of citizenship in the mother country . . . may be considered a genuine expansion of nationality.

(Hobson 1902: 6)

Hobson was explaining the economic emergence of late nineteenth-century **imperialism**, but the link between nation and expansion is much older – the emergence of the nation-state and the imperial-capitalist economies of post-Renaissance Europe being arguably inseparable. It is also arguable that without the provision of a greatly expanded source of supply for the dominant European standards of exchange (gold and silver) in the New World, the rapid development of long-distance trading ventures in the Renaissance period would not have occurred. Finally, this trade generated further demands for manufacture, and the raw materials for this expansion were supplied by the new economies of the colonized world, in the forms of plantations and mines which fuelled the industrialization of Europe.

This complex story which is here, of course, grossly simplified, became the basis for a narrative that acted to consolidate the interests of the new trading classes and which demanded new social formations that either integrated older forms (municipal kingdoms, city-states or city leagues) or developed new ones (oligarchic and radical republics) to represent the interests of the new trading classes whose wealth, derived from the distance trade with the colonies, replaced and challenged the power of the old feudal aristocracies. These new 'national' entities demanded a new national narrative, the 'Story of the Nation', which became disseminated through 'imagined communities' of speakers and listeners (or writers and readers) (Anderson 1983).

French Enlightenment thought heralded a shift in the theory of the 'nation', a shift that sought to relocate the legitimacy of the modern nation-state in a theory of the 'people' based on the idea of a universal set of principles (the 'Rights of Man') rather than on mythic and his-torical origins. In its strict form, the impulse to create such a Universal vision is transnational and its revolutionary tendency to cross borders can be seen in the effects of Enlightenment thinking on many nations in Europe and in the Americas in the eighteenth century. Despite the conservative reaction that set in throughout Europe after Napoleon's defeat, and the various attempts to resurrect the traditional monarchies, the states that emerged were in various ways based upon a modern concept of 'state-power' rather than on the traditional ideas of inherited authority such as divine kingship. Even authoritarian regimes such as modern Prussia connected the idea of a dominant, traditional figure of authority ('king' or 'emperor') to a modern and highly efficient state bureaucracy and to the empowerment, through this bureaucracy, of the interests of the state conceived as an abstraction rather than as a personal fiefdom.

Conversely, in the France of the Second and Third Republics the idea of a popular will was increasingly tied, not to a declaration of the struggle for universal human rights, but to a national vision of power and world expansion. Although, as Renan had noted, nations emerged only after the classical and mediaeval idea of an *imperium* (empire) had broken down, it was, ironically, the newly emergent nations of the post-Renaissance world that initiated the new, colonizing form of nineteenth-century imperialism. **Imperialism** now became an extension into the wider world of the ideology of a 'national' formation based on the unifying signifiers of language and race.

Significantly, the rump of the last of the mediaeval imperialisms, that of the Austro-Hungarian fragment of the erstwhile Holy Roman Empire, proceeded in the opposite direction, as it was increasingly assaulted from within by the demands of those who wished to develop political entities based upon racially and linguistically defined nationalities. On the other hand, the imperialisms of the second half of the nineteenth century were expressions of the need to generate unifying cohesive myths within the complex and heterogenous realities of the late nineteenth-century nation-states (such as England, France, Germany [Prussia], Russia, etc.) to prevent the re-emergence of older divisions based on earlier conceptions of the *natio* or to resist the emergence of new internal divisive forces based on theories of class. These were absolutely dependent on the expansionist vision which saw the home 'nation' as the centre of a larger formation and which defined itself specifically in opposition to the difference which that 'other' represented. In this sense, as Timothy Brennan has expressed it:

> Even though [nationalism] as an ideology . . . came out of the imperialist countries, these countries were not able to formulate their own national aspirations until the age of exploration. The markets made possible by European imperial penetration motivated the construction of the nation-state at home. European nationalism was motivated by what Europe was doing in its far-flung dominions. The 'national idea', in other words, flourished in the soil of foreign conquest.
>
> (Bhabha 1990: 59)

During the late imperial period the dominance of the idea of the nation was such that it was largely in terms of a resistant nationalism that the anti-colonial movements of the late nineteenth and early twentieth centuries came into being, even though it was that force of nationalism that had fuelled the growth of **colonialism** in the first place. **Anti-colonial** movements employed the idea of a pre-colonial past to rally their opposition through a sense of difference, but they employed this past not to reconstruct the pre-colonial social state but to generate support for the construction of post-colonial nation-states based upon the European nationalist model. Just as the modern European nation-states had come into being in the wake of the break up of the old imperial forms of the classical and mediaeval world, so the colonial empires these modern nations had constructed were now subject to a similar internal resistance and a demand for separation based on the construction of national entities and nationalist cultural constructions.

This is not just an ironic fact it also suggests that the bases of the **post-colonial state** were themselves far less radical than their early exponents believed, and the degree to which they incorporated models and institutions based on the European concept of a nation created the continuing linkages that allowed the **neo-colonialist** control of these states to operate so effectively. Few commentators have been prepared to argue that this process was a mistake, though Basil Davidson has done so in the case of Africa (1992). However, the use of nationalist myths and sentiments to control, suppress and discriminate against minority groups within many post-colonial states has been the subject of much recent comment, as these groups claim their distinctive place and argue for a greater tolerance and acceptance of cultural diversity.

The role of limited and biased versions of the past masquerading as national tradition has been attacked by many groups, including those who see these 'national traditions' as limited in various ways by gender, religion or ethnicity. In practice it is hard to see how the nation can cease to be employed as a definitive political entity within which these internal heterogeneities and differences can be resolved. Perhaps the issue is not whether we have nations but what kinds of nations we have, whether, that is, they insist on an exclusionary myth of national unity based in some abstraction such as race, religion or ethnic exclusivity, or they embrace plurality and multiculturalism.

Further reading: Anderson 1983; Basch 1994; Bhabha 1990; Blaut 1987; Boehmer 1991; Brennan 1989; Burton 2003; Chatterjee 1986, 1993; Cheah 2003; Chrisman 2002, 2004; Cooppan 1999; Davidson 1992; Franco 1997; Gikandi 2006; Hawley 1996; Hobsbawm 1990; Lazarus 1994, 1999; Leonard 2005; McClintock *et al.* 1997; Murray 1997; Paranjape 1998; Parker *et al.* 1992;

Perera 1998; Puri 2004; Ray 2000; Reiss 2004; San Juan 1996; Sivanandan 2004; Szeman 2003; Young 1998.

NATIONAL ALLEGORY

A term given some notoriety by Frederic Jameson in his essay 'Third World literature in an era of multinational capitalism'. Jameson argued that:

> What all third-world cultural productions have in common, and what distinguishes them radically from analogous cultural forms in the first world [is that] all third-world texts are necessarily . . . allegorical, and in a very specific way: they are to be read as what I will call *national allegories*, even when, or I should say particularly when, their forms develop out of predominantly western machineries of representation, such as the novel.
>
> (Jameson 1986: 67)

The reason for this, according to Jameson, is that capitalism has not yet split the private experience from the public sphere as it has in developed countries. Consequently, the 'story of the private individual destiny is always an allegory of the embattled structure of the public . . . culture and society' (67).

The sweeping nature of this claim drew strong criticism from Aijaz Ahmad who saw in it a totalizing and universalizing tendency that failed to take into account the specificity of Third World cultures. But while Jameson admits this claim is sweeping, he denies that it is totalizing. Rather, he insists that his thesis is an attempt to intervene in the dominance of First World criticism, an attempt to take on board *relational* ways of thinking about global culture and to give some exposure to the culturally diverse ways in which literary and cultural forms have been appropriated. Whatever the merits of Jameson's claim that private experience is represented as allegorical of the public and national destiny, it has aroused considerable discussion regarding the nature of post-colonial allegory, the construction of three worlds, and a questioning of the importance given to the nation over other social formations in the experience of Third World cultures.

Further reading: Ahmad 1992, 1995a; Beverley 2003; Buchanan 2003; Jameson 1986; San Juan 1996; Schmidt 2000; Szeman 2001.

NATIONAL LIBERATION MOVEMENTS

A series of movements that emerged in **Third World** countries in the 1960s which put into practice the Leninist doctrine that nationalism could be a progressive force for revolutionary change within colonized or neo-colonized societies. Although nationalism had been exposed by Marxist theory as a bourgeois social formation that masked capitalism, its necessity as a stage in the freeing of the world's workers had been recognized by Lenin as early as the First Party Congress in 1919. By the time of the Second Party Congress in 1920, Lenin enjoined every Communist party to 'demand the expulsion of their own imperialists from these colonies, to inculcate among the workers of their country a genuinely fraternal attitude to the working people of the colonies and the oppressed nations, and to carry on a systematic agitation among the troops of their country against any oppression of the colonial peoples' (Connor 1984: 56).

As a specialist on the 'nationalities question', Stalin had initiated a policy of brutally suppressing similarly counter-revolutionary nationalist aspirations in the Soviet Union's own satellite territories. However, with the emergence of the external threat posed by fascism in the 1930s he formulated a new ideological blend of the working class, the nation and the state in a call for a united national resistance to the threat of a fascist invasion. After the war, the Comintern continued to lend active support to a number of radical nationalist movements in locations across the world, ranging from Vietnam to Algeria. It distinguished these movements from classic bourgeois nationalism by the use of the term 'National Liberation Movements'. Led by local, Marxist-oriented intellectuals, these movements were epitomized by icons such as Ché Guevara, the Argentinian revolutionary companion of Cuban revolutionary Fidel Castro. Elsewhere, a series of significant nationalist leaders publicly embraced the aspirations of the National Liberation Movements to create free but revolutionary societies in the post-colonial world, for example, Sekou Touré and Kwame Nkrumah in Africa, and Ho Chi Minh in Vietnam. The movement also attracted some of the more significant intellectual figures to emerge in the **anticolonial** struggles of the period, such as Frantz Fanon in Algeria, Amilcar Cabral in Guinea-Bissau and Agostino Nero in Mozambique (see **Fanonism**).

Further reading: Alegría 1981; N. Alexander 1990; Amuta 1995; Balcárcel 1981; Blaut 1987; Connor 1984; Fanon 1959, 1964; Harlow 1987; Maolain 1985; Miller and Aya 1971; Moran 2006; Premnath 2002; San Juan 1991, 1991a; Sivandran 2004; Thayer 1989.

NATIVE

The use of the term 'native' to describe the indigenous inhabitants of colonies has a long and chequered history. The root sense of the term as those who were 'born to the land' was, in colonialist contexts, overtaken by a pejorative usage in which the term 'native' was employed to categorize those who were regarded as inferior to the colonial settlers or the colonial administrators who ruled the colonies. 'Native' quickly became associated with such pejorative concepts as **savage**, uncivilized or child-like in class nouns such as 'the natives'.

The idea that 'the natives' were members of a less developed culture that required colonial nurture to bring it to modernity and/or civilization permeated **colonial discourse**. In cases where the 'native' cultures were based on entirely different models, such as the hunter-gatherer cultures of some **settler colonies**, or cultures that did not share the signifiers of the European model of civilization such as writing, stone-buildings or industrial technology, the idea of the 'native' became part of a Darwinian characterization of the culture as 'primitive' or 'Stone Age'. Colonialist texts are replete with these kinds of characterizations of cultures as diverse as those of the Australian Aboriginal peoples, the New Zealand Maori, the Native American peoples of Canada and the many cultures of Africa or the South Pacific region whose complex and highly developed social and artistic forms were either not visible to the imperial gaze or were (and sometimes still are) deliberately obscured by such pejorative labelling.

Where cultures existed that clearly had, in European eyes, attained a high level of 'civilization', such as India and the South-East Asian region, the colonialist practice was to construe these as civilizations 'in decay', as manifestations of degenerate societies and races in need of rescue and rehabilitation by a 'civilized' Europe. Evidence of this social and moral degeneracy was perceived by the colonizers' obsessive focus on particular practices, such as sati or widow-burning, thuggee and ritual murder in India; or the supposedly characteristic forms of moral degeneracy on the part of specific races, evidenced in popular European representations of Malays 'running amok' in orgies of unmotivated violence.

The fear of contamination that is at the heart of colonialist discourse, and which results in the menacing ambivalence of **mimicry** or the obsessive colonialist fear of **miscegenation**, is often expressed through a fear amongst the colonizers of **going native**, that is, losing their distinctiveness and superior identity by contamination from native practices. The complexities of this can be seen in a text like Rudyard

Kipling's 'Kim' where Kim, an Indian-born English boy, is clearly distinguished from the native-born Indians in a discourse of racial superiority even though the text claims that his indigenous status gives him a special and superior insight into the culture and attitudes of Indians. In fact, for Kipling, the combination of racial superiority and local knowledge constructs an image of the ideal ruling figure for the colonial world in which being native-born can be achieved without the fear of racial contamination.

Further reading: Torgovnik 1990.

NATIVISM

A term for the desire to return to indigenous practices and cultural forms as they existed in pre-colonial society. The term is most frequently encountered to refer to the rhetoric of **decolonization** which argues that **colonialism** needs to be replaced by the recovery and promotion of pre-colonial, indigenous ways. The debate as to how far such a return or reconstruction is possible (or even desirable) has been a very vigorous one. Colonial discourse theorists such as Spivak and Bhabha argue strongly that such nativist reconstructions are inevitably subject to the processes of cultural intermixing that colonialism promoted and from which no simple retreat is possible. Spivak has more recently defended the use by post-colonial societies of a 'strategic' essentialism whereby the signifiers of indigenous (native) cultures are privileged in a process of negative discrimination. Such a strategy may allow these societies to better resist the onslaught of global culture that threatens to negate **cultural difference** or consign it to an apolitical and exotic discourse of **cultural diversity**. An even more positive defence of the nativist position has been mounted recently by Benita Parry (1994).

On the other hand, the multicultural nature of most post-colonial societies makes the issue of what constitutes the pre-colonial 'native' culture obviously problematic, especially where the current post-colonial nation-state defines itself in terms that favour a single dominant cultural group. Minority voices from such societies have argued that 'nativist' projects can militate against the recognition that colonial policies of transplantation such as **slavery** and **indenture** have resulted in racially mixed diasporic societies, where only a multicultural model of the post-colonial state can avoid bias and injustice to the descendants of such groups. Minorities from these areas have thus argued against the idea that the post-colonial oppressed form a homogenous group who can be decolonized and liberated by a nativist recovery of a pre-colonial culture.

The assumption of a homogeneous, unitary concept of the state is also challenged by the historical and cultural legacies of colonialism in the form of large and long-established **diasporic** communities in many multi-racial post-colonial states, such as Malaysia, Singapore and Fiji, and in the Caribbean, where the present racial mixture is profound and virtually every group is in one sense or another the product of a cultural diaspora, rather than being native or **indigenous** in origin. Models of culture and nationality that privilege one geographical or racial originary sign (e.g. Africa or blackness) have similar problems in addressing the diverse and often **creolized** nature of the population.

Even within less diverse states, minority religious and linguistic groups have faced similar difficulties with the simpler nativist projects of recuperation. The reconstruction of traditions based on supposed nativist models that enshrine a male, patriarchal vision of the pre-colonial, indigenous culture as **authentic** has necessarily aroused the resistance of women. For women, models of the traditional past have been seen as the product of present-day male practices which read the past through a biased sexist vision, and which are then used by a ruling élite to deny women their right to participate fully in the social model proposed (see Mba 1982; Stratton 1994) (see also **feminism** and **post-colonialism**). In practice, simple models of nativism, like simple models of **decolonization**, have raised as many issues as they have resolved.

Further reading: Baber 2002; Mamdani 2001; Michaels 1995; Mosley 1995; Parry 1994; Rodrigues 2004; Singer 2002.

NÉGRITUDE

A theory of the distinctiveness of African personality and culture. African Francophone writers such as Leopold Sédar Senghor and Birago Diop, and West Indian colleagues such as Aimé Césaire, developed the theory of négritude in Paris in the period immediately before and after the Second World War. These African and Caribbean intellectuals had been recruited under the French colonial policy of assimilation to study at the metropolitan French universities. The fact that they came from diverse colonies and that they were also exposed in Paris to influences from African American movements such as the

Harlem Renaissance, may have influenced them in developing a general theory of negro people that sought to extend the perception of a unified negro 'race' to a concept of a specifically 'African personality' (see **Black Atlantic**).

The négritudinist critics drew the attention of fashionable European intellectuals such as Jean Paul Sartre, who wrote an introduction, entitled 'Black Orpheus', to the first anthology of black African writing published in France, the *Anthologie de la nouvelle poésie négre et malgache de langue française* (1948). These critics insisted that African cultures and the literatures they produced had aesthetic and critical standards of their own, and needed to be judged in the light of their differences and their specific concerns rather than as a mere offspring of the parental European cultures.

The establishment of the critical magazine *Présence Africaine*, founded by Alioune Diop in Paris in 1947, had initiated a new critical interest in the French language writing of Africa and the Caribbean, and this important magazine became the vehicle for a number of crucial critical statements over the next twenty years or so, including Cheik Anta Diop's influential essay 'Nations, négres et culture' and Jacques Stephen Aléxis 'Of the magical realism of the Haitians' (see **magic realism**). With the decision in 1957 that future publications would be in French and English, *Présence Africaine* also became an important location for critical consideration of African writing in English (Mudimbe 1994). Négritude, and the work it developed, took as its territory not only Africa but the whole of **diasporic** African culture, since, as Senghor defined it, négritude encompassed 'the sum total of the values of the civilization of the African world' (Reed and Wake 1965: 99). For this reason it was the earliest and most important movement in establishing a wider awareness of Africa's claim to cultural distinctiveness.

The concept of 'négritude' implied that all people of negro descent shared certain inalienable essential characteristics. In this respect the movement was, like those of earlier race-based assertions of African dignity by such negro activists as Edward Wilmot Blyden, Alexander Crummell, W.E.B. Dubois and Marcus Garvey, both **essentialist** and **nativist**. What made the négritude movement distinct was its attempt to extend perceptions of the negro as possessing a distinctive 'personality' into all spheres of life, intellectual, emotional and physical.

Further reading: Ahluwalia 2001; Bernasconi 2002; Haddour 2005; Irele 2003; Jack 1996; Kemedjio 1999; Kennedy 1975; Mosley 1995; Munro 2004; Nkosi 2005; Senghor 1964; Wise 1995.

NEO-COLONIALISM/NEO-IMPERIALISM

Neo-colonialism meaning 'new colonialism' was a term coined by Kwame Nkrumah, the first President of Ghana, and the leading exponent of pan-Africanism in his *Neo-Colonialism: The Last Stage of Imperialism* (1965). This title, which echoed Lenin's definition of **imperialism** as the last stage of capitalism, suggested that, although countries like Ghana had achieved political independence, the ex-colonial powers and the newly emerging superpowers such as the United States continued to play a decisive role in their cultures and economies through new instruments of indirect control such as international monetary bodies, through the power of multinational corporations and cartels which artificially fixed prices in world markets, and through a variety of other educational and cultural NGOs (Non-Governmental Organizations). In fact, Nkrumah argued that neo-colonialism was more insidious and more difficult to detect and resist than the direct control exercised by classic colonialism.

The term has since been widely used to refer to any and all forms of control of the ex-colonies after political independence. Thus, for example, it has been argued by some that the new élites brought to power by independence, and often educated and trained by the colonialist powers, were unrepresentative of the people and acted as unwitting or even willing agents (**compradors**) for the former colonial rulers. In a wider sense the term has come to signify the inability of developing economies, the erstwhile so-called **Third World** economies to develop an independent economic and political identity under the pressures of **globalization**. Recently the term has been associated less with the influence of the former colonial powers and more with the role of the new superpower of the United States, whose expansionist policy past and present, it is argued, constitutes a new form of imperialism). In the same immediate post-Second World War period and through the use of different institutions such as Comintern and its economic wing, Comecon, as well as through loan organizations such as the International Bank for Economic Coperation, it has been argued that the role of the erstwhile Soviet Union in the period of the 'Cold War' mirrored the role of the United States, with aid and development programmes from both sides having many political strings attached, despite the claims of the Soviet Union at the time to be the leading supporter of the many **National Liberation** movements as these contesting powers extended their struggle into the rest of the world. China also participated in this process, as witness its role in parts of Africa in the period from the

1960s onwards. In many ways this process mirrored the way in which imperialist powers in the eighteenth and nineteenth century had also extended their struggle into the new regions opened up by colonial expansion.

Recently, with the demise of the Soviet Union and the rise of capitalism in China, the United States (the nation state most directly associated with **neo-liberal** capitalism) has become the primary concern of those who see globalization as continuing older forms of imperial control. Just as these theorists (Hardt and Negri 2001) have used the term **empire** to distinguish this new force from the classic **imperialism** of the era of direct colonization, so the term **neo-imperialism** has increasingly been used instead of **neo-colonialism** in a number of places, especially in material on the world wide web, to distinguish the ongoing control exercised over developing countries by a globalized capitalist economy often epitomized by the United States from earlier **neo-colonialism**. Although, of course, the main instruments of both were formed under the auspices of the United States after the end of the Second World War and in the aftermath of the Bretton Woods Conference in 1944. (See also **World System Theory**). The distinction draws attention to important shifts in the operation of global capital, but it should not be overlooked that many of the ways in which the new **empire** functions are directly analogous with operations in the era of classic imperialism, though the instruments may differ. Thus, for example, the role of modern NGO's (Non-Governmental Organizations) such as the World Bank, the International Monetary Fund, and especially non-governmental international aid and development organizations such as UNESCO operate in areas of concern and through practices very analogous to organizations in the colonial period such as missions. In fact it is arguable that missions and missionaries were the NGOs of their time. In the case of cultural organizations such as UNESCO, supporters have argued that the many benefits it brings may have been overlooked in the more radical objections to these global developments. In both cases the story is probably more complex than is sometimes recognized, with such organizations having both positive and negative impacts. (See **missions and colonialism**) Though it must be conceded that the claims of such Non-Governmental Organizations then and now to be acting independently of the existing global superpowers may also seem increasingly naïve. The negative view of these established international organizations has in recent times led to the setting up of counter organizations which have sought to speak for these more radical voices, notably the World Social Forum. Its charter claims that it represents

... an open meeting place for reflective thinking, democratic debate of ideas, formulation of proposals, free exchange of experiences and interlinking for effective action, by groups and movements of civil society that are opposed to **neo-liberalism** and to domination of the world by capital and any form of imperialism, and are committed to building a planetary society directed towards fruitful relationships among Mankind and between it and the Earth.

Its emergence may be viewed as a reaction by radical forces to the collapse of the earlier formal opposition from anti-capitalist states such as Russia and China in recent times, though it represents broader forces than the equivalent groups forged in the ideological conflicts of the post-war period including environmentalists and human rights activists.

Further reading: Benjamin, 2007; Denning 2004; French 2005; Gowda 1983; Nkrumah 1965; Pomeroy 1970; Rajen 1997; Saini 1981; Sen *et al.* 2004; Spivak 1999; B. Smith 1992; Thiong'o 1983; Woddis 1967.

NEO-LIBERALISM

A term used by many critics to refer to the theory and practice of an unfettered liberalization of market forces, sometimes regarded as synonymous with economic **globalization** or 'late capitalism'. Its major exponents over the last fifty years have been the IMF (International Monetary Fund) and World Bank but it has deep philosophical roots in historical liberalism and is a key feature of the **Washington Consensus**. It is significant for post-colonial studies because it has become the most obvious medium of **neo-colonial/neo-imperial** domination and of economic **globalization**.

Liberalism as a coherent social philosophy dates from the late eighteenth century. At first there was no distinction between political and economic liberalism, and classic liberal political philosophy contin-ued to develop after 1900 as pure conservative. Economic liberalization has always advocated the unrestrained operation of the market: free trade, absence of state intervention, or of any outside interference, the reliance on the processes of the market to create profit. Maynard Keynes' *General Theory*, published in the 1930s was revolutionary in its advocacy of state intervention and served to better explain the economy at that time, but philosophy of the totally free market reasserted itself very quickly – in an extreme form with Milton Friedman's monetarist principles. This belief in the free operation of market forces has become, in neo-liberalism, an end in itself, quite detached from the actual production of goods and services.

The term is of interest to post-colonial studies because economic liberalism has its origins in Adam Smith, whose view of the role of commodities in distinguishing the 'civilized' from the 'barbarous' is deeply embedded in the ideology of empire. For him the social body is a body composed of things, a web of commodities circulating in an exchange that connects people who do not see or know each other. These things make it a 'civilized' body. Having an abundance of 'objects of comfort' is the litmus test that distinguishes 'civilized and thriving nations' from 'savage' ones, 'so miserably poor' they are reduced to 'mere want' (1776: lx). It is trade that has caused certain parts of the world to progress, leaving others (such as Africa) in a 'barbarous and uncivilized state.' The unfettered flow of goods, and the free operation of the market, is thus attached, subtly but unshakably, to the idea of the 'civilizing mission' of empire.

This belief that the free market will lead to the greater happiness of all remains the dominant myth of neo-liberal philosophy in the 'neo-colonial' operation of late capitalism. Free trade has been the economic policy of choice for the British and US empires because free trade invariably favours the richest – those with most to trade. Arguably, economic liberalization is a consequence of the rising dominance of the British Empire, which went to war to maintain 'open markets'. Such 'open markets' had a catastrophic effect on the Indian textile industry and led to the Opium Wars with China.

The major features of economic liberalism remain the foundations of neo-liberal economics, but the rapidity and scale of the intensification of these principles characterizes the contemporary version. In general, neo-liberal economic philosophy is to intensify and expand the market by increasing the number, frequency, repeatability, and formalization of transactions. Clearly neo-liberal economic policies have become indistinguishable from economic globalization (which may nevertheless be distinguished from cultural, political and intellectual globalizations).

Ultimately, neo-liberalism is a philosophy in which the existence and operation of 'the market' are valued in themselves, quite apart from the production of goods and services. Consequently it can be seen, in its most extreme manifestations, to be a form of economic fundamentalism in which the operation of the market is an ethic in itself, capable of acting as a guide for all human action. Hence such statements as those of British Prime Minister Margaret Thatcher that 'there is no such thing as Society,' and 'there is no alternative.' The market becomes the fundamental and universal truth in terms of which all human action – political, social, economic and ultimately ethical – may be viewed.

Further reading: Harvey 2005; Scholte 2005; Hadiz 2006; Goodman and James 2007

NEW LITERATURES

A term used as an alternative to 'Commonwealth Literature' and later 'Post-Colonial Literatures', especially during the late 1970s and 1980s. 'New Literatures' stressed the emergent nature of work from post-colonized societies and connoted freshness and difference. It also avoided problems with the term 'Commonwealth', which had been criticized as glossing historical and persisting power inequalities between colonizers and the colonized.

It is still sometimes used as a synonym for the term 'post-colonial', but has been employed much less frequently in the 1990s. This is in part because of a sense expressed by some critics that the term has paternalistic overtones and fails to ground cultural production in the history and legacies of the colonial encounter. Its major disadvantage, however, is that many of the cultures to which it refers (such as those in India) have literary traditions far older than British literature itself. To avoid this problem, the term is generally used in the phrase 'New Literatures in English'. This is to emphasize the fact that it refers only to writing produced in English and not to writing available in classical languages like Sanscrit or in any of India's other languages. Arguably, this itself is problematic since it suggests that such writing exists in isolation from contemporary writing in the indigenous languages, or from the ongoing influence of oral practices. Interestingly, despite such problems, the term continues to be used outside of Europe for a variety of different reasons. Some critics, for instance, regard it as an 'emancipatory concept', and the African writer Ben Okri, distancing himself from the implication of 'coming after' in post-colonialism, declares a preference for 'new' as 'literatures of the newly ascendant spirit' (Boehmer 1995: 4).

Further reading: Boehmer 1995; Davis and Maes-Jelinek 1990; Gérard 1990;

Gurnah 2000; Jurak 1992; King 1980, 1996; Lim 2002; McLaren 1993; Nasta 2000; Nightingale 1986; Rutherford *et al.* 1992; Tiffin 1995; Walder 2000.

ORALITY

Post-colonial cultures have all, in various ways, been influenced by the interrelationship between orality and literacy. This is obvious, for example, in societies where oral culture predominated in the pre-colonial period, as in the case of some African societies, and in the indigenous cultures of all settler societies. In some parts of Africa, pre-colonial societies also had highly developed literary cultures in Arabic or employed the imported Arabic script to create the so-called *ajami* literatures in their own languages, and these had already led to complex interactions between written and oral cultural forms in these areas.

In the case of India, for example, where many highly developed pre-colonial literary cultures flourished, there were also vibrant oral folk cultures that remained a vigorous part of popular culture and inter-acted with the literary traditions. Interactions between both literary sources and oral traditions are a marked feature of the so-called *bhasa* literatures of South Asia. (See Devy 1992). In the West Indies, the presence of the cultures of the **slaves** and indentured labourers, transported there in their millions throughout the eighteenth and nineteenth centuries, was preserved largely in oral form. It was to this popular oral tradition that West Indian intellectuals looked in seeking both to recover fragmented African heritages and to discover a **'nation language'** for their region.

Post-colonial cultural studies have led to a general re-evaluation of the importance of orality and oral cultures and a recognition that the dominance of the written in the construction of ideas of civilization is itself a partial view of more complex cultural practices. Even highly literate cultures have vigorous popular oral cultures, as the discipline of cultural studies has convincingly demonstrated. In post-colonial societies, the dominance of writing in perpetuating European cultural assumptions and Euro-centric notions of civilization, as well as the view of writing as the vehicle of authority and truth, led to an under-valuing of oral culture, and the assumption that orality was a precondition for post-colonial writing, which subsequently subsumed it. Both of these misperceptions are being rapidly redressed in post-colonial theory.

151

The dominance of anthropological texts in the recording of 'oral' forms was part of this process of undervaluing, helping to convey the impression that the oral was not as socially or aesthetically valuable as the literary. In classic anthropology, orality was often designated as 'traditional' in a discourse that opposed it to the **'modern'**, and it was assumed to be both of the past and immutable. The practice of transcription also involved fixing the forms of the oral in ways inimical to its essentially performative mode, although recent anthropological accounts have sought to address and redress both of these limitations. In an attempt to combat this limited perception of oral 'texts' as social documents rather than complex aesthetic constructs, alternative terms were coined, such as 'orature', which sought to suggest that verbal and performative arts were as aesthetically rich and complex as written literature. But of course it can be argued that this very binary failed to dismantle the dependency model involved in the relationship between the two terms. The result was to denigrate the continuation and validity of orality into the present time and to deny its continuing significance in contemporary post-colonial cultures.

Recent studies (Barber and de Moraes-Farias 1989; Hofmeyer 1993) have stressed the fact that oral and literary cultures in colonial and post-colonial societies existed within unified social situations and were *mutually* interactive. Rather than being restricted to the past and therefore inferior to the written, oral forms in African societies, for instance, have a continuing and equal relationship with the written. This therefore challenges the simplistic and culture specific assumption of post-structuralist critics such as Derrida that the written has precedence over the oral (logo-centrism).

The present continuity and vigour of orality in post-colonial societies is demonstrated in the example of the West Indies, where the emergence of a vigorous post-colonial culture is as much the result of figures like reggae performer Bob Marley, 'dub' street poet Michael Smith, and the women storytellers and performers of the Sistren Collective, as of writers like Walcott, Harris, Brathwaite or Brodber. In South Africa, oral forms such as 'praise songs' have been adopted by such modern, European institutions as trade unions (for rallies) and have developed some of the formal and social aspects of literary texts and practices (see Gunner and Gwala 1991). In such cases not only is the work of the written culture increasingly modified by the existence of popular oral forms, but the oral cultures are themselves transformed by their ongoing interaction with the written cultures of the modern period.

Further reading: Adam 1996; Barber and de Moraes-Farias 1989; Casas 1998; Devy 1992; Gilroy 1993;Gunner and Gwala 1991; Gunner 1994; Gunner and Furniss 1995; Hofmeyer 1993; Hofmeyer 2004; Ong 1982; Swearingen 2004; Talib 2002; Zambare 2003.

ORIENTALISM

This is the term popularized by Edward Said's *Orientalism*, in which he examines the processes by which the 'Orient' was, and continues to be, constructed in European thinking. Professional Orientalists included scholars in various disciplines such as languages, history and philology, but for Said the discourse of Orientalism was much more widespread and endemic in European thought. As well as a form of academic discourse it was a style of thought based on 'the ontological and epistemological distinction between the "Orient" and the "Occident"' (Said 1978: 1). But, most broadly, Said discusses Orientalism as the corporate institution for dealing with the Orient 'dealing with it by making statements about it, authorizing views of it, describing it, by teaching it, settling it, ruling over it: in short, Orientalism as a Western style for dominating, restructuring, and having authority over the Orient' (3). In this sense it is a classic example of Foucault's definition of a discourse.

The significance of Orientalism is that as a mode of *knowing* the other it was a supreme example of the *construction* of the other, a form of authority. The Orient is not an inert fact of nature, but a phenomenon constructed by generations of intellectuals, artists, commentators, writers, politicians, and, more importantly, constructed by the naturalizing of a wide range of Orientalist assumptions and stereotypes. The relationship between the Occident and the Orient is a relationship of power, of domination, of varying degrees of a complex hegemony. Consequently, Orientalist discourse, for Said, is more valuable as a sign of the power exerted by the West over the Orient than a 'true' discourse about the Orient. Under the general heading of knowledge of the Orient, and within the umbrella of Western hegemony over the Orient from the eighteenth century onwards, there emerged 'a complex Orient suitable for study in the academy, for display in the museum, for reconstruction in the colonial office, for theoretical illustration in anthropological, biological, linguistic, racial, and historical theses about mankind and the universe' (7). Orientalism is not, however, a Western plot to hold down the 'Oriental' world. It is:

a *distribution* of geopolitical awareness into aesthetic, scholarly, economic, sociological, historical and philological texts; it is an *elaboration* not only of a basic geographical distinction . . . but also of a whole series of 'interests' which . . . it not only creates but maintains. It *is*, rather than expresses, a certain *will* or *intention* to understand, in some cases to control, manipulate, even incorporate, what is a manifestly different world

(Said 1978: 12).

Significantly, the discourse of Orientalism persists into the present, particularly in the West's relationship with 'Islam', as is evidenced in its study, its reporting in the media, its representation in general. But as a discursive mode, Orientalism models a wide range of institutional constructions of the colonial other, one example being the study, discussion and general representation of Africa in the West since the nineteenth century. In this sense, its practice remains pertinent to the operation of imperial power in whatever form it adopts; to know, to name, to fix the other in discourse is to maintain a far-reaching political control.

The generalized construction of regions by such discursive formations is also a feature of contemporary cultural life. (See Griffiths 2003). Oddly enough, Orientalism spills over into the realm of self-construction, so that the idea of a set of generalized 'Asian' values (e.g. Asian democracy) is promoted by the institutions and governments of peoples who were themselves lumped together initially by Orientalist rubrics such as 'the East' (Far East, Middle East, etc.), the Orient or Asia. Employed as an unqualified adjective, a term like 'Asia' is in danger of eroding and dismantling profound cultural, religious and linguistic differences in the countries where it is applied self-ascriptively in ways not dissimilar to the Orientalist discourses of the colonial period.

Further reading: Baber 2002; Ballantyne 2001; Boer 1994; Breckenridge and van der Veer 1993; Codell and Macleod 1998; Dallmayr 1996; Ezzaher 2003; Harlow and Carter 1999; R. King 1999; Lennon 2004; Lewis 1996; Lockman 2004; MacKenzie 1995; Moore-Gilbert 1996; Rotter 2000; Said 1978; Sardar 1999; Satchidanandan 2002; B.S. Turner 1994.

OTHER

In general terms, the 'other' is anyone who is separate from one's self. The existence of others is crucial in defining what is 'normal' and in locating one's own place in the world. The colonized subject is characterized as 'other' through discourses such as **primitivism** and **cannibalism**, as a means of establishing the **binary** separation of the colonizer and colonized and asserting the naturalness and primacy of the colonizing culture and world view.

Although the term is used extensively in existential philosophy, notably by Sartre in *Being and Nothingness* to define the relations between Self and Other in creating self-awareness and ideas of identity, the definition of the term as used in current post-colonial theory is rooted in the Freudian and post-Freudian analysis of the formation of **subjectivity**, most notably in the work of the psychoanalyst and cultural theorist Jacques Lacan. Lacan's use of the term involves a distinction between the 'Other' and the 'other', which can lead to some confusion, but it is a distinction that can be very useful in post-colonial theory.

In Lacan's theory, the other – with the small 'o' – designates the other who resembles the self, which the child discovers when it looks in the mirror and becomes aware of itself as a separate being. When the child, which is an uncoordinated mass of limbs and feelings sees its image in the mirror, that image must bear sufficient resemblance to the child to be recognized, but it must also be separate enough to ground the child's hope for an 'anticipated mastery'; this fiction of mastery will become the basis of the ego. This other is important in defining the identity of the subject. In post-colonial theory, it can refer to the colonized others who are marginalized by imperial discourse, identified by their difference from the centre and, perhaps crucially, become the focus of anticipated mastery by the imperial 'ego'.

The Other – with the capital 'O' – has been called the *grande-autre* by Lacan, the great Other, in whose gaze the subject gains identity. The Symbolic Other is not a real interlocuter but can be embodied in other subjects such as the mother or father that may represent it. The Symbolic Other is a 'transcendent or absolute pole of address, summoned each time that subject speaks to another subject' (Boons-Grafé 1992: 298). Thus the Other can refer to the mother whose separation from the subject locates her as the first focus of desire; it can refer to the father whose Otherness locates the subject in the Symbolic order; it can refer to the unconscious itself because the unconscious is structured like a language that is separate from the language of the subject. Fundamentally, the Other is crucial to the subject because the subject exists in its gaze. Lacan says that 'all desire is the metonym of the desire to be' because the first desire of the subject is the desire to exist in the gaze of the Other.

This Other can be compared to the imperial centre, imperial discourse, or the empire itself, in two ways: first, it provides the terms in which the colonized subject gains a sense of his or her identity as somehow 'other', dependent; second, it becomes the 'absolute pole of address', the ideological framework in which the colonized subject may come to understand the world. In colonial discourse, the subjectivity of the colonized is continually located in the gaze of the imperial Other, the *'grand-autre'*. Subjects may be **interpellated** by the ideology of the maternal and nurturing function of the colonizing power, concurring with descriptions such as 'mother England' and 'Home'.

On the other hand, the Symbolic Other may be represented in the Father. The significance and enforced dominance of the imperial language into which colonial subjects are inducted may give them a clear sense of power being located in the colonizer, a situation corresponding metaphorically to the subject's entrance into the Symbolic order and the discovery of the Law of the Father. The ambivalence of colonial discourse lies in the fact that *both* these processes of 'othering' occur at the same time, the colonial subject being both a 'child' of empire and a primitive and degraded subject of imperial discourse. The construction of the dominant imperial *Other* occurs in the same process by which the colonial *others* come into being.

Further reading: Boons-Grafé 1992; Fuss 1994; Lacan 1968; Nederveen Pieterse 1992; Sartre 1957; Spivak 1985a.

OTHERING

This term was coined by Gayatri Spivak for the process by which imperial discourse creates its 'others'. Whereas the Other corresponds to the focus of desire or power (the M–Other or Father – or Empire) in relation to which the subject is produced, the other is the excluded or 'mastered' subject created by the discourse of power. Othering describes the various ways in which colonial discourse produces its subjects. In Spivak's explanation, othering is a dialectical process because the colonizing *Other* is established at the same time as its colonized *others* are produced as subjects.

It is important to note that, while Spivak adheres faithfully to the Lacanian distinction between 'Other' and 'other', many critics use the spellings interchangeably, so that the Empire's construction of its 'others' is often referred to as the construction of 'the Other' (perhaps to connote an abstract and generalized but more symbolic representation of empire's 'others'). But in either case, the construction of the O/other is fundamental to the construction of the Self.

Spivak gives three examples of othering in a reading of Colonial Office dispatches between Captain Geoffrey Birch, his superior Major-General Ochterlony and *his* superior the Marquess of Hastings, Lord Moira. The first is a process of **worlding** whereby Captain Birch, riding across the Indian countryside, can be seen to be 'consolidating the self of Europe', that is, representing Europe as the Other in terms of which colonial subjectivity of the inhabitants will be produced. The second is an example of debasement whereby the hill tribes are described by General Ochterlony in terms of 'depravity', 'treachery', 'brutality' and 'perfidy', and the surrender of their lands to the crown an 'obligation' (Spivak 1985a: 134). He can be observed, says Spivak, in the act of creating the colonized 'other(s)' by making them the 'object[s] of imperialism'. The third is an example of the separation of native states and 'our (colonial) governments' in the reprimand given the general by the Marquess of Hastings for allowing half-pay subalterns to serve with regular troops in Native governments. All three are engaged in producing an 'other' text – the 'true' history of the native hill states – at the same time that they are establishing the Otherness of Empire (135).

The process of othering can occur in all kinds of colonialist narrative. Mary Louise Pratt detects an example of othering in John Barrow's *Account of Travels in the Interior of Southern Africa in the Years 1797 and 1798* in which

> The people to be othered are homogenized into a collective 'they,' which is distilled even further into an iconic 'he' (the standardized adult male specimen). This abstracted 'he'/ 'they' is the subject of verbs in a timeless present tense, which characterizes anything 'he' is or does not as a particular historical event but as an instance of a pregiven custom or trait.
>
> (Pratt 1985: 139)

Apart from its almost inevitable presence in travel and ethnographic writing, othering can take on more material and violent forms. In *Waiting for the Barbarians* (1980), South African novelist J.M. Coetzee demonstrates the ways in which imperial discourse constructs its others in order to confirm its own reality. In this novel, the magistrate who tells the story is situated at the edge of the 'empire' conducting the humdrum business of the outpost town in relative tranquillity, until Colonel Joll, a functionary of the 'Third Bureau', the secret police, arrives to extract, by torture, any information about the 'barbarians' that can be gathered from a ragtag collection of old men, women and children who are 'captured' on a prisoner-gathering foray. The fact that the whole enterprise is manifestly absurd because there is no threat from the barbarians, a nomadic people who come to town from time to time to trade, and there were no 'border troubles' before the arrival of the 'Third Bureau' (114) does not deter Colonel Joll. For the Colonel is in the business of *creating* the enemy, of delineating that opposition that must exist, in order that the empire might define itself by its geographical and racial others. This is an example of Othering. The Colonel is engaged in a process by which the empire can define itself against those it colonizes, excludes and marginalizes. It locates its 'others' by this process in the pursuit of that power within which its own subjectivity is established.

Further reading: Coetzee 1980; Olaniyan 1992; Pratt 1985; Spivak 1985a.

PALIMPSEST

Originally the term for a parchment on which several inscriptions had been made after earlier ones had been erased. The characteristic of the palimpsest is that, despite such erasures, there are always traces of previous inscriptions that have been 'overwritten'. Hence the term has become particularly valuable for suggesting the ways in which the traces of earlier 'inscriptions' remain as a continual feature of the 'text' of culture, giving it its particular density and character. Any cultural experience is itself an accretion of many layers, and the term is valuable because it illustrates the ways in which pre-colonial culture as well as the experience of colonization are continuing aspects of a post-colonial society's developing cultural identity. While the 'layering' effect of history has been mediated by each successive period, 'erasing' what has gone before, all present experience contains ineradicable traces of the past which remain part of the constitution of the present. Teasing out such vestigial features left over from the past is an important part of understanding the nature of the present.

An important use of the concept of the palimpsest has been made by Paul Carter in *The Road to Botany Bay* (1987a) in which he demonstrates how 'empty' uncolonized space becomes **place** through the process of textuality. Mapping, naming, fictional and non-fictional narratives create multiple and sometimes conflicting accretions which become the dense text that constitutes place. In short, empty space becomes place through language, in the process of being written and named. Place itself, in the experience of the post-colonial subject, is a palimpsest of a process in language: the naming by which **imperial** discourse brings the colonized space 'into being', the subsequent rewritings and overwritings, the imaging of the place in the consciousness of its occupants, all of which constitute the contemporary place observed by the subject and contested among them. The most challenging aspect of this thesis is that the ordinary social subject, when looking at the surrounding environment, does not simply take in what is there as purely visual data, but is located with that place in a cultural horizon, that is, the simply observed place is a cultural palimpsest built up over centuries and retaining the traces of previous engagements and inscriptions, including the influence of the observer who is constructed in the act of 'observing'.

Guyanese novelist and critic, and erstwhile Government surveyor and mapmaker, Wilson Harris also makes frequent use of this extended idea of the palimpsest in his critical writing, relating it through the metaphors of the layers of material that build up on the floor of a tropical rainforest and those of a fossil bed. Both are expressive of the engagement which occurs between subject and world, a process which engages what Harris has called the 'transformative imagination'. Thus he regards the process of 'fossilization,' not as a metaphor for dead forms but as a sign of the continuation of the forms of the past in the living present. No single feature of past or present can be singled out as an origin, since all are related to an endless and multiple set of processes, an 'infinite rehearsal' that never ends and in which 'history' is located as a transient structure. So in Harris's vision of the Guyanese world the palimpsestic metaphor is also applied to the many races whose traces are laid and overlaid in modern Caribbean societies, preventing the re-emergence of an oppressive single image of a 'pure' race or culture (see **catalysis**).

Much post-colonial discourse constitutes a struggle for the restitution of 'writings' and 'readings' of the land expunged by colonialist texts (see **orality**). Colonial discourse erased prior constructions of the land, allowing it to be seen as an empty space, ready to receive their own inscriptions. This occurred even in 'spaces' such as India where a body of complex textualities already existed, as these were displaced or denigrated *vis-à-vis* the colonial values and modes of representation. That this was a widespread and long-standing colonial historical practice is illustrated by Brian Friel's play *Translations*, which shows the process of reinscription in nineteenth-century Ireland as British imperial power consolidated itself over Ireland's Gaelic speaking west by renaming the Gaelic place names, thus suppressing the existence of a flourishing and highly literate Gaelic culture. In extreme cases where extensive colonial settlement required an even more radical **othering** of the existing indigenous cultures, the imperial doctrine of *terra nullius* invoked the complete erasure of the pre-colonial people and culture, a process that was helped by the dominance in imperial and colonial discourses of ideas of literacy over orality as a superior cultural mode.

The concept of the palimpsest is a useful way of understanding the developing complexity of a culture, as previous 'inscriptions' are erased and overwritten, yet remain as traces within present consciousness. This confirms the dynamic, contestatory and dialogic nature of linguistic, geographic and cultural space as it emerges in post-colonial experience.

Further reading: Carter 1987a; Harris 1983.

PIDGINS/CREOLES

Pidgins are languages serving as *lingua franca*, that is, they are used as a medium of communication between groups who have no other language in common. (However, while English may serve as a *lingua franca* in, for instance, the Indian Parliament, it is not a pidgin or a creole.) When 'two or more people use a language in a variety whose grammar and vocabulary are very much reduced in extent and which is native to neither side' (Hall 1988: xii) they are using a pidgin. A creole 'arises when a pidgin becomes the native language of a speech community, as in the Caribbean' (xii). Pidgins typically develop out of trade languages and may evolve into creoles' (Seymour-Smith 1986: 223–224).

However DeCamp (1977) draws attention to the continuing lack of agreement over precise definitions of pidgins and creoles, noting that

> some definitions are based on function, the role these languages play in the community. . . . Some are based on historical origins and development. . . . Some definitions include formal characteristics: restricted vocabulary, absence of gender, true tenses. . . . Some linguists combine these different kinds of criteria and include additional restrictions in their definitions.
> (DeCamp 1977: 3)

Most commentators agree that a Creole is a more developed language than a pidgin and, as Muysken and Smith argue, one vital difference between pidgins and Creoles is that 'pidgins do not have native speakers while Creoles do'. But they note that some extended pidgins are beginning to acquire native speakers, for example, Tok Pisin of Papua New Guinea, Nigerian Pidgin English and Sango (Central African Republic) (Muysken and Smith 1995: 3). Consequently, at this point in their development they are increasingly considered as Creoles.

Further reading: Alleyne 1980; Blake 1996; Bongie 1998; Caldwell 2003; Colás 1995; *Études Créoles*; C. Gilman 1985; Hall 1988; Holm 1988 and 1989; *Journal of Pidgin and Creole Languages*; Mulhausler 1986; Muysken and Smith 1995; Romain 1988; Seymour-Smith 1986; Simmons-McDonald 2003; Singh 2000; Singler 1990; Spears and Winford 1997; Todd 1984.

PLACE

The concepts of place and displacement demonstrate the very complex interaction of language, history and environment in the experience of colonized peoples and the importance of space and location in the process of identity formation. In many cases, 'place' does not become an issue in a society's cultural discourse until colonial intervention radically disrupts the primary modes of its representation by separating 'space' from 'place'. A sense of place may be embedded in cultural history, in legend and language, without becoming a concept of contention and struggle until the profound discursive interference of colonialism. Such intervention may disrupt a sense of place in several ways: by imposing a feeling of displacement in those who have moved to the colonies; by physically alienating large populations of colonized peoples through forced migration, slavery or indenture; by disturbing the representation of place in the colony by imposing the colonial language. Indeed in all colonial experience, colonialism brings with it a sense of dislocation between the environment and the imported language now used to describe it, a gap between the 'experienced' place and the descriptions the language provides.

One of the deepest reasons for the significance of place in colonized societies lies in the disruptions caused by **modernity** itself in the links between time, space and place in European societies. In pre-modern or pre-colonial times, as Giddens (1990) explains, all cultures had ways of calculating the time, but before the invention of the mechanical clock no one could tell the time without reference to other markers: 'when' was almost always connected to 'where'. The mechanical clock was instrumental in separating time from space, telling the time in a way that could allow the precise division of 'zones' of the day without reference to other markers. With the universalization of the calendar and the standardization of time across regions, the emptying of time (its severance from location) became complete and became the precondition for the 'emptying of space'. In pre-modern times, space and place are more or less synonymous with one another, but once relations with absent others were made possible by the invention of the clock, the calendar and the map, things changed radically. Locales became shaped by social influences quite distant from them, such as spatial technologies, colonizing languages, or, indeed, the very conception of place that those languages came to transmit.

The movement of European society through the world, the 'discovery' and occupation of remote regions, was the necessary basis for the creation of what could be called 'empty space'. **Cartography** and the creation of universal maps established space as a measurable, abstract concept independent of any particular place or region. Significantly, the severing of time from space provides a basis for their recombination in relation to social activity. For instance, a train timetable appears to be a temporal chart, but it is in fact a timespace ordering device. Consequently, while the separation of time and space allows social relations to be lifted out of their locale, 'place', which is in some senses left behind by modernity, becomes an anxious and contested site of the link between language and identity, a possible site of those local realities that the universal separation of time, space and place leaves virtually untouched.

In addition to the separation of space from place, brought about by European ways of measuring a 'universal' space and time that sever them from any particular location, place becomes an issue within language itself. A sense of displacement, of the lack of fit between language and place, may be experienced by those who possess English as a mother tongue or by those who speak it as a second language. In both cases, there appears to be a lack of fit between the place described in English and the place actually experienced by the colonized subject. This comes about firstly because the words developed to describe place originated in an alien European environment, and secondly because many of the words used by the colonizers described 'empty space' or 'empty time', and so had thrown off any connection to a particular locale. Place can thus be a constant trope of difference in post-colonial writing, a continual reminder of colonial ambivalence, of the separation yet continual mixing of the colonizer and colonized.

The concept of place itself may be very different in different societies and this can have quite specific political as well as literary effects in the extent of displacement. For instance, in Aboriginal societies, place is traditionally not a visual construct, a measurable space or even a topographical system but a tangible location of one's own dreaming, an extension of one's own being. A particular formation, like a stream or hill, for instance, may embody a particular dreaming figure, whose location on the dreaming track has a particular significance to a person's own life, 'totem', clan relationship and identity because that person may have been conceived near it. The idea of not owning the land but in some sense being 'owned by it' is a way of seeing the world that is so different from the materiality and commodification of a colonizing power, that effective protection of one's place is radically disabled when that new system becomes the dominant one.

This is perhaps the most extreme form of cultural disruption, but its general character is repeated throughout the colonial world because the colonizing powers brought with them a particular view of land that had a philosophical, legal and political provenance as well as an economic justification. The key to this attitude can be found in the idea of 'enclosure' that underlies the Western concept of property. John Locke's *Second Treatise of Government* (Book II Chapter 5 – 'Of Property') demonstrates the European rationale for the expropriation of lands by the 'advanced' agrarian communities from hunter gatherer societies. For Locke, the very mark of property is the enclosure: the defining, or bounding, of a place that signals the perceived settling, or cultivation, of that place. Indeed it is the figure of enclosure that marks the **frontier** between the **savage** and the civilized. Although nobody has an exclusive dominion over nature, says Locke, since the 'Fruits' of the earth and the 'Beasts' were given for the use of men, there must be a way to appropriate them before they can be of any use to a particular man, and this is the method of enclosure (Locke 1960: 330). Because it is man's labour that removes the products from nature and makes them his,

> *As much Land* as a Man Tills, Plants, Improves, Cultivates and can use the Product of, so much is his *Property*. He by his Labour does, as it were, inclose it from the Common . . . [For God] gave it to the use of the Industrious and Rational (and *Labour* was to be *his Title* to it).
>
> (Locke 1960: 333)

Quite apart from the ascription to God of the values of the European Enlightenment, the effect of this is to invalidate the claims over land of any people whose relationship with it does not involve agricultural 'improvement'. So powerful was the concept of property and its associated assumptions that the social reformer Thomas Fowell Buxton could say in the mid-nineteenth century that only the Bible and the plough could lead Africa on to a higher level of existence: for 'plough' meant agriculture, and agriculture meant property, and property meant civilization (Baumgart 1982: 14). Other colonists, of course, had a very different idea about the rights of African ownership of land, and the ideology of Social Darwinism as well as the long history of race thinking provided a justification for the long history of European land theft.

Superior military and economic strength enabled the colonizing power to establish its legal and economic perceptions of place as dominant, but it was the mode of representation, the language itself, that effected the most far-reaching pressure, which established the concept of place as a particularly complex site of colonial engagement. But at the same time it was language that enabled colonized peoples to turn displacement into a creative resistance. In many respects, the political economy of property is a much less complicated aspect of imperial dominance than the discursive activity of language and writing and its involvement in the concept of place.

The most concerted discussion of place and its location in language has come from **settler colony** writers for whom the possession of English as a first language has produced a particularly subtle, complex and creatively empowering sense of the lack of fit between the language available and the place experienced. Canadian Robert Kroestch, in 'Unhiding the hidden', suggests that the particular predicament of the Canadian writer, and perhaps all settler colony writers, is that they work in a language that appears to be authentically their own, and yet is not quite. For another Canadian writer, Dennis Lee, this experience has had a profound effect on his writing, even drying up his writing altogether at one stage because he felt he could not find the words to express his experience authentically (1974).

What becomes apparent in these writers is that 'place' is much more than the land. The theory of place does not propose a simple separation between the 'place' named and described in language, and some 'real' place inaccessible to it, but rather indicates that in some sense place *is* language, something in constant flux, a discourse in process. These writers become compelled to try to construct a new language that might fit the place they experience because the language does not simply report the visual or proximate experience but is implicated in its presence. Dennis Lee coins the term 'cadence' to describe this: 'a presence, both outside myself and inside my body opening out and trying to get into words' (1974: 397).

One of the most sustained discussions of the linguistic construction of place occurs in Paul Carter's *The Road to Botany Bay*, which proposes a concept he calls 'spatial history'. Such history examines place as a **palimpsest** on which the traces of successive inscriptions form the complex experience of place, which is itself historical. Imperial history, the teleological narrative of civilization and settlement, distinguishes itself by ignoring the place, the environment, as simply the empty stage on which the theatre of history is enacted. But if we see place as not simply a neutral location for the imperial project, we can see how intimately place is involved in the development of identity, how deeply it is involved in history, and how deeply implicated it is in the systems of representation – language, writing and the creative arts – that develop in any society but in colonized societies in particular.

Whatever the nature of the post-colonial society, language always negotiates a kind of gap between the word and its signification. In this sense, the dynamic of **naming** becomes a primary colonizing process because it appropriates, defines and captures the place in language. Perhaps the most comprehensive example of this is the drafting of the Mercator projection Atlas in 1636. The map demonstrates that geography, like place itself, 'is a series of erasures and overwritings which have transformed the world' (Rabasa 1993: 358). Our most profound, ubiquitous and unquestioned assumptions about the physical shape of the globe and its continents can thus be seen to be a specific evidence of the power of European discourse to naturalize its construction of the world itself.

The provision of names to the non-European world through exploration and 'discovery' is thus an elaboration of the dynamic of control that the Atlas presupposes. To name a place is to announce discursive control over it by the very act of inscription, because through names, location becomes metonymic of those processes of travel, annexation and colonization that effect the dominance of imperial powers over the non-European world. The control over place that the act of naming performs extends even to an **ecological imperialism** in which the fauna, flora and the actual physical character of colonized lands changes under the pressure of the practical outworking of the European concern with property: enclosure, agriculture, importation of European plants and weeds; the destruction of indigenous species; possibly even the changing of weather patterns.

Further reading: Ashcroft *et al*. 1995; Baucom 1999; Carter 1987a; Carter *et al*. 1993; Chrisman 1998; Clayton and Gregory 1996; Crosby 1986; Darian-Smith *et al*. 1996; Harris 1983; Longley 1997; Mignolo 1995c; Mitchell 1994; Prentice 1991; Rice 2003; Sheridan 2001; Supriya 2004; van der Veer 1995; Wright 2002.

POST-COLONIAL BODY

While there is no such thing as 'the post-colonial body', the body has been central to colonialist and post-colonial discourses of various kinds. Much post-colonial writing in recent times has contended that the body is a crucial site for inscription. How people are perceived controls how they are treated, and physical differences are crucial in such constructions. This view of the body as a site for representation and control is central to many early analysts of post-colonial experience, notably Frantz Fanon (1961), but also to the arguments of Edouard Glissant (1989). These early concerns with the body centred on ideas of colour and race (see **chromatism**). They emphasized the visibility of signs of difference when manifested in skin colour, hair type, facial features such as eye shape or nose shape, etc. Although such 'differences' do not constitute any decisive genetic dissimilarity, and certainly do not indicate the existence of sub-groups within a single human species (as theories of race have often erroneously asserted), they nevertheless became prime means of developing and reinforcing prejudices against specific groups.

Such prejudices were generated either for economic reasons (see **slavery**) or to control indigenous populations in colonial possessions by emphasizing their difference and constructing them as inferior (see **hegemony**). More recently, there has been an increased concern with, and understanding of, the special role played by gender in constructing images of colonial inferiority (the emasculation or feminization of post-colonial cultural representation in image, word, etc.) and in constructing a special 'double' colonization for women within the general field of colonial oppression. This has led to a greater concern with the body as a site for gendered readings of post-colonial subjectivity.

The body, and its importance in post-colonial representation, empha-sizes the very special nature of post-colonial discourses. For although the body is a text, that is, a space in which conflicting discourses can be written and read, it is a specially material text, one that demonstrates how **subjectivity**, however constructed it may in fact be, is 'felt' as inescapably material and permanent. This is important for post-colonial studies in that it reminds us that the discursive forces of imperial power operated on and through people, and it offers a ready corrective to the tendency to abstract ideas from their living context.

The location of the body as a site for discursive control has been examined in many ways in recent times. In museum studies and in fine arts, an interest in the representation and exhibition of people, their photographs and their preserved remains, is central to a radical rewriting of the history of ethnographic collections and public exhibitions (Coombes 1994; Maxwell 1998). The re-designing of exhibitions of such material to emphasize and deconstruct this bias is an important consequence of this kind of work; an example is the exhibition of Khoi-San bushmen and their preserved remnants in Cape Town in 1995 (See Skotnes 1996). The emphasis in both Native American and Australian Aboriginal communities upon the need to recover the bodies of ancestors converted by imperial museums into exotic 'exhibits', and their restoration to their proper place and role as revered human beings, is another example of this restitutive process in action.

But recent critical discussion of the body in post-colonial spaces has also stressed the complexity of the ways in which the body can be constructed, and has elaborated its ambivalent role in the maintenance of, and resistance to, colonizing power. Thus, for example, Kadiatu Kanneh has spoken of the complexity of the idea of the 'veil' in the construction of discourses of the Muslim female, emphasizing that the motive for Western liberal 'unveiling' may itself be in some circumstances a form of imperial control (Kanneh 1995). In a different vein, Gillian Whitlock has stressed how habits of prudence and sexual restraint may interfere with and limit even the most liberal attempts to detail the reality of female abuse in institutions such as slavery, emphasizing physical brutality but unable to acknowledge sexual abuse (Whitlock 1995). Analyses such as these warn us of the danger of simply assuming that the body is neutral (natural) and not itself part of more widespread and contesting cultural institutions and practices.

Post-colonialism, for example, may offer us quite new ways of thinking about the implications of the centrality of nudity in artistic traditions in Western Europe. It may reveal the ways in which the discourse works not only to read the culture of the colonized, but also to deconstruct the hidden codes and assumptions of the colonial powers and their traditions. Even basic Western assumptions about the representation of sexuality itself may be opened up to be read in more complex ways, for example, if we observe the ways in which representations of the body in non-Western traditions, such as some West African carvings, frequently employ markers of both genders in a single image of the body. The relatively recent re-emergence in Western representations of the body of non-realistic codes such as Cubism may well be dependent on the discovery of these alternative traditions, and they may be the source for a renewed awareness of the limitations of the dominant 'naturalist' idea of the human body, its shape, its colour and its gender as fixed and determinate (see **modernism, primitivism**).

Further reading: Ashcroft 1998; Coombes 1994; Crane and Mohanram 1996; Dale and Ryan 1998; R. Dixon 1997; Gilbert 1993; Katrak 2006; Keown 2005; Low 1996; McClintock 1995; Massad 2000; Maxwell 1998; Mehan 2001; S. Mishra 1996; Mohanram 1999; Schoene-Harwood 1998; Thomas 1995; Young 1995.

POST-COLONIALISM/POSTCOLONIALISM

Post-colonialism (or often postcolonialism) deals with the effects of colonization on cultures and societies. As originally used by historians after the Second World War in terms such as **the post-colonial state**, 'post-colonial' had a clearly chronological meaning, designating the post-independence period. However, from the late 1970s the term has been used by literary critics to discuss the various cultural effects of colonization.

Although the study of the controlling power of representation in colonized societies had begun in the late 1970s with texts such as Said's *Orientalism*, and led to the development of what came to be called colonialist discourse theory in the work of critics such as Spivak and Bhabha, the actual term 'post-colonial' was not employed in these early studies of the power of colonialist discourse to shape and form opinion and policy in the colonies and metropolis. Spivak, for example, first used the term 'post-colonial' in the collection of interviews and recollections published in 1990 called *The Post-Colonial Critic*. Although the study of the effects of colonial representation were central to the work of these critics, the term 'post-colonial' *per se* was first used to refer to cultural interactions within colonial societies in literary circles (e.g. Ashcroft *et al*. 1977). This was part of an attempt to politicize and focus the concerns of fields such as Commonwealth literature and the study of the so-called New Literatures in English which had been initiated in the late 1960s. The term has subsequently been widely used to signify the political, linguistic and cultural experience of societies that were former European colonies.

Thus the term was a potential site of disciplinary and interpretative contestation almost from the beginning, especially the implications involved in the signifying hyphen or its absence. The heavily post-structuralist influence of the major exponents of colonial discourse theory, Said (Foucault), Homi Bhabha (Althusser and Lacan) and Gayatri Spivak (Derrida), led many critics, concerned to focus on the material effects of the historical condition of colonialism, as well as on its discursive power, to insist on the hyphen to distinguish post-colonial studies *as a field* from colonial discourse theory *per se*, which formed only one aspect of the many approaches and interests that the term 'post-colonial' sought to embrace and discuss (Ashcroft 1996).

While this distinction in style still exists, the interweaving of the two approaches is considerable. 'Post-colonialism/ postcolonialism' is now used in wide and diverse ways to include the study and analysis of European territorial conquests, the various institutions of European colonialisms, the discursive operations of empire, the subtleties of subject construction in colonial discourse and the resistance of those subjects, and, most importantly perhaps, the differing responses to such incursions and their contemporary colonial legacies in both pre-and post-independence nations and communities. While its use has tended to focus on the cultural production of such communities, it is becoming widely used in historical, political, sociological and economic analyses, as these disciplines continue to engage with the impact of European imperialism upon world societies.

The prefix 'post' in the term also continues to be a source of vigorous debate amongst critics. The simpler sense of the 'post' as meaning 'after' colonialism has been contested by a more elaborate understanding of the working of post-colonial cultures which stresses the articulations between and across the politically defined historical periods, of pre-colonial, colonial and post-independence cultures. As a result, further questions have been asked about what limits, if any, should be set round the term. Aijaz Ahmad complains, for instance, that when the term 'colonialism' can be pushed back to the Incas and forward to the Indonesian occupation of East Timor, then it becomes 'a transhistorical thing, always present and always in process of dissolution in one part of the world or another' (1995: 9). It is clear, however, that post-colonialism as it has been employed in most recent accounts has been primarily concerned to examine the processes and effects of, and reactions to, European colonialism from the sixteenth century up to and including the **neo-colonialism** of the present day.

No doubt the disputes will continue, since, as Stephen Slemon has argued, 'post-colonialism', is now used in its various fields, to describe a remarkably heterogeneous set of subject positions, professional fields, and critical enterprises:

> It has been used as a way of ordering a critique of totalizing forms of Western historicism; as a portmanteau term for a retooled notion of 'class', as a subset of both postmodernism and post-structuralism (and conversely, as the condition from which those two structures of cultural logic and cultural

critique themselves are seen to emerge); as the name for a condition of nativist longing in post-independence national groupings; as a cultural marker of non-residency for a Third World intellectual cadre; as the inevitable underside of a fractured and ambivalent discourse of colonialist power; as an oppositional form of 'reading practice'; and – and this was my first encounter with the term – as the name for a category of 'literary' activity which sprang from a new and welcome political energy going on within what used to be called 'Commonwealth' literary studies.

(Slemon 1994: 16–17)

Yet the term still continues to be used from time to time to mean simply 'anti-colonial' and to be synonymous with 'post-independence', as in references to the **post-colonial state**. To further complicate the issue of how these overlapping projects continue to collide in recent discussions, Slemon notes also that the existence of the three over-lapping fields has led to a 'confusion . . . in which the project . . . of identifying the scope and nature of anti-colonialist resistance in writing has been mistaken for the project . . . which concerns itself with articulating the literary nature of Third and Fourth-World cultural groups' (Slemon 1990: 31). As he sees it, the second of these projects retains a concern with 'whole nations or cultures as [its] basic [unit]' and sets up comparisons or contrasts between these units, whereas the first project is concerned with 'identifying a social force, colonialism, and with the attempt to understand the resistances to that force wherever they may lie' (31). Slemon is well aware that this raises its own problems, problems that have been part of the recent debate. As he notes,

Colonialism, obviously is an enormously problematic category: it is by definition transhistorical and unspecific, and it is used in relation to very different kinds of historical oppression and economic control. [Nevertheless] like the term 'patriarchy', which shares similar problems in definition, the concept of colonialism . . . remains crucial to a critique of past and present power relations in world affairs.

(Slemon 1990: 31)

Slemon also makes the point in this same essay that an assumption that the reactions of oppressed peoples will always be resistant may actually remove agency from these people. Not only are they capable of producing 'reactionary' documents, but as Ahmad (1992) and others have insisted, post-colonial societies have their own internal agendas and forces that continue to interact with and modify the direct response to the colonial incursion. Clearly any definition of post-colonialism needs to include a consideration of this wider set of local and specific ongoing concerns and practices. It is unlikely that these debates will be easily resolved. At the present time, though, no matter how we conceive of 'the post-colonial', and whatever the debates around the use of the problematic prefix 'post', or the equally problematic hyphen, the grounding of the term in European colonialist histories and institutional practices, and the responses (resistant or otherwise) to these practices on the part of all colonized peoples, remain fundamental.

An equally fundamental constraint is attention to precise location. Every colonial encounter or 'contact zone' is different, and each 'post-colonial' occasion needs, against these general background principles, to be precisely located and analysed for its specific interplay. A vigorous debate has revolved around the potentially homogenizing effect of the term 'post-colonial' (Hodge and Mishra 1990; Chrisman and Williams 1993). The effect of describing the colonial experience of a great range of cultures by this term, it is argued, is to elide the differences between them. However, there is no inherent or inevitable reason for this to occur. The materiality and locality of various kinds of post-colonial experience are precisely what provide the richest potential for post-colonial studies, and they enable the specific analysis of the various effects of colonial discourse.

The theoretical issues latent in these two fundamentals – materiality and location – lie at the basis of much of the dispute over what the term references and what it should or should not include. Yet, despite these disputes and differences, signs of a fruitful and complementary relationship between various post-colonial approaches have emerged in recent work in the field. Whether beginning from a basis in discourse theory, or from a more materialist and historical reading, most recent discussions have stressed the need to retain and strengthen these fundamental parameters in defining the idea of the post-colonial/postcolonial. As critics like Young have indicated, the crucial task has been to avoid assuming that 'the reality of the historical conditions of colonialism can be safely discarded' in favour of 'the fantasmatics of colonial discourse' (Young 1995: 160). The most cogent criticism of discourse theory has been offered by materialist thinkers such as Mohanty, Parry and Ahmad who, as Young suggests, argue that it should not proceed 'at the expense of materialist historical enquiry' (161). On the other hand, as Young also warns, although the totalizing aspects of discourses of the postcolonial/post-colonial is of real concern, it is necessary to avoid a return to a simplified form of localized materialism that refuses entirely to recognize the existence of and effect of general discourses of colonialism on individual instances of colonial practice.

The project of identifying the general discursive forces that held together the imperial enterprise and that operated wherever colonization occurred is often in conflict with the need to provide detailed accounts of the material effect of those discourses as they operated in different periods and different localities. To suggest that colonialism or imperialism were not themselves multivalent forces, and operated differently according to the periods in which they occurred, the metropolitan cultures from which they proceeded, or the specific 'contact zones' in which they took effect, is clearly to over-simplify. But to suggest that it is impossible to determine widespread common elements within these local particularities, especially at the level of ideology and discursive formation, seems equally inadequate as a basis for any but the most limited accounts.

Not every colony will share every aspect of colonialism, nor will it share some essential feature since, like any category, it is, to use Wittgenstein's metaphor, a rope with many overlapping strands (1958: 87). Nevertheless, it is likely that, as Robert Young has said, the particular historical moment can be seen to interact with the general discourse of colonialism so that:

> The contribution of colonial discourse analysis [for example] is that it provides a significant framework for that other work by emphasising that all perspectives on colonialism share, and have to deal with a common discursive medium which was also that of colonialism itself: the language used to enact, enforce, describe or analyse colonialism is not transparent, innocent, ahistorical or simply instrumental.
>
> (Young 1958: 163)

Young concludes a discussion of these recent disputational positions with a wise conclusion.

> Yet at this point in the postcolonial era, as we seek to understand the operation and effects of colonial history, the homogenization of colonialism does also need to be set against its historical and geographical particularities. The question is whether it can maintain, and do justice to, both levels.
>
> (165)

It is likely that the debate will not be resolved finally in favour of either extreme position, but that the increasingly detailed archival work done on all aspects of colonial/post-colonial culture will continue to correct the more simplistic generalizations that characterize early formulations of the field without overthrowing the validity of a general, comparative methodology in framing important questions that a strictly local materialist analysis alone could neither pose nor answer.

Further reading: Ashcroft *et al.* 1989, 1995; Boehmer 1995; Brydon 2000; Castle 2001; Childs and Williams 1997; Chrisman 2003; Desai and Nair 2005; Gandhi 1998; Goldberg and Quayson 2002; Harrison 2003; Hawley 2001; Loomba 2005; Punter 2000; Quayson 2000; San Juan 1998; Spivak 1999; Venn 2006; Wisker 2007; Young 2001, 2003.

POST-COLONIAL READING

A way of reading and rereading texts of both metropolitan and colonial cultures to draw deliberate attention to the profound and inescapable effects of colonization on literary production; anthropological accounts; historical records; administrative and scientific writing. It is a form of deconstructive reading most usually applied to works emanating from the colonizers (but may be applied to works by the colonized) which demonstrates the extent to which the text contradicts its underlying assumptions (civilization, justice, aesthetics, sensibility, race) and reveals its (often unwitting) colonialist ideologies and processes. Examples of post-colonial readings of particular texts include Eric Williams' interrogation of the formerly authoritative texts of Caribbean history in *British Historians and the West Indies* (1966); contemporary rereadings of the works of canonical European anthropologists such as Malinowski; numerous post-colonial rereadings (and rewritings) of Shakespeare's *The Tempest* in French, English and Spanish; rereadings of Jane Austen's *Mansfield Park* (see **contrapuntal reading**); Jean Rhys' rereadings (and thus rewriting, in *Wide Sargasso Sea*) of Charlotte Bronte's *Jane Eyre*.

The notion of a 'post-colonial reading' need not be restricted to interrogating a body of works (for example, documents dealing with the European history of an area) nor to rereading and rewriting individual texts. A post-colonial rereading of, for instance, English literary history would (hypothetically) involve far greater stress on colonial relations between England and Scotland, Ireland and Wales, and the historical and contemporary effects of these relations on literary production and representation. It would also involve reconsidering English literature and literary production as less a series of domestically inspired changes and progressions than one emanating from and through the imperial process and/or colonial contacts. Thus, for instance, modernism can be argued to be the product of Europe's contact with the so-called 'savage' cultures of Africa and the South Pacific; while post-structuralist theories (such as that of Derrida) might be reread as less the products of the Parisian intellectual climate than inspired or significantly inflected by colonial experience.

Further reading: Dimitriadis 2001; Kaul 1996; Said 1993; Tiffin 1987; Trees 1997.

POST-COLONIAL STATE

The term 'post-colonial state' has often been used by historians, economists and political theorists as a synonym for 'post-independence state'. Its formation after independence is the clearest signal of the separation of the colonized from the imperial power. The independence of that newly formed state is the *sine qua non* of the claim to have left the power of the colonizer behind. However, in practice, such 'independence' may come to be seen as superficial, mainly because the dominance of the idea of the European concept of the **nation** in the minds of those who led the struggle for independence often meant that new post-colonial states were closely modelled on that of the former European powers. Post-colonial nation-states have usually (though not always) been coterminous with the boundaries of the colonial administrative units. Thus in Africa, for example, the extent of independent countries such as Nigeria and Ghana broadly reflects the colonial enclaves carved out from the pre-colonial societies of West Africa. By contrast, in the Indian subcontinent, the apparent colonial unity of the Indian Raj was replaced by a Partition into the separate states of India and Pakistan. The separately governed princely states of the Raj period were incorporated, often unwillingly, into the new post-colonial states so formed. In any case, the modern political entities bore only a notional relationship to the pre-colonial entities now incorporated as modern, post-colonial nation-states.

As in the case of the European nation-states on whose model they were created, the post-colonial nation-state was often created by a deliberate fusing or dividing of a number of already existing territories. In each case the glue that held them together was a constructed national mythology in which unifying symbols such as flags, names and national symbols were vital elements. Thus, for example, post-colonial states like Ghana adopted the name of a mediaeval kingdom whose physical boundaries had no congruence with that of the colonial enclave of the Gold Coast protectorate. In the case of Zimbabwe (literally Stone Town), the country took its name from the local name for the many archaeological ruins of the pre-colonial cultures in the region. In the case of Pakistan, the name was invented as an anagram of the principal Muslim regions of the old North-West of colonized India.

More importantly, perhaps, post-colonial states were often tied to former colonial administrative, legal and economic systems that limited their independent action. This effectively allowed the continued control of many of these states in the period after independence (see **neo-colonialism**). The resulting back-lash in the form of an assertion of **native/nativist** practices was understandable, but posed new prob-lems since no single, undisputed, national pre-colonial tradition could adequately represent the multiplicity of ethnicities and differences that made up most modern post-colonial states. In this the post-colonial states were not different from those of their erstwhile colonizers, but the fact that these had succeeded in constructing relatively successful myths of national homogeneity (partly by contrasting themselves as unified against the differentness of the **other** represented by the colonized world) ironically meant that the newly formed post-colonial states were often compared with the European models in a very unfair and unfavourable way. The task facing contemporary post-colonial states, then, is to construct an effective unity whilst avoiding the oppression of minority groups whose practices clash with those of the dominant national mythology, whether over religion, language or cultural mores. Significantly, in this sense, the imperial nations also face the same problem as they are forced to redefine themselves in terms of the new **ethnicities** created by the influx of peoples from the erstwhile colonial **margins**.

Further reading: Bhabha 1990; Chatterjee 1993; Davidson 1992; Premnath 2003; Stepputat and Hansen 2001.

POSTCOLONY

This term has been largely associated with the work of the Franco-phone Cameroonian critic Achille Mbembe who has written several influential accounts of how power and oppression actually work in the postcolonised states of Africa, the most influential of which has been the study translated into English as *On the Postcolony* (2001). Athough the term has also been used by others in different ways, which do not necessarily concur with Mbembe's views (e.g. Comaroff 2006). The term has been used so far principally in studies of African states and in studies of the ongoing violence perpetrated in those states by those in power during and after colonization.

Mbembe suggests that although in Africa the postcolony is chaotically pluralistic; it has nonetheless an internal coherence. It is a specific system of signs, a particular way of fabricating simulacra or re-forming stereotypes. It is not the economy of signs in which the power is mirrored and imagined self-reflectively. The postcolony is characterized 'by a distinctive style of political improvisation, by a tendency to excess and lack of proportion, as well as by distinctive ways identities are multiplied transformed and put into circulation.' (Mbembe 2001: 102). In response to this analysis Mbembe emphasizes the need to address the fields of daily practice through which Africans in the postcolony 'exercise existence – that is, live their lives out and confront the very forms of their death. On this basis, I then asked what is the set of particular signs that confers on the current African age its character of urgency, its distinctive mark, its eccentricities, its vocabularies, and its magic, and make it both a source of terror, astonishment, and hilarity at once? What gives this set of things significations that all can share? In what languages are these significations expressed? How can these languages be deciphered?' (15)

Mbembe's project is aimed towards a restorative goal, to restoring to Africans a sense of their wholeness, of their validity as 'autonomous African subject[s]'. As he suggests, 'On a sociological level attention must be given to the contemporary everyday practices through which Africans manage to recognise and to maintain with the world an unprecedented familiarity – practices through which they invent something that is their own and that beckons to the world in its generality' (258). The African subject has been dismembered, fragmented and effectively rendered 'non-existent' by the physical and psychic violence of slavery and colonization. These violences have been projected forward into the ongoing representations of Africa and Africans in the **neo-colonial** discourses of the post-colonial world. Thus Mbembe agrees with the emphasis in much **post-colonial** and **neo-colonial** theory on the ongoing effects of colonization but argues for a different emphasis in response, one which refocuses attention onto an analysis of the daily practices by which Africans have engaged with and negotiated the legacies of the processes of enslavement and colonization. In effect he moves the attention away from the process of overcoming the violence and disruption to social and cultural forms, which is the legacy of this history and refocuses on the ways in which Africans have taken these things on board and survive within and even through them. For example, in his analysis of the operation of power in the postcolony he argues that we need to move beyond the idea of a binary oppositional mode and embrace a more complex model in which the forces of oppressive power (the *commandemente* as he terms it) are revealed as symbolic languages, fetishised in a variety of daily rituals. Opposition to these modes of power may, often in startling ways, embrace these very rituals, engaging with them through laughter and mockery. Mbembe's analysis brings together the oppressor and the oppressed, the corrupt élite and their subjects in a process which he argues is continuous. Oppositionality is not an answer in itself since, he argues, the 'postcolonial relationship is not primarily a relationship of resistance or collaboration but can best be characterised as convivial, a relationship fraught by the fact of the *commandemente* and its "subjects" having to share the same living space.' (104) Mbembe concludes: 'Hence, it would seem wrong to continue to interpret postcolonial relations in terms of absolute resistance or absolute domination, or, as a function of the binary oppositions usually adduced in conventional analyses of movements of indiscipline and revolt (e.g. counter-discourse, counter-society, counter-hegemony. . . .).' (105) Instead he argues that 'the [analytical] emphasis should be on the logic of 'conviviality,' on the dynamics of domesticity and familiarity, inscribing the dominant and the dominated within the same episteme' (110) Direct or even indirect opposition is useless in the face of what Mbembe sees as a plurality which cannot be reduced to 'a single permanently stable system' (108), since the existence of such a stable system would be a prerequisite for successful formal opposition. Instead the mockery which the subject conducts from inside the fetishized system of power is both a condition of that power and a prerequisite of its exposure. Both ruler and ruled in the postcolony are engaged in the production of a regime of unreality in which the subject who simulates the official rituals, eg, hanging portraits of the ruler in their homes, wearing party uniforms, carrying party cards, etc. are '[saying] the unsayable and [recognising] the unrecognisable. . . . [Thus] . . . the fetish, seen for the sham it is, is made to lose its might and become a mere artefact.' (108) Mbembe clearly draws on the Bakhtinian idea of carnivale, (See Bakhtin 1941) though his critique differs from that of Bakhtin, in that he argues that in the postcolony the public space is not singular as it is in the classic state but rather is constituted in many overlapping domains 'each having its own logic yet liable to be entangled with other logics' (104).

Mbembe's work has been criticized as not leading to an active policy, which might address the issues of violence and oppression within the postcolony, displacing political action into the realm of the personal and the libidinous. In response Mbembe has argued that his analysis of the postcolony is apt since 'the usual categories of political economy are unable to highlight its complexities. In this kind of power formation, reality is each time erased, recreated, and duplicated. It is this power of proliferation (and its ability to obliterate the distinctions between truth and falsehood, the visible and the occult) that turns domination and subjection into a magical song, at that point where the originary arbitrariness produces terror and hilarity.' (Hoeller 2002). Despite this defence other commentators have suggested Mbembe's work is essentially pessimistic. For these critics Mbembe's work 'places Africa's dire predicament in perspective. But it offers no solution. (Jules-Rosette, 2002; see also Janz, 2002) Others, especially anthropologists and sociologists, have been even more directly critical, suggesting that Mbembe's claim that Africa 'stands out as the supreme receptacle of the West's obsession with and circular discourse about the facts of "absence", "lack", and "non-being," of identity and difference, of negativeness – in short nothingness' (5) grossly misrepresents the more complex analysis of Africa which their disciplines have produced. In this respect the debate about this text reflects the conflicting assessments of **ethnography** and of positivist scientific discourses over the effect of Eurocentric **surveillance** of the post-colonial subject. (See Keita 2006). Mbembe analyses the role of the IMF, the World Bank and other non-government organizations in a controversially different way to many other post-colonial intellectuals, (see **neo-colonialism/neo-imperialism**). Mbembe argues that despite their control by external powers and forces such as the US these institutions may act inadvertently to undermine power élites in the postcolony (the *commandement*) because they encourage economic conditions which 'have created the conditions for a *privitisation of sovereignity*' through the decentralization of fiscal power and the emergence of self-administered social programmes not dependent on state patronage (78). (For a useful discussion of this view, see Adeeko 2002). Mbembe's influential and controversial work has rekindled the debate on the nature and continuity of the African colonial legacy and the responses it has shaped in the region in a number of new ways.

Further reading: Adeeko 2002; Janz 2002; Keita 2006; Jules-Rosette, 2002; Hoeller 2002; Mbembe 2001; Mbembe 2003.

PRIMITIVISM

A term that has been widely used in art history and, to a lesser extent, in literary studies. It is used narrowly to identify a specific modern school of art and writing that emphasizes simplicity of form or theme. In this regard, in the history of modern European art it is associated with the work of sculptors such as Brancusi and painters such as Miro. In this narrow sense it is an ongoing and important influence on modern art. In modern writing, however, it is less frequently employed as a critical term, being associated with simplicity of style and a deliberate employment of simple themes and subjects (for example, the representation of peasant life). In some cases, notably in Latin American writing, it has had a radical association absent from most of its European uses. However, in many places it has formed part of a more general movement of national self-assertion, for example in Slavic countries in the second half of the nineteenth century when it fostered the recovery and employment of motifs and themes from peasant and folk art as nationalist symbols.

Its broader use defines a form or style perceived to represent an early stage of human cultural endeavour. Thus early human art is often described as primitive art. The problem with the term used in this way is that it assumes a linear, teleological unfolding of human history from simple to complex. Thus early or primitive art is seen as leading to a culmination and fulfilment in later sophisticated or civilized art. Even more dubiously, such criteria may lead to further categories. Thus uneducated, that is untrained and unschooled, artists whose work does not reflect the dominant artistic conventions, such as the Frenchman Henri Rousseau, or the American woman painter Granma Moses, or even trained artists who deliberately repudiate the conventions, such as the British painter Stanley Spencer, may be categorized as 'primitive'. Furthermore, whole alternative cultural and artistic traditions may be assigned to this category simply because their conventions do not match those of the dominant artistic codes of the West. This discrimination lends itself too easily to unfounded and often pejorative comparisons of the 'value' of different cultures. Thus African or Pacific Islander or Native American Indian or Australian Aboriginal art was often described as 'primitive' (implying a savage crudity and simplicity, if also a welcome freshness and a child-like vision) because its conventions did not match those of the dominant European tradition whose values were considered to establish the norms of civilized and mature art (see **universalism, savage**). Even the most positive descriptions based on the category of the primitive are in danger of exoticizing these cultures and **othering** them.

As these dominant European traditions associated with the **modernist** movement at the end of the nineteenth and early twentieth centuries became questioned and challenged, Western artists, such as Picasso, often deliberately sought to reproduce the innocence and 'child-like' qualities of primitive art. This was, in part, a repudiation of their own culture and did not necessarily involve an affirmation of the validity and difference of the cultures they employed as signifiers of the liberating force of the primitive. The signs of the primitive continued to be juxtaposed with icons of Western art, reinforcing the binary of primitive (savage) and modern (civilized), even as it sought to dismantle the claims of the latter. Thus, for example, in Picasso's famous and influential early painting *Les Demoiselles d'Avignon* (1907), the classical Greek icon of the three Graces in the grouping of the young women is juxtaposed against the image of an African mask which replaces the face of one of them. Such a juxtaposition may seek to dismantle the status of the classical tradition but does not necessarily affirm the value of the alter/native tradition it employs.

For these reasons, primitivism remains a problematic concept, and one that most post-colonial studies have treated with caution as a descriptive category, whilst recognizing that the artistic and social movements it describes have had powerful historical links with colonialist and post-colonialist discourses.

Further reading: Arac and Ritvo 1995; Barkan and Bush 1995; Consentino 2000; During 1994; Harrison *et al.* 1993; Hiller 1991; Rhodes 1994; Rubin 1984; Torgovnick 1990.

RACE

'Race' is a term for the classification of human beings into physically, biologically and genetically distinct groups. The notion of race assumes, firstly, that humanity is divided into unchanging natural types, recognizable by physical features that are transmitted 'through the blood' and permit distinctions to be made between 'pure' and 'mixed' races. Furthermore, the term implies that the mental and moral behaviour of human beings, as well as individual personality, ideas and capacities, can be related to racial origin, and that knowledge of that origin provides a satisfactory account of the behaviour.

Race is particularly pertinent to the rise of colonialism, because the division of human society in this way is inextricable from the need of colonialist powers to establish a dominance over subject peoples and hence justify the imperial enterprise. Race thinking and colonialism are imbued with the same impetus to draw a **binary** distinction between 'civilized' and 'primitive' and the same necessity for the hierarchization of human types. By translating the fact of colonial oppression into a justifying theory, however spurious, European race thinking initiated a hierarchy of human variation that has been difficult to dislodge. Although race is not specifically an invention of imperialism, it quickly became one of imperialism's most supportive ideas, because the idea of superiority that generated the emergence of race as a concept adapted easily to both impulses of the imperial mission: dominance and enlightenment.

In this respect, 'racism' is not so much a product of the concept of race as the very reason for its existence. Without the underlying desire for hierarchical categorization implicit in racism, 'race' would not exist. Racism can be defined as: a way of thinking that considers a group's unchangeable physical characteristics to be linked in a direct, causal way to psychological or intellectual characteristics, and which on this basis distinguishes between 'superior' and 'inferior' racial groups. Physical differences did not always represent an inferiority of culture or even a radical difference in shared human characteristics. In the period of the Crusades, the racial difference of black African Coptic saint-warrior St Maurice is clearly recorded without prejudice in a statue in Magdeburg Cathedral which shows him to be a black African, even including his facial lineage cuts (Davidson 1994: 330). But with the rise of European imperialism and the growth of Orientalism in the nineteenth century, the need to establish such a distinction between superior and inferior finds its most 'scientific' confirmation in the dubious analysis and taxonomy of racial characteristics.

'Race' is first used in the English language in 1508 in a poem by William Dunbar, and through the seventeenth and eighteenth centuries it remained essentially a literary word denoting a class of persons or things. It was only in the late eighteenth century that the term came to mean a distinct category of human beings with physical characteristics transmitted by descent. Humans had been categorized by Europeans on physical grounds from the late 1600s, when François Bernier postulated a number of distinctive categories, based largely on facial character and skin colour. Soon a hierarchy of groups (not yet termed races) came to be accepted, with white Europeans at the top. The Negro or black African category was usually relegated to the bottom, in part because of black Africans' colour and allegedly 'primitive' culture, but primarily because they were best known to Europeans as slaves.

Immanuel Kant's use of the German phrase for 'races of mankind' in his *Observations on the Feeling of the Beautiful and Sublime* (1764) was probably the first explicit use of the term in the sense of biologically or physically distinctive categories of human beings. Kant's stress on an intuitive, non-rational form of thought 'allowed the Romantics to posit the notion of an unchanging inner essence within human beings', an essence that 'found expression through the sense of "race"' (Malik 1996: 77). Debates about whether human variation was caused by descent or environment raged throughout the seventeenth and eighteenth centuries. But with the ascendancy of the biological sciences in the late nineteenth century, descent emerged as the predominant model. It was encapsulated in the transition of 'race' from signifying, in its literary sense, a line of descent that a group defined by historical continuity, to its scientific sense of 'race' as a zoologically or biologically defined group.

Despite its allegedly scientific grounding and application, the term 'race' has always provided an effective means of establishing the simplest model of human variation – colour difference. Colour became the means of distinguishing between groups of people and of identifying the behaviour to be expected of them. In 1805, the French anatomist Cuvier, who was particularly significant in the development of 'race' theory, postulated the existence of three major 'races': the white, the yellow and the black. The division of the whole of humanity into three such arbitrarily designated genetic groups seems so vague as to be entirely useless for any kind of analysis, but the concept has remained influential for the ideological reason that this typology rested upon a gradation from superior to inferior. Cuvier's typology of race influenced such works as Charles Hamilton Smith's (1848) *The Natural History of the Human Species*; Robert Knox's (1850) *The Races of Man*; Count de Gobineau's (1853) *Essai sur l'inégalité des Races humaines*; and Nott and Gliddon's (1854) *Types of Mankind*. The assumptions underlying this racial typology, though continually contradicted by actual observation, have remained stubbornly persistent to the present day, even when the categories are more elaborately defined as 'caucasoid', 'mongoloid' and 'negroid'. These assumptions are: first, that variations in the constitution and behaviour of individuals were to be explained as the expression of different biological types; second, that differences between these types explained variations in human cultures; third, that the distinctive nature of the types explained the superiority of Europeans and Aryans in particular; and fourth, that the friction between nations and individuals of different type emerged from innate characteristics.

The simple clarity of this view of race, more or less based on colour, was superseded by the implications of Darwin's *The Origin of Species* (1859). Natural selection now offered a mechanism for species alteration – either the superior races might be contaminated through contact with the inferior, or deliberate human intervention might maximize the benefits of selection and advance the emergence of pure races. In either case, the fundamental assumption of the hierarchy of races remained secure. Darwin's contribution was to provide the theory of race with a mechanism of change in the idea of natural selection, and consequently to offer the possibility for planned racial development (eugenics) – a central tenet of the school of thought that came to be known as Social Darwinism.

Social Darwinism, in both its positive and negative implications, concurred readily with imperial practice, particularly the paradoxical dualism that existed in imperialist thought between the *debasement* and the *idealization* of colonized subjects. On the one hand, the debasement of the primitive peoples could find in Social Darwinism a justification for the domination and at times extinction of inferior races as not only an inevitable but a desirable unfolding of natural law. On the other hand, the concept of racial improvement concurred with the 'civilizing mission' of imperial ideology, which encouraged colonial powers to take up the 'white man's burden' and raise up the condition of the inferior races who were idealized as child-like and malleable. The assumption of superiority thus supported by scientific racial theory could pursue its project of world domination with impunity.

The latter perception of blacks as helpless beings in need of care, protection and advancement was quickly overtaken in the nineteenth century by the former view of them as primitive and indolent savages, as colonial expansion found the need for increasing supplies of labour to service its enterprises. The evangelical anti-slavery impulse that had achieved the abolition of slavery in the 1830s began to give way to a virulent form of racial hostility. Thomas Carlyle's notorious *Occasional Discourse on the Nigger Question* (1849) vigorously propounded the right to coerce the 'indolent' black man into the service of colonial plantation agriculture, and by the 1870s, before the last phase of imperial expansion into Africa, such prejudice, supported as it was by Social Darwinism, had virtually overshadowed liberal brands of thought on issues of race.

The usefulness of the concept of race in both establishing the innate superiority of imperial culture as it approached its zenith, and at the same time lumping together the 'inferior' races under its control, can be seen in the example of English commentary on the 'races' of Britain itself – particularly the Irish. In early writings, although the Irish were initially seen to be physically much the same as the English, Irish culture was seen as alien and threatening. Rich (1986) traces the process from 1617 when Fynes Moryson found the language of the Irish crude, if indeed it was a language at all, their clothing almost animal-like and their behaviour shocking. Edmund Spenser refers to the 'bestial Irishmen', while William Camden in 1610 recounted the profanity, cannibalism, musicality, witchcraft, violence, incest and gluttony of the 'wilde and very uncivill' Irish. In this description the Irish sound remarkably like Africans as described by nineteenth-century English commentators. Indeed, by 1885, John Beddoe, president of the Anthropological Institute, had developed an 'index of Nigrescence' that showed the people of Wales, Scotland, Cornwall and Ireland to be racially separate from the British. More specifically, he argued that those from Western Ireland and Wales were 'Africanoid' in their jutting jaws' and 'long slitty nostrils', and thus originally immigrants of Africa (Szwed 1975: 20–1). Bizarre though this might seem, it is a consumate demonstration of the exclusionary impetus of imperialism that operates so energetically in the concept of race.

The linking of the Irish and Welsh with Africa demonstrates remarkably clearly how imperial ideology operates to exclude and marginalize colonized peoples, whether in Britain or the Empire. Such a racial hierarchy was integral to the extension of the Empire. Kipling's notorious formulation, in the poem 'Recessional' (1897: 328–329), of the non-Caucasian races as 'lesser breeds without the law' may stand as a classic instance:

> If, drunk with power we loose
> Wild tongues that have not Thee in awe,
> Such boastings as the Gentiles use,
> Or lesser breeds without the Law –
> Lord God of Hosts, be with us yet,
> Lest we forget – lest we forget.

The most energetic period of imperial expansion in the last decades of the nineteenth century saw a rapid increase in anthropometric investigation of race differences. Disputes about the form of racial 'types' had raged throughout the century, but by 1886 anthropologists in Britain had reached a general consensus on the 'cephalic index': the discrimination of racial identity in terms of skull shape. Francis Galton, the founder of eugenics, measured 9,000 people at the International Health Exhibition in London in 1884, and the anthropological interest in race in the imperial context was reinforced at an Anthropological

Conference on Native Races in British Possessions held in 1887 at the time of Queen Victoria's Golden Jubilee. By the late 1890s many popular works began to appear, illustrating with lavish detail the nature and diversity of human races and the implicit superiority of the white Anglo-Saxon races and civilization. Despite the appearance of greater scientific rigour, the description of the negroid had not advanced much past the stereotype compounded by Carlyle.

The twentieth century has seen great swings in the theoretical attitude to race, but the term continues to hold a resilient sway in the ordinary thinking of people throughout the world. The 1911 Universal Races Congress held in London was a major demonstration of liberal thought and the promotion of 'monogenism' – the idea that there was 'only one species of man living on earth today'. But the universalist creed of the Victorian liberal tradition was considerably shaken by the First World War and the emergence of colonial nationalism which eroded confidence in the power of reason to ensure a growing unity between different races in a single world order (see Rich 1986: 49). In the early decades of the twentieth century, 'race' continued to acquire a legitimacy through the 'scientific' study of racial variation, but the horror of the Second World War and the slaughter of millions of Jews, Slavs, Poles and gypsies on racial grounds led to the 1951 *Unesco Statement of the Nature of Race and Racial Difference* which pointed out that race, even from a strict biological standpoint, could *at most* refer to a group with certain distinctive gene concentrations. The statement asserts that mental characteristics should never be included in such classifications and that environment is far more important than inherited genetic factors in shaping behaviour.

However, in the 1960s there was an upsurge in biological thinking about human behaviour once again, with writers such as Lorenz, Ardry and Morris asserting that individual behaviour was largely controlled by ancient instincts that could at best be modified by culture. This led the way for an upsurge in race thinking in popular science in the 1970s: Eysenck's *Race, Intelligence and Education* (1971), Richardson and Spears's *Race, Culture and Intelligence* (1972), Baxter and Sansom's *Race and Social Difference* (1972) indicate some of a wide range of popular books that maintained the centrality of 'race' in debates about human variation. At the same time, the neo-biologism of the 1960s led to a much more rigorous development in the 1970s with the emergence of socio-biology, which views all individual behaviour, and cultures themselves, as the end products of biological selection processes. These developments lent an air of legitimacy to race thinking, which also analyses behaviour and performance in biological terms, and the relation between sociobiology and modern racism has been examined by Barker (1981).

It is significant that academic debate during these decades sustained *race* rather than **ethnicity** as the centre of discussion. The sense of permanency that a dubious biological explanation offered, through an inexorable genetic determination and transmission, consolidated the concept of race at this time, rather than the more complex concept of ethnicity with its inherent plasticity and its basis in culture. Yet the 1970s and 1980s saw the gradual growth of interest and research into ethnicity, a growth that perhaps has not been reflected in popular thinking. In practice, 'race' may be a major constitutive factor in determining ethnic categories, but to revive the idea that it is somehow 'objective' and less socially constructed than ethnicities founded on religious, linguistic or other more obviously culturally determined factors is to fail to recognize that race is a cultural rather than a biological phenomenon, the product of historical processes not of genetically determined physical differences.

The most important fact about race was, as Fanon was the first to notice, that however lacking in objective reality racist ideas such as 'blackness' were, the psychological force of their construction of self meant that they acquired an objective existence in and through the behaviour of people. The self-images and self-construction that such social pressure exerted might be transmitted from generation to generation, and thus the 'fact of blackness' came to have an objective determination not only in racist behaviour and institutional practices, but more insidiously in the psychological behaviour of the peoples so constructed. This **Fanonist** stress on the objective psychological fact of race as a determining part of the social process of constructing individuals' self-perceptions has been part of the response of many black commentators to the claims by critics such as Appiah that perceptions of race have acted only negatively in determining post-colonial responses to European domination. However fictional race may be shown to be as an objective category, its power as a discursive formation remains unabated.

Thus a fraught and volatile term, 'race', continues to hold centre stage while the theories on which concepts of race were established have become more and more blurred. In this way resistance becomes less and less able to dislodge the vague and untenable concept of race itself. Race in the time of neo-colonialism is just as vague and just as resilient as it was at the beginning of the history of European imperialism. It is perhaps up to the concept of *ethnicity* to change the direction of the debate.

Further reading: Baxter and Sansom 1972; Bremen 1990; Chrisman 2003;

Cooppan 1999; Fanon 1961; Frankenberg and Mani 1996; Gilroy 1996; Gunew 1997; Husband 1994; Malik 1996; McInturff 2000; Marriot 2000; S. Mishra 1993; Olson and Worsham 1999; Rich 1986; Ross 1982; H. Scott 2002; Sharpe 2000.

RASTAFARIANISM

A black nationalist religion that emerged in Jamaica in the 1930s. Its geneses are complex and include slave beliefs in the soul's return after death to Africa from exile in the Caribbean. Together with the visionary black restitutive politics of Marcus Garvey and the Ethiopeanism of Leonard Percival Howell, Rastafarianism drew its inspiration from the Old Testament prophecy that 'Princes shall come out of Egypt; Ethiopia shall soon stretch forth her hands unto God' (Psalm 68: 31). In 1930, Ras Tafari, great grandson of King Saheka Selassie of Shoa, was crowned Negus of Ethiopia, taking the name Haile Selassie, meaning 'Mighty of the Trinity'. To this title was added 'King of Kings' and 'Lion of the Tribe of Judah', which placed him in the legendary line of King Solomon (Barrett 1988: 81). Celebrating the coronation of Ras Tafari as Haile Selassie, Jamaican Rastafarians initially looked forward to a literal repatriation to their African ancestral homelands through the agency of the Ethiopian Emperor. Increasingly, however, African repatriation was regarded less as a literal return than a figurative one: a reclaiming by Jamaicans of their African ancestry, a heritage systematically denigrated under slavery and in European colonialist ideologies.

Initially a movement of the Jamaican underclass, Rastafarianism soon spread to sections of the middle class and to intellectuals, and across the Caribbean. It gained increasing popularity in other areas of the world, largely through the music and lyrics of Reggae star Bob Marley in the 1970s and 1980s, where its language and beliefs were co-opted in the fight against a wide variety of oppressions, both racial and economic. Rastafarians have always been acutely aware of the crucial connections between language and power, and in the cause of racial restitution have disrupted the rules of English grammar to refuse the 'objective case' (i.e. 'that which is acted upon') by eradicating the personal pronoun 'me' and insisting on 'I' no matter what the demands of conventional grammar.

Further reading: Barrett 1977, 1988; Campbell 1985; Cashmore 1979, 1983; Chevannes 1997; Clarke 2000; Collins 2000; Gossai and Murell 2000; Hodges 2000; King and Jensen 1995; King and Bays 2003; Miles 1978; Murrell and Spencer 1998; Oosthuizen 1993; Owens 1976; Pollard and Nettleford 2000; Savishinsky 1999; Somerson 1999.

RELIGION AND THE POST-COLONIAL

There has been no more dramatic shift in recent times in post-colonial studies than the growing awareness of the role religion has played in both the practices of colonization and the developments which have occurred since political independence in the post-colonial world. This takes many forms. First, there is a growing awareness of the complex role religion played in the history of imperialism, both directly through the impact of missions (See **missions and colonialism**) and indirectly, as religion acted to shape the responses of both colonizer and colonized. The religious practices of colonized peoples were often denigrated as mere superstition or openly attacked as heathenism, and so used to justify the so-called 'civilizing mission' (*mission civilatrice*) of the colonizer. This was particularly the case where these practices were not written down in forms (sacred texts), which Europeans could recognize. Even where their complexity and intellectual force was acknowledged (e.g. as in the case of cultures with written religious texts such as India) they were perceived to be decadent or decayed and in need of reform. So influential was this view that it even exerted force on the reformers sprung from within those cultures themselves in the colonial period, e.g. Tilak and Vivekananda in India. (See Viswanathan 1998; King 1999). Ironically, such reformers and the changes they effected went hand in hand with the development of secular anti-colonial resistances, which also borrowed forms from the practices of their colonizers, forms such as the European concept of the nation state (See **nation/nationalism**), and broader discourses of reform, progress and modernization. Of course, as several commentators have already argued, colonized societies were always changing and modernizing in their own terms both before and after the impact of colonization (Ahmad 1992). But resistance after colonization often took the form of appropriation of institutions modelled on those of the colonizers. This was as true of religious institutions as of secular ones. Religion could therefore act either as a means of hegemonic control or could be employed by the colonized as a means of resistance. If this were true of the responses to and within the pre-colonial religious practices of colonized peoples, it was also true of the ways in which the Christian practices introduced under colonialism developed in post-colonized spaces. Whilst for many Christianity was a means by which their own cultures were being overwritten and ignored, for others it became a vehicle for independent indigenous expression, at least when modified in an appropriated form. Christianity, which had been from its earliest years a religion of accretion and which thrived on the absorption of other practices and cultural modes, continued to change as it encountered the cultures of the colonized. In its most extreme form, notably in Africa, indigenous churches arose in which Christian and pre-colonial religions formed new synthesized forms. The leaders and 'prophets' of these new churches often played a vital role in the development of independence movements. This was aided by the fact that the rapid spread of Christianity in many areas of Latin America, Africa and Asia far outstripped the growth of these religions in Europe in the late nineteenth and twentieth century when religion in Europe was on the retreat (Van der Veer 2004). This rapid spread of Christianity beyond Europe was achieved not by the success of European proselytizers but by the work of indigenous evangelists. In fact, historians of religion now acknowledge that until indigenous evangelists emerged Europeans had little or no success in converting large numbers of peoples in many of these regions (Etherington 2006). Many of these indigenous evangelists worked within existing religious forms and churches, though none of these forms and churches remained unchanged by the encounters. Such changes were clearly much more marked in the synthetised churches, which openly combined Christianity with elements of the pre-colonial religions.

If there is now a growing acknowledgement of the neglect of religion in the accounts of colonial times, then more recently we have seen much more attention paid to the ongoing role of religion in the modern post-colony. Especially in North America and Canada, but increasingly elsewhere, indigenous scholars of religion have emphasized the role of religion in the modern era (Donaldson 2002; Treat 1996). As the balance of concern begins to swing away from Europe and America, scholars and politicians alike become increasingly aware that they are forced to engage with religious as well as other social and cultural practices within the framework of **globalization**. In fact, in the early twentieth century it becomes clear that religion has re-emerged as one of the key defining features of difference and that the role of religion has become central to the way in which Europeans and Americans think about identity with a force which it has not had for several centuries. This has resulted not from the growth of religious adherence in those areas (or at least not until very recently in the case of America) but in response to their awareness that for much of the world the secular model of post-Enlightenment Europe was never dominant except for a small minority of Western educated intellectuals, and that it has increasingly been on the wane as the populations in many areas reassert their identity by a renewed adherence to their own traditions. In the resurgence of fundamentalist forces within many religions such as Islam, Hinduism and Christianity itself in recent times, especially in America and in areas such as Africa and Asia, we see the most obvious and, some would argue, the most negative effect of this renewed stress on religion as a component in social and national as well as personal identity. Islamic fundamentalism in particular has emerged in the public domain as a force that asserts a shared identity above and beyond other cultural allegiances, causing direct confrontation to emerge in many societies with earlier markers of identity based on secular formations such as nationality and citizenship. Though this is the most discussed example, religious leaders in many other societies such as those of America and Europe, as well as in many parts of the post-colonial world, e.g. India, assert their right to engage directly in secular politics and recruit adherents to social and political parties and causes. As a result religious fundamentalism (a term whose origin, incidentally, is in the American Christian churches of the early twentieth century), that is religion offered as an alternative and indisputable form of personal and social identity and set over against ideas of secular reason and scientific evidence is likely to be an arena of confrontation in many of these societies for the foreseeable future. (See Pesso-Misquel and Stierstorfer 2006) More positively though, we might see the questioning of the more simplistic formulations of the ideas of the European enlightenment (based on the idea that Western science and rational logic is the only meaningful way of organizing societies and the only way of guaranteeing human development and progress) may yield to an acknowledgement that enlightenment reason too has had its dark side, not least in its embrace of a discourse of progress and science in forms inimical to older ideas of living in harmony with the environment rather than controlling and mastering it (See **ecological imperialism**). In this respect the re-emergence of religious thought is part of a broader post-humanist critique which has taken many forms in recent times (See Wolfe 2003).

Further reading: Ahmad 1992; Donaldson 2002; King 1999; Pesso-Misquel and Stierstorfer 2006; Sugirtharajah 2001; Treat 1996; Van der Veer 2004; Viswanathan 1998; Wolfe, Cary (2003).

RHIZOME

A botanical term for a root system that spreads across the ground (as in bamboo) rather than downwards, and grows from several points rather than a single tap root. The metaphor was first popularized by Deleuze and Guattari in their critiques of psychoanalysis (Deleuze and

Guattari 1972), but in post-colonial theory it has been used to contest the binary, centre/margin view of reality that is maintained by **colonial discourse**.

The key value of the term is to demonstrate that the repressive structures of imperial power themselves operate rhizomically rather than monolithically The reason we do not normally think of power operating in this way is that structures of power characterize *themselves* in terms of unities, hierarchies, binaries and centres. Power does not, however, operate in a simple vertical way from the institutions in which it appears to be constituted: it operates dynamically, laterally and inter-mittently. There is no 'master-plan' of imperialism, and its advance is not necessarily secured through violence and oppression. Cultural hegemony operates through an invisible network of filiative connec-tions, psychological internalizations, and unconsciously complicit associations. This is why the term 'post-colonial' is best understood to cover 'all the culture from the moment of colonization to the present' (Ashcroft *et al.* 1989: 2), because the complex operations of imperialism problematize the existence of simple political categories of response or identification such as 'resistance' or 'minority', 'black' or 'white', and arguably even 'colonizer' and 'colonized'. These positions are constantly diffused and intersecting within the rhizome of imperial contact. For colonized cultures, the intermittent and rhizomic nature of imperialism is the most difficult thing to combat because it operates alongside a mythology that asserts the presence of the tap root, the canon, the standard, the patented. It is this *myth* of monolithic power that the categories of marginality are addressing, not the intermittent, overlapping and intertwining nature of its actual operation. For this reason, however appealing certain **anti-colonialist** and **decolonizing** rhetorics may be in offering apparently powerful modes of resistance and opposition, they have sometimes been less than successful in combating older colonialist legacies and **neo-colonialism** whose practices inherit the rhizomic operations of imperialism itself.

Further reading: Deleuze and Guattari 1972, 1980.

SAVAGE/CIVILIZED

The concept of a savage/civilized dichotomy is traceable at least as far back as Homer's *Odyssey*. In English, the *OED* defines 'uncivilized' as 'existing in the lowest stage of culture (1588)'; 'pertaining to or characteristic of savages (1614)'. The notion of civilizing cultures (or persons) goes back at least to 1601: 'To make civil. To bring out a state of barbarism; to instruct in the arts of life; to enlighten and refine.'

The term 'savage' has performed an important service in Euro-centric epistemologies and imperial/colonial ideologies. As Marianna Torgovnik notes, terms like 'primitive, savage, pre-Colombian, tribal, third world, undeveloped, developing, archaic, traditional, exotic, "the anthropological record," non-Western and Other . . . all take the West as norm and define the rest as inferior, different, deviant, subordinate, and sub-ordinateable' (1990: 21).

In 'An Image of Africa', Chinua Achebe, citing Joseph Conrad's *Heart of Darkness*, notes how Africa is used by the West to define and establish its own superiority as a 'civilized' culture against the 'darkness' of a 'primitive' Africa (Achebe 1988). But in the modern world, the West's construction of itself may be regarded as being dependent on the savage/civilized dichotomy in more complex ways. As Torgovnik (speaking from a Western perspective) puts it, our sense of the savage impinges on our sense of ourselves, and it is bound up with the selves who act in the 'real' political world. Freud's map of the psyche placed the ego at the point that mediates between the civilizing super-ego and the 'primitive' libido (or id) (Torgovnik 1990: 17). Whether his map was accurate or not is less important than its strength as a meta-phor for the hierarchized relationship between Europe and its others. Contemporary Westerners thus understand themselves as poised between the 'civilized' and the 'savage', or as clinging to a veneer of civilization over a savage abyss. The Western conception of 'self, whether of 'itself' or of others, is thus forged within the dialectic of these terms.

Noble savage

The best-known expression of the idea of the 'noble savage' is in Rousseau's *A Discourse on Inequality* (1755). The concept arises in the eighteenth century as a European nostalgia for a simple, pure, idyllic state of the natural, posed against rising industrialism and the notion of overcomplications and sophistications of European urban society. This nostalgia creates an image of other cultures as part of Rousseau's criticism of the failure, as he perceived it, of modern European societies to preserve and maintain the natural innocence, freedom and equality of man in a 'natural' state. It creates images of the savage that serve primarily to re-define the European. The crucial fact about the construction is that it produces an ostensibly positive oversimplification of the 'savage' figure, rendering it in this particular form as an idealized rather than a debased stereotype.

Further reading: Barkan and Bush 1995; Jahoda 1999; Maes-Jelinek 1996; Mitchell and Hearn 1999; Nederveen Pieterse 1992; Sawyer 2003; Spurr 1993; Torgovnik 1990.

SETTLER

The *Shorter Oxford Dictionary* defines 'settler' as 'one who settles in a new country; a colonist' (1695) and 'generally: one who settles in a place as a resident' (1815). Within colonial discourse, the settlers generally referred to are Europeans who moved from their countries of origin to European colonies with the intention of remaining. Increasingly the term 'settler-invader' has been used to emphasize the less-than-benign repercussions of such 'settlement', particularly on indigenous peoples.

SETTLER COLONY

In post-colonial/colonial discourse, this term is often used to distinguish between two types of European colonies: settler (or settler-invader) colonies and colonies of occupation. Nigeria and India are examples of colonies of occupation, where indigenous people remained in the majority but were administered by a foreign power. Examples of settler colonies where, over time, the invading Europeans (or their descendants) annihilated, displaced and/or marginalized the indigenes to become a majority non-indigenous population, include Argentina, Australia, Canada and the United States. Like all such designations, however, 'settler colonies' and 'colonies of occupation' provide the abstract poles of a continuum rather than precise descriptive categories or paradigms. The countries of the Caribbean, for example, are not usually considered 'settler colonies', even though the indigenous Caribs and Arawaks were virtually annihilated one hundred years after Columbus' entry into the area. Here the European 'settlers' comprised a relatively small but powerful group of white planters, while the majority of 'settlers' were Africans kidnapped as slaves and forcibly 'settled' in the region. Kenya, Ireland, South Africa, Mozambique and Algeria also provide examples of colonies whose patterns of settlement and cultural and racial legacies fall somewhere between the abstract paradigms of settler colony and colony of occupation.

Many critics and writers have commented on the ambivalent position of settlers in settler colonies, especially where they constitute a racially distinct majority with regard to the indigenous inhabitants or where they have imposed a dominance through force of arms and political institutions (see **apartheid**). Settlers are displaced from their own point of origin and may have difficulties in establishing their identity in the new place (see **exile**). They are frequently constructed within a discourse of difference and inferiority by the colonizing power ('colonials/colonial') and so suffer discrimination as colonial subjects themselves.

At the same time, they act as the agents of that power, and their own identity depends in part, at least initially, on retaining their sense of difference from the 'native' population. In this sense they are simultaneously both colonized and colonizer. Settlers may seek to appropriate icons of the 'native' to their own self-representation, and this can, itself, be a form of oppression where such icons have sacred or social significance alienated by their new usages. On the positive side, as settlers themselves become indigenes in the literal sense, that is, born within the new space, they begin to forge a distinctive and unique culture that is neither that of the metropolitan culture from which they stem, nor that of the 'native' cultures they have displaced in their early colonizing phase. The new culture may, and indeed often does, involve borrowings from both of these prior social and cultural forms. Post-colonial theorists have responded to these new societies and cultures in a wide variety of ways, ranging from those who stress the complicit nature of these cultures and suggest that this is somehow absolute and inescapable (Hodge and Mishra 1990; Mukherjee 1990) to those who see them as defining examples of the rejection of a 'pure' model of culture, a model that is at the heart of the colonial process itself and its sustaining ideology (Brydon 1991; Slemon 1990; Lawson 1991).

Further reading: Ahluwalia 2001; Brydon and Tiffin 1993; Dalziell 2004; Denoon 1979, 1983; Evans 2003; van Herk 1996; Lawson 1995; Lodge 1986; Matthews 1962; Maxwell 1994; Moses 2004; Pearson 2001; Prentice 2004; Russell 2001; Stasiulis and Yuval-Davis 1995; Wolfe 1999.

SLAVE/SLAVERY

Although the institution of slavery has existed since classical times and has occurred in many forms in different societies, it was of particular significance in the formation of many post-colonial societies in Africa and the Caribbean.

Columbus' arrival in the Caribbean in 1492 initiated a period of genocide and enslavement of the native Amerindian peoples. But in 1503, Bishop Las Casas (protector of the Amerindians) proposed an alternative to indigenous labour in the form of systematic importation of blacks, initially to work in the mines. Building on an earlier Spanish and Portuguese practice of enslaving Africans along the Atlantic coast, Charles V granted a patent to a Flemish merchant in 1517 to import 4,000 black slaves per year into Hispaniola, Cuba and Jamaica. The organization of European slavery over the next three centuries has its genesis in this trading concession. It has been estimated that during 300 years of its operation, over 12 million blacks were forcibly shipped in chains across the infamous Atlantic 'Middle Passage' to Brazil, the Caribbean and the United States. Some historians estimate the figure to be much larger. The **'Middle Passage'** was so called because it formed the central section of the euphemistically termed 'triangular trade', whereby goods were bought from Europe to exchange for people at 'factories' on the African coast. On arrival in the Americas, slaves were sold and products such as indigo and sugar were transported back to Europe, the 'hypotenuse' of this triangle.

The negro slave system that was employed and refined over this 300 year period was the extreme form known as commercial slavery, in which slaves were not just made to labour in domestic capacities or forced into concubinage but provided the dominant work-force of entire economies. Early forms of slavery (e.g. Greek and Roman) often granted slaves a much higher degree of freedom, and sometimes even permitted them to be integrated into the social or family group in ways that allowed them to be assimilated and even to acquire power and wealth. The European institutionalization of commercial slavery in the late sixteenth century offered colonizing powers a seemingly endless source of plantation labour, exploited by an ideology of absolute possession in which Africans became objects of European exchange. Commercial slavery was the logical extension both of the need to acquire a cheap labour force for burgeoning planter economies, and of the desire to construct Europe's cultures as 'civilized' in contrast to the **native**, the **cannibal**, and the **savage**.

Although slavery existed in many periods and in many societies (e.g. many African societies had 'slaves'), they were not commercial slaves in this modern sense. Slavery was often associated with exogamous groups, captives or members of other groups outside the community, but the post-Renaissance development of an intense ideology of **racism** produced the peculiarly destructive modern form of commercial, chattel slavery in which all rights and all human values were set aside and from which only a few could ever hope to achieve full manumission (legal freedom). Many of the pseudo-objective, 'scientific' discourses by which colonialism justified its practices flowed from the need to rationalize such an indefensible commercial exploitation and oppression, on a mass scale, of millions of human beings. It has been suggested by some commentators that slavery gave birth to racism, at least in its modern form, just as racism became the excuse for slavery's excesses (Davidson 1994). **Race** and racial prejudice in their modern forms have thus been intimately bound up with the colonial form of the institution of slavery, to the degree that it seems almost impossible to disentangle them.

The slave trade was abolished by most European parliaments in the early 1800s, but the European powers often found it difficult to enforce the new laws, and this was not very successful as each power had a different set of laws and ways of enforcing them. For example, a variety of national laws as to what constituted evidence of a ship engaging in slaving meant that in practice it was hard to prove the offence. Without a ban on the *institution* of slavery, bans on its trade were unlikely to be successful. Yet there were often long delays between these two bans on the trade and on the owning of slaves. Britain, for example, abolished the trade in 1807 but did not outlaw slavery in its possessions until 1833. As a result, the slave system (i.e. plantation slavery) persisted in the Caribbean and some South American areas until the 1830s. France had banned slavery early as the result of its revolutionary liberationist sentiment, but when the freed slaves asserted their independence from central control, as in the case of Toussaint L'Ouverture's revolt in Haiti, the retaliation from the government was swift. As South American countries became independent, they too banned slavery. By 1840, Spain and Portugal had also officially abolished traffic in slaves, but Portuguese ships continued their crossings, remaining a major source of smuggled slaves until late into the nineteenth century. In the newly independent United States, where slavery was a crucial element in the economy, especially of the South, although abolitionism began in the 1830s the banning of slavery did not occur until after the outbreak of the American Civil War. The North proclaimed slaves free in 1861, but only ratified this formally by the 13th amendment to the Constitution in 1865.

When slavery was finally outlawed in colonial systems such as Britain's, it was replaced by an extension of a system of employment called **indentured labour**. Although, as the term implies, indenture contracts were apparently voluntarily entered into, in practice this operated as a system of forced labour, with many of the labourers impressed rather than recruited. Indenture became the main means of securing cheap labour after 1833, supplying the workers for British colonial plantations in locations as widespread as Fiji, Malaya, Northern Queensland and, of course, the Caribbean. Many **diasporic** groups, notably Indians and Chinese, were transported under this system. Consequently, even after the formal abolition of slavery, various forms of forced or contracted labour, such as indenture in English colonies, and debt peonage in Latin America, meant that oppressive labour habits died hard in these regions, where the forms of agriculture developed under the slave system required a continued supply of cheap and controlled labour.

Further reading: Blackburn 1988; Berlin 2004; Berman 2006; Davidson 1994; Durrant 2003; Horton 2004; Klein and Miers 1999; Mackenthun 2000; Manning 1990; Mayer 2000; Plasa and Ring 1994; Sandiford 2000; Thompson 1987; Walvin 1992, 1996.

SPECIESISM

'Speciesism' is the term coined by animal rights philosopher and activist Peter Singer, to designate the belief of most human cultures that they are superior to and very different from other animals. This belief enables humans to justify their killing, eating, abuse, enslavement and experimentation on non-human animals. Peter Singer uses the comparison with human racism to explain the concept:

> Racists violate the principle of equality by giving greater weight to the interests of members of their own race where there is a clash between their interests and the interests of those of another race. Racists of European descent typically have not accepted that pain matters as much when it is felt by Africans, for example, as when it is felt by Europeans. Human speciesists do not accept that pain is as bad when it is felt by pigs or mice as when it is felt by humans.
>
> (Singer 2003: 34)

Though Singer coined the term, he was by no means the first to make such a comparison. Jeremy Bentham, writing at a time when human slavery was still condoned or accepted by most Europeans wrote:

> The day may come when the rest of the animal creation may acquire those rights which never could have been witholden from them but by the hand of Tyranny. The French have already discovered that the blackness of the skin is no reason why a human should be abandoned without redress to the caprice of a tormentor.
>
> (quoted in Singer: 33)

It is important to note, however, that speciesism and racism are not mere analogues. As Jacques Derrida and others have pointed out, racism is actually *predicated* on speciesism, species being the philosophical and instrumental premise of racism. Citing Jacques Derrida and Georges Bataille, Cary Wolfe explains why: 'Our humanist concept of subjectivity is inseparable from the discourse and institution of speciesism' since the 'human' is *by definition* the *not* animal or 'animalistic.' This in turn makes possible a symbolic economy in which we can engage in 'a non-criminal putting to death,' as Derrida phrases it, not only of animals, but of other humans as well by marking them as animals (Wolfe ? 40). It is (and was) by marking 'others' (of whatever sort) as 'animal' that conquest and colonization (as well as other forms of domination) have been, and continue to be justified and prosecuted – on other peoples as well as on non-human animals themselves.

Thus the interrogation of the history, concept and uses of the 'species boundary' is an urgent task for the dismantling of racism as well as speciesism.

Further reading: Crosby 1986; Singer 2003; Wolfe 2003

SUBALTERN

Subaltern, meaning 'of inferior rank', is a term adopted by Antonio Gramsci to refer to those groups in society who are subject to the **hegemony** of the ruling classes. Subaltern classes may include peasants, workers and other groups denied access to 'hegemonic' power. Since the history of the ruling classes is realized in the state, history being the history of states and dominant groups, Gramsci was interested in the historiography of the subaltern classes. In 'Notes on Italian history' (1934–5) he outlined a six point plan for studying the history of the subaltern classes which included: (1) their objective formation; (2) their active or passive affiliation to the dominant political formations; (3) the birth of new parties and dominant groups; (4) the formations that the subaltern groups produce to press their claims; (5) new formations within the old framework that assert the autonomy of the subaltern classes; and other points referring to trade unions and political parties (Gramsci 1971: 52).

Gramsci claimed that the history of the subaltern classes was just as complex as the history of the dominant classes (52), although the history of the latter is usually that which is accepted as 'official' history. For him, the history of subaltern social groups is necessarily fragmented and episodic (54), since they are always subject to the activity of ruling groups, even when they rebel. Clearly they have less access to the means by which they may control their own representation, and less access to cultural and social institutions. Only 'permanent' victory (that is, a revolutionary class adjustment) can break that pattern of subordination, and even that does not occur immediately.

The term has been adapted to post-colonial studies from the work of the Subaltern Studies group of historians, who aimed to promote a systematic discussion of subaltern themes in South Asian Studies. It is used in *Subaltern Studies* 'as a name for the general attribute of sub-ordination in South Asian society whether this is expressed in terms of class, caste, age, gender and office or in any other way' (Guha 1982: vii). The group – formed by Ranajit Guha, and initially including Shahid Amin, David Arnold, Partha Chatterjee, David Hardiman and Gyan Pandey – has produced five volumes of *Subaltern Studies*: essays relating to the history, politics, economics and sociology of subalterneity 'as well as the attitudes, ideologies and belief systems – in short, the culture informing that condition' (vii).

The purpose of the Subaltern Studies project was to redress the imbalance created in academic work by a tendency to focus on élites and élite culture in South Asian historiography. Recognizing that sub-ordination cannot be understood except in a binary relationship with dominance, the group aimed to examine the subaltern 'as an objective assessment of the role of the élite and as a critique of élitist intepretations of that role' (vii). The goals of the group stemmed from the belief that the historiography of Indian nationalism, for instance, had long been dominated by élitism – colonialist élitism and bourgeoise-nationalist élitism – both the consequences of British colonialism. Such historiography suggested that the development of a nationalist consciousness was an exclusively élite achievement either of colonial administrators, policy or culture, or of élite Indian personalities, insti-tutions or ideas. Consequently, asserts Guha, such writing cannot acknowledge or interpret the contribution made by people *on their own*, that is, independently of the élite. What is clearly left out by the class outlook of such historiography is a 'politics of the people' (4), which, he claims, is an autonomous domain that continued to operate when the élite politics became outmoded.

One clear demonstration of the difference between the élite and the subaltern lies in the nature of political mobilization: élite mobilization was achieved vertically through adaptation of British parliamentary institutions, while the subaltern relied on the traditional organization of kinship and territoriality or class associations. Popular mobilization in the colonial period took the form of peasant uprisings, and the contention is that this remains a primary locus of political action, despite the change in political structure (6). This is very different from the claims of élite historiography that Indian nationalism was primarily an idealist venture in which the indigenous élite led the people from subjugation to freedom.

Despite the great diversity of subaltern groups, the one invariant feature was a notion of resistance to élite domination. The failure of the bourgeoisie to speak for the nation meant that the nation of India failed 'to come into its own', and for Guha 'it is the study of this failure which constitutes the central problematic of Indian historiography' (7). Clearly the concept of the subaltern is meant to cut across several kinds of political and cultural binaries, such as colonialism vs. nationalism, or imperialism vs. indigenous cultural expression, in favour of a more general distinction between subaltern and élite, because, suggests Guha, this subaltern group is invariably overlooked in studies of political and cultural change.

The notion of the subaltern became an issue in post-colonial theory when Gayatri Spivak critiqued the assumptions of the Subaltern Studies group in the essay 'Can the subaltern speak?' This question, she claims, is one that the group *must* ask. Her first criticism is directed at the Gramscian claim for the *autonomy* of the subaltern group, which, she says, no amount of qualification by Guha – who concedes the diversity, heterogeneity and overlapping nature of subaltern groups – can save from its fundamentally essentialist premise. Second, no methodology for determining who or what might constitute this group can avoid this essentialism. The 'people' or the 'subaltern' is a group defined by its difference from the élite.

To guard against essentialist views of subalterneity Guha suggests that there is a further distinction to be made between the subaltern and dominant indigenous groups at the regional and local levels. However, Guha's attempt to guard against essentialism, by specifying the range of subaltern groups, serves only, according to Spivak, to problematize the idea of the subaltern itself still further. 'The task of research is to investigate, identify and measure the *specific* nature of the degree of *deviation* of [the dominant indigenous groups at the regional and local level] from the ideal [the subaltern] and situate it historically' (Spivak 1985b: 27). But, asks Spivak, 'what taxonomy can fix such a space?' For the 'true' subaltern group, she says, whose identity is its difference, there is no unrepresentable subaltern subject that can know and speak itself. One cannot construct a category of the subaltern that has an effective voice clearly and unproblematically identifiable as such, a voice that does not at the same time occupy many other possible speaking positions.

Spivak goes on to elaborate the problems of the category of the subaltern by looking at the situation of gendered subjects and of Indian women in particular, for 'both as an object of colonialist historiography and as a subject of insurgency, the ideological construction of gender keeps the male dominant' (28). For if 'in the context of colonial production, the subaltern has no history and cannot speak, the subaltern as female is even more deeply in shadow' (28). Spivak examines the position of Indian women through an analysis of a particular case, and concludes with the declaration that 'the subaltern cannot speak'. This has sometimes been interpreted to mean that there is no way in which oppressed or politically marginalized groups can voice their resistance, or that the subaltern only has a dominant language or a dominant voice in which to be heard. But Spivak's target is the concept of an unproblematically constituted subaltern identity, rather than the subaltern subject's ability to give voice to political concerns. Her point is that no act of dissent or resistance occurs on behalf of an essential subaltern subject entirely separate from the dominant discourse that provides the language and the conceptual categories with which the subaltern voice speaks. Clearly, the existence of post-colonial discourse itself is an example of such speaking, and in most cases the dominant language or mode of representation is **appropriated** so that the **marginal** voice can be heard.

Further reading: Beverley 1999, 2004b; Chakrabarty and Bhabha 2002; Coronil 1999; Davis and Gross 1994; Gopal 2004; Gramsci 1971; Guha 1982, 1997, 2001; Guha and Spivak 1988; Koshy 2005; Mignolo 1994, 2000a, 2000b; Moraña and Hallstead 2004; Prakash *et al.* 1999; Spivak 1985b, 2003.

SUBJECT/SUBJECTIVITY

The question of the subject and subjectivity directly affects colonized peoples' perceptions of their identities and their capacities to resist the conditions of their domination, their 'subjection'. The status of the human individual was one of the key features of Enlightenment philosophy. Descartes' declaration that 'I think, therefore I am' confirmed the centrality of the autonomous human individual, a founding precept of humanism, a precept that effectively separated the subject from the object, thought from reality, or the self from the other. The individual, autonomous 'I' was one that operated in the world according to this separation and was no longer to be seen as merely operated upon by divine will or cosmic forces. The individual self was separate from the world and could employ intellect and imagination in understanding and representing the world. The autonomous human consciousness was seen to be the source of action and meaning rather than their product. This is a position referred to as 'Cartesian individualism', one that tended to overlook or downplay the significance of social relations or the role of language in forming the self.

Although debate about subject–object relations continued in European philosophy throughout the nineteenth century, with the critique of subject-centred reason culminating in Nietzsche's philosophy, the most influential contemporary shift in this Enlightenment position began in the thinking of Freud and Marx. Freud's theories of the unconscious dimensions of the self revealed that there were aspects of the individual's formation that were not accessible to thought, and which thus blurred the distinction between the subject and object. Marx, in assessing the importance of the economic structure of society to the lives of individual workers, made the famous claim that 'It is not the consciousness of men that determines their being, but, on the contrary, their social being that determines their consciousness.' The combined effect of these two thinkers upon twentieth-century thought was radically to disturb the notion of the integrity and autonomy of the human individual, the theory of subjectivity becoming more formally elaborated by their followers.

The concept of subjectivity problematizes the simple relationship between the individual and language, replacing human nature with the concept of the production of the human subject through ideology, discourse or language. These are seen as determining factors in the construction of individual identity, which itself becomes an *effect* rather than a cause of such factors. The overlap between theories of ideology, psychoanalysis and post-structuralism has amounted to a considerable attack upon the Enlightenment assertion of individual autonomy, and continuing debate centres on the capacity of the subject so formed by these broad social and cultural forces either to disrupt or to undermine them.

Ideology

The most influential development of Marx's notion of 'social being' was Louis Althusser's theory of the subject's construction by ideology. Ideology is the system of ideas that explains, or makes sense of, a society, and according to Marx is the mechanism by which unequal social relations are reproduced. The ruling classes not only rule, they rule as thinkers and producers of ideas so that they determine how the society sees itself (*hegemony*). This 'misrepresentation' of meaning and social relations is referred to by Marx as 'false consciousness', or a false view of one's 'true' social condition, something that has a coercive power over the subordinate classes. But for Althusser, ideology is not just a case of the powerful imposing their ideas on the weak: subjects are 'born into' ideology, they find subjectivity within the expectations of their parents and their society, and they endorse it because it provides a sense of identity and security through structures such as language, social codes and conventions. In ideology, the subjects also represent to themselves 'their relation to those conditions of existence which is represented to them there' (Althusser 1984: 37). That is, subjects collude with ideology by allowing it to provide social meaning.

Ideology is perpetuated, according to Althusser, by ideological state apparatuses such as church, education, police, which **interpellate** subjects, that is, apparatuses that 'call people forth' as subjects, and which provide the conditions by which, and the contexts in which, they obtain subjectivity. Interpellation has been explained in the following way: when a policeman hails you with the call 'Hey you!', the moment you turn round to acknowledge that you are the object of his attention, you have been interpellated in a particular way, as a particular kind of subject. Ideological State Apparatuses interpellate subjects in this way. For Althusser, the subject is the individual's self-consciousness as constructed by those institutions. Despite what many critics have seen as the extreme functionalism of this view of subjectivity, the concept of interpellation is still useful for describing how the 'subject' is located and constructed by specific ideological and discursive operations, particularly formations such as **colonial discourse**. Although ideology serves the interests of the ruling classes, it is not static or unchangeable, and its materiality has certain important consequences. For while ideology is dominant, it is also contradictory, fragmentary and inconsistent and does not necessarily or inevitably blindfold the 'interpellated' subject to a perception of its operations.

Psychoanalysis

Perhaps the most influential development of Freud's theories of the unconscious was made by Jacques Lacan's combination of psychoanalysis and structuralist analysis of language. He contended that Freud's major insight was not that the unconscious exists, but that it has a structure – the 'unconscious is structured like a language,' but it is a 'language which escapes the subject in its operation and effects'. The similarity to the structure of language was crucial to Lacan because the subject itself is produced through language in the same way that language produces meaning.

The subject is formed through a series of stages. In an initial stage the infant exists as a dependent and uncoordinated complex of limbs and sounds that can form no distinction between self and other. In the second stage, the 'mirror stage', the infant begins to distinguish itself from the other by perceiving a split between the 'I' that looks, and the 'I' that is reflected in the mirror. While this need not refer to an actual mirror, the 'other' who is perceived as separate from the self appears to have the unity and control of itself that the perceiving 'I' lacks. Although such control is *imaginary*, the infant nevertheless desires that which it lacks and sees it in the image of the other. Because the child is held up to the mirror by the mother, or sees itself 'reflected', so to speak, in the gaze of the mother, it also sees its similarity to, and difference from, the mother, who becomes the first love object, the first locus of desire. The final stage is an entry into language, a passing from the imaginary phase to the symbolic order in which the subject comes to discover that the locus of power is now located in the 'phallus'. This principle is also called the Law of the Father, and Lacan's theory asserts that the subject obtains an understanding of its gender at the same time as it enters into language. Entering this stage, the subject is both *produced* in language and *subjected* to the laws of the symbolic that pre-exist it. The laws of language are themselves metonymic of the cultural complex of laws and rules and conventions into which the subject moves and through which it obtains identity.

Though the subject may speak, it does so only in terms that the laws of language allow. Just as Saussure had argued that the signs that make up a language do not name a pre-existing reality but *produce* it through a system of differences, so Lacan argues that the position of the 'I' within language, the subject, does not simply represent the presence of a subject that pre-exists it, but produces it by a system of differentiations between the 'I' and that which is not 'I'. This distinction is not static but continuous, the subject being in a continual process of development.

Such a process forms a basis for Derrida's rejection of the concept of 'presence'. Both subjectivity and the language that produces it constitute a process in which meaning is never fully present in any utterance but is continually deferred.

Lacan's theory of the development of the subject has given rise to other approaches, notably those of feminist critics such as Kristeva, Cixous and Irigary, who concede the importance of language to subjectivity but who contest Lacan's privileging of the phallus, despite its imaginary status. These theorists emphasize the 'feminine' or androgynous aspects of pre-Oedipal language and its potential for development outside the confines of the patriarchally dominated symbolic order.

Discourse

The construction of subjectivity within certain historical, social and cultural systems of knowledge in a society has been elaborated in the work of Michel Foucault. Just as the subject, in psychoanalytical terms, is produced by, and must operate within, the laws of language, so discourse produces a subject equally dependent upon the rules of the system of knowledge that produces it. In this respect, discourse is both wider and more varied than either ideology or language, different subjects being produced by different discourses, but the processes by which the subject is produced is the same. An example of Foucault's approach to subjectivity was his rejection of the author as an originator of meaning. In the essay 'What is an author?' he argues that 'it is a matter of depriving the subject (or its substitute) of its role as originator, and as analysing the subject as a variable and complex function of discourse' (1979: 209). In regard to the authors of texts, we now need to understand how the author function is situated in discourse. 'The author function is therefore characteristic of the mode of existence, circulation, and functioning of certain discourses within the society' (202).

Similarly, other subjects are constructed by the circulation of certain systems of knowledge. Foucault provides detailed analyses of the ways in which power is exercised to produce and control (to 'subject') individual subjects through systems of knowledge about the 'criminal', the 'pervert' and the 'lunatic' within the discourses of criminality, sexuality and psychiatry. Within any historical period, various discourses compete for control of subjectivity, but these discourses are always a function of the power of those who control the discourse to determine knowledge and truth. Thus, while a person may be the subject of various discourses, subjectivity will be produced by the discourse that dominates at the time.

Post-structuralism

In structuralist and post-structuralist thought, then, the subject could be thought of as a 'site' rather than a 'centre' or a 'presence', something where things happen, or upon which things happen, rather than something that made things happen. Culler, for example, suggests that as the self is broken down into component systems and is deprived of its status as a source and master of meaning, it comes to seem more and more like a construct. 'Even the idea of personal identity emerges through the discourse of a culture: the "I" is not something given but comes to exist as that which is addressed by and related to others' (1981: 33).

Derrida's critique of logo-centrism and the metaphysics of presence has led to perhaps the most radical view of the subject: the claim that any 'concept of a (conscious or unconscious) subject necessarily refers to the concept of substance — and thus of presence — out of which it was born' (Smith 1988: 46). So there can be no concept at all of subjectivity without a partaking in the same metaphysics of presence that under-lies the notion of the autonomous individual. In this sense, Derrida appears to be aiming to undermine not only the Cartesian notion of individuality but any notion of a fixed subject. Paul Smith has indicated the great contradiction this produces in Derrida's own work when we begin to think of the position of the deconstructive critic: 'The supposed agent of deconstructive practice is then, paradoxical insofar as it acts, has effects, produces texts, and so on; but still its role is passively to encounter forces which do not depend on it' (50).

The problems inherent in a view of subjectivity as *produced* by broader social forces focus at precisely this point. For if the subject is produced by ideology, discourse or language, is it trapped in this subjectivity beyond the power of choice, recognition or resistance? Frantz Fanon refers to a version of the process by which subjects are produced by ideology or discourse when he says that 'Colonialism is fighting . . . to maintain the identity of the image it has of the Algerian and the depreciated image that the Algerian has of himself (Fanon 1959: 30). Colonial discourse constructs a particular kind of subject with which the subject itself can and often does concur because of its powerlessness. The fact that a statement such as Fanon's can be made suggests that the process of subject construction by discourse can be recognized and therefore contested. Whether the subject can do so in isolation from the social construction and political organization of resistance is a matter of debate. Fanon was the first to examine the psychology of colonialism and its effects on the colonized, and in

EILLANCE

the conclusion to *Black Skin: White Masks* he rhetorically proclaims an almost Cartesian **agency** for the colonized subject: 'I am my own foundation. And it is by going beyond the historical, instrumental hypothesis that I will initiate the cycle of my freedom' (Fanon 1952: 231). And again, 'It is through the effort to recapture the self and to scrutinize the self, it is through the lasting tension of their freedom that men will be able to create the ideal conditions of existence for a human world' (232).

Further reading: Ashcroft 2000; Bhabha 1994; Bhatt 2002; Buchholtz 2004; Easthope and McGowan 1992; Fanon 1952, 1959; Foster 1999; Green *et al.* 1996; Michel 1995; P.K. Mishra 2000; Ray 1999; Smith 1988; Varadharajan 1995; Werbner and Stoller 2002.

SURVEILLANCE

One of the most powerful strategies of imperial dominance is that of surveillance, or observation, because it implies a viewer with an elevated vantage point, it suggests the power to process and understand that which is seen, and it objectifies and **interpellates** the colonized subject in a way that fixes its identity in relation to the surveyor. The importance of the gaze has been emphasized by Lacan, since the gaze of the mother in the mirror phase is the initial process by which identity is achieved (see **subject/subjectivity**; **Other/other**; **Othering**). This gaze corresponds to the 'gaze of the *grande-autre*' within which the identification, objectification and subjection of the subject are simultaneously enacted: the imperial gaze defines the identity of the subject, objectifies it within the identifying system of power relations and confirms its subalterneity and powerlessness.

Foucault in his *Discipline and Punish* describes the profound importance of the introduction of surveillance into the prison system by means of the 'panopticon' – Jeremy Bentham's eighteenth-century design for a circular prison divided into individual cells, all of which could be observed from a single vantage point. This was a form of prison architecture in which guards could maintain constant vigil over the imprisoned. Such surveillance revolutionized the effectiveness of incarceration because its power came from the assumption of the incarcerated that they were always under surveillance and therefore must always act as if they were. For the observer, sight confers power; for the observed, visibility is powerlessness. Clearly, the discipline instilled by the panopticon, and its imposition of 'constant' surveillance, provides a powerful metaphor for the 'disciplinary' operation of dominant discourse of all kinds.

The panopticon remains a powerful metaphor for the surveillance of inmates in all 'total institutions' such as mental asylums, whatever their physical architecture. One consequence of such surveillance is termed 'conversion' by Erving Goffman. This is the process where-by 'the inmate appears to take over the official or staff view of himself and tries to act out the role of the perfect inmate . . . presenting him-self as someone whose institutional enthusiasm is always at the disposal of the staff' (1961:63). In this case the 'official view' is directly connected to the power exerted by the institution over the inmate's actions. The process of conversion in colonization is far more subtle but just as potent. Whereas imperial power over the colonized subject may not be necessarily as direct and physical as it is in a 'total' institution, power over the subject may be exerted in myriad ways, enforced by the threat of subtle kinds of cultural and moral disapproval and exclusion. The colonized subject may accept the imperial view, including the array of values, assumptions and cultural expectations on which this is based, and order his or her behaviour accordingly. This will produce colonial subjects who are 'more English than the English', those whom V.S. Naipaul called 'The Mimic Men' in the novel of that name. More often, such conversion will be ambivalent, attenuated, intermittent and diffused by feelings of resistance to imperial power, leading to what Homi Bhabha calls 'mimicry', a 'conversion' that always teeters on the edge of menace.

Surveillance of colonial space is a regular feature of **exploration and travel** writing. The emergence of 'landscape' and the concomitant desire for a commanding view that could provide a sweeping visual mastery of the scene was an important feature of eighteenth- and nineteenth-century poetry and fiction. It became a significant method by which European explorers and travellers could obtain a position of panoramic observation, itself a representation of knowledge and power over colonial space. The desire for a literal position of visual command is metaphoric of the 'panoptic' operation of the imperial gaze in which the observed find themselves constituted. When a writer takes this position, as occurs time and again in **Orientalist** discourse, the invulnerable position of the observer affirms the political order and the binary structure of power that made that position possible. As in the panopticon, the writer 'is placed either above or at the centre of things, yet apart from them so that the organization and classification of things takes place according to the writer's own system of value' (Spurr 1993: 16).

The writing of explorers and travellers in the nineteenth century who adopted the motif of 'monarch of all I survey' gives clearest evidence of the panoramic nature of the imperial gaze, but it may be found also in the description of interiors or in accounts of the surveillance of the body itself. David Spurr gives this account of a passage from the explorer Stanley's journal:

> She is of light brown complexion, with broad round face, large eyes and small but full lips. She had a quiet modest demeanour, though her dress was but a narrow fork clout of bark cloth. . . . I notice when her arms are held against the light, a whitey-brown fell on them. Her skin has not the silky smoothness of touch common to the Zanzibaris, but altogether she is a very pleasing little creature.
>
> (Spurr 1993: 23)

'The eye treats the body as a landscape: it proceeds systematically from part to part, quantifying and spatializing, noting color and texture, and finally passing an aesthetic judgement which stressed the body's role as object to be viewed' (23). The woman has been captured during a skirmish, a reminder that the freedom of the gaze depends on the security of the position from which it is being directed.

This concept of the gaze becomes important for post-colonial discourse because such surveillance, which corresponds to and confirms the gaze of colonial authority, may be reversed. This is, in Bhabha's formulation, a particularly potent aspect of the menace in **mimicry**: the displacing gaze of the disciplined, where the observer becomes the observed and 'partial' representation rearticulates the whole notion of *identity* and alienates it from its essence. The metaphoric displacing and returning of the imperial gaze is a fundamental operation of the **appropriation** of imperial technologies, discourses and cultural forms. The colonized subject not only alters these to local needs but uses them to direct the gaze upon the colonizer and thus reverse the orientation of power in the relationship.

Further reading: Foucault 1977; Johnston 2002; Roy 1995; Spurr 1993.

SYNCRETISM

A term sometimes used to avoid the problems some critics have associated with the idea of **hybridity** in identifying the fusion of two distinct traditions to produce a new and distinctive whole (see **synergy**). The term is often used in religious studies, but it has also found favour in theatre criticism with references to a syncretic performance tradition or a syncretic ritual.

SYNERGY

A term used to emphasize that post-colonial cultures are the product of a number of forces variously contributing to a new and complex cultural formation. Synergy, referring to the product of two (or more) forces that are reduceable to neither is perhaps a way of escaping from some of the less fortunate aspects of the term **hybridity**, which, as critics such as Robert Young have shown, has a complex and limiting history in nineteenth-century colonial usage (Young 1995). Other terms such as syncretic have occasionally been essayed to avoid the problem some critics perceive to exist with the term hybridity. But the widespread usage of the term syncretic in religious and theological texts has also tended to make its usage limited by its strong associations with these specialist fields. Synergy seems to offer some advantages, as it emphasizes the positive and energetic aspects of the process of **transculturation** and the equal but different elements that the various historical periods and forces have contributed in forming the modern post-colonial condition.

TESTIMONIO

A *testimonio* is a novel or novella–length narrative, told in the first person by a narrator who is also the actual protagonist or witness of the events she or he recounts. The unit of narration is usually a life or a significant life episode, such as the experience of being a prisoner. Since in many cases the narrator is someone who is either functionally illiterate, or, if literate, not a professional writer or intellectual, the production of a *testimonio* generally involves the recording, transcription and editing of an oral account by an interlocutor who is a journalist, writer or social activist (Beverley and Zimmerman 1990: 173). It is a particular and effective example of a form of writing that **appropriates** dominant forms of imperial discourse to create powerful **subaltern** voices.

The aspects of its production, its **oral** nature, its mediation through an intermediary, usually a First World interlocutor, are the source of most of the theoretical issues raised by this genre, particularly the question of **authenticity** and the effect of the interlocutor on the text, because 'the contradictions of sex, class, race, age that frame the narrative's production can also reproduce themselves in the relation of the narrator to this direct interlocutor' (176).

Generally associated with Latin America, *testimonio* coalesces as a clearly defined genre around the decision in 1970 of Cuba's cultural centre, *Casa de las Américas*, to begin awarding a prize in this category in their annual literary contest (173). However, *Testimonio*-like texts have existed for a long time (though without that name) at the margins of literature in many post-colonial cultures, representing in particular those subjects – the child, the 'native', the woman, the insane, the criminal, the proletarian – excluded from authorized representation when it was a question of speaking or writing for themselves. For example, missionary tracts dealing with native life or with the stories of ex-slaves who have converted are frequently cast in the form of such accounts of native life as 'told to' or as 'transcribed by' the missionary author.

The word testimony suggests the act of testifying or bearing witness in a legal or religious sense, distinguishing it from simple recorded participant narrative. In René Jara's phrase it is a '*narración de urgencia*' – a story that needs to be told – involving a problem of repression, poverty, subalterneity, exploitation, or simply struggle for survival, which is implicated in the act of narration itself (Vidal and Jara 1986: 3). The existence of the genre at the margins of literature, its occupation of a zone of indeterminacy between speaking and writing, between literature and history, between autobiography and communal record, between the personal and the political statement, makes it most interesting for comparison with other post-colonial interventions into imperial discourse. More recently the relations of texts produced by interlocutors have been developed into broader ways of considering the complex role of oral testimony and narratives in establishing the **agency** of the indigenous voice in other post-colonial **contact zones** where societies were characterized by orality e.g. Africa. Although the term *testimonio* has not usually been applied to these texts, they represent a similar stage in the process of relations between post-colonial subjects and the texts in which they are voiced. Although the earliest life stories and personal accounts of such societies and their people were produced under the controlling **patronage** of First World interlocutors (e.g. **missionaries**) recent accounts have stressed that even under these most unpromising of conditions these texts can reveal the hidden subjects of the text, uncovering the controlling inscriptive practices of the inter-locutor and revealing the occluded voice of the indigenous subject (see Griffiths 2000; 2004; 2005).

Further reading: Bartow 2005; Behr 2004; Beverley 1989, 2004a; Beverley and Zimmerman 1990; De Costa 2002; Denegri 2003; Dulfano 2004; Gugelberger 1996; Gugelberger and Kearney 1991; Liano 2003; Nance 2006.

THIRD WORLD (FIRST, SECOND, FOURTH)

The term 'Third World' was first used in 1952 during the so-called Cold War period, by the politician and economist Alfred Sauvy, to designate those countries aligned with neither the United States nor the Soviet Union. The term 'First World' was used widely at the time to designate the dominant economic powers of the West, whilst the term 'Second World' was employed to refer to the Soviet Union and its satellites, thus distinguishing them from the First World. The wider political and economic base of the concept was established when the First World was sometimes used also to refer to economically successful ex-colonies such as Canada, Australia and, less frequently, South Africa, all of which were linked to a First World network of global capitalism and Euro-American defence alliances.

Very quickly, 'Third World images' became a journalistic cliché invoking ideas of poverty, disease and war and usually featuring pictures of emaciated African or Asian figures, emphasizing the increasing racialization of the concept in its popular (Western) usage. The term was, however, also used as a general metaphor for any underdeveloped society or social condition anywhere: 'Third World conditions', Third World educational standards', etc., reinforcing the pejorative stereotyping of approximately two-thirds of the member nations of the United Nations who were usually classified as Third World countries. As obvious economic differentials began to emerge within this group, with economic developments in the various regions, notably Asia, the term 'Fourth World' was introduced by some economists to designate the lowest group of nations on their economic scale.

Recent post-colonial usage differs markedly from this classic use in economics and development studies, with the term 'Third World' being less and less in evidence in the discourse. This has been defended by some post-colonial critics on the grounds that the term is essentially pejorative. But in the United States in particular the increasing tendency to avoid the term in post-colonial commentary, as well as the decline in the use of terms such as anti-colonial in course descriptions and in academic texts, has sometimes been criticized as leading to a de-politicization of the decolonizing project. The term 'Second World' has been employed also in recent post-colonial criticism by some **settler colony** critics to designate settler colonies such as Australia and Canada (Lawson 1991, 1994; Slemon 1990) to emphasize their differ-ence from colonies of occupation. The term 'Fourth World' is also now more commonly employed to designate those groups such as pre-settler **indigenous peoples** whose economic status and oppressed condition, it is argued, place them in an even more marginalized position in the social and political hierarchy than other post-colonial peoples (Brotherston 1992).

Further reading: Brotherston 1992; Deena 1997; Dirlik 1996; Harris 1992; Hasseler 1997; Katrak 2006; Larsen 1997; Lazarus 2004; Prasad 1997; R.S. Rajan 1997; San Juan 1995a; Sauvy 1952; Shohat 1997.

TRANSCULTURATION

This term refers to the reciprocal influences of modes of representa-tion and cultural practices of various kinds in colonies and metropoles, and is thus 'a phenomenon of the contact zone', as Mary Louise Pratt puts it. The term has been used by ethnographers to describe how subordinated or marginal groups select and invent from materials transmitted to them by a dominant or metropolitan culture (e.g. Taussig 1993). The word was coined in the 1940s by Cuban sociologist Fernando Ortiz (1978) in relation to Afro-Cuban culture. Uraguayan critic Angel Rama incorporated the term into literary studies in the 1970s. Ortiz proposed the term to replace the paired concepts of accul-turation and deculturation that described the transference of culture in reductive fashion, one imagined from within the interests of the metropoles (Pratt 1992: 228). Though such influences may be 'recip-rocal', Pratt is careful to note that 'contact zones' are social spaces where 'disparate cultures meet, clash and grapple with each other, often in highly asymmetrical relations of dominance and subordination – like colonialism, slavery, or their aftermaths as they are lived out across the globe today' (4).

The concept raises several sets of questions, according to Pratt: How are metropolitan modes of representation received and appropriated at the periphery? How does one speak of transculturation from the colonies to the metropolis? How have Europe's constructions of subordinated others been shaped by those others? How have those constructions been shaped by the constructions of themselves and their habitats that they presented to the Europeans?

> While the imperial metropolis tends to understand itself as determining the periphery (in the emanating glow of the civilizing mission or the cash flow of development), it habitually blinds itself to the ways in which the periphery determines the metropolis, beginning, perhaps with the latter's obsessive need to present and represent its peripheries and its others continually to itself.
>
> (Pratt 1992: 6)

Further reading: Cornejo Polar and Dennis 2004; Fitz 2001; García 2006; Kokotovic 2005; Medeiros-Lichem 2004; Mignolo 2003; Monasterios 2004; Ortiz 1978; Pratt 1992; Rama 1982; Spitta 1995; Taylor 2003.

TRANSNATIONAL LITERATURES

A term that is rapidly increasing in use in response to deficiencies observed in the terms 'post-colonial literatures' and 'diasporic literatures' in referring to cross-cultural literary writing. In general the term refers to literature written by people who have immigrated or in some other way travelled from a homeland; to literatures written in a second language; or to literatures with a cross-cultural theme. These literatures may be produced in situations that are neither a direct consequence of colonialism, nor comply with the major features of diaspora. For example, literatures written by South Asians or South-East Asians in America, although written in a language that has resulted from a history of colonialism, cannot said to be 'post-colonial' in the same way as literatures written in those locations. But neither are they 'diasporic' in the ways in which that term is usually understood – as subjects who are fundamentally 'absent' from their home nation. Although their themes may revolve around similar issues of dislocation, ambivalence, cultural clash and loss, this is not necessarily always the case. Such literatures are produced by writers who are generally more affluent, more mobile than populations regarded as diasporic, who may feel 'at home' in several locations rather than 'exiled' from home and who spend time travelling, and even living in two or more locations. In this respect the term takes better account of the increasing fluidity of global populations. Furthermore, transnational literatures generally have better access to major metropolitan publishing houses and authors who are more attuned to global issues. It is probably true, however, that the term continues to refer to the same constituencies as post-colonial and diasporic writing. Although equally applicable, the term is less likely to be used with regard to an Italian writing in Russia than to a Sri Lankan writing in America.

Further reading: Jackson, Crang and Dwyer (2004); Lionnet and Shu-mei (2005); Levitt and Waters (2002)

TRANSLATION

The interpretation of the meaning of a text in one language (the 'source text') and the production, in another language, of an equivalent text (the 'target text,' or 'translation'), which ostensibly communicates the same message. Translation has long been a contentious area of literary study and questions of felicity or faithfulness to the original versus beauty, or the adequate transference of aesthetic form have received increased and especially nuanced attention in post-colonial theory. The process of translation must take into account a number of factors, including context, the rules of grammar of both languages, their writing conventions, and the cultural nuances of the translated text. An accepted convention of translation studies is that a translation is always more effective if undertaken by a translator in the target language into which the text is being translated. In post-colonial situations however (such as in India), many translators may be equally fluent in both source and target languages.

Translation has become an issue of growing importance in post-colonial studies, particularly with regard to the translation of literary texts from local languages to world languages such as English. It has emerged as a contentious issue in response to the tendency of post-colonial literary studies to concentrate on writing in English. Post-colonial studies themselves emerged from Anglophone literature departments and apart from the tension this has caused amongst Francophone and Latin American theorists, the ignoring of local literatures has led to the vigorous entry of translation into the post-colonial theoretical landscape. As a result the principle of translating indigenous and local literatures has become an important issue in the debate about the dominance of English. For some writers and critics in post-colonial societies the dominance of English texts in post-colonial theory has led to a negative characterization of post-colonial theory. This is especially so in regions where vigorous traditions of writing in the pre-colonial languages continued to exist before and after colonization, e.g. India and South-East Asia. In parts of Africa where oral traditions were very developed and where these led to writing in local languages during and after the colonial period a similar response has occurred (see Barber 1995, Barber and Furniss 2006, Ngugi 1981a). These writers argue that post-colonial critics with a Euro-American orientation in their work have acted to focus attention on English texts and so divert attention from texts in local languages. They contend that this continues to reflect the power relations of colonizer and colonized and the patronage systems for the publication and distribution of texts this engendered. Thus translation is also seen as problematic in so far as it continues to privilege English texts over those in local languages with a flow-on effect for the status of those langauges within their own communities. This is underpinned by the fact that English (or another colonial language) tends to be the language used by the post-colonial élite and secures them in power (Ngugi 1981b, 1986). Local language groups see the production of literatures in their languages as a precious, vast and untapped cultural resource. Nevertheless, others have argued that in post-colonial terms the translation of a large number of indigenous novels into English opens up a potentially huge readership both in the post-colonial countries themselves, e.g. India and the world. Such a cultural resource becomes, through translation, a vehicle of cultural communication, and perhaps a mode of cultural survival.

Further reading: Barber 1995; Barber and Furniss 2006; Bassnett 2002; Bassnett and Trivedi; Munday 2001; Rahmen 2002; Robinson 2000; Venuti 2004.

UNIVERSALISM/UNIVERSALITY

The assumption that there are irreducible features of human life and experience that exist beyond the constitutive effects of local cultural conditions. Universalism offers a **hegemonic** view of existence by which the experiences, values and expectations of a dominant culture are held to be true for all humanity. For this reason, it is a crucial feature of imperial hegemony, because its assumption (or assertion) of a common humanity – its failure to acknowledge or value cultural difference – underlies the promulgation of imperial discourse for the 'advancement' or 'improvement' of the colonized, goals that thus mask the extensive and multifaceted exploitation of the colony.

One of the most persistent examples of this phenomenon occurs in English literature, where the value or 'greatness' of a writer's work is proven by the extent to which it depicts the 'universal human condition'. By this means, the link between the universal and the Euro-centric, and in particular the link between universality and the canon of texts that represents English literature, remains intact as an implicit feature of the discourse wherever it is taught. It was the power of this discourse to present the English subject as both attractive and universal that rendered it such an effective tool of socio-political control in India in the nineteenth century and in other colonies in the nineteenth and twentieth centuries, and it is the resilience of this notion of the universal that has maintained a cultural hegemony long after independence throughout the post-colonial world (Viswanathan 1989).

As Homi Bhabha points out, the effects of universalism upon reading are not only that some immanent, universal meaning is produced in the text but that it constructs the reader as someone in whom all conflict is resolved, a reading subject who cannot see how it might itself be ideologically implicated in the historical conflicts it sees in the text:

> Universalism does not merely end with a view of immanent 'spiritual' meaning produced in the text. It also interpellates, for its reading, a subject positioned at the point where conflict and difference resolves and all ideology ends. It is not that the Transcendental subject cannot *see* historical conflict or colonial difference as mimetic structures or themes in the text. What it cannot conceive is how it is itself structured ideologically and discursively in relation to those processes of signification which do not then allow for the possibility of whole or universal meanings.
>
> (Bhabha 1984a: 104)

Therefore not only is the subject of English literature the universal human subject, but the reader is the universal ('cultured') reader, removed from any consideration of the material conditions of the local and present experience of colonization and exploitation.

Charles Larson gives an account of his teaching a Thomas Hardy novel to African students, and recounts the ways in which his initial universalist cultural assumptions were exposed by local experience. Larson was stunned when asked the question 'What is a kiss?' What is natural in one society is not 'natural' at all, he discovered, but cultural. 'How was one to read a Thomas Hardy novel with all those frustrated kisses,' he asks, 'without ever having been kissed?'

One of the more intriguing examples of universalism is indicated by Alan Bishop, who points out that the apparently culture-free discourse of mathematics, whose universal truths appear indisputable, is actually a very culturally determined mode of imperialist discourse. Certainly, Bishop argues, wherever you are in the world, the degrees in a triangle add up to 180; but, he asks,

> Where do degrees come from? Why is the total 180? Why not 200, or 100? Indeed, why are we interested in triangles and their properties at all? The answer to all of these questions is, essentially, 'because some people determined it should be that way'. Mathematical ideas, like my other ideas, are humanly constructed. They have a cultural history.
>
> (Bishop 1990: 52)

Not only are there many different forms of mathematics, but the mathematics that are now held to be universal are constituted by certain cultural modes of thought such as rationalism, atomism and objectism, which are particularly characteristic of the philosophical traditions of European societies. One of the most interesting things about universalism is its pervasiveness and the subtlety with which it re-emerges, even in those sensitive to cultural differences and strongly disposed to radical analysis. David Suzuki's study, for instance, which attempts to draw epistemological parallels between native American cosmology and Western science, fails to question why such a comparison should be desirable or necessary. Such parallelism becomes, in its unreflexive nature, a mode of universalism that cannot escape holding Western science as a 'real' ground of comparison, or assuming that the native American and Western worlds are the same.

Further reading: Achebe 1988; Anderson 1998; Assiter 2003; Bishop 1990; Browning 2006; Chakrabarty 2000; Larson 1973; Lawson 2006; Lazarus *et al.* 1995; Lionnet 1998; Lott 2000; Newman 2000; Palumbo-Liu 1995; Rasmussen 1990; Richter 2004; Robotham 2005; Schulze-Engler 1996; Szegedy-Maszák 1996.

WASHINGTON CONSENSUS

This is a term coined in 1990 to describe the general agreement among economists and Wall Street bankers about the best means to procure global economic growth. It was called the 'Washington Consensus' because Washington is the headquarters of most global financial institutions. The foundation was laid in 1990 by a World Bank economist, John Williamson, who compiled a list of the most widely recommended market-oriented policies: (1) Fiscal discipline (2) A redirection of public expenditure priorities toward fields offering both high economic returns and the potential to improve income distribution, such as primary health care, primary education, and infrastructure (3) Tax reform (to lower marginal rates and broaden the tax base) (4) Interest rate liberalization (5) A competitive exchange rate (6) Trade liberalization (7) Liberalization of inflows of foreign direct investment (8) Privatization (9) Deregulation (to abolish barriers to entry and exit (10) Secure property rights.

The language of this list spans the philosophical terrain of **neo-liberalism**, with its insistence on the unfettered operation of the market. Although the principles would be unremarkable to many economists they encompass a programme that many critics have argued is designed to both obfuscate and cement the power of the West. The term 'Washington Consensus' provides a useful description of World Bank and IMF 'one size fits all' prescriptive economic policies. It is of interest to post-colonial studies first, because it summarises neo-liberal economic policy which itself has its origins in imperial expansion, and second, because it demonstrates the way in which neo-imperial power is maintained by a persuasive ideological language, working in tandem with powerful global institutions.

Williamson originally compiled this list as a reflection of the thinking at Washington-based international financial institutions about the policies needed to reduce Latin America's chronic debt. But even he was surprised to see his list being applied globally in the 1990s in places as diverse as Indonesia and Kazakhstan. His reply to criticisms was that 'the "consensus" should not be taken on as an ideology' (2002) a defence that many critics rejected on the basis that the list summarized the ideology of neo-liberalism quite comprehensively. One critic declared that the list of measures 'was a perfect guide to making an economy attractive to foreign capital.' (Ramo 2004). The model not only failed basic tests of suitability for most countries, but often proved socially and economically disastrous, most notably (in the short term at least), for Russia.

The Washington Consensus, which explains the behaviour of the IMF and World Bank in the latter half of the twentieth century, also explains why economic globalization is so often confused with US imperialism. The US is the largest contributor to the IMF and the only member with an effective veto. In many cases, the effects of structural adjustments in small economies do more for Wall Street bankers than for poor farmers. The response of the IMF to the Asian Financial Crisis for instance was to impose 'cookie cutter' SAPs (Structural Adjustment Packages), which forced debtor nations to behave in exactly the opposite way that the US behaved when it entered recession in 2001. Michel Chossudovsky in *The Globalization of Poverty* shows that World Bank and IMF programmes create economic strait-jackets that do more to impoverish the recipients and cast them in the yoke of international division of labour than to promote economic growth. Meant to balance national budgets, rectify market imbalances and make the economy more competitive, the unexpected effect of these policies has often been to impoverish the working and middle classes and cause economies to plunge into a serious economic depression due to shrinking internal demand.

Further reading: Chossudovsky 1997; Ramo 2004; Stiglitz 2002; Williamson 2002.

WHITENESS

Although **Race** has been a dominant feature of social construction since the late eighteenth century it is significant that whiteness as a defining racial category has only recently emerged in the range of **chromatic** ideas of human difference. Since European and later American races occupied the dominant pole in the binaries of race in the post-slavery era and African, Asian and Amerindian peoples were the majority constituents of the subaltern pole, the category white was effectively occluded, naturalized as an always already-given category against which other races could be distinguished and so not needing to be constituted in a specific way as a separate race grouping. In fact, of course, like all chromatic typologies the terms employed in these racist discourses: black, brown, red, yellow and so forth were designed to homogenize the complexities of difference which exist within the single human species. But the category of white has a special force, since it is un-stated, set apart by its force as the normative. Recent critical accounts have sought to expose this false naturalizing of the category by investigating the different ways whiteness has been employed as a social discriminator. These vary greatly in different places and times, though all seek to construct a unified grouping to oppose against those others which the 'whites' seek to exclude and control. Mike Hill has summarized this 'first wave of work on the topic [as an attempt] to break what Frantz Fanon referred to as the 'ontogenic' seal of white normativity'. The most formal modern recognitions of the category include the use of the term white within the discriminatory legislation associated with **apartheid**. But US scholarship has also pointed to the growth of the term in multicultural societies such as the US, where racialist groups defending the possibility of 'whites' becoming a minority swamped by racial admixture have employed the term whiteness as a rallying call. Early commentators on this phenomenon, such as Roederer and Hill himself, have always been cautious of the term 'whiteness studies', feeling that 'a critical rush to whiteness would be symptomatic of the very problem of **hegemony** [such studies] sought to demolish' (Hill 2004a). For this reason Hill, for example, has emphasized that the task is to uncover the power of the term in a world where official and unofficial typologies of racial and ethnic identity are moving rapidly to a position where isolated racial categories are being dismantled, for example in crucial instruments where social control and self-ascription collide, such as the National Census. While this may seem to be a development progressive thinkers might applaud, Hill shows how in practice it can lead to the diminishing of the power of such racial groups as African Americans or Latinos as effective social forces and political lobbyists. Beyond these practical issues lie the more crucial epistemological issues which haunt all such categories. As Hill has summarized this:

> The ambivalent prospect of an end to whiteness haunts progressive scholarship on race as much as it haunts the paranoid visions of white-collar racists on the other side of the ethnographic looking-glass. For both groups, ironically, whiteness is both gone and still very much here. And if such a body of discourse called whiteness studies actually exists, there is a sense that the blind proliferation of this work creeps towards an ugly metamorphosis that will keep it from progressive goals.
>
> (Hill 2004a: 9)

Hill concludes, 'Perhaps whiteness studies might better be dubbed *after-*whiteness studies, thus keeping the temporary irony of its absent presence at the forefront and in play.' (ibid.).

It's a manner of inquiry I find revealing, one that secretly knows that critical knowledge sustains the phantasmagoric form of the very thing it wants to deconstruct. That we feel shame about such knowledge and try to hide rather than mobilize its contradictions, and that folks exploit such shame across the political spectrum, is the worse part of the whiteness studies game. What people who continue to write on whiteness tend not to realize is that they too are writing from a position that's inherently self-effacing, since their object of study disappears the moment they start working, then comes back, but in ways that are unwanted or unexpected. It's that ghostly encounter with absence I alluded to before. Rather than just scary or impolitic, I find in this hour of ruin a little bit of hope. That white folk are at last in an epistemologically fatal position goes to the very root of the concept of potential.

(Hill 2004b)

In this respect whiteness studies faces a problem similar to that which haunts many contemporary academic fields, including **post-colonial** studies itself, that is that its existence as a field of study preserves the very concept (**colonialism**) it seeks to dismantle.

Although whiteness is a category which is grounded in racist discourses and practices it also impinges on discourses of **class** and gender (see **feminism and postcolonialism** and **transcultural feminism**). Whiteness has frequently been employed in territories as diverse as South Africa, Australia and the US as a means of recruiting the economically disadvantaged segments of the so-called white population to support national or social programmes which are to their disadvantage in that they divert their attention from the actual causes of their poverty in the broader economic practices of capital.

Parties which emphasize 'family values' and thus the need to protect the 'traditional' roles of the genders have also embraced racist discourses which emphasize the threat changes to gender patterns pose to so-called 'core national values', which values they identity with those of the cultural groupings which have embraced the signifier of 'whiteness', e.g. the emergence of just such an alliance of practices in groupings such as One Nation in Australia, which enjoyed a brief electoral success in many areas in the late 1990s. In the US the recently emerged fundamentalist Christian groups, while asserting their lack of political or racial bias ('It's not a black thing, or a white thing, it's a Jesus thing') have often been racially discriminatory as well as politically conservative in their actual practice. They have often shown little regard for the alleviation of minority-group poverty, manifested in their overt opposition to 'welfare' or support for programmes of reform of the ongoing effects of racial bias in educational and training opportunities, employment patterns, etc. In this regard they have moved away from earlier Christian traditions of anti-slavery advocacy and social reformism. **Religion** has re-emerged in recent times as a force which may create new forms of discrimination against groups such as Muslims, though these are often masked as attacks only on fundamentalist minorities. The identification of 'white' national values with Christianity by those who peddle these simplistic models of religion and its role in the formation of national cultural identities poses a threat of further social divisions along lines which collapse religion and race into new discriminatory signifiers of difference.

Further reading: Burrows 2004; Hill 1997; Hill 2004a; Hill 2004b; Mohanram 2007; Roediger 2002; Young 1990.

WORLD SYSTEM THEORY

A theory of the operation of the world economic, social and political system, formulated by Immanuel Wallerstein (1974a; 1974b). The chief assertion of this theory is that the capitalist system has been the world economic system since the sixteenth century and that one cannot talk about economies in terms of the nation-state, nor of 'society' in the abstract, nor of 'stages' of development, because each society is affected by, indeed is a part of, the capitalist world economy.

> It was only with the emergence of the modern world economy in sixteenth-century Europe that we saw the full develop-ment and economic predominance of market trade. This was the system called capitalism. Capitalism and world economy (that is, a single division of labour, but multiple polities and cultures) are obverse sides of the same coin. One does not cause the other.
>
> (Wallerstein 1974b: 391)

World system theory emerged as a refutation of modernization theory, which tended to (a) concentrate on the nation-state, (b) assume that all countries follow a similar path of growth, (c) disregard transnational structures and (d) base explanations on ahistorical ideal types. The proposition of one world capitalist system in operation since the sixteenth century radically affects how we view not only world economics but also national politics, class, ethnicity and international relations in general. For instance, the theory rejects the concept of a 'society' as a unit of analysis in favour of two systems of production:

'mini-systems' that are localized and of short duration, and the world system itself (Wallerstein 1976).

A demonstration of how this theory works can be seen in its approach to the feudal-like economies of Latin America. One traditional Marxist view of economic development sees all economies as passing through a series of stages, so it would regard these economies as existing at a pre-bourgeois, pre-industrialized stage of development. But world system theory holds that these economies are already a part of the capitalist world system. They are not an earlier stage of a transition to industrialization, but are undeveloped because they are 'peripheral, raw-material producing' areas, on the margins of, and exploited by, the industrialized world and hence in a state of **dependency**. Such societies may, or may not, develop an industrial base. But whether they do or not depends upon how well they resist dominant states and **appropriate** the capitalist world system (or, as Wallerstein would contend, purely as a result of structural changes in the system) rather than any inevitable process of development. Industrialization can thus be seen as, above all, a political phenomenon.

The world system is primarily a political system, rather than one determined by 'neutral' economic factors, and in this sense overlaps theories of **neo-colonialism** and **decolonization**. The capitalist world system emerged at the same time as the modern European imperial dominance of the world. This had two major consequences: the establishment of the world as a spatio-temporal site of imperial power, and the perpetuation of the imperial **binarism** between colonizing and colonized countries. Although Wallerstein does not develop the link between the capitalist world system and imperialism (since he regards individual world empires as subsidiary to the capitalist world system), it is clear that the world system is intimately tied up with European expansion and that the history of colonization has a great deal of bearing upon which countries are industrialized today, and which are maintained as resource-producing areas (see **globalization**).

According to Wallerstein, the three structural positions in the world economy – core, periphery and semi-periphery – had become stabilized by about 1640. Northwest Europe was the core, specializing its agriculture and adding industries such as textiles, ship building and metal production; Eastern Europe and the Western hemisphere were the periphery, providing exports of grain, bullion, wood, cotton and sugar; and Mediterranean Europe was the semi-peripheral region specializing in high cost industrial products. Capitalism was from the beginning an affair of the world economy and not of nation-states. The particular geographical location of these structural positions may change, but not their basic function in the system.

Clearly, although Wallerstein sees the capitalist world system as one that overrides any other world system, such as imperialism, the imperial expansion of Europe, its cultural and political, as well as economic dominance, in short the emergence of **modernity** itself, are inextricable from the rise and dominance of a world economic system. Dominant core states may change, but the structure of the world system, and the dynamics of capital accumulation on which it rests, remain in place. The theory does not explain, nor is it interested in, human subjectivity, the politics of colonization, the continued dominance of certain discursive forms of imperial rhetoric, nor the particular and abiding material consequences of colonialism in individual societies. It offers no place for individual political agency, nor is it concerned with the local dynamics of cultural change, nor even with the operation of 'societies', all these things being subsidiary to the broad structural forces of the world system.

More recently (1991), Wallerstein has addressed the relationship of culture to the world system, contending that culture, both as that which creates distinctions within groups ('Culture'), and that which distinguishes between groups such as nations ('cultures'), are actually 'the consequence of the historical development of [the world] system and reflect its guiding logic' (1991: 32). Both forms of culture serve to mystify people about the world system and thus keep it in place. In this scheme of things, even 'anti-systemic' movements are a product of the world system.

Further reading: De Santillana 1955; Hopkins 1982; Lane 2006; Lawson 2006; Moretti 2006; Robertson 1992; Spivak 2006; Wallerstein 1974a, 1974b, 1976, 1980, 1991.

WORLDING

A term coined by Gayatri Spivak to describe the way in which colonized space is brought into the 'world', that is, made to exist as part of a world essentially constructed by **Euro-centrism**:

> If . . . we concentrated on documenting and theorizing the itinerary of the consolidation of Europe as sovereign subject, indeed sovereign and subject, then we would produce an

alternative historical narrative of the 'worlding' of what is today called 'the Third World.'

(Spivak 1985a: 128)

Alluding to Heidegger's essay 'The Origin of the Work of Art', Spivak describes the process as the 'worlding of the world on uninscribed earth', which may be described in other terms as the 'inscribing' of imperial discourse upon the colonized 'space'. This kind of inscription is most obviously carried out by activities such as mapping, both by putting the colony on the map of the world and by mapping it internally so as to name it, and by naming it to know it, and hence, control it. But the process of 'worlding' also occurs in much more subtle ways: Spivak offers examples of the ways in which imperialism works to overwrite the colonized place by simply being there, pointing to the example of the solitary British soldier walking across the countryside of India in the early nineteenth century:

> He is actually engaged in consolidating the self of Europe by obliging the native to cathect the space of the Other on his home ground [that is, he is obliging the native to experience his home ground as imperial space]. He is worlding *their own world*, which is far from mere uninscribed earth. . . . [He is effectively and violently sliding one discourse under another.]
>
> (Spivak 1985a: 133)

This is one of the many different processes of **othering**, which characterize colonial contact. The point Spivak is making here is that the imperial project itself is far from monolithic, that its 'class composition and social positionality are necessarily heterogeneous' (133). This 'cartographic transformation' was not only achieved by the policy makers, but also, and more importantly, by the little people like the solitary soldier – and the thousands of colonists who followed people like him to places that are colonized by an imperial society.

Further reading: Spivak 1985a.

BIBLIOGRAPHY

Abernethy, D. B. (2000) *The Dynamics of Global Dominance: European Overseas Empires, 1415–1980*, New Haven: Yale University Press.

Achebe, C. (1988) *Hopes and Impediments,* London and New York: Doubleday.

Adam, I. (1996) 'Oracy and Literacy: A Postcolonial Dilemma?' *The Journal of Commonwealth Literature* 31(1): 97–109.

Adams, W. and M. Mulligan (2003) *Decolonizing Nature: Strategies for Conservation in a Post-Colonial Era*, London, Sterling VA: Earthscan Publications.

Adeeko, Adeleke (2002). 'Bound to Violence?: Achille Mbembe's *On the Postcolony*', *West Africa Review*: 3, 2.

Ahluwalia, P. (2001) *Politics and Post-Colonial Theory: African Inflections*, London and New York: Routledge.

Ahmad, A. (1992) *In Theory: Classes, Nations, Literatures*, London: Verso.

Ahmad, A. (1995) 'The Politics of Literary Postcoloniality', *Race and Class* (36) 3.

Ahmad, A. (1995a) 'Jameson's Rhetoric of Otherness and the "National Allegory"', in B. Ashcroft, G. Griffiths and H. Tiffin (ed.) *The Post-Colonial Studies Reader*, London: Routledge.

Albrow, M. (1994) *Globalization: Myths and Realities,* Inaugural Lecture, London: Roehampton Institute.

Albrow, M. and King, E. (1990) (eds) *Globalization, Knowledge and Society,* London: Sage in association with the International Sociological Association.

Alegría, C. (1981) 'Literatura y liberación nacional en El Salvador', *Casa de las Americas* 21(126): 12–16.

Alexander, F. (1969) *Moving Frontiers: An American Theme and its Application to Australian History,* Port Washington, NY: Kennikat Press.

Alexander, M. J. and Mohanty, C. T. (1997) (eds) *Feminist Genealogies, Colonial Legacies, Democratic Futures,* New York and London: Routledge.

Alexander, N. (1990) *Education and the Struggle for National Liberation in South Africa: Essays and Speeches*, Braamfontein: Skotaville, Educational Division.

Alexander, T. (1996) *Unravelling Global Apartheid: An Overview of World Politics*, Cambridge, Massachusetts: Polity Press.

Alexis, J. S. (1956) 'Of the Magical Realism of the Haitians', *Presence Africaine* 8–10.

Alleyne, M. C. (1980) 'Theoretical Orientations in Creole Studies' in A. Valdman and A. Highfield (eds), *Theoretical Orientations in Creole Studies*, New York: Academic Press.

Alonso, A. M. (2004) 'Conforming Disconformity: "Mestizaje", Hybridity, and the Aesthetics of Mexican Nationalism', *Cultural Anthropology* 19(4): 459–490.

Altbach, P. G. (1975) 'Literary Colonialism: Books in the Third World', *Harvard Educational Review* 15 (2) (May).

Althusser, L. (1984) *Essays on Ideology*, London: Verso. Anderson, B. (1983) *Imagined Communities: Reflections on the Origin and Spread of Nationalism*, London: Verso.

Amur, G. S., V. R. N. Prasad, *et al.* (1985) *Indian Readings in Commonwealth Literature*, New York: Apt.

Amuta, C. (1995) 'Fanon, Cabral and Ngugi on National Liberation' in B. Ashcroft, G. Griffiths and H. Tiffin (ed.), *The Post-Colonial Studies Reader*, London: Routledge: 158–163.

Anderson, A. (1991) *Race Against Time: The Early Maori-Pakeha Families and the Development of the Mixed-Race Population in Southern New Zealand*, Dunedin, N. Z: Hocken Library, University of Otago.

Anderson, A. (1998) 'Cosmopolitanism, Universalism, and the Divided Legacies of Modernity' in P. Cheah and B. Robbins (eds) *Cosmopolitics: Thinking and Feeling beyond the Nation*, Minneapolis, MN, University of Minnesota Press: 265–289.

Anderson, B. (1983) *Imagined Communities: Reflections on the Origin and Spread of Nationalism*, London: Verso.

Ansell-Pearson, K., B. Parry, *et al.* (1997) (eds) *Cultural Readings of Imperialism: Edward Said and the Gravity of History*, New York: St. Martin's.

Anzaldua, Gloria (1987) *Borderlands/La Frontera: The New Mestiza*, San Francisco: Aunt Lute.

Appadurai, A. (1986) *The Social Life of Things: Commodities in Cultural Perspective*, Cambridge: C.U.P.

Appadurai, A. (1991) 'Global Ethnoscapes. Notes and Queries for a Trans-national Anthropology', in R. Fox (ed.) *Recapturing Anthropology: Working in the Present*, Santa Fe, NM: School of American Research Press.

Appadurai, Arjun (1996), *Modernity at Large: Cultural Dimensions of Globalization*, Minneapolis: University of Minnesota Press.

Appiah, K. A. (1992) *In My Father's House: Africa in the Philosophy of Culture*, London: Methuen.

Appiah, K. A. and H. L. Gates. (1995) (eds) *Identities*, Chicago: University of Chicago Press.

Arac, J. and Ritvo, H. (1995) (eds) *Macropolitics of Nineteenth-century Literature: Nationalism, Exoticism, Imperialism*, Durham, NC: Duke University Press.

Armstrong, C. I. and A. Hestertun (2006) *Postcolonial Dislocations: Travel, History and the Ironies of Narrative*, Oslo, Norway: Novus Press.

Arnold, A. J. (2003) 'Perilous Symmetry: Exoticism and the Geography of Colonial and Postcolonial Culture' in F. G. Henry and J. Garane (eds) *Geo/Graphies: Mapping the Imagination in French and Francophone Literature and Film*, Amsterdam, Netherlands: Rodopi: 1–28.

Asad, T. (1973) (ed.) *Anthropology and the Colonial Encounter,* London: Ithaca.

Ashcroft, B., Griffiths, G. and Tiffin, H. (1989) *The Empire Writes Back: Theory and Practice in Post-Colonial Literatures,* London: Routledge.

Ashcroft, B., Griffiths, G. and Tiffin, H. (1995) *The Post-Colonial Studies Reader,* London: Routledge.

Ashcroft, B., Griffiths, G. and Tiffin H. (2002) *The Empire Writes Back: Theory and Practice in Post-colonial Literatures,* London: Routledge. 2nd Edition.

Ashcroft, B. (1989) 'Intersecting Marginalities: Post-Colonialism and Feminism', *Kunapipi* Vol. XI, No. 2: 23–43.

Ashcroft, B. (1994) 'Interpolation and Post-Colonial Agency', *New Literatures Review* 28–29: 176–189.

Ashcroft, B. (1996) 'On the Hyphen in Post-Colonial', *New Literatures Review* 32: 23–32.

Ashcroft, B. (1998) 'Constructing the Post-Colonial Male Body' in L. Dale and S. Ryan (eds) *The Body in the Library*, Amsterdam, Netherlands: Rodopi: 207–223.

Ashcroft, B. (1999) 'The Rhizome of Post-Colonial Discourse' in R. Luckhurst and P. Marks (eds) *Literature and the Contemporary: Fictions and Theories of the Present*, Harlow, England: Longman: 111–125.

Ashcroft, B. (2000) 'Primitive and Wingless: The Colonial Subject as Child' in W. S. Jacobson (ed.) *Dickens and the Children of Empire*, New York: Palgrave.

Ashcroft, B. (2001a), *Post-Colonial Transformation*, London: Routledge.

Ashcroft, B. (2001) *On Post-Colonial Futures: Transformations of Colonial Culture*, London: Continuum.

Ashcroft, B. (2005) 'Modernity's First Born: Latin America and Postcolonial Transformation' in P. McCallum and W. Faith (eds) *Linked Histories: Postcolonial Studies in Globalized World*, Calgary, AB: University of Calgary Press: 189–207.

Ashcroft, W. D., Cotter, M., Docker, J. and Nandan, S. (1977) *New Literature Review* 2 'Special issue: post-colonial literature'.

Ashcroft, W. D. (1989a) 'Intersecting marginalities: post-colonialism and feminism', *Kunapipi* (11) 2.

Ashcroft, W. D. (1989b) 'Is that the Congo? Language as Metonymy in the Postcolonial Text', *World Literature Written in English* (29) 2 (Autumn).

Assiter, A. (2003) *Revisiting Universalism*, New York: Palgrave Macmillan.

Baber, Z. (2002) 'Orientalism, Occidentalism, Nativism: The Culturalist Quest for Indigenous Science and Knowledge', *European Legacy: Toward New Paradigms* 7(6): 747–758.

Bahri, D. (2004) 'Feminism in/and Postcolonialism' in N. Lazarus (ed.) *The*

Cambridge Companion to Postcolonial Literary Studies, Cambridge, England: Cambridge University Press: 199–220.

Baker, H. A., M. Diawara, *et al.* (1996) (eds) *Black British Cultural Studies: A Reader*, Chicago: University of Chicago Press.

Baker, S. (1991) 'Magic Realism as a Postcolonial Strategy: The Kadaitcha Sung', *SPAN: Journal of the South Pacific Association for Commonwealth Literature and Language Studies* 32: 55–63.

Bakhtin, M. (1981) *The Dialogic Imagination: Four Essays,* edited by Michael Holquist; translated by Caryl Emerson and Michael Holquist, Austin: University of Texas Press.

Bakhtin, M. (1984) *Rabelais and His World*, trans. Helene Iswolsky, Bloomington: Indiana UP, [1941].

Bakhtin, M. (1994) *The Bakhtin Reader: Selected Writings of Bakhtin, Medvedev and Voloshinov,* edited by Pam Morris; with a glossary compiled by Graham Roberts, London: Edward Arnold.

Balcárcel, J. L. (1981) 'Literatura y liberaci by Graham Roberts', London: *Casa de las Americas* 21(126): 17–25.

Ball, J. C. (2004) *Imagining London: Postcolonial Fiction and the Transnational Metropolis*, Toronto, ON: University of Toronto Press.

Ballantyne, T. (2001) *Orientalism, Racial Theory and British Colonialism: An Aryan Empire*, Basingstoke: Palgrave.

Barber, K. (1991) *I Could Speak until Tomorrow: Oriki, Women and the Past in a Yoruba Town,* Edinburgh: Edinburgh University Press for the International African Institute.

Barber, Karin (1995) 'African-language Literature and Postcolonial Criticism', *Research in African Literatures*, Winter 1995 26(4) 3.

Barber, Karin and Graham Furniss (2006) 'African Language Writing', *Research in African Literatures*, Fall, Vol. 37, Issue 3, pp. 1–14.

Barber, K. and De Moraes-Farias, P.F. (1989) (eds) *Discourse and its Disguises: The Interpretation of African Oral Texts,* Birmingham: University of Birmingham, Centre of West African Studies.

Barkan, E. and R. Bush, (1995) (eds) *Prehistories of the Future: The Primitivist Project and the Culture of Modernism*, Stanford, California: Stanford University Press.

Barkan, E. and M.D. Sheltòn (1998) (eds) *Borders, Exiles, Diasporas*, Stanford, California: Stanford University Press.

Barker, F., P. Hulme, *et al.* (1994) *Colonial Discourse, Postcolonial Theory*, Manchester: Manchester University Press.

Barker, M. (1981) *The New Racism: Conservatives and the Ideology of the Tribes,* London: Junction Books.

Barker, M. (1982) *The New Racism: Conservatives and the Ideology of the Tribe,* Frederick, MD: Aletheia Books.

Barlow, T. E. (2005) 'Eugenic Woman, Semicolonialism, and Colonial Modernity as Problems for Postcolonial Theory' in A. Loomba, S. Kaul, M. Bunzl, A. Burton and J. Esty (eds) *Postcolonial Studies and Beyond*, Durham, NC: Duke University Press: 359–384.

Barrett, L. E. (1977) *The Rastafarians: The Dreadlocks of Jamaica*, Kingston, Jamaica: Sangster's Book Store.

Barrett, L. E. (1988) *The Rastafarians: Sounds of Cultural Dissonance*, Boston: Beacon Press.

Barringer, T. J. and T. Flynn. (1998) (eds) *Colonialism and the Object: Empire, Material Culture, and the Museum*, London: Routledge.

Barrington, L. W. (2006) (ed.) *After Independence: Making and Protecting the Nation in Postcolonial and Postcommunist States*, Ann Arbor: University of Michigan Press.

Barrios de Chungara, D. (1977) *Let Me Speak: Testimony of Domatila, a Woman of the Bolivian Mines*, translated by Victoria Ortiz, London: Monthly Review Press.

Bartolovich, C. and N. Lazarus (2002) (eds) *Marxism, Modernity, and Postcolonial Studies*, Cambridge, England: Cambridge University Press.

Bartow, J. R. (2005) *Subject to Change: The Lessons of Latin American Women's Testimonio for Truth, Fiction, and Theory*, Chapel Hill, NC: University of North Carolina Press.

Basch, L. G. (1994) *Nations unbound: transnational projects, postcolonial predicaments, and deterritorialized nation-states*, S.I: Gordon and Breach.

Bassnett, Susan (2002) *Translation Studies* London: Routledge.

Bassnett, Susan and Harish Trivedi (1999) (eds) *Post-Colonial Translation*, London: Routledge.

Battiste, Marie and Jean Barman (1995) (eds) *First Nations Education in Canada*, Vancouver: UBC Press.

Baucom, I. (1999) *Out of Place: Englishness, Empire, and the Locations of Identity*, Princeton, NJ: Princeton University Press.

Baugh, E. (2000) 'Postcolonial/Commonwealth Studies in the Caribbean: Points of Difference' in R. Smith (ed.) *Postcolonizing the Commonwealth: Studies in Literature and Culture*, Waterloo, ON: Wilfrid Laurier University Press.

Bauman, E. (1998) 'Re-Dreaming Colonial Discourse: Postcolonial Theory and the Humanist Project' *Critical Quarterly* 40(3): 79–89.

Bauman, Zygmunt (1998), *Globalization: The Human Consequences*, New York: Columbia University Press.

Baumgart, W. (1982) *Imperialism: The Idea and Reality of British and French Colonial Expansion 1880–1914*, translated by Ben V. Mast, Oxford: Oxford University Press.

Baxter, P. and Sansom, B. (1972) *Race and Social Difference: Selected Readings*, Harmondsworth: Penguin.

Behdad, A. (2005) 'On Globalization, Again!' in A. Loomba, S. Kaul, M. Bunzl, A. Burton and J. Esty (eds) *Postcolonial Studies and Beyond*, Durham: Duke University Press.

Behr, M. (2004) 'Postcolonial Transformations in Canadian Inuit Testimonio' in A. A. Lunsford and L. Ouzgane (eds) *Crossing Borderlands: Composition and Postcolonial Studies*, Pittsburgh, PA: University of Pittsburgh Press.

Bennett, B. (2003) *Resistance and Reconciliation: Writing in the Commonwealth*,

Canberra: ACLALS in association with The School of Language, Literature and Communication, University of New South Wales at ADFA.

Berglund, J. (2006) *Cannibal Fictions: American Explorations of Colonialism, Race, Gender and Sexuality*, Madison: University of Wisconsin Press.

Benjamin, Bret (2007*) Invested Interests: Capital, Culture and the World Bank*, Minneapolis, University of Minnesota Press.

Berkhofer, R. F. (1978) *The White Man's Indian: Images of the American Indian from Columbus to the Present*, New York: Knopf.

Berlin, I. (2004) *American Slavery in History and Memory/by Ira Berlin*, Melbourne: La Trobe University History Programme.

Berman, C. V. (2006) *Creole Crossings: Domestic Fiction and the Reform of Colonial Slavery*, Ithaca, NY: Cornell University Press.

Bernasconi, R. (2002) 'The Assumption of Negritude: Aimé Césaire, Frantz Fanon, and the Vicious Circle of Racial Politics', *Parallax* 8(2 [23]): 69–83.

Bery, A., P. Murray, *et al.* (2000) *Comparing Postcolonial Literatures: Dislocations*, Basingstoke, England: Macmillan.

Betts, R. F. (2004) *Decolonization*, New York: Routledge.

Beverley, J. (1989) 'The Margin at the Center: On *testimonio* (testimonial narrative)', *Modern Fiction Studies* (35) 1 (Spring).

Beverley, J. (1999) 'On the Subject of "Studies": Subaltern, Cultural, Women's, Ethnic, etc.' *Journal of Iberian and Latin American Studies* 5(2): 45–63.

Beverley, J. (2003) 'Adiós: A National Allegory (Some Reflections on Latin American Cultural Studies)', in S. Hart and R. Young (eds) *Contemporary Latin American Cultural Studies*, London, England: Arnold: 48–60.

Beverley, J. (2004a) *Testimonio: On the Politics of Truth*, Minneapolis, MN: University of Minnesota Press.

Beverley, J. (2004b) 'Writing in Reverse: On the Project of the Latin American Subaltern Studies Group' in A. Del Sarto, A. Ríos and A. Trigo (eds) *The Latin American Cultural Studies Reader*, Durham, NC: Duke University Press.

Beverley, J. and Zimmerman, M. (1990) *Literature and Politics in the Central American Revolutions,* Austin: University of Texas Press.

Bhabha, H. K. (1983) 'Difference, Discrimination and the Discourse of Colonialism' in F. Barker, P. Hulme, M. Iverson and D. Loxley (eds) *The Politics of Theory*, Colchester: University of Essex.

Bhabha, H. K. (1984a) 'Of Mimicry and Man: The Ambivalence of Colonial Discourse', *October* 28 (Spring) (reprinted as Ch. 4 of Bhabha 1994).

Bhabha, H. K. (1984b) 'Representation and the Colonial Text: A Critical Exploration of Some Forms of Mimeticism', in F. Glover Smith (ed.) *The Theory of Reading,* Brighton: Harvester.

Bhabha, H. K. (1985) 'Signs Taken for Wonders: Questions of Ambivalence and Authority under a Tree Outside Delhi, May 1817', *Critical Inquiry* (12) 1 (Autumn) (reprinted as Ch. 6 of Bhabha 1994).

Bhabha, H. K. (1988) The Commitment to Theory', *New Formations 5,* 5–23 (also appears in an altered form in J.Pines and P.Willemen (eds) *Questions of Third Cinema,* British Film Institute, 1989 and subsequently reprinted as Ch. 1 of Bhabha 1994).

Bhabha, H. K. (1990) (ed.) *Nation and Narration,* London and New York: Routledge.

Bhabha, H. K. (1994) *The Location of Culture,* London: Routledge.

Bhabha, H. K. (1996) 'The Other Question: Difference, Discrimination, and the Discourse of Colonialism' in H. A. Baker, Jr, M. Diawara, R. H. Lindeborg and S. Best (eds) *Black British Cultural Studies: A Reader,* Chicago, Illinois: University of Chicago Press.

Bharucha, N. E. (1997) 'Bombay to Mumbai: Postcolonial Repossessions and Hegemonies.' *SPAN: Journal of the South Pacific Association for Commonwealth Literature and Language Studies* 45: 13–36.

Bhatt, C. (2002) 'Primordial Being: Enlightenment and the Indian Subject of Postcolonial Theory' in P. Osborne and S. Sandford (eds) *Philosophies of Race and Ethnicity,* London: Continuum.

Biddiss, M.D. (1970) *Father of Racist Ideology: The Social and Political Thought of Count Gobineau,* London: Weidenfeld & Nicholson.

Billington, R.A. (1966) (ed.) *The Frontier Thesis: Valid Interpretation of American History?,* New York: Holt, Rinehart.

Bishop, A. (1990) 'Western Mathematics: The Secret Weapon of Cultural Imperialism', *Race and Class* 32 (2).

Blackburn, R. (1988) *The Overthrow of Colonial Slavery, 1776–1848,* London and New York: Verso.

Blake, R. (1996) 'Barbadian Creole English: Insights into Linguistic and Social Identity', *Journal of Commonwealth and Postcolonial Studies* 4(1): 37–54.

Blassingame, J. W. (1971) (ed.) *New Perspectives on Black Studies,* Urbana, IL.: University of Illinois Press.

Blaut, J. M. (1987) *The National Question: Decolonizing the Theory of Nationalism,* preface by Juan Mari Bras, London: Zed Books.

Blaut, J. M. (1993) *The Colonizer's Model of the World: Geographical Diffusionism and Eurocentric History,* New York: Guilford Press.

Blomstrom, M. and Hettne, B. (1984) *Development Theory in Transition: The Dependency Debate and Beyond: Third World Responses,* London: Zed Books.

Blundell, Valda (2000) *Changing Perspectives in the Anthropology of Art,* Ottawa: Golden Dog Press.

Blundell, Valda and Donny Woolagoodja (2005) *Keeping the Wanjinas Fresh: Sam Woolagoodja and the Enduring Power of Lalai,* Fremantle Arts Centre Press, Fremantle.

Blunt, A. and C. McEwan (2002) *Postcolonial Geographies,* New York: Continuum.

Bochner, S. (1982) (ed.) *Cultures in Contact: Studies in Cross-Cultural Interaction,* Oxford and New York: Pergamon Press.

Boehmer, E. (1991) 'Stories of Women and Mothers: Gender and Nationalism in the Early Fiction of Flora Nwapa' in Susheila Nasta *Motherlands,* London: Women's Press.

Boehmer, E. (1995) *Colonial and Postcolonial Literature: Migrant Metaphors,* Oxford: Oxford University Press.

Boehmer, E. (1998) *Empire Writing: An Anthology of Colonial Literature, 1870–1918,* Oxford: Oxford University Press.

Boehmer, E. (2005) *Stories of Women: Gender and Narrative in the Postcolonial Nation,* Manchester, England: Manchester University Press.

Boer, I. E. (1994) 'This Is Not the Orient: Theory and Postcolonial Practice' in M. Bal, I. E. Boer and J. Culler (eds) *The Point of Theory: Practices of Cultural Analysis,* New York: Continuum: 211–219.

Bongie, C. (1998) *Islands and Exiles: The Creole Identities of Post/Colonial Literature,* Stanford, CA: Stanford University Press.

Boon, J.A. (1982) *Other Tribes, Other Scribes: Symbolic Anthropology in the Comparative Study of Cultures, Histories, Religions, and Texts,* Cambridge: Cambridge University Press.

Boons-Grafé, M.-C. (1992) 'Other/other', (translated by Margaret Whitford) in Elizabeth Wright (ed.) *Feminism and Psychoanalysis: A Critical Dictionary,* Oxford: Blackwell.

Bracey, E. N. (2003) *On Racism: Essays on Black Popular Culture, African American Politics, and the New Black Aesthetics,* Lanham: University Press of America.

Brah, A. (1996) *Cartographies of Diaspora: Contesting Identities,* London: Routledge.

Brahms, F. (1995) 'Entering Our Own Ignorance: Subject-Object Relations in Commonwealth Literature' in B. Ashcroft, G. Griffiths and H. Tiffin (eds) *The Post-Colonial Studies Reader,* London: Routledge.

Brathwaite, E. K. (1971) *The Development of Creole Society in Jamaica, 1770–1820,* Oxford: Oxford University Press.

Brathwaite, E. K. (1974) *Contradictory Omens: Cultural Diversity and Integration in the Caribbean,* Mona, Jamaica: Savacou Publications.

Brathwaite, E. K. (1981) 'English in the Caribbean: Notes on Nation Language and Poetry: An Electronic Lecture' in L. A. Fiedler and H. A. Baker, Jr (eds) *English Literature: Opening Up the Canon,* Baltimore: Johns Hopkins University Press: 15–53.

Brathwaite, E. K. (1984) *History of the Voice: The Development of Nation Language in Anglophone Caribbean Poetry,* London: New Beacon Books. Cited in Ashcroft *et al.* (1995) pp. 309–313.

Brathwaite, E. K. (1995) 'Creolization in Jamaica' in B. Ashcroft, G. Griffiths and H. Tiffin (eds) *The Post-Colonial Studies Reader,* London: Routledge: 202–205.

Brathwaite, E. K. (1995a) 'Nation Language' in B. Ashcroft, G. Griffiths and H. Tiffin (eds) *The Post-Colonial Studies Reader,* London: Routledge: 309–313.

Bray, T. and Middleton, R. (1979) *Contemporary Modernism,* Milton Keynes: Open University Press.

Braziel, J. E. and A. Mannur, (2003) (eds) *Theorizing Diaspora: A Reader,* Malden, Massachussets: Blackwell.

Breckenridge, C. A. and P. v. d. Veer (1993) (eds) *Orientalism and the Postcolonial Predicament: Perspectives on South Asia*, Philadelphia, PA: University of Pennsylvania Press.

Bremen, J. (1990) (ed.) *Imperial Monkey Business: Racial Supremacy in Social Darwinist Theory and Colonial Practice*, CASA Monographs 3, Amsterdam: VU University Press.

Brennan, T. (1989) *Salman Rushdie and the Third World: Myths of the Nation*, London: Macmillan.

Brennan, T. (2004) 'From Development to Globalization: Postcolonial Studies and Globalization Theory' in N. Lazarus (ed.) *The Cambridge Companion to Postcolonial Literary Studies*, Cambridge: Cambridge University Press.

Brennan, T. (2005) 'The Economic Image-Function of the Periphery' in A. Loomba, S. Kaul, M. Bunzl, A. Burton and J. Esty (eds) *Postcolonial Studies and Beyond*, Durham: Duke University Press.

Brotherston, G. (1992) *Book of the Fourth World: Reading the Native Americas through their Literature*, Cambridge: Cambridge University Press.

Brown, R.H. and Coelho, G.V. (1987) (eds) *Migration and Modernization: The Indian Diaspora in Comparative Perspective*, Williamsburg, VA: Department of Anthopology, College of William and Mary.

Browning, D. S. (2006) (ed.) *Universalism vs. Relativism: Making Moral Judgments in a Changing, Pluralistic, and Threatening World*, Plymouth: Rowman & Littlefield.

Brydon, D. (1984) 'Re-writing *The Tempest*', *World Literature Written in English* (23) 1 (Winter).

Brydon, D. 'The White Inuit Speaks: Contamination as Literary Strategy' in I. Adam and H. Tiffin (eds) *Past the Last Post: Theorising Post-Colonialism and Post-Modernism*, New York and London: Harvester Wheatsheaf.

Brydon, D. (ed.) (2000) *Postcolonialism: Critical Concepts in Literary and Cultural Studies*, London: Routledge.

Brydon, D. (2001a) 'Global Designs, Postcolonial Critiques: Rethinking Canada in Dialogue with Diaspora', *Ilha do Desterro: A Journal of Language and Literature* 40: 61–84.

Brydon, D. (2001b) 'Mobilizing Globalization's Undertow', *Ilha do Desterro: A Journal of Language and Literature* 40: 125–126.

Brydon, D. and Tiffin, H. (1993) *Decolonising Fictions*, Aarhus: Dangaroo.

Buchanan, I. (2003) 'National Allegory Today: A Return to Jameson' *New Formations: A Journal of Culture/Theory/Politics* 51: 66–79.

Buchholtz, M. (2004) *Postcolonial Subjects: Canadian and Australian Perspectives*, Torun, Poland: Wydawnictwo Uniwersytetu Mikolaja Kopernika.

Buell, Lawrence (1995) *The Environmental Imagination: Thoreau, Nature Writing and the Formation of American Culture*, Cambridge MA: Harvard UP.

Buell, Lawrence (2005), *The Future of Environmental Criticism* Malden MA: Blackwell.

Bulbeck, C. (1998) *Re-orienting Western Feminisms: Women's Diversity in a Postcolonial World*, Cambridge: Cambridge University Press.

Blundell, Valda (2000) *Changing Perspectives in the Anthropology of Art*, Ottawa, Golden Dog Press.

Blundell, Valda and Donny Woolagoodja (2005) *Keeping the Wanjinas Fresh: Sam Woolagoodja and the Enduring Power of Lalai*, Fremantle Arts Centre Press, Fremantle.

Burton, A. M. (2003) (ed.) *After the Imperial Turn: Thinking With and Through the Nation*, Durham: Duke University Press.

Burton, G. C. (2004) *Ambivalence and the Postcolonial Subject: The Strategic Alliance of Juan Francisco Manzano and Richard Robert Madden*, New York: Peter Lang.

Butler, J. (1997) 'Gender Is Burning: Questions of Appropriation and Subversion' in A. McClintock, A. Mufti and E. Shohat (eds) *Dangerous Liaisons: Gender, Nation, and Postcolonial Perspectives*, Minneapolis: University of Minnesota Press.

Butler, J. E. (1981) *Black Studies – Pedagogy and Revolution: A Study of Afro-American Studies and the Liberal Arts Tradition Through the Discipline of Afro-American Literature*, Washington, D.C: University Press of America.

Cabral, A. (1973) *Return to the Sources: Selected Speeches,* New York and London: Monthly Review Press.

Caldwell, R. C., Jr (2003) 'For a Theory of the Creole City: Texaco and the Postcolonial Postmodern' in M. Gallagher (ed.) *Ici-Lá : Place and Displacement in Caribbean Writing in French*, Amsterdam, Netherlands: Rodopi: 25–39.

Campbell, H. (1985) *Rasta and resistance: from Marcus Garvey to Walter Rodney*, Dar es Salaam: Tanzania Publishing House.

Campbell, Kofi Omoniyi Sylvanus (2006) *Literature and Culture in the Black Atlantic,* New York: Palgrave/Macmillan.

Campbell-Praed, Mrs (1881) *Policy and Passion*, London: Richard Bentley and Sons.

Carby, H. (1982) 'White woman listen! Black feminism and the boundaries of sisterhood' in *The Empire Strikes Back: Race and Racism in 70s Britain,* Centre for Contemporary Cultural Studies, University of Birmingham, London: Hutchinson.

Carothers, J. C. (1953) *The African Mind in Health and Disease: A Study in Ethnopsychiatry,* Geneva: World Health Organization.

Carruthers, Jane (2006) 'Contesting Cultural Landscapes in South Africa and Australia' in David Trigger and Gareth Griffiths (eds.) *Disputed Territories: Land, Culture and Identity in Settler Societies*, Hong Kong: Hong Kong University Press.

Carter, E., Donald, J. and Squires, J. (1993) (eds) *Space and Power: Theories of Identity and Location,* London: Lawrence & Wishart.

Carter, M. (1996) *Voices from Indenture: Experiences of Indian Migrants in the British Empire,* New York: Leicester University Press.

Carter, P. (1987) *The Road to Botany Bay,* London: Faber & Faber.

Carter P. (1992) *Living in a New Country: History, Traveling and Language,* London: Faber and Faber.

Carter, P. (1996) *The Lie of the Land,* London: Faber & Faber.

Casas, M. d. l. C. (1998) 'Orality and Literacy in a Postcolonial World.' *Social Semiotics* 8(1): 5–24.

Cashmore, E. (1979) *Rastaman: the Rastafarian movement in England*, London: Unwin Paperbacks.

Cashmore, E. (1983) *Rastaman: The Rastafarian Movement in England,* London and Boston: Unwin.

Castillo, D. A. (1999) 'Border Theory and the Canon' in D. L. Madsen (ed.) *Postcolonial Literatures: Expanding the Canon*, London: Pluto.

Castle, G. (ed.) (2001) *Postcolonial discourses: an anthology* Malden, MA: Blackwell.

Castro-Klarén, S. (1999) 'Mimicry Revisited: Latin America, Post-Colonial Theory and the Location of Knowledge' in A. d. Toro and F. d. Toro (eds) *El debate de la postcolonialidad en Latinoamérica: Una postmodernidad periférica o cambio de paradigma en el pensamiento latinoamericano*, Madrid: Iberoamericana: 137–164.

Célestin, R. (1996) *From Cannibals to Radicals: Figures and Limits of Exoticism,* Minneapolis and London: University of Minnesota Press.

Chakrabarty, D. (2000) *Provincializing Europe: Postcolonial Thought and Historical Difference*, Princeton, N.J: Princeton University Press.

Chakrabarty, D. (2000a) 'Universalism and Belonging in the Logic of Capital', *Public Culture* (12) 3 [32]: 653–678.

Chakrabarty, D. and H. K. Bhabha (2002) *Habitations of Modernity: Essays in the Wake of Subaltern Studies*, Chicago, IL: University of Chicago Press.

Chamberlain, M. E. (1999) *Decolonization: The Fall of the European Empires*, Malden, MA: Blackwell Publishers.

Chambers, I. and L. Curti, (eds) (1996) *The Post-Colonial Question: Common Skies, Divided Horizons*, London: Routledge.

Chanady, A. (1995) 'The Formation of National Consciousness in Latin America: Mestizaje and Monolithic Cultural Paradigms' in M. E. d. Valdés, M. Valdés and R. A. Young (eds) *Latin America and Its Literature*, Whitestone, NY: Council on National Literatures: 170–180.

Chanady, A. (2003) 'Identity, Politics and Mestizaje' in S. Hart and R. Young (eds) *Contemporary Latin American Cultural Studies*, London: Arnold: 192–202.

Chang, E. K. (2001) 'Last Past the Post: Theory, Futurity, Feminism' in M. Dekoven (ed.) *Feminist Locations: Global and Local, Theory and Practice*, New Brunswick, NJ: Rutgers University Press: 60–74.

Chatterjee, P. (1986) *Nationalist Thought and the Colonial World: A Derivative Discourse,* London: Zed Books.

Chatterjee, P. (1993) *The Nation and its Fragments: Colonial and Postcolonial Histories,* Princeton, NJ: Princeton University Press.

Cheah, P. (1999) 'Spectral Nationality: The Living On [Sur-Vie] of the Postcolonial Nation in Neocolonial Globalization', *Boundary 2: An International Journal of Literature and Culture* 26(3): 225–252.

Cheah, P. (2003) *Spectral Nationality: Passages of Freedom from Kant to Postcolonial Literatures of Liberation*, New York, NY: Columbia University Press.

Chevannes, B. (1997) (ed.) *Rastafari and Other African-Caribbean Worldviews*, New Brunswick, NJ: Rutgers University Press.

Childs, P. and Williams, P. (1997) *An Introduction to Post-Colonial Theory*, London and New York: Prentice Hall/Harvester Wheatsheaf.

Childs, P., J. J. Weber, *et al.* (2006) *Post-Colonial Theory and Literatures: African, Caribbean and South Asian*, Trier, Germany: Wissenschaftlicher.

Chin, T. (2006) 'Transnationalism, Diaspora, Politics and the Caribbean Postcolonial', *Small Axe: A Caribbean Journal of Criticism* 19: 189–197.

Chossudovsky, Michel (1997) *The Globalization of Poverty: Impacts of IMF and World Bank Reforms*, London and New Jersey: Zed Books.

Chow, R. (1993) *Writing Diaspora: Tactics of Intervention in Contemporary Cultural Studies*, Bloomington: Indiana University Press.

Chrisman, L. (1998) 'Imperial Space, Imperial Place: Theories of Empire and Culture in Frederic Jameson, Edward Said and Gayatri Spivak', *New Formations: A Journal of Culture/Theory/Politics* 34: 53–69.

Chrisman, L. (2000) 'Rethinking Black Atlanticism', *Black Scholar: Journal of Black Studies and Research* 30(3–4): 12–17.

Chrisman, L. (2002) 'Rethinking Race and Nation' *New Formations: A Journal of Culture/Theory/Politics* 47: 67–143.

Chrisman, L. (2003) *Postcolonial Contraventions: Cultural Readings of Race, Imperialism, and Transnationalism*, Manchester: Manchester University Press.

Chrisman, L. (2004) 'Nationalism and Postcolonial studies' in N. Lazarus (ed.) *The Cambridge Companion to Postcolonial Literary Studies*, Cambridge, England: Cambridge University Press: 183–198.

Chrisman, L. (2005) 'Beyond Black Atlantic and Postcolonial Studies: The South African Differences of Sol Plaatje and Peter Abrahams' in A. Loomba. *et al.* (eds) *Postcolonial Studies and Beyond*, Durham: Duke University Press.

Chrisman, L. and Williams, P. (1993) (eds) *Colonial Discourse and Postcolonial Theory: A Reader,* Hemel Hempstead: Harvester Wheatsheaf.

Clark, S. (1999) (ed.) *Travel Writing and Empire: Postcolonial Theory in Transit*, London, England: Zed.

Clarke, S. (2000) 'Dreams of Home: Rastafari's Imagining Community for the African Diaspora', *BMA: The Sonia Sanchez Literary Review* 6(1): 91–108.

Clayton, D. and Gregory, D. (1996) (eds) *Colonialism, Postcolonialism and the Production of Space,* Oxford: Blackwell.

Clifford, J. (1986) (ed.) *Writing Culture: The Poetics and Politics of Ethnography*. A School of American Research Advanced Seminar, Berkeley: University of California Press.

Clifford, J. (1988) *The Predicament of Culture,* Cambridge, MA: Harvard University Press.

Clifford, J. (1997) *Routes: Travel and Translation in the Late Twentieth Century*, Cambridge, Massachusetts: Harvard University Press.

Codell, J. F. and D. S. Macleod (1998) , (eds) *Orientalism Transposed: The Impact of the Colonies on British Culture*, Aldershot, England: Ashgate.

Coetzee, J. M. (1980) *Waiting for the Barbarians*, Harmondsworth: Penguin.

Coetzee, J. M. (1989) *White Writing: The Culture of Letters in South Africa*, Yale, MA: Yale University Press.

Colás, S. (1995) 'Of Creole Symptoms, Cuban Fantasies, and Other Latin American Postcolonial Ideologies', *PMLA: Publications of the Modern Language Association of America* 110(3): 382–396.

Colás, S. (2001) 'From Caliban to Cronus: A Critique of Cannibalism as Metaphor for Cuban Revolutionary Culture' in K. Guest and M. Kilgour (eds) *Eating Their Words: Cannibalism and the Boundaries of Cultural Identity*, New York: State University of New York Press.

Collett, A. (2002) 'South Africa Post-Apartheid.' *Kunapipi: Journal of Post-Colonial Writing* 24(1–2): 1–300.

Collins, L. (2000) 'Daughters of Jah: The Impact of Rastafarian Womanhood in the Caribbean, the United States, Britain, and Canada' in H. Gossai and N. S. Murrell (eds) *Religion, Culture, and Tradition in the Caribbean*, New York: St. Martin's.

Comaroff, J. and J. Comaroff (1993) *Modernity and Its Malcontents: Ritual and Power in Postcolonial Africa*, Chicago, IL: University of Chicago Press.

Comaroff, Jean (2006) *Law and Disorder in the Postcolony*, Chicago: University of Chicago Press. Connor, W. (1984) *The National Question in Marxist-Leninist Theory and Strategy*, Princeton: Princeton University Press.

Consentino, D. A. (2000) 'Under the Shadow of God: Roots of Primitivism in Early Colonial Mexico' in E. Camayd-Freixas and J. E. González (eds) *Primitivism and Identity in Latin America: Essays on Art, Literature, and Culture*, Tucson, AZ: University of Arizona Press: 41–52.

Coombes, A. E. (1994) *Reinventing Africa: Museums, Material Culture and Popular Imagination*, New Haven and London: Yale University Press.

Coombes, A. E. (2003) *History After Apartheid: Visual Culture and Public Memory in a Democratic South Africa*, Durham: Duke University Press.

Cooppan, V. (1999) 'W(h)ither Post-colonial Studies? Towards the Trans-national Study of Race and Nation' in L. Chrisman and B. Parry (eds) *Postcolonial Theory and Criticism*, Cambridge: Brewer: 1–35.

Cornejo Polar, A. (1997) 'Mestizaje e hibridez: Los riesgos de las metáforas: Apuntes' *Revista Iberoamericana* 63(180): 341–344.

Cornejo Polar, A. and C. Dennis (2004a) 'Mestizaje and Hybridity: The Risks of Metaphors-Notes' in A. Del Sarto, A. Ríos and A. Trigo (eds) *The Latin American Cultural Studies Reader*, Durham, NC: Duke University Press: 760–764.

Cornejo Polar, A. and C. Dennis (2004b) 'Mestizaje, Transculturation, Heterogeneity' in A. Del Sarto, A. Ríos and A. Trigo (eds) *The Latin American Cultural Studies Reader*, Durham, NC: Duke University Press: 116–119.

Coronil, F. (1999) 'Listening to the Subaltern: Postcolonial Studies and the Neocolonial Poetics of Subaltern States' in L. Chrisman and B. Parry (ed.) *Postcolonial Theory and Criticism*, Cambridge, England: Brewer.

Coutinho, E. F. (1992) 'El discurso crítico-teórico latinoamericano y la cuestión de la descolonización cultural', *Casa de las Americas* 32(187): 61–79.

Crane, R. and R. Mohanram (1996) 'The Postcolonial Body.' *SPAN: Journal of the South Pacific Association for Commonwealth Literature and Language Studies* 42–43: 1–173.

Crawford, N. (2002) *Argument and Change in World Politics: Ethics, Decolonization, and Humanitarian Intervention*, Cambridge: Cambridge University Press.

Croizier, R. C., G. Blue, *et al.* (2002) (eds) *Colonialism and the Modern World: Selected Studies*, Armonk, New York: M.E. Sharpe.

Crosby, A. W. (1986) *Ecological Imperialism: The Biological Expansion of Europe, 900–1900,* Cambridge: Cambridge University Press.

Culler, J. (1981) *The Pursuit of Signs: Semiotics, Literature, Deconstruction,* London: Routledge.

Dale, L. and Ryan, S. (1998) (eds) *The Body in the Library,* Amsterdam: Rodopi.

Dallmayr, F. R. (1996) *Beyond Orientalism: Essays on Cross-Cultural Encounter*, Albany: State University of New York Press.

Dalziell, T. (2004) *Settler romances and the Australian Girl*, Fremantle, W. A: UWA Press.

Dangaremba, Titsi (1988) *Nervous Conditons*, London: The Women's Press.

D'Andrade, R. G. (1995) *The Development of Cognitive Anthropology*, Cambridge and New York: Cambridge University Press.

Darby, P. (1997) (ed.) *At the Edge of International Relations: Postcolonialism, Gender, and Dependency*, London: Pinter.

Darby, P. (1998) *The Fiction of Imperialism: Reading Between International Relations and Postcolonialism*, London: Cassell.

Darian-Smith, K., Gunner, L. and Nuttall, S. (1996) (eds) *Text, Theory, Space: Land, Literature and History in South Africa and Australia,* London: Routledge.

Darias Beautell, E. (2000) 'Writing Back and Beyond: Postcoloniality, Multiculturalism, and Ethnicity in the Canadian Context' in R. G. Davis and R. Baena (eds) *Tricks with a Glass: Writing Ethnicity in Canada*, Amsterdam, Netherlands: Rodopi: 19–35.

Dash, J. M. (1992) *Discours Antillais: Caribbean Discourse: Selected Essays by Edouard Glissant,* translated and with an introduction by J. Michael Dash, Charlottesville: University Press of Virginia.

Dash, J. M. (1995) *Edouard Glissant,* Cambridge and New York: Cambridge University Press.

Dash, J. M. (2003) 'Postcolonial Caribbean Identities' in F. A. Irele and S. Gikandi (eds) *The Cambridge History of African and Caribbean Literature*, Cambridge: Cambridge University Press.

Davidson, B. (1992) *The Black Man's Burden: Africa and the Curse of the Nation-state,* London: James Currey.

Davidson, B. (1994) *The Search for Africa, History, Culture, Politics,* New York: Random House.

Davis, G. V. and H. Maes-Jelinek (1990) *Crisis and Creativity in the New Literatures in English: Cross/Cultures*, Amsterdam: Rodopi.

Davis, J. and Hodge, B. (1985) (eds) *Aboriginal Writing Today*, Canberra: Australian Institute of Aboriginal Studies.

Davis, R. C. and D. S. Gross (1994) 'Gayatri Chakravorty Spivak and the Ethos of the Subaltern' in J. S. Baumlin and T. F. Baumlin (eds) *Ethos: New Essays in Rhetorical and Critical Theory*, Dallas: Southern Methodist University Press.

D'Cruz, C. (2001) '"What Matter Who's Speaking?": Authenticity and Identity in Discourses of Aboriginality in Australia', *Jouvert: A Journal of Postcolonial Studies* 5(3).

DeCamp, D. (1977) 'The development of pidgin and Creole studies' in A.Valman (ed.) *Pidgin and Creole Linguistics*, Bloomington: Indiana University Press.

De Costa, E. (2002) 'Voices of Conscience: The Power of Language in the Latin American Testimonio' in I. M. F. Blayer and M. Sanchez (eds) *Storytelling: Interdisciplinary and Intercultural Perspectives*, New York: Peter Lang.

Deena, S. (1997) 'Colonial and Canonical Control over Third World Writers' in R. K. Dhawan (ed.) *Postcolonial Discourse: A Study of Contemporary Literature*, New Delhi, India: Prestige.

DeFoigny, G. (1995) *The Southern Land, Known,* translated by D. Fausett, Syracuse, NY: Syracuse University Press.

Deleuze, G. and Guattari, F. (1972) *Anti-Oedipus: Capitalism and Schizophrenia,* translated by Robert Hurley, Mark Seem and Helen R. Lane, New York: Viking; reprinted Minneapolis: University of Minnesota Press, 1987.

Deleuze, G. and Guattari, F. (1980) *A Thousand Plateaus: Capitalism and Schizophrenia,* translated and foreword by Brian Massumi, London: Athlone Press.

de Moraes-Farias, P. F. and Barber, K. (1990) *Self-Assertion and Brokerage: Early Cultural Nationalism in West Africa,* University of Birmingham African Studies Series 2, Birmingham: Centre of West African Studies.

Denegri, F. (2003) 'Testimonio and Its Discontents' in S. Hart and R. Young (eds) *Contemporary Latin American Cultural Studies*, London: Arnold.

Denning, Michael (2004) *Culture in the Age of Three Worlds*, London: Verso.

Denoon, D. (1979) 'Understanding Settler Societies', *Historical Studies* (18) 73: 511–527.

Denoon, D. (1983) *Settler Capitalism: The Dynamics of Dependent Development in the Southern Hemisphere,* Oxford: Clarendon.

Derrida, J. (1986) 'Racism's last word' *(Le Dernier mot du Racisme)* translated by Peggy Kamuf in Henry Louis Gates (ed.) *'Race,' Writing and Difference,* Chicago: University of Chicago Press.

Desai, G. and S. Nair (2005) *Postcolonialisms: An Anthology of Cultural Theory and Criticism*, New Brunswick, NJ: Rutgers University Press.

De Santillana, G. (1955) *Dialogue on the Great World Systems*, Chicago, IL.

Devy, G. N. (1992) *After Amnesia: Tradition and Change in Indian Literary Criticism,* Hyderabad: Orient Longman and Sangam Books.

Dimitriadis, G. (2001) *Reading and Teaching the Postcolonial: From Baldwin to Basquiat and Beyond*, New York: Teachers College Press.

Dirlik, A. (1996) 'The Postcolonial Aura: Third World Criticism in the Age of Global Capitalism' in P. Mongia (ed.) *Contemporary Postcolonial Theory: A Reader*, London: Arnold.

Dirlik, A. (1999) 'Is There History after Eurocentrism? Globalism, Postcolonialism, and the Disavowal of History' *Cultural Critique* 42(0): 1–34.

Dirlik, A. (2005) 'The End of Colonialism? The Colonial Modern in the Making of Global Modernity', *Boundary 2: An International Journal of Literature and Culture* 32(1): 1–31.

Dissanayake, W. and C. Wickramagamage (1993) *Self and Colonial Desire: Travel Writings of V.S. Naipaul*, New York: Peter Lang.

Dixon, C. J. and M. J. Heffernan (1991) *Colonialism and Development in the Contemporary World*, London: Mansell.

Dixon, R. (1997) 'Prosthetic Gods: The Australian Colonial Body and Melanesia, 1930–1950', *Southern Review: Literary and Interdisciplinary Essays* 30(2): 130–145.

Docker, J. (1978) 'The Neo-Colonial Assumption in University Teaching of English' in Chris Tiffin (ed.) *South Pacific Images*, St Lucia, Queensland: *Journal of the South Pacific Association for Commonwealth Literature and Language Studies*.

Docker, J. (1992) *Dilemmas of Identity: The Desire for the Other in Colonial and Postcololonial Cultural History*, London: Sir Robert Menzies Centre for Australian Studies, Institute of Commonwealth Studies, University of London.

Donaldson, L. (1993) *Decolonizing Feminisms,* London and New York: Routledge.

Donaldson, Laura and Kwok Pui-Lan (2002) (eds) *Postcolonialism, Feminism and Religious Discourse*, London and New York: Routledge.

Döring, T. (2002) *Caribbean-English Passages: Intertextuality in a Postcolonial Tradition*, New York: Routledge.

Douglas, M. (1991) *Purity and Danger: An Analysis of the Concepts of Pollution and Taboo*, London: Routledge.

Drescher, S. (1987) *Capitalism and Antislavery: British Mobilisation in Comparative Perspective,* Oxford: Oxford University Press.

Drew, J. (1999) 'Cultural Composition: Stuart Hall on Ethnicity and the Discursive Turn' in G. A. Olson and L. Worsham (eds) *Race, Rhetoric, and the Postcolonial*, Albany, NY: State University of New York Press: 205–239.

Duara, P. (2003) (ed.) *Decolonization: Perspectives from Now and Then*, New York: Routledge.

DuCille, A. (1996) *Skin Trade,* Cambridge, MA: Harvard University Press.

Dulfano, I. (2004) 'Testimonio: Present Predicaments and Future Forays' in L. S. Maier and I. Dulfano (eds) *Woman as Witness: Essays on Testimonial Literature by Latin American Women*, New York: Peter Lang.

Dunn, R. S. (1973) *Sugar and Slaves: The Rise of the Planter Class in the English West Indies 1624–1713,* New York: Norton.

During, S. (1994) 'Rousseau's Patrimony: Primitivism, Romance and Becoming Other' in F. Barker, P. Hulme and M. Iversen (eds) *Colonial Discourse/Postcolonial Theory,* Manchester: Manchester University Press: 47–71.

Durix, J.-P. (1998) *Mimesis, Genres, and Post-Colonial Discourse: Deconstructing Magic Realism,* Basingstoke, England: Macmillan.

Durrant, S. (2003) *Postcolonial Narrative and the Work of Mourning: J. M. Coetzee, Wilson Harris, and Toni Morrison,* Albany, NY: State University of New York Press.

Dussel, E. (1993) 'Eurocentrism and Modernity (Introduction to the Frankfurt Lectures)' *Boundary 2: An International Journal of Literature and Culture* 20(3): 65–76.

Dussel, E. and E. Mendieta (1998) 'Beyond Eurocentrism: The World-System and the Limits of Modernity' in F. Jameson and M. Miyoshi (ed.) *The Cultures of Globalization,* Durham, NC: Duke University Press: 3–31.

Eagleton, T. (1990) *Nationalism, Colonialism, and Literature,* Minneapolis: University of Minnesota Press.

Easthope, A. and McGowan, K. (1992) *A Critical and Cultural Theory Reader,* Sydney: Allen & Unwin.

Easton, S. C. (1964) *The Rise and Fall of Western Colonialism: A Historical Survey from the Early Nineteenth Century to the Present,* New York: Praeger.

Echeverría, I. (1998) 'Los rastros de un mestizaje' *Cuadernos Hispanoamericanos* 579: 7–15.

Eddy, J. and Schreuder, D. (1988) (eds) *The Rise of Colonial Nationalism: Australia, New Zealand, Canada and South Africa First Assert Their Nationalities 1880–1914,* Sydney: Allen & Unwin.

Elder, G., J. Wolch and J. Emel (1998) 'Race, Place and the Bounds of Humanity', *Society and Animals* 6 (2).

Emberley, J. (1993) *Thresholds of Difference: Feminist Critique, Native Women's Writings, Postcolonial Theory,* Toronto: University of Toronto Press.

Esty, J. (2004) *A Shrinking Island: Modernism and National Culture in England,* Princeton, NJ: Princeton University Press.

Etherington, Norman (2005) *Missions and Imperialism,* Companion Volume, Oxford History of the British Empire, Oxford: OUP.

Evans, J. (2003) (ed.) *Equal Subjects, Unequal Rights: Indigenous Peoples in British Settler Colonies, 1830–1910,* Manchester: Manchester University Press.

Eysteinsson, A. (1990) *The Concept of Modernism,* Ithaca: Cornell University Press.

Ezzaher, L. E. (2003) *Writing and Cultural Influence: Studies in Rhetorical History, Orientalist Discourse, and Post-Colonial Criticism,* New York: Peter Lang.

Fanon, F. (1952) *Black Skin: White Masks,* translated by Charles Lam Markmann, London: MacGibbon and Kee (1968).

Fanon, F. (1959) *Studies in a Dying Colonialism,* translated by Haakon Chevalier, New York: Grove (1965, reissued 1970).

Fanon, F. (1961) *The Wretched of the Earth,* translated by Constance Farrington, New York: Grove. Cited in Ashcroft *et al.* 1995.

Fanon, F. (1964) *Towards the African Revolution,* translated by Haakon Chevalier, Harmondsworth: Penguin (1967).

Fardon, R. (1990) (ed.) *Localizing Strategies: Regional Traditions of Ethnographic Writing,* Edinburgh: Scottish Academic Press.

Faris, W. B. (2004) *Ordinary Enchantments: Magical Realism and the Remystification of Narrative,* Nashville: Vanderbilt University Press.

Fazzini, M. (2004) *Resisting Alterities: Wilson Harris and Other Avatars of Otherness,* Amsterdam, Netherlands: Rodopi.

Featherstone, M. (1990) (ed.) *Global Culture: Nationalism, Globalization and Modernity,* London: Sage.

Featherstone, M., Lash, S. and Robertson, R. (1995) (eds) *Global Modernities,* London: Sage.

Fee, M. (1989) 'Why C. K. Stead didn't like Keri Hulme's *the bone people:* who can write as other?', *Australian and New Zealand Studies in Canada* 1.

Fenwick, M. (2000) 'A Vision of Unity: Braithwaite, Ngugi, Rushdie and the Quest for Authenticity' in R. Smith (ed.) *Postcolonizing the Commonwealth: Studies in Literature and Culture,* Waterloo, ON: Wilfrid Laurier University Press.

Ferguson, M. (1993a) 'The Myth about Globalization', *European Journal of Communication* (7): 69–93.

Ferguson, M. (1993b) *Colonialism and Gender Relations from Mary Wollstonecraft to Jamaica Kincaid: East Caribbean Connections,* New York: Columbia University Press.

Ferguson, J. (2005) 'Decomposing Modernity: History and Hierarchy after Development' in A. Loomba, S. Kaul, M. Bunzl, A. Burton and J. Esty (eds) *Postcolonial Studies and Beyond,* Durham, NC: Duke University Press: 166–181.

Ferguson, R. *et al.* (1990) (eds) *Out There: Marginalization and Contemporary Cultures,* foreword by Marcia Tucker, images selected by Felix Gonzalez-Torres, New York: New Museum of Contemporary Art, Cambridge, MA: MIT Press.

Ferro, M. (1997) *Colonization: A Global History,* London and New York: Routledge.

Fieldhouse, D. K. (1981) *Colonialism 1870–1945: An Introduction,* London: Weidenfeld & Nicolson.

Fishman, J. A. (1985) *The Rise and Fall of the Ethnic Revival: Perspectives on Language and Ethnicity,* Berlin and New York: Mouton.

Fitz, E. E. (2002) 'From Blood to Culture: Miscegenation as Metaphor for the Americas' in M. Kaup and D. J. Rosenthal (eds) *Mixing Race, Mixing Culture: Inter-American Literary Dialogues,* Austin, TX: University of Texas Press: 243–272.

Fitz, K. (2001) *Negotiating History and Culture: Transculturation in Contemporary Native American Fiction,* Frankfurt, Germany: Peter Lang.

Flint, H. (2006) 'Toni Morrison's Paradise: Black Cultural Citizenship in the American Empire.' *American Literature*, Duke University Press. 78: 585–612.

Fokkema, D. W. (1984) *Literary History, Modernism, and Postmodernism*, Amsterdam and Philadelphia: J. Benjamins.

Forsdick, C. (2001) 'Travelling Concepts: Postcolonial Approaches to Exoticism', *Paragraph: A Journal of Modern Critical Theory* 24(3): 12–29.

Foster, G. A. (1999) *Captive Bodies: Postcolonial Subjectivity in Cinema*, Albany, NY: State University of New York Press.

Foucault, M. (1971) 'Orders of Discourse: inaugural lecture delivered at the Collège de France', *Social Science Information* (10) 2: 7–30 .

Foucault, M. (1977) *Discipline and Punish: The Birth of the Prison*, translated by Alan Sheridan, New York: Vintage.

Foucault, M. (1979) 'What is an Author?', translated by Joseph Harari, in David Lodge (ed.) *Modern Criticism and Theory: A Reader*, London and New York: Longman.

Fox, R. G. (1990) (ed.) *Nationalist Ideologies and the Production of National Cultures*, Washington DC: American Anthropological Association.

Franco, J. (1975) 'Dependency Theory and Literary History: The Case of Latin America', *Minnesota Review* 5: 65–80.

Franco, J. (1997) 'The Nation as Imagined Community' in A. McClintock, A. Mufti and E. Shohat (eds) *Dangerous Liaisons: Gender, Nation, and Postcolonial Perspectives*, Minneapolis: University of Minnesota Press.

Frank, A. G. (1979) *Capitalism and Underdevelopment in Latin America*, Harmondsworth: Penguin.

Frankenberg, R. and L. Mani (2001) 'Crosscurrents, Crosstalk: Race, "Post-Coloniality" and the Politics of Location' in K.-K. Bhavnani (ed.) *Feminism and Race*, Oxford, England: Oxford University Press: 479–491.

French, J. L. (2005) *Nature, Neo-Colonialism, and the Spanish American Regional Writers*, (Re-Encounters with Colonialism series) Hanover, NH: Dartmouth College Press/University Press of New England.

Friedman, S. S. (2006) 'Periodizing Modernism: Postcolonial Modernities and the Space/Time Borders of Modernist Studies', *Modernism/Modernity* 13(3): 425–443.

Friel, B. (1981) *Translations*, London and Boston: Faber & Faber. (First performed in September 1980.) .

Fuchs, J. (2000) 'Postcolonial Mock-Epic: Abrogation and Appropriation.' *Studies in the Literary Imagination* 33(2): 23–43.

Fuss, D. (1994) 'Interior Colonies: Frantz Fanon and the Politics of Identification', *Diacritics* (24) 2–3 (Summer/Fall): 20–42.

Gandhi, L. (1998) *Postcolonial Theory: A Critical Introduction*, New York: Columbia University Press.

Gandhi, L. (2006) *Affective Communities: Anticolonial Thought, Fin-de-Siècle Radicalism, and the Politics of Friendship*, Durham: Duke University Press.

Ganguly, K. (2002) 'Adorno, Authenticity, Critique' in C. Bartolovich and N. Lazarus (eds) *Marxism, Modernity, and Postcolonial Studies*, Cambridge: Cambridge University Press.

García, O. (2006) 'Lost in Transculturation: The Case of Bilingual Education in New York City' in M. Pütz, J. A. Fishman, J. Neff-van Aertselaer and C. Baker (eds) *'Along the Routes to Power': Explorations of Empowerment through Language*, Berlin, Germany: Mouton de Gruyter: 157–177.

Gardiner, M. (2001) 'Postcolonial Theory, Modernity and Scottish Cultural Identity' in A. Blake and J. Nyman (eds) *Text and Nation: Essays on Post-Colonial Cultural Politics*, Joensuu, Finland: Faculty of Humanities, University of Joensuu: 73–86.

Gates Jnr, H. L. (1986) *'Race', Writing and Difference*, Chicago and London: University of Chicago Press.

Gates Jnr, H .L. (1991) 'Critical Fanonism', *Critical Inquiry* 17 (Spring).

Gellner, E. (2006) *Nations and Nationalism*, Oxford: Blackwell.

George, O. (2003) *Relocating Agency: Modernity and African Letters*, Albany, NY: State University of New York Press.

Gérard, A. (1990) 'Literature, Language, Nation and the Commonwealth' in G. V. Davis and H. Maes-Jelinek (eds) *Crisis and Creativity in the New Literatures in English: Cross/Cultures*, Amsterdam: Rodopi: 93–101.

Ghosh, A (2004), *The Hungry Tide*, New York: Penguin.

Ghosh, B. N. (2000) *Dependency Theory Revisited*, Aldershot: Ashgate.

Gibson, R. (1992) *South of the West: Postcolonialism and the Narrative Construction of Australia*, Bloomington: Indiana University Press.

Giddens, A. (1990), *The Consequences of Modernity*, Cambridge: Polity Press.

Gikandi, S. (1992) 'The Politics and Poetics of National Formation: Recent African Writing' in Anna Rutherford (ed.) *From Commonwealth to Post-Colonial*, Aarhus and Sydney: Dangaroo Press.

Gikandi, S. (2000) 'Reading the Referent: Postcolonialism and the Writing of Modernity' in S. Nasta (ed.) *Reading the "New" Literatures in a Postcolonial Era*, Cambridge, England: Brewer: 87–104.

Gikandi, S. (2001) 'Globalization and the Claims of Postcoloniality', *South Atlantic Quarterly* 100(3): 627–658.

Gikandi, S. (2004) 'Poststructuralism and Postcolonial Discourse' in N. Lazarus (ed.) *The Cambridge Companion to Postcolonial Literary Studies*, Cambridge: Cambridge University Press: 97–119.

Gikandi, S. (2006) 'Postcolonial Theory and the Specter of Nationalism', *CLIO: A Journal of Literature, History, and the Philosophy of History* 36(1): 69–84.

Gilbert, H. (1993) 'Postcolonial Grotesques: Re-Membering the Body in Louis Nowra's Visions and The Golden Age.' *SPAN: Journal of the South Pacific Association for Commonwealth Literature and Language Studies* 36: 618–633.

Gilman, C. (1985) *Pidgin Languages: Form Selection or Simplification?* Bloomington: Indiana University Linguistics Club.

Gilman, S. L. (1985) 'Black Bodies, White Bodies: Toward an Iconography of Female Sexuality in Nineteenth-century Art, Medicine, and Literature' in Henry Louis Gates (ed.) *'Race', Writing, and Difference*, Chicago and London: University of Chicago Press.

Gilroy, Paul (1987) *There Ain't No Black in the Union Jack: The Cultural Politics of Race and Nation*, London: Hutchinson.

Gilroy, Paul (1993) *The Black Atlantic, modernity and modern consciousness*, New York: Verso.

Gilroy, P. (1996) '"The Whisper Wakes, the Shudder Plays": "Race," Nation and Ethnic Absolutism' in P. Mongia (ed.) *Contemporary Postcolonial Theory: A Reader*, London: Arnold: 248–274.

Gilroy, P. (2002) 'The End of Antiracism' in Philomena Essed and David Theo Goldberg (eds), *Race Critical Theories: Text and Context*, pp. 249–264. Malden, Mass. and Oxford: Blackwell.

Gilroy, P. (2004) *After Empire: Melancholia or Convivial Culture?*, Abingdon, Oxfordshire: Routledge.

Glissant, E. (1989) *Caribbean Discourse: Selected Essays,* translated by J. Michael Dash, Charlottesville: University Press of Virginia. (French version, Paris: Editions Seuill 1981) .

Gobineau J. A., comte de (1853–5) *Essai sur l'inégalité des Races humaines,* (4 vols.) Paris: Firmin Didot.

Gobineau, J. A., comte de (1856) *The Moral and Intellectual Diversity of Races (Essai sur l'inégalité des Races Humaines),* New York: Garland 1984 (originally published Philadelphia: Lippincott 1856).

Goffinan, E. (1961) *Asylums: Essays on the Social Situation of Mental Patients and Other Inmates,* Harmondsworth: Penguin.

Gòkè-Paríolá, A. (1996) 'African American Vernacular English in Colonial and Postcolonial Perspectives: The Linguistic Paradox', *Journal of Commonwealth and Postcolonial Studies* 4(1): 14–23.

Goldberg, D. T. and A. Quayson (2002) *Relocating Postcolonialism*, Malden, MA: Blackwell Publishers.

Goodman, James and Paul James (2007), *Nationalism and Global Solidarities: Alternative Projections to Neoliberal Globalization*, London: Routledge.

Goodwin, K. (1992) 'Studying Commonwealth Literature', *College Literature* 19–20(3–1 [Double issue]): 142–151.

Gopal, P. (2004) 'Reading Subaltern Histor' in N. Lazarus (ed.) *The Cambridge Companion to Postcolonial Literary Studies*, Cambridge: Cambridge University Press.

Gossai, H. and N. S. Murrell (2000) *Religion, Culture, and Tradition in the Caribbean*, New York: St. Martin's.

Goswami, M. (2005) 'Autonomy and Comparability: Notes on the Anticolonial and the Postcolonial', *Boundary 2: An International Journal of Literature and Culture* 32(2): 201–225.

Gowda, H. H. A. (1983) *The Colonial and the Neo-Colonial Encounters in Commonwealth Literature*, Mysore: Prasaragana University.

Gramsci, A. (1971) *Selections from the Prison Notebooks,* edited and translated by Quintin Hoare and Geoffrey Nowell Smith, London: Lawrence & Wishart.

Gramsci, A. (1988) *A Gramsci Reader: Selected Writings 1916–1935,* edited by David Forgacs, London: Lawrence & Wishart.

Gramsci, A. (1991) *Prison Notebooks*, New York: Columbia University Press.

Green, M. J., K. Gould, *et al.* (1996) (eds) *Postcolonial Subjects: Francophone Women Writers*, Minneapolis: University of Minnesota Press.

Griffiths, G. (1994) 'The Myth of Authenticity' in C. Tiffin and A. Lawson (eds) *De-scribing Empire: Postcolonialism and Textuality*, London: Routledge.

Griffiths, G. (1997) 'Writing, Literacy and History in Africa' in M.-H. Msiske and P. Hyland (eds) *Writing and Africa*, London: Longman.

Griffiths, Gareth (2000) *African Literatures in English (East and West)*, London: Longman.

Griffiths, Gareth (2003) '"Anglophonic" Culture in the New Milllennium: Inter-Cultural Words and Images in the Cyberage in the Asian Region' in *Anglophone Cultures in Southeast Asia* (eds) Ahrens *et al.*, Universitätsverlag Winter: Heidelberg.

Griffiths, Gareth (2005) '"Trained to Tell the Truth": Missionaries, Converts and Narration' in Etherington, Norman (2005) *Missions and Imperialism*, Companion Volume, Oxford History of the British Empire, Oxford: Oxford University Press.

Griffiths, Gareth and J. V. Singler (eds) (2004) *Guanya Pau: The Story of an African Princess (1891)*, Peterborough, ON, Canada: Broadview Editions, Broadview Press.

Griffiths, Gareth (2007) 'Sites of Purchase: Slavery, Missions and Tourism on Two Tanzanian Sites' in *Economies of Representation, 1790–2000: Colonialism and Commerce,* ed. Leigh Dale and Helen Gilbert, Burlington, Vermont, Ashgate.

Grove, R. (1994) *Green Imperialism,* Cambridge: Cambridge University Press.

Gruesser, J. C. (2005) *Confluences: Postcolonialism, African American Literary Studies and the Black Atlantic*, Athens, Georgia: University of Georgia Press.

Gualtieri, C. (1996) 'The Colonial Exotic Deconstructed: A Suggested Reading Paradigm for Post-Colonial Texts' in W. Zach and K. L. Goodwin (eds) *Nationalism vs. Internationalism: (Inter)National Dimensions of Literatures in English*, Tübingen, Germany: Stauffenburg: 47–53.

Gugelberger, G. (1996) *The Real Thing,* Durham and London: Duke University Press.

Gugelberger, G. and Kearney, M. (1991) (eds) 'Voices for the Voiceless: Testimonial Literature in Latin America', *Latin American Perspectives*, Issue 70, (18) 3 (Summer); Issue 71, (18) 4 (Fall).

Guha, R. (1997) (ed.) *A Subaltern studies reader, 1986–1995*, Minneapolis: University of Minnesota Press.

Guha, R. (2001) 'Subaltern Studies: Projects for Our Time and Their Convergence' in I. Rodríguez (ed.) *The Latin American Subaltern Studies Reader*, Durham, NC: Duke University Press.

Guha, R. and J. Martinez-Alier (1997) *Varieties of Environmentalism* London, Sterlin VA.: Earthscan.

Guha, R. and G. C. Spivak. (1988) (eds) *Selected Subaltern studies*, New York: Oxford University Press.

Gunew, S. (1994) *Framing Marginality: Multicultural Literary Studies,* Carlton, Victoria: Melbourne University Press.

Gunew, S. (1997) 'Postcolonialism and Multiculturalism: Between Race and Ethnicity', *Yearbook of English Studies* 27: 22–39.

Gunew, S. (2004) *Haunted Nations: The Colonial Dimensions of Multiculturalisms,* London: Routledge.

Gunner, E. and Gwala, M. (1991) (trans. and eds) *Musho! Zulu Popular Praises,* East Lansing: Michigan State University Press. Gunner, E. (1994) *Politics and Performance,* Johannesburg: Wits University Press.

Gunner, E. and Furniss, G. (1995) *Power, Marginality and African Oral Literature,* Cambridge and New York: Cambridge University Press.

Gunner, E. (2004) 'Africa and Orality', Chapter 1, pp.1–18 in Abiola Irele and Simon Gikandi (eds), *The Cambridge History of African and Caribbean Literature* Vol 1, Cambridge: Cambridge University Press.

Gurnah, A. (2000) 'Imagining the Postcolonial Writer' in S. Nasta (ed.) *Reading the 'New' Literatures in a Postcolonial Era,* Cambridge: Brewer: 73–86.

Gurr, A. (1981) *Writers in Exile: The Identity of Home in Modern Literature,* Brighton: Harvester.

Habermas, J. (1981) 'Modernity versus Postmodernity', *New German Critique* 22.

Habermas, J. (1987) *The Philosophical Discourse of Modernity,* Cambridge: Polity.

Haddour, A. (2005) 'Sartre and Fanon: On Negritude and Political Participation', *Sartre Studies International: An Interdisciplinary Journal of Existentialism and Contemporary Culture* 11(1–2): 286–301.

Hadiz, Vedi R. (2006), *Empire and Neoliberalism in Asia,* London: Routledge.

Hadjor, K. B. (1992) *Dictionary of Third World Terms,* Harmondsworth: Penguin.

Hall Jnr, R. A. (1988) *Pidgin and Creole Languages,* London and New York: Longman Linguistics Library.

Hall, C. M. and H. Tucker (2004) *Tourism and Postcolonialism: Contested Discourses, Identities and Representations,* London: Routledge.

Hall, S. (1989) 'New Ethnicities' in *Black Film, British Cinema,* ICA Documents 7, London: Institute of Contemporary Arts.

Hall, S. (1991) 'The Local and the Global: Globalisation and Ethnicity' in A. King (ed.) *Culture Globalization and the World System,* London: Macmillan.

Hall, S. (1996) 'Cultural Identity and Diaspora' in P. Mongia (ed.) *Contemporary Postcolonial Theory: A Reader,* London: Arnold: 110–121.

Hammersley, M. and Atkinson, P. (1983) *Ethnography: Principles in Practice,* London and New York: Tavistock.

Hanchard, M. (1997) 'Identity, Meaning, and the African-American' in A. McClintock, A. Mufti and E. Shohat (eds) *Dangerous Liaisons: Gender, Nation, and Postcolonial Perspectives,* Minneapolis: University of Minnesota Press.

Harding, S. G. and U. Narayan, (eds) (2000) *Decentering the Center: Philosophy for a Multicultural, Postcolonial, and Feminist World*, Bloomington, Indiana: Indiana University Press.

Hardt, Michael and Antonio Negri (2001), *Empire*, Cambridge, Mass., London: Harvard University Press.

Harlow, B. (1987) *Resistance Literature,* New York: Methuen.

Harlow, B. and M. Carter (1999) (eds) *Imperialism and Orientalism: A Documentary Sourcebook*, Malden, Massachussetts: Blackwell Publishers.

Harris, M. (1992) *Outsiders & Insiders: Perspectives of Third World Culture in British and Post-Colonial Fiction*, New York: Peter Lang.

Harris, W. (1970) *Ascent to Omai*, London: Faber.

Harris, W. (1981) *Explorations: A Selection of Talks and Articles 1966–1981,* edited by Hena Maes-Jelinek, Aarhus, Denmark: Dangaroo.

Harris, W. (1983) *The Womb of Space: The Cross-Cultural Imagination,* Westport, CT: Greenwood.

Harris, W. (2004) 'Resistances to Alterities' in M. Fazzini (ed.) *Resisting Alterities: Wilson Harris and Other Avatars of Otherness*, Amsterdam, Netherlands: Rodopi.

Harrison, C., Frascina, F. and Perry, G. (1993) *Primitivism, Cubism, Abstraction: The Early Twentieth Century,* New Haven: Yale University Press, in association with the Open University.

Harrison, N. (2003) *Postcolonial Criticism: History, Theory and the Work of Fiction*, Cambridge: Polity Press in association with Blackwell Publishers.

Hart, J. (1997) 'Translating and Resisting Empire: Cultural Appropriation and Postcolonial Studies' in B. Ziff and P. V. Rao (eds) *Borrowed Power: Essays on Cultural Appropriation*, New Brunswick, New Jersey: Rutgers University Press.

Hart, J. (2003) *Comparing Empires: European Colonialism from Portuguese Expansion to the Spanish-American War*, New York: Palgrave Macmillan.

Harvey, David (2005), *A Brief History of Neoliberalism* Oxford, New York: Oxford University Press.

Hasseler, T. A. (1997) 'Articulating Feminist Causes and Democratic Futures in Western and Third World Feminism.' *ARIEL: A Review of International English Literature* 28(4): 154–168.

Havinden, M. and Meredith, D. (1993) *Colonialism and Development: Britain and its Tropical Colonies, 1850–1960,* London: Routledge.

Hawes, C. (2003) 'Periodizing Johnson: Anticolonial Modernity as Crux and Critique' in A. Burton (ed.) *After the Imperial Turn: Thinking With and Through the Nation*, Durham: Duke University Press.

Hawley, J. C. (1996) *Writing the Nation: Self and Country in the Post-Colonial Imagination*, Amsterdam: Rodopi.

Hawley, J. C. (2001) *Encyclopedia of Postcolonial Studies*, Westport, CT: Greenwood.

Hayes Edwards, B. (2003) *The Practice of Diaspora: Literature, Translation, and the Rise of Black Internationalism*, Cambridge, MA: Harvard University Press.

Head, D. (1999), 'The (im)possibility of Ecocriticism' in R. Kerridge and N. Sammells (eds) *Writing the Environment: Ecocriticism and Literature* London: Zed Books.

Head, D. (2006) *The Cambridge Guide to Literature in English*, Cambridge: Cambridge University Press.

Healy, C. (1997) *From the Ruins of Colonialism: History as Social Memory*, Cambridge: Cambridge University Press.

Healy, J. J. (1979) *Literature and the Aborigine in Australia*, St Lucia: University of Queensland Press (2nd ed. 1989).

Hennessy, Rosemary with Martha Ojeda (2007) *NAFTA From Below: Maquiladora Workers, Campesinos, and Indigenous Communities Speak Back*, San Antonio, Texas: The Coalition for Justice in the Maquiladoras.

Herk, A v. (1996) 'Pioneers and Settlers' in B. King (ed.) *New National and Post-Colonial Literatures: An Introduction*, Oxford: Clarendon.

Hiatt, A. (2005) 'Mapping the Ends of Empire' in A. J. Kabir and D. Williams (eds) *Postcolonial Approaches to the European Middle Ages: Translating Cultures*, Cambridge: Cambridge University Press.

Higman, B.W. (1984) *Slave Populations in the British Caribbean 1807–1834*, London and Baltimore: Johns Hopkins University Press.

Hildebrant, M. (1992) 'Mestizaje lingüístico en un vocabulario del siglo XVII.' *Boletín de la Academia Argentina de Letras* 57(223–224): 9–30.

Hill, Mike (1997) *Whiteness: A Critical Reader*, New York: New York University Press.

Hill, Mike (2004a) *After Whiteness: Unmaking An American Majority*, New York, New York University Press.

Hill, Mike (2004b) 'Interview with Damien W. Riggs', *Borderlands-ejournal*, Vol 3, No. 2004.

Hiller, S. (1991) (ed.) *The Myth of Primitivism: Perspectives on Art*, London and New York: Routledge.

Hobsbawm, E. J. (1968) *Industry and Empire: An Economic History of Britain since 1750*, London: Weidenfeld & Nicolson.

Hobsbawm, E. J. (1990) *Nations and Nationalism Since 1780*, Cambridge: Canto (Cambridge University Press).

Hobson, J. A. (1902) *Imperialism*, Ann Arbor: University of Michigan Press.

Hodge, B. and Mishra, V. (1990) *The Dark Side of the Dream: Australian Literature and the Postcolonial Mind*, Sydney: Allen & Unwin.

Hodges, H. (2000) 'The Far Eye: Rastafarian Historicism in West Indian Literature', *In Process: A Journal of African American and African Diasporan Literature and Culture* 2: 114–136.

Hoeller Christian (2002) 'Africa in Motion' (interview with Achille Mbembe) *Springerin*, No. 3.

Hofmeyer, I. (1993) *We Spend Our Years As a Tale that is Told: Oral Historical Narrative in a South African Chiefdom*, Johannesburg: Witwatersrand University Press; New Haven: Heinemann.

Hofmeyer, I. (2004) *The Portable Bunyan: A Transnational History of 'The Pilgrims Progress*, Princeton N.J.: Princeton University Press.

Hogan, P. C. (2000) *Colonialism and Cultural Identity: Crises of Tradition in the Anglophone Literatures of India, Africa, and the Caribbean*, New York: State University of New York Press.

Holm, J. A. (1988) *Pidgins and Creoles: Theory and Structure*, Vol. I, Cambridge Language Surveys, Cambridge: Cambridge University Press 1–12.

Holm, J. A. (1989) *Pidgins and creoles*, Cambridge: Cambridge University Press.

Holquist, M. (1984) 'Introduction' to Mikhail Bakhtin *Rabelais and his World*, translated by Hélène Iswolsky, Bloomington: Indiana University Press.

Holst-Petersen, K. and Rutherford, A. (1985) *A Double Colonization: Colonial and Post-Colonial Womens' Writing*, Aarhus, Denmark: Dangaroo.

Hoogvelt, A. M. M. (2001) *Globalization and the Postcolonial World: The New Political Economy of Development*, Basingstoke: Palgrave.

hooks, b. (1997) 'Sisterhood: Political Solidarity between Women' in A. McClintock, A. Mufti and E. Shohat (ed.) *Dangerous Liaisons: Gender, Nation, and Postcolonial Perspectives*, Minneapolis, MN: University of Minnesota Press: 396–411.

Hopkins, T. K. (1982) *World-Systems Analysis: Theory and Methodology*, Beverly Hills, California: Sage Publications.

Horton, J. O. (2004) *Slavery and the Making of America*, New York: Oxford University Press.

Huggan, G. (1989) 'Decolonizing the map: post-colonialism, post-structuralism and the cartographic connection', *Ariel* 20 (4): 115–131.

Huggan, G. (1994) 'A Tale of Two Parrots: Walcott, Rhys, and the Uses of Colonial Mimicry', *Contemporary Literature* 35(4): 643–660.

Huggan, G. (1997) '(Post)Colonialism, Anthropology, and the Magic of Mimesis', *Cultural Critique* 38(0): 91–106.

Huggan, G. (2000) 'Counter-Travel Writing and Post-Coloniality' in L. Glage (ed.) *Being/s in Transit: Travelling, Migration, Dislocation*, Amsterdam, Netherlands: Rodopi: 37–59.

Huggan, G. (2001) *The Postcolonial Exotic: Marketing the Margins*, London: Routledge.

Huggan, G. (2004) 'Postcolonialism, Globalization, and the Rise of (Trans)Cultural Studies' in G. V. Davis, P. H. Marsden, B. Ledent and M. Delrez (eds) *Towards a Transcultural Future: Literature and Society in a 'Post'-Colonial World*, Amsterdam, Netherlands: Rodopi.

Hulme, P. (1986) *Colonial Encounters: Europe and the Native Caribbean 1492–1797*, London: Methuen (reissued Routledge 1992).

Hulme, P. (1989) 'Subversive Archipelagos: Colonial Discourse and the Break-Up of Continental Theory', *Dispositio/n: American Journal of Cultural Histories and Theories* 14(36–38): 1–23.

Hulme, P. (2000) *Remnants of Conquest: The Island Caribs and Their Visitors 1877–1998*, Oxford: Oxford University Press.

Hulme, P. (2005) 'Beyond the Straits: Postcolonial Allegories of the Globe' in A. Loomba *et al.* (eds) *Postcolonial Studies and Beyond*, Durham: Duke University Press.

Husband, C. (1994) *'Race' and Nation: The British Experience,* Perth, WA: Paradigm.

Hyam, R. (1990) *Empire and Sexuality: The British Experience,* Manchester and New York: Manchester University Press.

Ingold, T. (1996) (ed.) *Key Debates in Anthropology,* London and New York: Routledge.

Institute of Commonwealth Studies (1982) *The Diaspora of the British,* London: University of London (Institute of Commonwealth Studies).

Irele, F. A. (2003) 'The Harlem Renaissance and the Negritude Movement' in F. A. Irele and S. Gikandi (eds) *The Cambridge History of African and Caribbean Literature,* Cambridge, England: Cambridge University Press: 759–784.

Isajaw, W. W. (1974) 'Definitions of Ethnicity' *Ethnicity* (1) 2: 111–174.

Jacobs, J. (2004) 'Writing Reconciliation: South African Fiction after Apartheid' in M. Fazzini (ed.) *Resisting Alterities: Wilson Harris and Other Avatars of Otherness,* Amsterdam, Netherlands: Rodopi.

Jack, B. E. (1996) *Negritude and Literary Criticism: The History and Theory of 'Negro-African' Literature in French,* Westport, CT: Greenwood Press.

Jackson, Peter, Phillip Crang and Claire Dwyer eds. (2004) *Transnational Spaces* London: Routledge.

Jahoda, G. (1999) *Images of Savages: Ancients [sic] Roots of Modern Prejudice in Western Culture,* London: Routledge.

Jameson, F. (1986) 'Third World Literature in the Era of Multinational Capitalism', *Social Text* 15 (Fall).

Janiewski, D. E. (1998) '"Confusion of Mind": Colonial and Post-Colonial Discourses about Frontier Encounters', *Journal of American Studies* 32(1): 81–103.

JanMohammed, A.R. (1983) *Manichean Aesthetics: The Politics of Literature in Colonial Africa,* Amherst: University of Massachusetts Press.

JanMohammed, A. R. (1985) 'The Economy of Manichean Allegory: The Function of Racial Difference in Colonialist Literature', *Critical Inquiry* 12 (1). In Ashcroft *et al.* 1995, pp. 18–23.

Janz, Bruce (2002) Review of Achille Mbembe's *On the Postcolony,* H-Africa Net, March. http://www.h-net.org/reviews/showrev.cgi?path=122821 016818245.

Jarratt, S. C. (2004) 'Beside Ourselves: Rhetoric and Representation in Postcolonial Feminist Writing' in A. A. Lunsford and L. Ouzgane (eds) *Crossing Borderlands: Composition and Postcolonial Studies,* Pittsburgh, PA: University of Pittsburgh Press: 110–128.

Johnson, G. A. and Smith, M. B. (1990) (eds), *Ontology and Alterity in Merleau-Ponty,* Evanston, IL.: Northwestern.

Johnston, A. (2002) 'Tahiti, "the Desire of Our Eyes": Missionary Travel Narratives and Imperial Surveillance' in H. Gilbert and A. Johnston (eds) *In Transit: Travel, Text, Empire,* New York: Peter Lang.

Jones, J. (1965) *Terranglia: The Case for English as World Literature,* New York: Twayne.

Jordan, G. and Weedon, C. (1995) *Cultural Politics: Class, Gender, Race, and the Postmodern World*, Oxford, UK and Cambridge, MA: Blackwell.

Joyce, J. A. (2005) *Black Studies as Human Studies: Critical Essays and Interviews*, Albany, NY: State University of New York Press.

Jules-Rosette, Benetta (2002) 'Afro-Pessimism's Many Guises', *Public Culture* 14.3 (2002.

Jurak, M. (1992) 'The Role of New Literatures in the Framework of English Studies' in M. Jurak (ed.) *Literature, Culture and Ethnicity: Studies on Medieval, Renaissance and Modern Literatures*, Ljubljana: Author: 45–49.

Kanneh, K. (1995) *The Difficult Politics of Wigs and Veils: Feminism and the Colonial Body* (paper presented at the Conference on Gender and Colonialism, U. C. Galway, May 1992, in Ashcroft *et al.* (1995).

Kanth, R. K. (2005) *Against Eurocentrism: A Transcendent Critique of Modernist Science, Society, and Morals: A Discursus on Human Emancipation: Purporting to be a Speculative Critique and Resolution of the Malaise of Modernism*, New York: Palgrave Macmillan.

Katrak, K. H. (1996) 'Post-Colonial Women Writers and Feminisms' in B. King (ed.) *New National and Post-Colonial Literatures: An Introduction*, Oxford: Clarendon: 230–244.

Katrak, K. H. (2006) *Politics of the Female Body: Postcolonial Women Writers of the Third World*, New Brunswick, N.J: Rutgers University Press.

Kaul, S. (1996) 'Colonial Figures and Postcolonial Reading', *Diacritics: A Review of Contemporary Criticism* 26(1): 74–89.

Keita, Lansana (2006) Review 'On the Postcolony (Mbembe)', *Transforming Anthropology*, April 2005, Vol. 13, No. 1, pp. 67–68.

Kemedjio, C. (1999) *De la négritude á la créolité: Edouard Glissant, Maryse Condé et la malédiction de la théorie*, Hamburg, Germany: LIT.

Kennedy, E. C. (1975) (ed. and introd.) *The Negritude Poets: An Anthology of Translations from the French*, New York: Viking.

Kent, J. (1992) *The Internationalization of Colonialism: Britain, France, and Black Africa, 1939–1956*, Oxford: Clarendon Press.

Keown, M. (2005) *Postcolonial Pacific Writing: Representations of the Body*, London: Routledge.

Kilgour, M. (1993) *From Communion to Cannibalism: An Anatomy of Metaphors of Incorporation*, Princeton, NJ: Princeton University Press.

Kincaid, J. (1985) *Annie John*, London: Picador.

Kincaid, J. (1988) *A Small Place*, London: Virago.

King, A. D. (1991) (ed.) *Culture Globalization and the World System*, London: Macmillan.

King, B. (1974) (ed.) *Literatures of the World in English*, London: Routledge.

King, B. (1980) *The New Literatures in English*, London: Macmillan.

King, B. (1983) 'Nationalism, Internationalism, Periodisation and Common-wealth Literature' in D. Riemenschneider (ed.) *The History and Historiography of Commonwealth Literature*, Tübingen: Narr.

King, B. (1996) (ed.) *New National and Post-Colonial Literatures: An Introduction*, Oxford: Clarendon.

King, R. (1999) *Orientalism and Religion: Postcolonial Theory, India and 'The Mystic East'*, London and New York: Routledge.

King, S. and R. J. Jensen (1995) 'Bob Marley's "Redemption Song": The Rhetoric of Reggae and Rastafari', *Journal of Popular Culture* 29(3): 17–36.

King, S. A., B. T. I. Bays, *et al.* (2003) (eds) *Reggae, Rastafari, and the Rhetoric of Social Control*, Jackson, MS: University Press of Mississippi.

Kipling, R. (1889) 'The Ballad of East and West' in *Rudyard Kipling's Verse: The Definitive Edition*, London: Hodder & Stoughton (1940).

Kipling, R. (1897) 'Recessional' in *Rudyard Kipling's Verse: The Definitive Edition*, London: Hodder & Stoughton (1940).

Kipling, R. (1899) 'The White Man's Burden: The United States and the Philippine Islands' in *Rudyard Kipling's Verse: The Definitive Edition*, London: Hodder & Stoughton (1940).

Klein, M. A. and S. Miers. (1999) (eds) *Slavery and Colonial Rule in Africa*, Portland, OR: Frank Cass.

Klor de Alva, J. J. (1995) 'The Postcolonization of the (Latin) American Experience: A Reconsideration of "Colonialism," "Postcolonialism," and "Mestizaje"' in G. Prakash (ed.) *After Colonialism: Imperial Histories and Postcolonial Displacements*, Princeton, N.J: Princeton University Press: NP.

Koebner, R. (1961) *Empire*, Cambridge: Cambridge University Press.

Koebner, R. and Schmidt, H.D. (1964) *Imperialism: The Story and Significance of a Political Word, 1840–1960,* Cambridge: Cambridge University Press.

Kofman, E. and Youngs, G. (1996) *Globalization: Theory and Practice,* London: Pinter.

Kokotovic, M. (2005) *The Colonial Divide in Peruvian Narrative: Social Conflict and Transculturation*, Brighton, England: Sussex Academic.

Kroestch, R. (1974) 'Unhiding the Hidden: Recent Canadian Fiction', *Journal of Canadian Fiction,* (3) 3. Cited in Ashcroft *et al.* (1995) pp. 394–396.

Korte, B. (2001) 'Exploring without a Mission? Postcolonial Travel in a Global World' in G. Stilz (ed.) *Colonies, Missions, Cultures in the English Speaking World: General and Comparative Studies*, Tübingen, Germany: Stauffenburg: 383–395.

Korte, B. and C. Matthias (2000) *English Travel Writing from Pilgrimages to Postcolonial Explorations*, Basingstoke, England: Macmillan.

Koshy, S. (2005) 'The Postmodern Subaltern: Globalization Theory and the Subject of Ethnic, Area, and Postcolonial Studies' in F. Lionnet and S.-m. Shih (eds) *Minor Transnationalism*, Durham: Duke University Press.

Koundoura, M. (2002) 'Reoccupying the Space of Culture: Greece and the Postcolonial Critique of Modernity', *Journal x: A Journal in Culture and Criticism* 6(2): 127–140.

Kraniauskas, J. (2004) 'Hybridity in a Transnational Frame: Latin Americanist and Postcolonial Perspectives on Cultural Studies' in A. Del Sarto, A. Ríos and A. Trigo (eds) *The Latin American Cultural Studies Reader*, Durham, NC: Duke University Press.

Kroestch, R. (1974) 'Unhiding the Hidden: Recent Canadian Fiction', *Journal of Canadian Fiction,* (3) 3. Cited in Ashcroft *et al.* (1995) pp. 394–396.

Kumar, Amitava (2003) (ed.) *World Bank Literature*, Minneapolis: University of Minnesota.

Lacan, J. (1966) *Ecrits,* Paris: Editions du Seuil.

Lacan, J. (1968) *The Language of the Self: The Function of Language in Psychoanalysis,* translated with notes and commentary, by Anthony Wilden, Baltimore, MD: Johns Hopkins University Press.

Lacan, J. (1977) *Ecrits: A Selection,* translated by Alan Sheridan, London: Tavistock.

Lane, J.-E. (2006) *Globalization and Politics: Promises and Dangers*, Aldershot: Ashgate.

Lang, G. (2000) *Entwisted Tongues: Comparative Creole Literatures*, Amsterdam: Rodopi.

Lapping, B. (1987) *Apartheid: A History,* London: Paladin.

Larson, C. (1973) 'Heroic Ethnocentrism: The Idea of Universality in Literature', *The American Scholar* (42) 3 (Summer).

Larsen, N. (1997) 'Poverties of Nation: The Ends of the Earth, "Monetary Subjects without Money," and Postcolonial Theory', *Cultural Logic: An Electronic Journal of Marxist Theory and Practice* 1(1).

Lawson, A. (1991) 'A Cultural Paradigm for the Second World', *Australian–Canadian Studies* (9) 1–2: 67–78.

Lawson, A. (1994) 'Un/settling Colonies: The Ambivalent Place of Discursive Resistance' in Chris Worth *et al.* (eds) *Literature and Opposition,* Clayton, Victoria: Centre for Comparative and Cultural Studies, Monash University.

Lawson, A. (1995) 'Postcolonial Theory and the "Settler" Subject', *Essays on Canadian Writing* 56 (Fall): 20–36.

Lawson, S. (2006) *Culture and Context in World Politics*, New York: Palgrave Macmillan.

Lazarus, N. (1993) 'Disavowing Decolonization: Fanon, Nationalism, and the Problematic of Representation in Current Theories of Colonial Discourse', *Research in African Literatures* 24(4): 69–98.

Lazarus, N. (1994) 'National Consciousness and the Specificity of (Post) Colonial Intellectualism' in F. Barker, P. Hulme and M. Iversen (eds) *Colonial Discourse/Postcolonial Theory*, Manchester: Manchester University Press: 197–220.

Lazarus, N. (1999) *Nationalism and Cultural Practice in the Postcolonial World*, Cambridge: Cambridge University Press.

Lazarus, N. (2002) 'The Fetish of "the West" in Postcolonial Theory' in C. Bartolovich and N. Lazarus (eds) *Marxism, Modernity, and Postcolonial Studies*, Cambridge: Cambridge University Press: 43–64.

Lazarus, N. (2004) 'Fredric Jameson on "Third-World Literature": A Qualified Defense' in D. Kellner and S. Homer (eds) *Fredric Jameson: A Critical Reader*, Basingstoke, England: Palgrave Macmillan.

Lazarus, N. (2005) 'The Politics of Postcolonial Modernism' in A. Loomba, S. Kaul, M. Bunzl, A. Burton and J. Esty (eds) *Postcolonial Studies and Beyond*, Durham, NC: Duke University Press: 423–438.

Lazarus, N., S. Evans, *et al.* (1995) 'The Necessity of Universalism', *Differences: A Journal of Feminist Cultural Studies* (7) 1: 75–145.

Lee, D. (1974) 'Cadence, Country, Silence: Writing in Colonial Space', *Boundary* 2 (3) 1 (Fall). Cited in Ashcroft *et al.* 1995 pp. 397–401.

Leer, M. (1992) 'Europe, the Orient and the New World: Conceptual Geography and Historical Cosmology 1492–1992', *Kunapipi* 14(2): 22–34.

Lefevere, A. (1983) 'Interface: Some Thoughts on the Historiography of African Literature Written in English' in Dieter Riemenschneider (ed.) *The History and Historiography of Commonwealth Literature,* Tübingen: Gunter Narr Verlag.

Lemire, E. (2002) *'Miscegenation': Making Race in America*, Philadelphia, PA: University of Pennsylvania Press.

Lenin, V. I. (1916) 'Imperialism, the Highest Stage of Capitalism' in *Collected Works of V.I. Lenin,* Moscow: Foreign Language House, 1960–1969.

Lennon, J. (2004) *Irish Orientalism: A Literary and Intellectual History*, Syracuse, NY: Syracuse University Press.

Leonard, P. (2005) *Nationality between Poststructuralism and Postcolonial Theory: A New Cosmopolitanism*, New York: Palgrave Macmillan.

Levitt, Peggy and Mary C. Waters, eds (2002) *The Changing Face of Home: the Transnational Lives of the Second Generation.* New York: Russell Sage Foundation.

Lewis, R. (1996) *Gendering Orientalism: Race, Femininity, and Representation*, New York: Routledge.

Liano, D. (2003) 'Sobre el testimonio y la literatura' in P. Collard, R. d. Maeseneer and R. Vázquez Díaz (eds) *Murales, figuras, fronteras: Narrativa e historia en el Caribe y Centroamérica*, Madrid: Iberoamericana.

Lichteim, G. (1971) *Imperialism,* London: Allen Lane.

Lim, S. G.-l. (2002) 'New Literatures in English and Postcolonial Writers in the Age of Globalization' in G. Collier and F. Schulze-Engler (eds) *Crabtracks: Progress and Process in Teaching the New Literatures in English*, Amsterdam, Netherlands: Rodopi: 141–152.

Lionnet, F. (1995) *Postcolonial Representations: Women, Literature, Identity*, Ithaca, NY: Cornell University Press.

Lionnet, F. (1998) 'Performative Universalism and Cultural Diversity: French Thought and American Contexts' in J.-J. Goux and P. R. Wood (ed.) *Terror and Consensus: Vicissitudes of French Thought*, Stanford, CA: Stanford University Press: 119–132.

Lionnet, Françoise and Shu-mei Shih eds. (2005) *Minor Transnationalism* Durham: Duke University Press.

Lloyd, D. (2003) 'Ireland's Modernities' *Interventions: International Journal of Postcolonial Studies* 5(3): 317–474.

Locke, J. (1960) *Two Treatises of Government,* introduced by Peter Laslet, Cambridge: Cambridge University Press.

Lockman, Z. (2004) *Contending Visions of the Middle East: The History and Politics of Orientalism*, Cambridge: Cambridge University Press.

Lodge, T. (1986) (ed.) *Resistance and Ideology in Settler Societies*, Johannesburg: Ravan Press.

Longley, K. (1997) 'Places of Refuge: Postcolonial Spaces.' *Journal of the South Pacific Association for Commonwealth Literature and Language Studies* 44: 8–21.

Loomba, A. (2005) (ed) *Colonialism-Postcolonialism*, New York: Routledge.

Loomba, A. *et al* (2005) (eds) *Postcolonial Studies and Beyond*, Durham, Duke University Press.

Lott, E. (2000) 'After Identity, Politics: The Return of Universalism', *New Literary History: A Journal of Theory and Interpretation* (31) 4: 665–680.

Low, G. C.-L. (1996) *White Skins, Black Masks: Representation and Colonialism*, London: Routledge.

McCallum, P. and W. Faith (2005) *Linked Histories: Postcolonial Studies in Globalized World*, Calgary, AB: University of Calgary Press.

McClintock, A. (1995) *Imperial Leather: Race, Gender, and Sexuality in the Colonial Contest*, New York: Routledge.

McClintock, A., A. Mufti, *et al.* (1997) *Dangerous Liaisons: Gender, Nation, and Postcolonial Perspectives*, Minneapolis, MN: University of Minnesota Press.

McDougall, R. (1998) 'Walter Roth, Wilson Harris, and a Caribbean/ Postcolonial Theory of Modernism', *University of Toronto Quarterly: A Canadian Journal of the Humanities* 67(2): 567–591.

McGee, P. (1992) *Telling the Other: The Question of Value in Modern and Postcolonial Writing*, Ithaca: Cornell University Press.

McHoul, A. and Grace, W. (1993) *A Foucault Primer: Discourse, Power and the Subject*, Melbourne: Melbourne University Press.

McInturff, K. (2000) 'Disciplining Race: Crossing Intellectual Borders in African American and Postcolonial Studies', *Canadian Review of American Studies* 30(1): 73.

Mackenthun, G. (2000) 'Postcolonial Masquerade: Antebellum Sea Fiction and the Transatlantic Slave Trade' in K. H. Schmidt and F. Fleischman (ed.) *Early America Re-Explored: New Readings in Colonial, Early National, and Antebellum Culture*, New York: Peter Lang.

Mackenzie, J. M. (1989) *The Empire of Nature: Hunting, Conservation and British Imperialism*, Manchester: Manchester University Press.

MacKenzie, J. M. (1995) *Orientalism: History, Theory, and the Arts*, Manchester: Manchester University Press.

McLaren, J. (1993) *New Pacific Literatures: Culture and Environment in the European Pacific*, New York: Garland Publishers.

McLeod, J. (2004) *Postcolonial London: Rewriting the Metropolis*, London: Routledge.

McNeill, W. H. (1983) *The Great Frontier: Freedom and Hierarchy in Modern Times*, Princeton, NJ: Princeton University Press.

McQuillan, M. (2002) 'Irish Eagleton: Of Ontological Imperialism and Colonial Mimicry', *Irish Studies Review* 10(1): 29–38.

Maes-Jelinek, H. (1996) 'Another Future for Post-Colonial Studies? Wilson Harris' Post-Colonial Philosophy and the "Savage Mind"', *Wasafiri: Journal of Caribbean, African, Asian and Associated Literatures and Film* 24: 3–8.

Malik, K. (1996) *The Meaning of Race: Race, History and Culture in Western Society,* New York: New York University Press.

Mamdani, M. (2001) *When Victims Become Killers: Colonialism, Nativism and the Genocide in Rwanda,* Oxford: James Currey.

Mann, H. S. (1995) 'Women's Rights versus Feminism? Post-Colonial Perspectives' in G. Rajan and R. Mohanram (eds) *Postcolonial Discourse and Changing Cultural Contexts: Theory and Criticism,* Westport, CT: Greenwood: 69–88.

Manning, P. (1990) *Slavery and African Life: Occidental, Oriental and African Slave Trades,* Cambridge: Cambridge University Press.

Maolain, C. O. (1985) (ed.) *Latin American Political Movements,* Harlow: Longman.

Marriott, D. (2000) 'Border Anxieties: Race and Psychoanalysis' in A. Bery, P. Murray and W. Harris (eds) *Comparing Postcolonial Literatures: Dislocations,* Basingstoke, England: Macmillan.

Marshall, P. (1968) *The Chosen Place, The Timeless People,* New York: Vintage (1984).

Massad, J. (2000) 'The "Post-Colonial" Colony: Time, Space, and Bodies in Palestine/Israel' in F. Afzal-Khan and K. Seshadri-Crooks (eds) *The Pre-Occupation of Postcolonial Studies,* Durham, NC: Duke University Press: 311–346.

Matthews, J. P. (1962) *Tradition in Exile,* Toronto: University of Toronto Press.

Maxwell, A. (1994) 'Revisionist Histories and Settler Colonial Societies', *Southern Review: Literary and Interdisciplinary Essays* 27(4): 383–402.

Maxwell, A. (1998) *Colonial Photography and Exhibitions,* London: Cassell.

Mayer, R. (2000) '"Africa as an Alien Future": The Middle Passage, Afro-futurism, and Postcolonial Waterworlds.' *Amerikastudien/American Studies* 45(4): 555–566.

Mba, E. (1982) *Nigerian Women Mobilised: Women's Political Activity in Southern Nigeria 1900–1965,* Berkeley, Institute of International Studies, University of California.

Mbembe, Achille (2001) *On the Postcolony,* Berkeley and Los Angeles: University of California Press.

Mbembe, Achille (2003) 'Necropolitics', *Public Culture,* Winter 15: 11–40.

Medeiros-Lichem, M. T. (2004) 'Amerindian Rhythms in Polylogues: From Transculturation to the Global Presence of Hybrid Cultures', *Trans: Internet-Zeitschrift fur Kulturwissenschaften* (15).

Mehan, U. S. (2001) 'Transgressing Bodies in Postcolonial Fiction', *Journal of Comparative Literature and Aesthetics* 24(1–2): 1–13.

Memmi, A. (1965) *The Colonizer and the Colonized,* translated by Howard Greenfield, Boston: Beacon Press.

Menon, N. (2005) 'Between the Burqa and the Beauty Parlor? Globalization, Cultural Nationalism, and Feminist Politics' in A. Loomba, S. Kaul, M. Bunzl, A. Burton and J. Esty (eds) *Postcolonial Studies and Beyond,* Durham, NC: Duke University Press: 206–229.

Mercer, K. (1994) *Welcome to the Jungle: New Positions in Black Cultural Studies,* New York: Routledge.

Meyer, S. (1996) *Imperialism at Home: Race and Victorian Womens' Fiction,* Ithaca and London: Cornell University Press.

Michaels, W. B. (1995) *Our America: Nativism, Modernism, and Pluralism,* Durham: Duke University Press.

Michel, M. (1995) 'Positioning the Subject: Locating Postcolonial Studies.' *Ariel: A Review of International English Literature* 26(1): 83–99.

Middleton, R. (1979) *The Meaning of Modernism,* Milton Keynes: Open University Press.

Mies, M. and V. Shiva (1993), *Ecofeminism* Melbourne: Spinifex.

Mignolo, W. D. (1994) 'Are Subaltern Studies Postmodern or Postcolonial? The Politics and Sensibilities of Geo-Cultural Locations', *Dispositio/n: American Journal of Cultural Histories and Theories* 19(46): 45–73.

Mignolo, W. (1995a) *The Darker Side of the Renaissance: Literacy, Territoriality, and Colonization,* Ann Arbor: University of Michigan Press.

Mignolo, W. D. (1995b) 'La razón postcolonial: Herencias coloniales y teorías postcoloniales' *Revista Chilena de Literatura* 47: 91–114.

Mignolo, W. D. (1995c) 'Afterword: Human Understanding and (Latin) American Interests: The Politics and Sensibilities of Geocultural Locations', *Poetics Today* 16(1): 171–214.

Mignolo, W. D. (2000a) *Local Histories/Global Designs: Coloniality, Subaltern Knowledges, and Border Thinking,* Princeton, New Jersey: Princeton University Press.

Mignolo, W. D. (2000b) '(Post)Occidentalism, (Post)Coloniality, and (Post)-Subaltern Rationality' in F. Afzal-Khan and K. Seshadri-Crooks (eds) *The Pre-Occupation of Postcolonial Studies,* Durham, NC: Duke University Press.

Mignolo, W. D. (2001) 'Coloniality at Large: The Western Hemisphere in the Colonial Horizon of Modernity', *CR: The New Centennial Review* 1(2): 19–54.

Mignolo, W. D. (2003) 'Double Translation: Transculturation and the Colonial Difference' in F. Schiwy, T. Maranhao and B. Streck (eds) *Translation and Ethnography: The Anthropological Challenge of Intercultural Understanding,* Tucson, AZ: University of Arizona Press: 3–29.

Mignolo, W. D. and F. Schiwy (2003) 'Double Translation: Transculturation and the Colonial Difference' in T. Maranhao and B. Streck (eds) *Translation and Ethnography: The Anthropological Challenge of Intercultural Understanding,* Tucson, AŻ: University of Arizona Press: 3–29.

Miles, R. (1978) *Between Two Cultures?: The Case of Rastafarianism,* Bristol: S.S.R.C. Research Unit on Ethnic Relations, University of Bristol.

Miller, M. G. (2004) *Rise and Fall of the Cosmic Race: The Cult of Mestizaje in Latin America,* Austin, TX: University of Texas Press.

Miller, N. and Aya, R. (1971) (eds), introduction by Eric R. Wolf, *National Liberation: Revolution in the Third World,* New York: Free Press.

Mills, S. (1991) *Discourses of Difference: An Analysis of Women's Travel Writing and Colonialism,* London: Routledge.

Mills, S. and R. Lewis, (2003) (eds) *Feminist Postcolonial Theory: A Reader*, New York, NY: Routledge.

Minh-ha, Trinh T. (1995) 'Writing Postcoloniality and Feminism' in B. Ashcroft, G. Griffiths and H. Tiffin (eds) *The Post-Colonial Studies Reader*, London: Routledge: 264–268.

Mishra, P. K. (2000) 'English Language, Postcolonial Subjectivity, and Globalization in India.' *Ariel: A Review of International English Literature* 31(1–2): 383–410.

Mishra, S. (1993) 'Haunted Lines: Postcolonial Theory and the Genealogy of Racial Formations in Fiji', *Meanjin* 52(4): 623–634.

Mishra, S. (1996) 'Frantz Fanon, Aimé Césaire, Roberto Retamar: Estranged and Estranging Bodies; or, Gazing on Caliban: An Essay against Hybridity', *UTS Review: Cultural Studies and New Writing* 2(2): 108–128.

Mishra, S. (2006) *Diaspora Criticism*, Edinburgh: Edinburgh University Press.

Mishra, V. (1996a) 'The Diasporic Imaginary: Theorising the Indian Diaspora', *Textual Practice* 10: 421–427.

Mishra, V. (1996b) '(B)ordering Naipaul: Indenture History and Diasporic Poetics', *Diaspora* 5 (2) Fall: 189–237.

Mitchell, D. T. and M. Hearn (1999) 'Colonial Savages and Heroic Tricksters: Native Americans in the American Tradition.' *Journal of Popular Culture* 32(4): 101–117.

Mitchell, W. J. T. (1992) 'Postcolonial Culture, Postimperial Criticism', *Transition* 56. Cited in Ashcroft *et al.* 1995, pp. 475–480.

Mitchell, W. J. T. (1994) *Landscape and Power,* Chicago and London: Chicago University Press.

Mohanram, R. (1999) *Black Body: Women, Colonialism and Space*, Minneapolis: University of Minnesota Press (Public World Series).

Mohanram, R. (2007) *Imperial White: Race, Diaspora and the British Empire*, Minneapolis: University of Minnesota Press.

Mohanram, R. and G. Rajan (1996) *English Postcoloniality: Literatures from Around the World*, Westport, Connecticut: Greenwood Press.

Mohanty, C. T. (1984) 'Under Western eyes: Feminist Scholarship and Colonial Discourse', *Boundary* 2 (Spring/Fall): 71–92.

Mohanty, C. T. (1995) 'Under Western Eyes: Feminist Scholarship and Colonial Discourses' in B. Ashcroft, G. Griffiths and H. Tiffin (eds) *The Post-Colonial Studies Reader*, London: Routledge: 259–263.

Mohanty, C. T, Russo, A. and Torres, L. (eds) (1991) *Third World Women and the Politics of Feminism,* Bloomington: Indiana University Press.

Moikabu, J. M. (1981) *Blood and Flesh: Black American and African Identifications,* Westport, CT: Greenwood Press.

Molloy, S. (2005) 'Postcolonial Latin America and the Magic Realist Imperative: A Report to an Academy' in S. Bermann and M. Wood (eds) *Nation, Language, and the Ethics of Translation*, Princeton, NJ: Princeton University Press.

Monasterios, E. (2004) 'Rethinking Transculturation and Hybridity: An

Andean Perspective' in I. M. F. Blayer and M. C. Anderson (eds) *Latin American Narratives and Cultural Identity: Selected Readings*, New York: Peter Lang: 94–110.

Moodie, S. (1852) *Roughing it in the Bush*, Toronto: McLelland and Stewart (1962).

Moore, H. and T. Sanders (2001) *Magical Interpretations, Material Realities: Modernity, Witchcraft and the Occult in Postcolonial Africa*, London, England: Routledge.

Moore, S. (2000) '"Anglo-Irish" Hybridity: Problems in Miscegenation, Representation, and Postcolonialism in Irish Studies', *Journal of Commonwealth and Postcolonial Studies* 7(1): 75–110.

Moore-Gilbert, B. (1996) 'Beyond Orientalism? Culture, Imperialism and Humanism', *Wasafiri: Journal of Caribbean, African, Asian and Associated Literatures and Film* 23: 8–13.

Mongia, P. (1996) (ed.) *Contemporary Postcolonial Theory: A Reader*, London: Arnold.

Moran, D. (2006) *Wars of National Liberation*, London: Cassell/Collins.

Moraña, M. (2002) 'De metáforas y metonimias: Antonio Cornejo Polar en la encrucijada del latinoamericanismo internacional' in M. Moraña and J. Beverley (eds) *Nuevas perspectivas desde/sobre América Latina: El desafío de los estudios culturales*, Pittsburgh, PA: Instituto Internacional de Literatura Iberoamericana, University of Pittsburgh: 261–270.

Moraña, M. and S. Hallstead (2004) 'The Boom of the Subaltern' in A. Del Sarto, A. Ríos and A. Trigo (eds) *The Latin American Cultural Studies Reader*, Durham, NC: Duke University Press.

Moreiras, A. (2004) 'On Infinite Decolonization', *English Studies in Canada* 30(2): 21–28.

Moretti, F. (2006) 'Evolution, World-Systems, Weltliteratur' in G. Lindberg-Wada (ed.) *Studying Transcultural Literary History*, Berlin, Germany: de Gruyter: 113–121.

Morgan, S. (2006) *The Feminist History Reader*, London: Routledge.

Moses, A. D. (2004) (ed.) *Genocide and Settler Society: Frontier Violence and Stolen Indigenous Children in Australian History*, New York: Berghahn Books.

Mosley, A. G. (1995) (ed.) *African Philosophy: Selected Readings*, Englewood Cliffs, NJ: Prentice Hall.

Mostern, K. (2000) 'Postcolonialism after W. E. B. Du Bois' in A. Singh and P. Schmidt (eds) *Postcolonial Theory and the United States: Race, Ethnicity, and Literature*, Jackson, MS: University Press of Mississippi.

Motohashi, T. (1999) 'The Discourse of Cannibalism in Early Modern Travel Writing' in S. Clark (ed.) *Travel Writing and Empire: Postcolonial Theory in Transit*, London: Zed.

Msiska, M.-H. and Hyland, P. (1997) (eds) *Writing and Africa*, London: Longman.

Muckle, Robert J. (1998), *The First Nations of British Columbia: An Anthropological Survey* Vancouver: UBC Press.

Mudimbe, V. Y. (1992) (ed.) *The Surreptitious Speech: Presence Africaine and the Politics of Otherness, 1947–1987,* Chicago: University of Chicago Press.

Mudimbe, V. Y. (1994) *The Idea of Africa,* Bloomington: Indiana University Press/London: J.Currey.

Mudrooroo (1990) *Writing from the Fringe: A Study of Modern Aboriginal Writing,* South Yarra, Vic.: Hyland House.

Mukherjee, A. (1990) 'Whose Post-Colonialism and Whose Post-Modernism?', *WLWE* 30 (2): 1–9.

Mulhausler, P. (1986) *Pidgin and Creole Linguistics,* Oxford: Blackwell.

Munday, J. (2001), *Introducing Translation Studies: Theories and Applications* London, New York: Routledge.

Munro, M. (2004) 'Can't Stand Up for Falling Down: Haiti, Its Revolutions, and Twentieth-Century Negritudes' *Research in African Literatures* 35(2): 1–17.

Murdoch, H. A. (1999) 'Exploring the Margin: Models of Cultural Identity in the Postcolonial French Caribbean', *Journal of Commonwealth and Postcolonial Studies* 6(1): 153–184.

Murray, S. (1997) (ed.) *Not on Any Map: Essays on Post-Coloniality and Cultural nationalism,* Exeter: Exeter University Press.

Murray, S. (1997a) 'Postcoloniality/Modernity: Wilson Harris and Postcolonial Theory' *Review of Contemporary Fiction* 17(2): 53–58.

Murray, P. (2000) 'The Trickster at the Border: Cross-Cultural Dialogues in the Caribbean' in A. Bery, P. Murray and W. Harris (eds) *Comparing Postcolonial Literatures: Dislocations,* Basingstoke, England: Macmillan.

Murrell, N., W. D. Spencer, *et al.* (1998) (eds) *Chanting Down Babylon: The Rastafari Reader,* Philadelphia, PA: Temple University Press.

Muysken, P. and Smith, N. (1995) 'The Study of Pidgin and Creole Languages' in J. Arends, P. Muysken and N. Smith (eds) *Pidgins & Creoles: An Introduction,* Amsterdam and Philadelphia: John Benjamins, pp. 3–14.

Naipaul, V. S. (1967) *The Mimic Men,* London: André Deustch.

Nance, K. A. (2006) *Can Literature Promote Justice? Trauma Narrative and Social Action in Latin American Testimonio,* Nashville, TN: Vanderbilt University Press.

Nasta, S. (2000) *Reading the 'New' Literatures in a Postcolonial Era,* Cambridge: Brewer.

Nederveen Pieterse, J. (1992) *White on Black: Images of Africa and Blacks in Western Popular Culture,* New Haven and London: Yale University Press.

Nederveen Pieterse, J. (1995) *The Development of Development Theory Towards Critical Globalism,* Working Paper Series, The Hague: Institute of Social Studies.

Nederveen Pieterse, J. and B. C. Parekh, (1995) (eds) *The Decolonization of Imagination: Culture, Knowledge and Power,* London: Zed Books.

Nelson, E. S. (1993) (ed.) *Writers of the Indian Diaspora: A Bio-bibliographical Critical Sourcebook,* Westport, CT: Greenwood Press.

New, W. H. (1975) *Among Worlds,* Erin, Ontario: Press Porcepic.

Newman, S. (2000) 'Universalism/Particularism: Towards a Poststructuralist Politics of Universality.' *New Formations: A Journal of Culture/Theory/Politics* (41): 95–108.

Newsom, D. D. (2001) *The Imperial Mantle: The United States, Decolonization, and the Third World,* Bloomington: Indiana University Press.

Ngugi, wa T. (1981a) *De-Colonising the Mind: The Politics of Language in African Literature,* London: James Currey.

Ngugi, wa T. (1981b) *Writers in Politics,* London: Heinemann.

Ngugi, wa T. (1983) *Barrel of a Pen: Resistance to Repression in Neo-colonial Kenya,* London: New Beacon Books.

Ngugi, wa T. (1986) *Writing against Neocolonialism,* Wembley: Vita Books.

Ngugi, wa T. (1993) *Moving the Centre: The Struggle for Cultural Freedoms,* London: J.Currey/Portsmouth, NH: Heinemann.

Nightingale, P. (1986) (ed.) *A Sense of Place in the New Literatures in English* St. Lucia, Qld: University of Queensland Press.

Nkosi, L. (2005) 'Negritude: New and Old Perspectives' in L. Stiebel and L. Gunner (eds) *Still Beating the Drum: Critical Perspectives on Lewis Nkosi,* New York: Rodopi: 267–290.

Nkrumah, K. (1965) *Neo-colonialism: The Last Stage of Imperialism,* London: Nelson.

Nunes, Z. (1994) 'Anthropology and Race in Brazilian Modernism' in F. Barker, P. Hulme and M. Iversen (eds) *Colonial Discourse/Postcolonial Theory,* Manchester: Manchester University Press: 115–125.

Obeyesekere, G. (1992) 'British Cannibals: Contemplation of an Event in the Death and Resurrection of James Cook, Explorer', *Critical Inquiry* 18 (Summer).

Okonkwo, C. (1999) *Decolonization Agonistics in Postcolonial Fiction,* New York: St. Martin's.

Olaniyan, T. (1992) 'The Poetics and Politics of "Othering": Contemporary African, African-American, and Caribbean Drama and the Invention of Cultural Identities', *Cultural Critique* 34(0): 2922A.

Olson, G. A. and L. Worsham, (1999) (eds) *Race, Rhetoric, and the Postcolonial,* Albany: State University of New York Press.

Ong, W. J. (1982) *Orality and Literacy: The Technologizing of the Word,* London and New York: Methuen.

Oosthuizen, G. C. (1993) 'The Rastafarian Movement and Its Appearance in South Africa', *Syzygy: Journal of Alternative Religion and Culture* 2(3–4): 243–266.

Orgun, G. (2000) 'Marginality, Cosmopolitanism and Postcoloniality', *Commonwealth Essays and Studies* 23(1): 111–124.

Ortiz, F. (1978) *Contrapunto Cubano (1947–1963),* Caracas: Biblioteca Ayacucho.

Owens, J. D. (1976) *The Rastafarians of Jamaica,* London: Heinemann.

Palumbo-Liu, D. (1995) 'Universalisms and Minority Culture', *Differences: A Journal of Feminist Cultural Studies* (7) 1: 188–208.

Papastergiadis, N. (1996) 'Ambivalence in Cultural Theory: Reading Homi Bhabha's Dissemi-Nation' in J. C. Hawley (ed.) *Writing the Nation: Self and Country in the Post-Colonial Imagination*, Amsterdam: Rodopi.

Paranjape, M. (1998) 'Theorising Postcolonial Difference: Culture, Nation, Civilization' *Journal of the South Pacific Association for Commonwealth Literature and Language Studies* 47: 1–17.

Parker, A., Russo, M., Sommer, D. and Yaeger, P. (1992) *Nationalism and Sexuality*, London and New York: Routledge.

Parkinson, L. and Faris, W.B. (1995) (eds) *Magical Realism: Theory, History, Community*, Durham, NC: Duke University Press.

Parry, B. (1987) 'Problems in Current Discourse Theory', *Oxford Literary Review* 9: 27–58.

Parry, B. (1994) 'Resistance Theory/Theorising Resistance: Two Cheers for Nativism' in F. Barker, P. Hulme and M. Iversen (eds) *Colonial Discourse/ Postcolonial Theory*, Manchester and New York: Manchester University Press.

Parry, B. (1995) 'Problems in Current Theories of Colonial Discourse' in B. Ashcroft, G. Griffiths and H. Tiffin (eds) *The Post-Colonial Studies Reader*, London: Routledge.

Parry, B. (2002) 'Fanon and the Trauma of Modernity' *New Formations: A Journal of Culture/Theory/Politics* 47: 24–29.

Parry, B. (2002a) 'Liberation Theory: Variations on Themes of Marxism and Modernity' in C. Bartolovich and N. Lazarus (eds) *Marxism, Modernity, and Postcolonial Studies*, Cambridge, England: Cambridge University Press: 125–149.

Patterson, O. (1967) *The Sociology of Slavery: An Analysis of the Origins, Development and Structure of Negro Slave Society in Jamaica*, London: MacGibbon and Kee.

Pearson, D. (2001) *The Politics of Ethnicity in Settler Societies: States of Unease*, Basingstoke: Palgrave.

Pechey, G. (1994) 'Post-Apartheid Narratives' in F. Barker, P. Hulme and M. Iversen (eds) *Colonial Discourse/Postcolonial Theory*, Manchester: Manchester University Press.

Pennycook, A. (1998) *English and the discourses of colonialism*, London: Routledge.

Pennycook, A. (2002) 'Ruptures, Departures and Appropriations: Post-colonial Challenges to Language Development' in C. D. Villareal, L. R. R. Tope and P. M. B. Jurilla (eds) *Ruptures and Departures: Language and Culture in Southeast Asia*, Quezon City, Philippines: University of the Philippines Press.

Perera, N. (1998) *Society and Space: Colonialism, Nationalism and Postcolonial Identity in Sri Lanka*, Boulder, Colorado: Westview Press.

Peretti, B. W. (1995) 'Plantation Cafés: Jazz, Postcolonial Theory, and Modernism' in G. Rajan and R. Mohanram (eds) *Postcolonial Discourse and Changing Cultural Contexts: Theory and Criticism*, Westport, CT: Greenwood: 89–99.

Pérez-Torres, R. (2006) *Mestizaje: Critical Uses of Race in Chicano Culture,* Minneapolis, MN: University of Minnesota Press.

Pesso-Miquel, Catherine and Klaus Stierstorfer (eds), *Fundamentalism and Literature,* New York: Palgrave Macmillan, 2006.

Phillips, A. A. (1958) *The Australian Tradition: Studies in a Colonial Culture,* Melbourne: F.W.Cheshire.

Phillips, A. A. (1979) *Responses: Selected Writings,* introduction and checklist by Brian Kiernan, Kew, Vic.: Australia International Press & Publications.

Philp, K. R. (1986) (ed.) *Indian Self-rule: First-hand Accounts of Indian–White Relations from Roosevelt to Reagan,* Salt Lake City, Utah: Howe Bros.

Philp, K. R. and West, E. (1976) (eds) *Essays on Walter Prescott Webb,* Austin: University of Texas Press.

Pidd, M., (ed). (2004) *Systems Modelling: Theory and Practice,* Chichester, England: John Wiley & Sons.

Plasa, C. and Ring, B. J. (1994) (eds) *The Discourse of Slavery: Aphra Behn to Toni Morrison,* London and New York: Routledge.

Plumwood, V. (1993), *Feminism and the Mastery of Nature* London and New York: Routledge.

Plumwood, V. (2002), *Environmental Culture: the Ecological Crisis of Reason* London and New York: Routledge.

Pollard, V. and R. Nettleford (2000) *Dread Talk: The Language of Rastafari,* Kingston, Jamaica; Montreal, QC: Canoe; McGill-Queen's University Press.

Pomeroy, W. J. (1970) *American Neo-Colonialism: Its Emergence in the Philippines and Asia,* New York: International Publishers.

Prakash, G. (1995) *After colonialism: imperial histories and postcolonial displacements,* Princeton, New Jersey: Princeton University Press.

Prakash, G. (1997) 'Postcolonial Criticism and Indian Historiography' in A. McClintock, A. Mufti and E. Shohat (eds) *Dangerous Liaisons: Gender, Nation, and Postcolonial Perspectives,* Minneapolis: University of Minnesota Press.

Prakash, G., S. Tharu, *et al.* (1999) (eds) *Subaltern Studies X: writings on South Asian history and society,* New Delhi: Oxford University Press.

Prasad, M. (1997) 'On the Question of a Theory of (Third) World Literature' in A. McClintock, A. Mufti and E. Shohat (eds) *Dangerous Liaisons: Gender, Nation, and Postcolonial Perspectives,* Minneapolis, MN: University of Minnesota Press.

Pratt, M. L. (1985) 'Scratches on the face of the country; or, what Mr Barrow saw in the land of the bushmen', *Critical Inquiry* (12) 1 Autumn: 138–162. Reprinted in Gates 1986.

Pratt, M. L. (1991) 'Arts of the Contact Zone' in *Ways of Reading,* 5th edition, ed. David Bartholomae and Anthony Petroksky, New York: Bedford/St. Martin's (1999).

Pratt, M. L. (1992) *Imperial Eyes: Travel Writing and Transculturation,* London: Routledge.

Pratt, M. L. (2004) 'The Anticolonial Past.' *Modern Language Quarterly: A Journal of Literary History* 65(3): 443–456.

Premnath, G. (2002) 'The Afterlife of National Liberation: Fanon Today' *New Formations: A Journal of Culture/Theory/Politics* 47: 43–45.

Premnath, G. (2003) 'The Weak Sovereignty of the Postcolonial Nation-State' in A. Kumar, J. Berger and B. Robbins (eds) *World Bank Literature*, Minneapolis, MN: University of Minnesota Press: 253–264.

Prentice, C. (1991) 'The Interplay of Place and Placelessness in the Subject of Post-Colonial Fiction.' *SPAN: Journal of the South Pacific Association for Commonwealth Literature and Language Studies* 31: 63–80.

Prentice, C. (1994) 'Some Problems of Response to Empire in Settler Post-Colonial Societies' in C. Tiffin and A. Lawson (eds) *De-Scribing Empire: Post-Colonialism and Textuality*, London: Routledge.

Press, J. (1965) (ed.) *Commonwealth: Unity and Diversity Within Common Culture*, London: Heinemann.

Price, R. and Rosberg, C. G. (1980) *The Apartheid Regime,* Berkeley: University of California Press.

Punter, D. (2000) *Postcolonial Imaginings: Fictions of a New World Order,* Edinburgh: Edinburgh University Press.

Puri, S. (2004) *The Caribbean Postcolonial: Social Equality, Post-Nationalism, and Cultural Hybridity*, New York: Palgrave Macmillan.

Quayson, A. (2000) *Postcolonialism: Theory, Practice or Process?*, Cambridge: Polity.

Rabasa, J. (1993) *Inventing A>M>E>R>I>C>A: Spanish Historiography and the Formation of Eurocentrism,* Norman Okla and London: University of Oklahoma Press. Cited in Ashcroft *et al.* 1995: 358–364.

Radford, D. (1982) *Edouard Glissant,* Paris: Seghers.

Radhakrishnan, R. (2000) 'Adjudicating Hybridity, Co-ordinating Between-ness' *Jouvert: A Journal of Postcolonial Studies* 5(1).

Raheja, G. G. (2002) 'The Erasure of Everyday Life in Colonial Ethnography' in D. P. Mines and S. Lamb (eds) *Everyday Life in South Asia*, Bloomington, IN: Indiana University Press: 199–213.

Rahmen, Anisur (2002), *Translation: Poetics and Practice* New Delhi: Creative Books.

Rajadhyaksha, A. (1998) 'Realism, Modernism, and Post-Colonial Theory' in J. Hill, P. C. Gibson, R. Dyer, E. A. Kaplan and P. Willemen (eds) *The Oxford Guide to Film Studies*, New York, NY: Oxford University PressModernism: 413–425.

Rajan, R.S. (1993) *Real and Imagined Women: Gender, Culture and Post-colonialism,* London and New York: Routledge.

Rajan, R. S. (1997) 'The Third World Academic in Other Places: Or, the Postcolonial Intellectual Revisited' *Critical Inquiry* 23(3): 596–616.

Rajan, G. and Mohanram, R. (1995) (eds) *Postcolonial Discourse and Changing Cultural Contexts: Theory and Criticism,* Westport, CT: Greenwood Press.

Rajen, H. (1997) *Twentieth Century Imperialism: Shifting Contours and Changing Conceptions*, New Delhi: Sage Publications.

Rama, A. (1982) *Transculturacion narrativa en America Latin*, Mexico City: Siglo 21.

Ramazani, J. (2001) *The Hybrid Muse: Postcolonial Poetry in English*, Chicago: University of Chicago Press.

Ramazani, J. (2006) 'Modernist Bricolage, Postcolonial Hybridity' *Modernism/Modernity* 13(3): 445–463.

Ramo, Joshua Cooper (2004), *The Beijing Consensus* London: Foeign Policy Centre.

Ramraj, V. J. (1996) 'Diasporas and Multiculturalism' in B. King (ed.) *New National and Post-Colonial Literatures: An Introduction*, Oxford: Clarendon: 214–229.

Rasmussen, D. M. (1990) (ed.) *Universalism vs. Communitarianism: Contemporary Debates in Ethics*. Cambridge, Massachussetts: MIT Press.

Rath, S. P. (2000) 'Home(s) Abroad: Diasporic Identities in Third Spaces' *Jouvert: A Journal of Postcolonial Studies* 4(3).

Ray, S. (1999) 'The Postcolonial Critic: Shifting Subjects, Changing Paradigms' in C. Hendricks and K. Oliver (eds) *Language and Liberation: Feminism, Philosophy, and Language*, Albany, NY: State University of New York Press.

Ray, S. (2000) *En-gendering India: Woman and Nation in Colonial and Postcolonial Narratives*, Durham, NC: Duke University Press.

Reed, J. and Wake, C. (1965) (eds) *Senghor: Prose and Poetry,* London: (reissued 1976).

Reiss, T. J. (2004) 'Mapping Identities: Literature, Nationalism, Colonialism' in C. Prendergast (ed.) *Debating World Literature*, London, England: Verso.

Reynolds, H. (1982) *The Other Side of the Frontier: Aboriginal Resistance to the European Invasion of Australia,* Ringwood, Vic.: Penguin.

Rhodes, C. (1994) *Primitivism and Modern Art,* London: Thames & Hudson.

Rice, L. (2003) 'Of Heterotopias and Ethnoscapes: The Production of Space in Postcolonial North Africa', *Critical Matrix: The Princeton Journal of Women, Gender, and Culture* 14: 36–75.

Rich, P. B. (1986) *Race and Empire in British Politics,* Cambridge and New York: Cambridge University Press.

Richards, D. (2000) '"Canvas of Blood": Okigbo's African Modernism' in A. Bery, P. Murray and W. Harris (eds) *Comparing Postcolonial Literatures: Dislocations*, Basingstoke, England: Macmillan: 229–239.

Richardson, H. H. (1917) *The Fortunes of Richard Mahony,* London: Heinemann.

Richmond, A. H. (1994) *Global Apartheid: Refugees, Racism, and the New World Order*, New York: Oxford University Press.

Richter, V. (2004) 'A New Desire for the Grands Récits? Propositions for a Critical Universalism' in G. V. Davis, *et al* (eds) *Towards a Transcultural Future: Literature and Society in a "Post"-Colonial World*, Amsterdam, Netherlands: Rodopi: 93–104.

Riemenschneider, D. (1983) (ed.) *The History and Historiography of Commonwealth Literature*, Tübingen: Narr.

Robertson, R. (1992) *Globalization: Social Theory and Global Culture,* London: Sage.

Robertson, Roland, (1995) 'Glocalization,' in Mike Featherstone, Scott Lash and Roland Robertson (eds) *Global Modernities* London: Sage: 25–44.

Robinson, Douglas (2000) *What is Translation?*, Kent, Ohio: Kent Sate University Press.

Robinson, R. and Gallagher, J. (1981) *Africa and the Victorians: the Official Mind of Imperialism,* with Alice Denny, 2nd edn, London: Macmillan.

Robotham, D. (2005) 'Cosmopolitanism and Planetary Humanism: The Strategic Universalism of Paul Gilroy.' *South Atlantic Quarterly* (104) 3: 561–582.

Rodrigues, Á. L. (2004) 'Beyond Nativism: An Interview with Ngugi wa Thiong'o' *Research in African Literatures* 35(3): 161–167.

Roediger, David (2002) *Colored White: Transcending the Racial Past*, Berkeley: University of California Romaine, S. (1988) *Pidgin and Creole Languages,* London and New York: Longman.

Ross, R. (1982) (ed.) *Racism and Colonialism,* Leyden: Martinus Nijhoff.

Rothermund, D. (2006) *The Routledge Companion to Decolonization*, London: Routledge.

Rotter, A. J. (2000) 'Saidism without Said: Orientalism and U.S. Diplomatic History', *American Historical Review* 105(4): 1205–1217.

Rousseau, J. J. (1755) *A Discourse on Inequality,* translated by Maurice Cranston, London: Penguin (1988).

Roy, A. (1995) 'Postcoloniality and the Politics of Identity in the Diaspora: Figuring "Home," Locating Histories' in G. Rajan and R. Mohanram (eds) *Postcolonial Discourse and Changing Cultural Contexts: Theory and Criticism*, Westport, CT: Greenwood: 101–115.

Roy, T. (1995) 'Disciplining the Printed Text: Colonial and Nationalist Surveillance of Bengali Literature' in P. Chatterjee (ed.) *Texts of Power: Emerging Disciplines in Colonial Bengal*, Minneapolis: University of Minnesota Press.

Rubin, W. (1984) (ed.) *Primitivism in 20th-century Art: Affinity of the Tribal and The Modern,* New York: Museum of Modern Art.

Russell, L. (2001) *Colonial Frontiers: Indigenous-European Encounters in Settler Societies*, Manchester: Manchester University Press.

Russell, L. (2006) (ed.) *Boundary Writing: An Exploration of Race, Culture, and Gender Binaries in Contemporary Australia*, Honolulu: University of Hawaii Press.

Rutherford, A., Holst Petersen, K. and Maes Jelinek, H. (1992) (eds) *From Commonwealth to Post-Colonial,* Aarhus and Sydney: Dangaroo.

Ruthven, K. K. (1968) 'Yeats, Lawrence and the Savage God', *Critical Quarterly* (10) 1 and 2 (Spring/Summer).

Ryan, S. (1994) 'Inscribing the Emptiness: Cartography, Exploration and the Construction of Australia' in C. Tiffin and A. Lawson (eds) *De-Scribing Empire: Post-Colonialism and Textuality*, London: Routledge: 115–130.

Said, E. (1978) *Orientalism: Western Conceptions of the Orient,* London: Penguin (1991).

Said, E. (1983) *The World, the Text, and the Critic,* Cambridge, MA: Harvard University Press.

Said, E. (1984) 'The Mind of Winter: Reflections on Life in Exile', *Harper's* 269: 49–55.

Said, E. (1993) *Culture and Imperialism,* London: Chatto & Windus.

Said, E. (1994), *Representations of the Intellectual* New York: Pantheon.

Said, E. W. (1999) *Out of Place: A Memoir,* New York: Knopf.

Saini, M. K. (1981) *Politics of Multinationals: A Pattern in Neo-colonialism,* foreword by Rasheeduddin Khan, New Delhi: Gitanjali Prakashan.

Sanborn, G. (1998) *The Sign of the Cannibal: Melville and the Making of a Postcolonial Reader,* Durham: Duke University Press.

Sanday, P. R. (1986) *Divine Hunger: Cannibalism as a Cultural System,* Cambridge: Cambridge University Press.

Sandiford, K. A. (2000) *The Cultural Politics of Sugar: Caribbean Slavery and Narratives of Colonialism,* Cambridge: Cambridge University Press.

San Juan, E. (1991) 'Philippine Writing in English: Postcolonial Syncreticism versus a Textual Practice of National Liberation', *Ariel: A Review of International English Literature* 22(4): 69–88.

San Juan, E., Jr (1991a) *Writing and National Liberation: Essays in Critical Practice,* Quezon City: University of the Philippines Press.

San Juan, E. (1995) *Hegemony and Strategies of Transgression: Essays in Cultural Studies and Comparative Literature,* Albany: State University of New York Press.

San Juan, E., Jr (1995a) 'On the Limits of "Postcolonial" Theory: Trespassing Letters from the "Third World"', *Ariel: A Review of International English Literature* 26(3): 89–115.

San Juan, E., Jr (1996) 'From Postcolonial to Alter/Native National Allegory: Dialectics of Nation/People and World-System in Philippine Writing' in W. Zach and K. L. Goodwin (eds) *Nationalism vs. Internationalism: (Inter)National Dimensions of Literatures in English,* Tübingen, Germany: Stauffenburg.

San Juan, E., Jr (1998) *Beyond Postcolonial Theory,* New York: St. Martin's.

Sardar, Z. (1999) *Orientalism,* Buckingham: Open University Press.

Sarkowsky, K. (2002) 'Beyond Margins and Centres: First Nations Literature and the Challenge to Postcolonial Theory' in G. Collier and F. Schulze-Engler (eds) *Crabtracks: Progress and Process in Teaching the New Literatures in English,* Amsterdam, Netherlands: Rodopi.

Sartre, J.-P. (1957) *Being and Nothingness: An Essay on Phenomenological Ontology,* translated by Hazel E. Barnes, London: Methuen.

Satchidanandan, K. (2002) 'Orientalism Revisited.' *Indian Literature* 46(3 [209]): 8–12.

Sauvy, A. (1952) *General Theory of Population,* translated by Christophe Campos, London: Methuen.

Savishinsky, N. J. (1999) 'Transnational Popular Culture and the Global Spread of the Jamaican Rastafarian Movement' in M. Klass and M. Weisgrau (eds) *Across the Boundaries of Belief: Contemporary Issues in the Anthropology of Religion,* Boulder, CO: Westview.

Sawyer, M. (2003) 'The Noble Savage as Hegelian Hero: Dialectic Process and Postcolonial Theory', *Hispanic Journal* 24(1–2): 65–74.

Schaffer, K. (1989) *Women and the Bush: Forces of Desire in the Colonial Cultural Tradition,* Cambridge: Cambridge University Press.

Schaffer, K. (1995) *In the Wake of First Contact: The Eliza Fraser Stories,* Cambridge: Cambridge University Press.

Schermerhorn, R. A. (1970) *Comparative Ethnic Relations: A Framework for Theory and Research,* New York: Random House.

Schermerhorn, R. A. (1974) 'Ethnicity in the Perspective of the Sociology of Knowledge', *Ethnicity* (1) 1 (April).

Schmidt, F. (2000) 'Literaturas heterogéneas y alegorías nacionales: ¿Paradigmas para las literaturas poscoloniales?', *Revista Iberoamericana* 66(190): 175–185.

Schoene-Harwood, B. (1998) '"Emerging as the Others of Our Selves": Scottish Multiculturalism and the Challenge of the Body in Postcolonial Representation', *Scottish Literary Journal* 25(1): 54–72.

Scholte, J. A. (1996) 'Beyond the Buzzword: Towards a Critical Theory of Globalization' in E. Kofman and G. Youngs *Globalisation: Theory and Practice,* London: Pinter.

Scholte, Jan Aart (2005), *The Sources of Neoliberal Globalization,* Geneva: United Nations Research Institute for Social Development.

Schueller, M. J. (2003) 'Articulations of African-Americanism in South Asian Postcolonial Theory: Globalism, Localism, and the Question of Race', *Cultural Critique* 55: 35–62.

Schulze-Engler, F. (1996) 'Universalism with a Difference: The Politics of Postcolonial Theory' in W. Zach and K. Goodwin (eds) *Nationalism vs. Internationalism: (Inter)National Dimensions of Literatures in English,* Tübingen, Germany: Stauffenburg: 41–46.

Scott, D. (1996) 'The Aftermaths of Sovereignty: Postcolonial Criticism and the Claims of Political Modernity', *Social Text* 48: 1–26.

Scott, Jamie S. and Gareth Griffiths (eds.) (2005) *Mixed Messages: Materiality, Textuality, Missions,* New York: Palgrave/Macmillan.

Scott, J. S. and P. Simpson-Housley (2001) *Mapping the Sacred: Religion, Geography and Postcolonial Literatures,* Amsterdam, Netherlands: Rodopi.

Scott, H. (2002) 'Was There a Time before Race? Capitalist Modernity and the Origins of Racism' in C. Bartolovich and N. Lazarus (eds) *Marxism, Modernity, and Postcolonial Studies,* Cambridge: Cambridge University Press: 167–182.

Seers, D. (1981) *Dependency Theory: A Critical Re-assessment* London: Pinter.

Senghor, L. S. (1964) '*Négritude et* humanisme', Ch. 1, *Liberté 1,* Paris: Seuil.

Seymour-Smith, C. (1986) *Dictionary of Anthropology,* Boston, MA: G.K. Hall.

Sharpe, J. (2000) 'Is the United States Postcolonial? Transnationalism, Immigration, and Race' in C. R. King (ed.) *Postcolonial America,* Urbana, IL: University of Illinois Press: 103–121.

Shaw, R. (2001) 'Cannibal Transformations: Colonialism and Commodification in the Sierra Leone Hinterland' in H. Moore and T. Sanders (eds)

Magical Interpretations, Material Realities: Modernity, Witchcraft and the Occult in Postcolonial Africa, London: Routledge.

Sheridan, J. (2001) '"When First unto This Country a Stranger I Came": Grey Owl, Indigenous Lessons of Place, and Postcolonial Theory', in J. S. Scott and P. Simpson-Housley (eds) *Mapping the Sacred: Religion, Geography and Postcolonial Literatures*, Amsterdam, Netherlands: Rodopi: 419–439.

Shi-xu, M. Kienpointner, *et al.* (2005) (eds) *Read the Cultural Other: Forms of Otherness in the Discourses of Hong Kong's Decolonization*, Berlin, Germany: Mouton de Gruyter.

Shoemaker, A. (1989) *Black Words, White Page: Aboriginal Literature 1929–1988*, St. Lucia, Queensland: University of Queensland Press.

Shoemaker, A. (1990) *Swimming in the Mainstream: Australian Aboriginal and Canadian Indian Drama*, London: Sir Robert Menzies Centre for Australian Studies, Institute of Commonwealth Studies, University of London.

Shohat, E. (1994) *Unthinking Eurocentrism: Multiculturalism and the Media*, London and New York: Routledge.

Shohat, E. (1997) 'Framing Post-Third-Worldist Culture: Gender and Nation in Middle Eastern/North African Film', *Jouvert: A Journal of Postcolonial Studies* 1(1).

Simmons-McDonald, H. (2003) 'Decolonizing English: The Caribbean Counter-Thrust' in C. Mair (ed.) *The Politics of English as a World Language: New Horizons in Postcolonial Cultural Studies*, Amsterdam, Netherlands: Rodopi: 179–201.

Simpson, L. R. (2004) 'Anticolonial Strategies for the Recovery and Maintenance of Indigenous Knowledge', *American Indian Quarterly* 28(3–4): 373–384.

Singer, E. (2002) *Moving Beyond Nativism: Eine Betrachtung des irischen Gegenwartsromans aus dem Blickwinkel postkolonialer Theorien*, Frankfurt, Germany: Peter Lang.

Singer, P. (2003), 'Practical Ethics' in S. Armstrong and R. Botzler, (eds) *The Animal Ethics Reader*, London and New York: Routledge.

Singh, A. and P. Schmidt (2000) *Postcolonial Theory and the United States: Race, Ethnicity, and Literature*, Jackson, MS: University Press of Mississippi.

Singh, I. (2000) *Pidgins and Creoles: An introduction*, London: Arnold.

Singler, J. V.(1990) *Pidgin and Creole Tense-Mood-Aspect Systems*, Amsterdam/Philadelphia: J. Benjamins.

Sivanandan, T. (2004) 'Anticolonialism, National Liberation, and Postcolonial Nation Formation' in N. Lazarus (ed.) *The Cambridge Companion to Postcolonial Literary Studies*, Cambridge: Cambridge University Press: 41–65.

Skotnes, Pippa (1996) *Miscast: Negotiating the Presence of the Bushman*, Cape Town: University of Cape Town Press.

Slemon, S. (1987a) 'Monuments of Empire: Allegory/Counter-Discourse/Postcolonial Writing', *Kunapipi* (9) 3: 1–16.

Slemon, S. (1987b) 'Cultural Alterity and Colonial Discourse', *Southern Review* 20 (March).

Slemon, S. (1988a) 'Magical Realism as Post-Colonial Discourse', *Canadian Literature* 116 (Spring).

Slemon, S. (1988b) '*Carnival* and the Canon', *Ariel*, (19) 3 (July).

Slemon, S. (1990) 'Unsettling the Empire: Resistance Theory for the Second World', *World Literature Written in English* (30) 2: 30–41.

Slemon, S. (1992) 'Bones of Contention: Post-Colonial Writing and the "Cannibal Question"' in *Literature and the Body,* edited by Anthony Purdy, Amsterdam: Rodopi.

Slemon, S. (1994) 'The scramble for post-colonialism' in C. Tiffin and A. Lawson (eds) *De-scribing Empire: Postcolonialism and Textuality,* London: Routledge.

Slemon, S. (1995) 'Magic Realism as Postcolonial Discourse' in L. P. Zamora and W. B. Faris (eds) *Magical Realism: Theory, History, Community,* Durham, NC: Duke University Press.

Smith, A. (1776) *An Inquiry into the Nature and Causes of the Wealth of Nations,* edited by Edwin Cannan, New York: Modern Library (1994).

Smith, A. (2004) 'Migrancy, Hybridity, and Postcolonial Literary Studies' in N. Lazarus (ed.) *The Cambridge Companion to Postcolonial Literary Studies,* Cambridge: Cambridge University Press.

Smith, B. (1992) *Modernism and Post-modernism: A Neo-colonial Viewpoint,* London: Sir Robert Menzies Centre for Australian Studies, Institute of Commonwealth Studies, University of London.

Smith, B. C. (2003) *Understanding Third World Politics: Theories of Political Change and Development,* Basingstoke: Palgrave Macmillan.

Smith, J. D. (ed). (1993) *Racial Determinism and the Fear of Miscegenation, Post-1900,* New York: Garland Publishing.

Smith, P. (1988) *Discerning the Subject,* Minneapolis: University of Minnesota Press.

Smyth, G. (2000) 'The Politics of Hybridity: Some Problems with Crossing the Border' in A. Bery, P. Murray and W. Harris (eds) *Comparing Postcolonial Literatures: Dislocations,* Basingstoke, England: Macmillan.

Sollors, W. (1986), *Beyond Ethnicity: Consent and Descent in American Culture,* Oxford and New York: Oxford University Press.

Sollors, W. (1996) (ed.) *Theories of Ethnicity: A Classical Reader,* New York: New York University Press.

Somerson, W. (1999) 'Becoming Rasta: Recentering White Masculinity in the Era of Transnationalism', *Comparatist: Journal of the Southern Comparative Literature Association* 23: 128–140.

Somerville, Margaret and Tony Perkins (2003) 'Border Work in the Contact Zone: Thinking Indigenous/Non-Indigenous Collaboration Spatially', *International Journal of Intercultural Studies,* 24/3.

Sono, T. (1999) *Race Relations in Post-Apartheid South Africa,* Johannesburg: South African Institute of Race Relations.

Spears, A. K. and D. Winford (1997) *The Structure and Status of Pidgins and Creoles: Including Selected Papers from the Meetings of the Society for Pidgin and Creole Linguistics,* Amsterdam: J. Benjamins.

Spengler, O. (1926) *The Decline of the West,* translated by Charles Francis Atkinson, London: Allen & Unwin.

Spitta, S. (1995) *Between Two Waters: Narratives of Transculturation in Latin America,* Houston, TX: Rice University Press.

Spivak, G. (1984–5) 'Criticism, Feminism and the Institution', interview with Elizabeth Gross, *Thesis Eleven* 10/11 (November/March): 175–187.

Spivak, G. (1985a) 'The Rani of Simur' in Francis Barker *et al.* (eds) *Europe and Its Others Vol. 1 Proceedings of the Essex Conference on the Sociology of Literature,* Colchester: University of Essex.

Spivak, G. (1985b) 'Can the Subaltern Speak? Speculations on Widow Sacrifice', *Wedge* (7) 8 (Winter/Spring). Cited in Ashcroft *et al* 1995.

Spivak, G. (1985c) 'Three Women's Texts and a Critique of Imperialism', *Critical Inquiry* (18) 4 (Summer): 756–769.

Spivak, G. (1987) *In Other Worlds: Essays in Cultural Politics,* New York: Methuen.

Spivak, G. (1990) *The Post-colonial Critic: Interviews, Strategies, Dialogues,* edited by Sarah Harasym, New York: Routledge.

Spivak, G. (1991) 'Identity and Alterity: An Interview' (with Nikos Papastergiadis) *Arena* 97: 65–76.

Spivak, G. C. (1993) 'The Burden of English' in C. A. Breckenridge and P. van der Veer (eds) *Orientalism and the Postcolonial Predicament: Perspectives on South Asia,* Philadelphia: University of Pennsylvania Press: 134–157.

Spivak, G. C. (1996) 'Poststructuralism, Marginality, Postcoloniality and Value' in P. Mongia (ed.) *Contemporary Postcolonial Theory: A Reader,* London: Arnold.

Spivak, G. C. (1999) *A Critique of Postcolonial Reason: Toward a History of the Vanishing Present,* Cambridge: Harvard University Press.

Spivak, G. C. (2000) 'Translation as Culture', *Parallax* 6(1 [14]): 13–24.

Spivak, G. C. (2003) 'Subaltern Studies: Deconstructing Historiography' in J. Culler (ed.) *Deconstruction: Critical Concepts in Literary and Cultural Studies: Volume 4,* New York: Routledge.

Spivak, G. C. (2005) 'Commonwealth Literature and Comparative Literature' in S. Duangsamosorn (ed.) *Re-Imagining Language and Literature for the 21st Century,* Amsterdam, Netherlands: Rodopi.

Spivak, G. C. (2006) 'World Systems and the Creole', *Narrative* (14) 1: 102–112.

Springhall, J. (2001) *Decolonization since 1945: The Collapse of European Overseas Empires,* Houndmills, England: Palgrave.

Spurr, D. (1993) *The Rhetoric of Empire: Colonial Discourse in Journalism, Travel Writing and Imperial Administration,* Durham and London: Duke University Press.

Spybey, T. (1996) *Globalization and World Society,* Cambridge: Polity.

Stallybrass, P. and White, A. (1986) *The Politics and Poetics of Transgression,* London: Methuen.

Stasiulis, D. K. and N. Yuval-Davis. (1995) (ed.) *Unsettling Settler Societies: articulations of gender, race, ethnicity and class,* London: Sage.

Stepputat, F. and T. B. Hansen (2001) *States of Imagination: Ethnographic Explorations of the Postcolonial State*, Durham, NC: Duke University Press.

Stiglitz, Joseph (2002). Globalization and its Discontents New York: Norton.

Stocking, G. W. (1983) (ed.) *Observers Observed: Essays on Ethnographic Fieldwork*, Madison, WI: University of Wisconsin Press.

Stoneham, G. (2000) '"It's a Free Country": Visions of Hybridity in the Metropolis' in A. Bery, P. Murray and W. Harris (eds) *Comparing Postcolonial Literatures: Dislocations*, Basingstoke, England: Macmillan.

Stratton, F. (1994) *African Literature and the Politics of Gender*, London and New York: Routledge.

Sugirtharajah, R. S. (2001) *The Bible in the Third World: Precolonial, Colonial, Postcolonial Encounter*, Cambridge: Cambridge U.P.

Suleri, S. (1992) 'Woman Skin Deep: Feminism and the Postcolonial Condition', *Critical Inquiry* (18) 4 (Summer): 756–769.

Supriya, K. E. (2004) *Remembering Empire: Power, Memory, and Place in Postcolonial India*, New York: Peter Lang.

Swearingen, C. J. (2004) 'The New Literacy/Orality Debates: Ebonics and the Redefinition of Literacy in Multicultural Settings' in A. A. Lunsford and L. Ouzgane (eds) *Crossing Borderlands: Composition and Postcolonial Studies*, Pittsburgh, PA: University of Pittsburgh Press: 238–254.

Szegedy-Maszák, M. (1996) 'Universalism and Cultural Relativism' in H. Hendrix, J. Kloek, S. Levie and W. v. Peer (eds) *The Search for a New Alphabet: Literary Studies in a Changing World*, Amsterdam: Benjamins: 239–244.

Szeman, I. (2001) 'Who's Afraid of National Allegory? Jameson, Literary Criticism, Globalization.' *South Atlantic Quarterly* 100(3): 803–827.

Szeman, I. (2003) *Zones of Instability: Literature, Postcolonialism, and the Nation*, Baltimore, MD: Johns Hopkins University Press.

Szeman, I. (2006) 'Who's Afraid of National Allegory? Jameson, Literary Criticisim, Globalization' in C. Irr and I. Buchanan (eds) *On Jameson: From Postmodernism to Globalization*, Albany, New York: State University of New York Press.

Szwed, J. F. (1975) 'Race and the Embodiment of Culture', *Ethnicity* (2): 19–33.

Talib, I. S. (2002) *The language of postcolonial literatures: an introduction*, London: Routledge.

Taussig, M. (1993) *Mimesis and Alterity*, New York: Routledge.

Taylor, D. (2003) *The Archive and the Repertoire: Performing Cultural Memory in the Americas*, Durham Duke University Press.

Taylor, G. R. (1971) (ed.) *The Turner Thesis: Concerning the Role of the Frontier in American History*, Lexington, MA: Heath.

Taylor, P. (1995) 'Rereading Fanon, Rewriting Caribbean History' in G. Rajan and R. Mohanram (eds) *Postcolonial Discourse and Changing Cultural Contexts: Theory and Criticism*, Westport, CT: Greenwood.

Terdiman, R. (1985) *Discourse/Counter-Discourse: The Theory and Practice of*

Symbolic Resistance in Nineteenth-Century France, Ithaca and London: Cornell University Press.

Thayer, C. A. (1989) *War by Other Means: National Liberation and Revolution in Viet-Nam 1954–60,* Sydney: Allen & Unwin.

Thieme, J. (1996) *The Arnold Anthology of Post-Colonial literatures in English,* London: Arnold.

Thomas, N. (1994) *Colonialism's Culture: Anthropology, Travel and Government,* Oxford: Polity Press.

Thomas, S. (ed.) 'Decolonising Bodies', Special Issue *New Literatures Review* 30 (Winter).

Thompson, V. B. (1987) *The Making of the African Diaspora in theAmericas, 1441–1900,* Harlow, Essex and New York: Longman.

Thorpe, B. (1996) *Colonial Queensland: Perspectives on a Frontier Society,* St Lucia, Qld: University of Queensland Press.

Tiffin, H. (1983) 'Commonwealth Literature: Comparison and Judgement' in D. Riemenschneider (ed.) *The History and Historiography of Commonwealth Literature,* Tübingen: Narr.

Tiffin, H. (1984) 'Commonwealth Literature and Comparative Methodology.' *World Literature Written in English* 23(1): 26–30.

Tiffin, H. (1987) 'Comparative Literature and Post-Colonial Counter-Discourse', *Kunapipi* (9) 3.

Tiffin, H. (1995) 'Post-Colonial Literatures and Counter-Discourse' in B. Ashcroft, G. Griffiths and H. Tiffin (eds) *The Post-Colonial Studies Reader,* London: Routledge: 95–98.

Todd, L. (1984) *Modern Englishes: Pidgins and Creoles,* Oxford: Basil Blackwell.

Todorov, T. (1984) *Mikhail Bakhtin: The Dialogical Principle,* Minneapolis: University of Minnesota.

Torgovnik, M. (1990) *Gone Primitive: Savage Intellects, Modern Lives,* Chicago: Chicago University Press.

Trees, K. (1997) 'The Politics of Post-Colonial Reading Practices as They Relate to the Work of Aboriginal Writers' in A. Collett, L. Jensen, A. Rutherford and B. Thogersen (eds) *Teaching Post-Colonialism and Post-Colonial Literatures,* Aarhus, Denmark: Aarhus University Press: 155–159.

Treat, James (1996) (ed.) *Native and Christian: Indigenous Voices on Religious History in the United States and Canada,* New York: Routledge.

Trigger, D. S. (1992) *Whitefella Comin': Aboriginal Responses to Colonialism in Northern Australia,* Cambridge and Sydney: Cambridge University Press.

Turner, B. S. (1990) (ed.) *Theories of Modernity and Postmodernity,* London: Sage.

Turner, B. S. (1994) *Orientalism, Postmodernism, and Globalism,* London: Routledge.

Turner, F. J. (1961) *Frontier and Section: Selected Essays of Frederick Jackson Turner,* Englewood Cliffs, NJ: Prentice-Hall.

Turner, F. J. (1962) *The Frontier in American History,* with a foreword by Ray Allen Billington, New York: Holt, Rinehart.

Ukai, S. and L. E. Harrington (2005) 'Colonialism and Modernity' in R. F. Calichman (ed.) *Contemporary Japanese Thought*, New York: Columbia University Press.

Van der Veer, Peter 'Global Conversions' in Scott, Jamie S. and Gareth Griffiths (2005) (eds.) *Mixed Messages: Materiality, Textuality Missions*, New York: Palgrave/Macmillan.

Varadharajan, A. (1995) *Exotic Parodies: Subjectivity in Adorno, Said, and Spivak*, Minneapolis, MN: University of Minnesota Press.

Veer, P. v. d. (1995) (ed.) *Nation and Migration: The Politics of Space in the South Asian Diaspora* Philadelphia: University of Philadelphia Press.

Venn, C. (2006) *The Postcolonial Challenge: Towards Alternative Worlds*, London: Sage.

Venuti, Lawrence (2004), *The Translation Studies Reader*, London: Routledge.

Verdesio, G. (2002) 'The Original Sin behind the Creation of a New Europe: Economic and Ecological Imperialism in the River Plate' in S. Arias and M. Meléndez (ed.) *Mapping Colonial Spanish America: Places and Commonplaces of Identity, Culture, and Experience*, Lewisburg, PA: Bucknell University Press: 137–158.

Vidal, H. and Jara, R. (1986) (eds) *Testimonio y Literatura*, Minneapolis: Institute for the Study of Ideologies and Literature.

Vilanova, M. (1977) 'Mestizaje y marginación: El laberinto de la identidad en la America latina', *Cuadernos Hispanoamericanos: Revista Mensual de Cultura Hispanica* 320–321: 285–299.

Viswanathan, G. (1987) 'The beginnings of English literary study in India', *Oxford Literary Review* (9) 1 and 2.

Viswanathan, G. (1989) *Masks of Conquest: Literary Study and British Rule in India*, New York: Columbia University Press.

Viswanathan, Gauri (1998) *Outside the Fold: Conversion, Modernity and Belief*, New Jersey, Princeton U.P.

Walcott, D. (1974) 'The Muse of History' in O. Coombes (ed.) *Is Massa Day Dead? Black Moods in the Caribbean*, New York, Doubleday.

Walder, D. (2000) 'The Necessity of Error: Memory and Representation in the New Literatures' in S. Nasta (ed.) *Reading the 'New' Literatures in a Postcolonial Era*, Cambridge: Brewer: 149–170.

Wallerstein, I. (1974a) *The Modern World System: Capitalist Agriculture and the Origin of the European World-Economy in the Sixteenth Century*, New York: Academic Press.

Wallerstein, I. (1974b) 'The Rise and Future Demise of the World Capitalist System: Concepts for Comparative Analysis', *Comparative Studies in Society and History* (16) 3: 387–415.

Wallerstein, I. (1976) 'A World-System Perspective on the Social Sciences', *British Journal of Sociology* (27) 3: 343–352.

Wallerstein, I. (1980) *The Capitalist World Economy*, Cambridge: Cambridge University Press.

Wallerstein, I. (1991) *Geopolitics and Geoculture: Essays on the Changing World System*, Cambridge: Cambridge University Press.

Walvin, J. (1992) *Black Ivory: A History of British Slavery*, London, Harper Collins.

Walvin, J. (1996) *Questioning Slavery*, London: Routledge.

Ward, P. (2002) *Exile, Emigration, and Irish Writing*, Dublin: Irish Academic Press.

Ware, V. (1993) *Beyond the Pale: White Women, Racism and History*, London: Verso.

Wasserman, R. (1984) 'Re-inventing the New World: Cooper and Alencar', *Comparative Literature* (36) 2 (Spring).

Warren, K. J. (2000), *Ecofeminist Philosophy: a Western Perspective on What it is and Why it Matters*, Lanham Md.: Rowman and Littlefield.

Wasserman, R. (1994) *Exotic nations: Literature and Cultural Identity in the United States and Brazil, 1830–1930*, Ithaca: Cornell University Press.

Watt, I. (1957) *The Rise of the Novel*, London: Chatto & Windus.

Weber, D. J. and Rausch, J. M. (1994) (eds) *Where Cultures Meet: Frontiers in Latin American History*, Wilmington, DE: SR Books.

Weber, M. (1968a) *Max Weber on Charisma and Institution Building: Selected Papers*, edited with introduction by S. N. Eisenstadt, Chicago: University of Chicago Press.

Weber, M. (1968b) *Economy and Society* Vol. 1, New York: Bedminster Press.

Weber, M. (1970) *Max Weber: The Interpretation of Social Reality*, edited with an introduction by J. E. T. Eldridge, London: Joseph.

Weber, M. (1983) *Max Weber on Capitalism, Bureaucracy, and Religion: A Selection of Texts*, edited and in part newly translated by Stanislav Andreski, London and Boston: Allen & Unwin.

Weedon, C. (1999) *Feminism, Theory, and the Politics of Difference*, Malden, Massachusetts: Blackwell Publishers.

Weisbord, R. G. (1973) *Ebony Kinship: Africa, Africans, and the Afro-American*, Westport, CT: Greenwood Press.

Werbner, R. P. and P. Stoller (2002) (ed.) *Postcolonial Subjectivities in Africa*, New York: Zed Books.

Wesseling, H. L. (1997) *Imperialism and Colonialism: Essays on the History of European Expansion*, Westport, Connecticut: Greenwood Press.

West-Pavlov, R. (2005) *Transcultural Graffiti: Diasporic Writing and the Teaching of Literary Studies*, Amsterdam, Netherlands: Rodopi.

Weston, R. (1996) *Modernism*, London: Phaidon.

White, J. (1985) *Black Leadership in America, 1895–1968*, London and New York: Longman.

Whitlock, G. (1995) *Outlaws of the Text: Women's Bodies and the Organisation of Gender in Imperial Space*. Paper presented at the Australia/Canada: Postcolonialism and Women's Texts research seminar, Calgary Institute for the Humanities, February, 1992; reproduced in Ashcroft *et al.* 1995.

Williams, D. W. (1969) 'Image and Idea in the Arts of Guyana', Georgetown, Guyana: Edgar Mittelholzer Memorial Lectures, National History and Arts Council, Ministry of Information.

Williams, E. (1964) *Capitalism and Slavery*, London: André Deutsch.

Williams, E. (1966) *British Historians and the West Indies,* London: André Deutsch.

Williamson, John (2002), 'Did the Washington Consensus Fail?', Centre for Strategic and International Studies. Washington DC http://www.iie.com/publications/papers/paper.cfm?ResearchID=488.

Wise, C. (1995) 'The Dialectics of Négritude: Or, The (Post)Colonial Subject in Contemporary African-American Literature' in G. Rajan and R. Mohanram (eds) *Postcolonial Discourse and Changing Cultural Contexts: Theory and Criticism,* Westport, CT: Greenwood.

Wisker, G. (2000) *Postcolonial and African American Women's Writing: A Critical Introduction,* Basingstoke: Macmillan.

Wisker, G. (2007) *Key Concepts in Postcolonial Literature,* Basingstoke: Palgrave Macmillan.

Wittgenstein, L. (1958) *The Blue and Brown Books,* Oxford: Blackwell (1975).

Woddis, J. (1967) *Introduction to Neo-colonialism,* New York: International Publishers (1972).

Wolfe, Cary (2003) *Animal Rites: American Culture, the Discourse of Species and Posthumanist Theory,* Chicago and London: University of Chicago Press.

Wolfe, P. (1999) *Settler Colonialism and the Transformation of Anthropology: The Politics and Poetics of an Ethnographic Event,* London: Cassell.

Woods, D. (1986) *Apartheid: A Graphic Guide,* illustrated by Mike Bostock, London: Camden Press.

Wright, C. (2002) 'Centrifugal Logics: Eagleton and Spivak on the Place of "Place" in Postcolonial Theory', *Culture, Theory, and Critique* 43(1): 67–82.

Wynter, S. (1990) 'Beyond Miranda's Meanings' in Carol Boyce Davies and Elaine Savory Fido (eds) *Out of the Kumbla: Caribbean Women and Literature,* Trenton, New Jersey: Africa World Press. Reprinted in Alison Donnell and Sarah Lawson Welsh (eds) *The Routledge Reader in Caribbean Literature,* London and New York: Routledge (1996).

Young, R. J. C. (1990) *White Mythologies: Writing History and the West,* London: Routledge.

Young, R. J. C. (1995) *Colonial Desire: Hybridity in Theory, Culture and Race,* London: Routledge.

Young, R. J. C. (1998) 'The Overwritten Unwritten: Nationalism and Its Doubles in Post-Colonial Theory' in T. D'haen (ed.) *(Un)Writing Empire,* Amsterdam, Netherlands: Rodopi: 15–34.

Young, R. (2001) *Postcolonialism: An Historical Introduction,* Oxford: Blackwell.

Young, R. J. C. (2003) *Postcolonialism: A Very Short Introduction,* Oxford, England: Oxford University Press.

Zambare, A. V. (2003) 'The Orality of Information Culture: An Interface between Hypertextual and Postcolonial Narrative', *Journal of Commonwealth and Postcolonial Studies* 10(2): 55–71.

Zamora, L. P. and Faris, W. B. (eds) *Magical Realism: Theory, History,* Durham, NC: Duke University Press.

Zavala, I. M. (1992) *Colonialism and Culture: Hispanic Modernisms and the Social Imaginary,* Bloomington: Indiana University Press.

Zeigler, M. B. (1996) 'Postcolonial Contexts of African American Vernacular English', *Journal of Commonwealth and Postcolonial Studies* 4(1).

Zeigler, M. B. and V. Osinubi (2002) 'Theorizing the Postcoloniality of African American English', *Journal of Black Studies* 32(5): 588.

Ziff, B. H. and P. V. Rao. (1997) (eds) *Borrowed Power: Essays on Cultural Appropiation*, New Brunswick, New Jersey: Rutgers University Press.

NAME INDEX

SUBJECT INDEX

NB: Page numbers in **bold** refer to main entries.

287